THE GALE
ENCYCLOPEDIA
OF THE UNUSUAL
AND
UNEXPLAINED

BRAD STEIGER

AND

SHERRY
HANSEN
STEIGER

THE GALE ENCYCLOPEDIA OF THE UNUSUAL AND UNEXPLAINED

2

GALE®

THOMSON

GALE

Detroit • New York • San Diego • San Francisco • Cleveland • New Haven, Conn. • Waterville, Maine • London • Munich

Gale Encyclopedia of the Unusual and Unexplained

Brad E. Steiger and Sherry Hansen Steiger

Project Editor
Jolen Marya Gedridge

Editorial
Andrew Claps, Lynn U. Koch, Michael Reade

Permissions
Lori Hines

Imaging and Multimedia
Dean Dauphinais, Lezlie Light

Product Design
Tracey Rowens

Manufacturing
Rhonda A. Williams

LIBRARY OF CONGRESS CATALOGING-IN-PUBLICATION DATA

Steiger, Brad.
    Gale encyclopedia of the unusual and unexplained / Brad E. Steiger and Sherry Hansen Steiger.
        p. cm.
Includes bibliographical references and index.
    ISBN 0-7876-5382-9 (set : hardcover : alk. paper) — ISBN 0-7876-5383-7 (v. 1 : alk. paper) — ISBN 0-7876-5384-5 (v. 2 : alk. paper) — ISBN 0-7876-5385-3 (v. 3 : alk. paper)
    1. Parapsychology—Encyclopedias. 2. Occultism—Encyclopedias. 3. Supernatural—Encyclopedias. I. Title: Encyclopedia of the unusual and unexplained. II. Steiger, Sherry Hansen. III. Title.
    BF1025.S79 2003
    130'.3—dc21

2003003995

This title is also available as an e-book
ISBN 0-7876-7764-7
Contact your Gale representative for ordering information

Printed in the United States of America
10 9 8 7 6 5 4 3 2 1

Table of Contents

PREFACE

The Gale Encyclopedia of the Unusual and Unexplained (GEUU) presents comprehensive and objective information on unexplained mysteries, paranormal abilities, supernatural events, religious phenomena, magic, UFOs, and myths that have evolved into cultural realities. This extensive three-volume work is a valuable tool providing users the opportunity to evaluate the many claims and counterclaims regarding the mysterious and unknown. Many of these claims have been brought to the forefront from television, motion pictures, radio talk shows, best-selling books, and the Internet.

There has been a conscious effort to provide reliable and authoritative information in the most objective and factual way possible, to present multiple viewpoints for controversial subject topics, and to avoid sensationalism that taints the credibility of the subject matter. The manner of presentation enables readers to utilize their critical thinking skills to separate fact from fiction, opinion from dogma, and truth from legend regarding enigmas that have intrigued, baffled, and inspired humankind over the centuries.

ABOUT THE AUTHORS AND ADVISORS

Brad E. Steiger has written over 150 books with over 17 million copies in print. His vast writing experience includes biographies, books of inspiration, phenomenon and the paranormal, spirituality, UFO research, and crimes. His first articles on the paranormal appeared in 1954 and, today, he has produced over 2,000 articles on such themes. Steiger has appeared on such television programs as *Nightline with Ted Koppel*, *ABC Evening News with Peter Jennings*, *NBC Evening News with Tom Brokaw*, *This Week* (with David Brinkley, Sam Donaldson, and Cokie Roberts), *The Mike Douglas Show*, *The David Susskind Show*, *The Joan Rivers Show*, *Entertainment Tonight*, *Haunted Hollywood*, *Inside Edition*, *The Unexplained*, and *Giants: The Myth and the Mystery*. Sherry Hansen Steiger is a co-author of 24 books on a variety of topics on the unusual and unexplained with her husband Brad. Her continual studies in alternative medicine and therapies led to the 1992 official creation of The Office of Alternative Medicine under the Institutes of Health, Education and Welfare in Bethesda, Maryland. Both Steigers have served as consultants for such television shows as *Sightings* and *Unsolved Mysteries*.

The advisors for *GEUU* are Judy T. Nelson, the Youth Services Coordinator for the Pierce County Library System in Tacoma, Washington; Lee Sprince, former Head of Youth Services for the Broward County Main Library in Fort Lauderdale, Florida; and Brad E. Steiger, author of Gale's former Visible Ink Press title *The Werewolf Book: The Encyclopedia of Shape-Shifting Things*. For *GEUU*, both Nelson and Sprince were consulted on *GEUU*'s subject content, its appropriateness, and format; Steiger advised on the content's organization before he became the author of *GEUU*.

FORMAT

The *Gale Encyclopedia of the Unusual and Unexplained* consists of fourteen broad-subject chapters covering a wide range of high-interest topics: Afterlife Mysteries; Mediums and Mystics; Religious Phenomena; Mystery Religions and Cults; Secret Societies; Magic and Sorcery; Prophecy and Divination; Objects of Mystery and Power; Places of Mystery and Power; Ghosts and Phantoms; Mysterious Creatures; Mysteries of the Mind; Superstitions, Strange Customs, Taboos, and Urban Legends; and Invaders from Outer Space. Each chapter begins with an **Overview** that summarizes the chapter's concept in a few brief sentences. Then the **Chapter Exploration** provides a complete outline of the chapter, listing all topics and subtopics therein, so that the user can understand the interrelationships between the chapter's topics and its subtopics. An **Introduction** consisting of 6 to 12 paragraphs follows; it broadly describes the chapter's theme. Then each topic is explored, along with each subtopic, developing relevant concepts, geographic places, persons, practices, etc. After each topic, a **Delving Deeper** section provides complete bibliographical citations of books, periodicals, television programs, Internet sites, movies, and theses used, and provides users with further research opportunities. **Boldfaced cross-references** are used to guide users from the text to related entries found elsewhere in the three volumes. Sidebars supplement the text with unusual facts, features, and biographies, as well as descriptions of web sites, etc.

Each chapter contains photographs, line drawings, and original graphics that were chosen to complement the text; in all three volumes, over 250 images enliven the text. Many of these images are provided by Fortean Picture Library—"a pictorial archive of mysteries and strange phenomena"—and from the personal archives of the author, Brad Steiger. At the end of each chapter, a glossary, called **Making the Connection**, lists significant terms, theories, and practices mentioned within the text. A comprehensive glossary of the terms used throughout all three volumes can be found at the end of each volume.

Each volume has a cumulative **Table of Contents** allowing users to see the organization of each chapter at a glance. The **Cumulative Index**, found in each volume, is an alphabetic arrangement of all people, places, images, and concepts found in the text. The page references to the terms include the volume number as well as the page number; images are denoted by italicized page numbers.

USER COMMENTS ARE WELCOME

Users having comments, corrections, or suggestions can contact the editor at the following address: *Gale Encyclopedia of the Unusual and Unexplained*, The Gale Group, Inc., 27500 Drake Rd., Farmington Hills, MI 48331-3535.

Introduction

Understanding the Unknown

The belief in a reality that transcends our everyday existence is as old as humanity itself and it continues to the present day. In fact, in recent years there has been a tremendous surge of interest in the paranormal and the supernatural. People speak freely of guardian angels, a belief in life after death, an acceptance of extrasensory perception (ESP), and the existence of ghosts. In a Gallup Poll released on June 10, 2001, the survey administrators found that 54 percent of Americans believe in spiritual or faith healing; 41 percent acknowledge that people can be possessed by the devil; 50 percent accept the reality of ESP; 32 percent believe in the power of prophecy; and 38 percent agree that ghosts and spirits exist.

What are the origins of these age-old beliefs? Are they natural phenomenon that can be understood by the physical sciences? Some scientists are suggesting that such mystical experiences can be explained in terms of neural transmitters, neural networks, and brain chemistry. Perhaps the feeling of transcendence that mystics describe could be the result of decreased activity in the brain's parietal lobe, which helps regulate the sense of self and physical orientation. Perhaps the human brain is wired for mystical experiences and the flash of wisdom that illuminated the Buddha, the voices that Mohammed and Moses heard in the wilderness, and the dialogues that Jesus had with the Father were the result of brain chemistry and may someday be completely explained in scientific terms.

Perhaps the origin of these beliefs is to be found in psychology? Humankind's fascination with the unknown quite likely began with the most basic of human emotions—fear. Early humans faced the constant danger of being attacked by predators, of being killed by people from other tribes, or of falling victim to the sudden fury of a natural disaster, such as flood, fire, or avalanche. Nearly all of these violent encounters brought about the death of a friend or family member, so one may surmise that chief among the mysteries that troubled early humans was the same one that haunts man today: What happens when someone dies?

But belief in the unknown may be more than brain chemistry or a figment of our fears. Perhaps there is some spiritual reality that is outside of us, but with which one can somehow communicate? Perhaps the physical activity of the brain or psychological state (the two are of course related) may be only a precondition or a conduit to a transcendent world? The central mystery may always remain.

GHOSTLY ENTITIES AND URBAN LEGENDS

There is not a single known culture on planet Earth that does not have its ghost stories, and one can determine from Paleolithic cave paintings that the belief that there is something within the human body that survives physical death is at least 50,000 years old. If there is a single unifying factor in the arena of the unknown and the unexplained it is the universality of accounts of ghostly entities. Of course, not everyone agrees on the exact nature of ghosts. Some insist that the appearance of ghosts prove survival after death. Others state that such phenomena represent other dimensions of reality.

And then there are the skeptics who group most ghost stories in the category of "Urban Legends," those unverifiable stories about outlandish, humorous, frightening, or supernatural events. In some instances, the stories are based on actual occurrences that have in their telling and retelling been exaggerated or distorted. Other urban legends have their origins in people misinterpreting or misunderstanding stories that they have heard or read in the media or from actual witnesses of an event. There is usually some distance between the narrator and his tale; all urban legends claim that the story always happened to someone else, most often "a friend of a friend."

THE ROOTS OF SUPERSTITION

Whatever their basis in reality, certain beliefs and practices of primitive people helped ease their fear and the feeling of helplessness that arose from the precariousness of their existence. Others in the community who took careful note of their behavior ritualized the stories of those who had faced great dangers and survived. In such rituals lies the origin of "superstition," a belief that certain repeated actions or words will bring the practitioner luck or ward off evil. Ancient superstitions survive today in such common practices as tossing a pinch of salt over the shoulder or whispering a blessing after a sneeze to assure good fortune.

The earliest traces of magical practices are found in the European caves of the Paleolithic Age, c. 50,000 B.C.E. in which it seems clear that early humans sought supernatural means to placate the spirits of the animals they killed for food, to dispel the restless spirits of the humans they had slain, or to bring peace to the spirits of their deceased tribal kin. It was at this time that early humans began to believe that there could be supernatural powers in a charm, a spell, or a ritual to work good or evil on their enemies. Practices, such as imitating the animal of the hunt through preparatory dance, cutting off a bit of an enemy's hair or clothing to be used in a charm against him, or invoking evil spirits to cause harm to others, eventually gained a higher level of sophistication and evolved into more formal religious practices.

As such beliefs developed, certain tribal members were elevated in status to shaman and magician because of their ability to communicate with the spirit worlds, to influence the weather, to heal the sick, and to interpret dreams. Shamans entered a trance-like condition separating them from life's mundane existence and allowing them to enter a state of heightened spiritual awareness. According to anthropologists, shamanic methods are remarkably similar throughout the world. In our own time, Spiritualist mediums who claim to be able to communicate with the dead remain popular as guides for contemporary men and women, and such individuals as John Edward, James Van Praagh, and Sylvia Browne issue advice from the Other Side on syndicated television programs.

MONSTERS AND NIGHT TERRORS

Stone Age humans had good reason to fear the monsters that emerged from the darkness. Saber-tooth tigers stalked man, cave bears mauled them, and rival hominid species—many appearing more animal-like than human—struggled against them for dominance. The memories of the ancient night terrors surface in dreams and imagination, a kind of psychic residue of primitive fears. Anthropologists have observed that such half-human, half-animal monsters as the werewolf and other werecreatures were painted by Stone Age artists more than 10,000 years ago. Some of the world's oldest art found on ancient sites in Europe, Africa, and Australia depict animal-human hybrids. Such "therianthropes," or hybrid beings, appear to be the only common denominator in primitive art around the planet. These werewolves, were-lions, and werebats belonged to an imagined world which early humans saw as powerful, dangerous, and frightening.

Images of these creatures persisted into the historical period. The ancient Egyptians often depicted their gods as human-animal hybrids. Pharaoh identified himself with the god Horus, who could be represented as a falcon or a falcon-headed human. Anubis, the god of the necropolis, can be shown as a jackal-headed man, probably because such carrion-eating jackals prowled Egyptian cemeteries. Many other civilizations felt the power of these kinds of images. For example, the ancient Greeks fashioned the minotaur (half-human, half-bull), the satyr (half-human, half-goat), the harpy (half-woman, half-bird) and a host of other hybrid entities—the vast majority unfavorably disposed toward humankind. Examples could be found in other cultures as well.

CUSTOMS AND TABOOS

In 2001, scientists were surprised when bits of stone etched with intricate patterns found in the Blombos Cave, east of Cape Town on the southern African shores of the Indian Ocean, were dated at 77,000 years old, thereby indicating that ancient humans were capable of complex behavior and abstract thought thousands of years earlier than previously believed. In Europe, numerous sites have been excavated and artifacts unearthed that prove that structured behavior with customs and taboos existed about 40,000 years ago.

Customs are those activities that have been approved by a social group and have been handed down from generation to generation until they have become habitual. When an action or activity violates behavior considered appropriate by a social group, it is labeled a "taboo," a word borrowed from the Polynesians of the South Pacific. An act that is taboo is forbidden, and those who transgress may be ostracized by others or, in extreme instances, killed.

However, customs vary from culture to culture, and customary actions in one society may be considered improper in another. While the marriage of near-blood relations is prohibited in contemporary civilization, in earlier societies it was quite common. The ancient brother and sister gods of Egypt, Osiris and Isis, provided an example for pharaohs, who at times married their sisters. Polygamy, the marriage of one man and several women or one woman and several men, is prohibited in modern civilization, but there are still religious groups in nearly every nation who justify plural marriages as being ordained by the deity they worship. Adultery, an act of infidelity on the part of a married individual, is one of the most universal taboos. The code of Moses condemned both parties involved in the act to be stoned to death. Hindu religious doctrines demand the death, mutilation, or humiliation of both men and women, depending upon the caste of the guilty parties.

Taboos can change within a society over time. Many acts that were once considered forbidden have developed into an acceptable social activity. While some of the old customs and taboos surrounding courtship and marriage, hospitality and etiquette, and burials and funerals may seem amusing or quaint, primitive or savage, certain elements of such acts as capturing one's bride have been preserved in many traditions that are still practiced in the modern marriage ceremony.

BELIEF IN AN AFTERLIFE

Belief in the survival of some part of us after death may also be as old as the human race. Although one cannot be certain the earliest members of man's species (*Homo sapiens* c. 30,000 B.C.E.) conducted burial rituals that would qualify them as believers in an afterlife, one does know they buried their dead with care and consideration and included food, weapons, and various personal belongings with the body. Anthropologists have also discovered the Neanderthal species (c. 100,000 B.C.E.) placed food, stone implements, and decorative shells and bones with the deceased. Because of the placement of such funerary objects in the graves, one may safely conjecture that these prehistoric people believed death was not the end. There was some part of the deceased requiring nourishment, clothing, and protection in order to journey safely in another kind of existence beyond the grave. This belief persisted into more recent historical times. The ancient Egyptians had a highly developed concept of life after death, devoting much thought and effort to their eternal wellbeing, and they were not the only early civilization to be concerned about an afterlife.

With all their diversity of beliefs, the major religions of today are in accord in one essential teaching: Human beings are immortal and their spirit comes from a divine world and may eventually return there. The part of the human being that survives death is known in Judaism, Christianity, and Islam as the soul—the very essence of the individual person that must answer for its earthly deeds, good or bad. Hinduism perceives this spiritual essence as the divine Self, the *Atman*, and Buddhism believes it to be the summation of conditions and causes. Of the major world religions, only Buddhism does not perceive an eternal metaphysical aspect of the human personality in the same way that the others do. However, all the major faiths believe that after the spirit has left the body, it moves on to another existence. The physical body is a temporary possession that a human has, not what a person is.

The mystery of what happens when the soul leaves the body remains an enigma in the teachings of the major religions; however, as more and more individuals are retrieved from clinical death by the miracles of modern medicine, literature describing near-death-experiences has arisen which depicts a transition into another world or dimension of consciousness wherein the deceased are met by beings of light. Many of those who have returned to life after such an experience also speak of a life-review of their deeds and misdeeds from childhood to the moment of the near-death encounter.

PROPHECY AND DIVINATION

The desire to foresee the future quite likely began when early humans began to perceive that they were a part of nature, subject to its limitations and laws, and that they were seemingly powerless to alter those laws. Mysterious supernatural forces—sometimes benign, often hostile—appeared to be in control of human existence.

Divination, the method of obtaining knowledge of the future by means of omens or sacred objects, has been practiced in all societies, whether primitive or civilized. The ancient Chaldeans read the will of the gods in the star-jeweled heavens. The children of Israel sought the word of the Lord in the jewels of the Ephod. Pharaoh elevated Joseph from his prison cell to the office of chief minister of Egypt and staked the survival of his kingdom on Joseph's interpretation of his dreams. In the same land of Egypt, priests of Isis and Ra listened as those deities spoke through the unmoving lips of the stone Sphinx.

Throughout the centuries, soothsayers and seers have sought to predict the destiny of their clients by interpreting signs in the entrails of animals, the movements of the stars in the heavens, the reflections in a crystal ball, the spread of a deck of cards, and even messages from the dead. All of these ancient practices are still being utilized today by those who wish to know the future.

Objects and Places of Mystery and Power

Objects of mystery and power that become influential in a person's life can be an everyday item that an individual has come to believe will bring good fortune, such as an article of clothing that was worn when some great personal success was achieved or an amulet that has been passed on from generation to generation. In addition to such items of personal significance, some individuals have prized objects that reportedly brought victory or good fortune to heroes of long ago. Still others have searched for mysterious relics filled with supernatural attributes that were credited with accomplishing miracles in the past. No physical evidence is available to determine that such an object as the Ark of the Covenant ever existed, but its present location continues to be sought. The Holy Grail, the cup from which Jesus drank at the Last Supper, is never mentioned in the Bible, but by medieval times it had been popularized as the holiest relic in Christendom.

In addition to bestowing mystery and power upon certain objects, humans have always found or created places that are sacred to them—sites where they might gather to participate in religious rituals or where they might retreat for solitude and reflection. In such places, many people claim to experience a sense of the sublime. Others, while in a solemn place of worship or in a natural setting, attest to feeling a special energy that raises their consciousness and perhaps even heals their physical body.

Mysterious megaliths (large stones) were those placed at a special location by ancient people. Such sites include the standing stones of Brittany, the Bighorn Medicine Wheel in Wyoming, and the monuments of Easter Island. All of these places were ostensibly significant to an ancient society or religion, but many were long abandoned by the time they became known to today's world and their significance remains unexplained.

The most well-known megalithic structures are Stonehenge in Great Britain and the complex of pyramids and the Great Sphinx in Egypt. Like many such ancient places, those sites have been examined and speculated upon for centuries, yet they still continue to conceal secrets and occasionally yield surprising information that forces new historical interpretations of past societies.

There are other places that have become mysterious sites because of unusual occurrences. The claimed miraculous healing at Lourdes, France, the accounts of spiritual illumination at Jerusalem and Mecca, and the sacred visions at Taos, New Mexico, provide testimonies of faith and wonder that must be assessed by each individual.

There are also the "lost" civilizations and mysterious places that may never have existed beyond the human imagination. More than 2,500 years ago, legends first began about Atlantis, an ideal society that enjoyed an abundance of natural resources, great military power, splendid building and engineering feats, and intellectual achievements far advanced over those of other lands. This ancient society was described as existing on a continent-sized area with rich soil, plentiful pure water, abundant vegetation, and such mineral wealth that gold was inlaid in buildings. In the ensuing centuries, no conclusive evidence of Atlantis has been found, but its attributes have expanded to include engineering and technological feats that enhance its legendary status.

Sometimes legends come to life. The Lost City of Willkapanpa the Old, a city rumored to consist primarily of Incan rulers and soldiers, was not discovered until 1912 when a historian from Yale University found the site now known as Machu Picchu hidden at 8,000 feet in altitude between two mountains, Huayana Picchu ("young mountain") and Machu Picchu ("ancient mountain") in Peru.

Mystery Schools and Cults

Once a religion has become firmly established in a society, dissatisfied members often will break away from the larger group to create what they believe to be a more valid form of religious expression. Sometimes such splinter groups are organized around the revelations and visions of a single individual, who is recognized as a prophet by his or her followers. Because the new teachings may be judged as heretical to the original body of worshippers, those who follow the new revelations are branded as cultists or heretics.

Even in ancient times, the dissenters were forced to meet in secret because of oppression by the established group or because of their desire to hide their practices. Since only devotees could know the truths of their faith, adherents were required to maintain the strictest silence regarding their rites and rituals. The term "mysteries" or "mystery religion" is applied to these beliefs. The word "mystery" comes from the Greek word *myein*, "to close," referring to the need of the *mystes*, the initiate, to close his or her eyes and the lips and to keep secret the rites of the cult.

In ancient Greece, postulants of the mystery religions had to undergo a rigorous initiation that disciplined both their mind and body. In order to attain the self-mastery demanded by the priests of the mysteries, the neophytes understood that they must restructure their physical, moral, and spiritual being to gain access to the hidden forces in the universe. Only through complete mastery of oneself could one see beyond death and perceive the pathways of the after-life. Many times these mysteries were taught in the form of a play and were celebrated in sacred groves or in secret temples away from the cities.

In contemporary usage, the word "cult" generally carries with it negative connotations and associations. In modern times, a number of apocalyptic cults, such as the Branch Davidians and the People's Temple, have alarmed the general population by isolating themselves and preparing for Armageddon, the last great battle between good and evil. The mass suicides carried out by members of Heaven's Gate, People's Temple, and Order of the Solar Temple have also presented alarming images of what many believe to be typical cultist practice. Recent statistics indicate that there are 2,680 religions in the United States. Therefore, one must be cautious in labeling any seemingly unorthodox religion as a cult, for what is regarded as anti-social or blasphemous expression by some may be hailed as sincere spiritual witness by others.

SECRET SOCIETIES AND CONSPIRACIES

There will always be envious individuals who believe that wealthy and powerful members of society have been able to acquire their position only because of secret formulas, magical words, and supernatural rituals. Rumors and legends of secret societies have fueled the imaginations, fears, and envy of those on the outside for thousands of years. Many secret societies, such as the Assassins, the Garduna, the Thuggee, and the Tongs, were made up of highly trained criminals who were extremely dangerous to all outsiders. Others, such as the Knights Templar, the Illuminati, and the Rosicrucians, were said to possess enough ancient secrets of power and wealth to control the entire world.

Conspiracy enthusiasts allege that there are clandestine organizations which for centuries have remained a threat to individual freedoms, quietly operating in the shadows, silently infiltrating political organizations, and secretly manipulating every level of government and every facet of society. One of the favorites of conspiracy theorists, the Freemasons, while once a powerful and influential group throughout the Western world, is today regarded by many as simply a philanthropic and fraternal organization. Another secret society, the Illuminati, deemed by many conspiracy buffs to be the most insidious of all, faded into obscurity in the late eighteenth century. However, there is always a new secret society that seeks to divine arcane and forbidden avenues to wealth and power.

SORCERY, ALCHEMY AND WITCHCRAFT

Although Christianity affirms the existence of a transcendent reality, it has always distinguished between *religio* (reverence for God) and *superstitio*, which in Latin means "unreasonable religious belief." Christianity became the state religion of the Roman Empire in 395 C.E., and in 525 the Council of Oxia prohibited Christians from consulting sorcerers, diviners, or any kind of seer. A canon passed by the Council of Constantinople in 625 prescribed excommunication for a period of six years for anyone found practicing divination or who consulted with a diviner.

Although the Church had issued many canons warning against the practice of witchcraft or magic, little action was taken against those learned men who experimented with alchemy or those common folk who practiced the old ways of witchcraft. In 906 C.E., Abbot Regino of Prum recognized that earlier canon laws had done little to eradicate the practices of magic and witchcraft, so he issued his *De ecclesiaticis disciplinis* to condemn as heretical any belief in witchcraft or the power of sorcerers. In 1,000 C.E., Deacon Burchard, who would later become archbishop of Worms, published *Corrrector* which updated Regino's work and stressed that only God had the power to transform matter. Alchemists could not change base metals into gold, and witches could not shapeshift into animals.

In spite of such decrees, a lively belief in a world of witches and ghosts persisted throughout the Middle Ages and co-existed in the minds of many of the faithful with the miracle stories of the saints. To the native beliefs were added those of non-Christian peoples who either lived in Europe or whom Europeans met when they journeyed far from home, as when they went on the Crusades. By the twelfth century, magical practices based upon the arcane systems of the Spanish Moors and Jewish Kabbalah were established in Europe. The Church created the Inquisition in the High Middle Ages in response to unorthodox religious beliefs that it called heresies. Since some of these involved magical practices and witchcraft, the occult also became an object of persecution. The harsh treatment of the Manichaean Cathars in southern France is an example of society's reaction to those who mixed arcane practice with heterodox theology.

In spite of persecution, the concept of witchcraft persisted and even flourished in early modern times. At least the fear of it did, as the Salem witch trials richly illustrate. In the early decades of the twentieth century, schools of pagan and magical teachings were reborn as Wicca. Wiccans, calling themselves "practitioners of the craft of the wise," would resurrect many of the old ways and infuse them with modern thoughts and practices. Whatever its origin, the occult seems to be an object of permanent fascination to the human race.

ARE WE ALONE?

Is the earth the only inhabited planet? Imagine the excitement if contact is made with intelligent extraterrestrial life forms and humankind discovers that it is part of a larger cosmic community. It would change the way we think of ourselves and of our place in the universe. Or is the belief in extraterrestrials a creation of our minds? The universe is so vast we may never know, but the mysteries of outer space have a grip on the modern psyche, since it seems to offer the possibility of a world that may be more open to scientific verification than witchcraft.

PURPOSE OF BOOK

Whatever the origin and veracity of the unusual, these beliefs and experiences have played a significant role in human experiences and deserve to be studied dispassionately. These volumes explore and describe the research of those who take such phenomena seriously; extraterrestrials, ghosts, spirits, and haunted places are explored from many perspectives. They are part of the adventure of humanity.

ACKNOWLEDGEMENTS

Compiling such an extensive work as a three-volume encyclopedia of the unusual and unexplained proved many times to be a most formidable task. During those moments when I felt the labor pains of giving birth to such a large and exhausting enterprise might be beyond me, I was able to rely upon a number of wonderful midwives. My agent Agnes Birnbaum never failed to offer encouragement and support; my remarkably resourceful and accomplished editor Jolen Marya Gedridge continued to assure me that there truly was light at the end of the tunnel and that the great enterprise would one day be completed; the always pleasant and helpful staff at Gale—Julia Furtaw, Rita Runchock, Lynn Koch, and Nancy Matuszak—stood by to offer assistance; and most of all, I am forever indebted to my wife Sherry Hansen Steiger for her tireless compiling of the glossaries, her efforts in writing sidebars, her invaluable talents as a researcher, her patience and love, and her always providing a shoulder to cry on during the all-night writing sessions.

—*Brad E. Steiger*

CHAPTER 5
SECRET SOCIETIES

Many people have a deep-seated belief that they could more easily obtain power, wealth, and prestige if they could only be made privy to certain secrets for success that are possessed by mysterious societies that choose to keep their methods hidden from the larger society. Throughout the centuries, such secret societies have taunted outsiders with their forbidden knowledge and, on occasion, frightened or even assassinated those whose persistence in seeking access to their mysteries were unwelcome.

INTRODUCTION

In this chapter a number of secret societies will be examined that have fueled the imaginations, fear, and envy of those on the outside of the mysterious organizations for hundreds of years. One of the favorites of paranoid conspiracy theorists, the Freemasons, while once powerful and influential throughout the Western world, is today regarded by many as little more than a social relic of the past. Another secret society, the Illuminati, deemed by many conspiracy buffs to be the most insidious of all, faded into obscurity in the late eighteenth century. For conspiracy enthusiasts, however, both societies remain a threat to individual freedoms, allegedly operating in the shadows, silently infiltrating political organizations, secretly manipulating every level of government and every facet of society.

Almost without exception, each of the secret societies presented in this chapter began with serious religious aspirations, which slowly disintegrated into political ambitions, and eventually deteriorated into criminal activities. The Garduna and the Holy Vehm had their birth in mystical visions and a passion to defend Christianity from those who would seek to destroy it. Regardless of its founders' noble intentions, both groups were used to further political ambitions and soon become nothing more than outlaw gangs. The Chinese Tongs and Triads began as protective associations for merchants and laborers who were being exploited by the ruling establishment or, in the United States, by the dominant white society. In some cities the Tongs remain primarily private social clubs engaged in such victimless crimes as illegal gambling. The Triad, however, has grown into one of the largest of the worldwide crime organizations.

There will always be those envious and unsuccessful individuals who believe that the rich and successful have acquired their wealth and power only through their possession of secret formulas, utterance of magical words, and performance of supernatural rituals. Those same individuals will seek desperately to become members of groups that they believe have such mystical powers or they will become

obsessed in their efforts to destroy them. The Knights Templar gained status as an order of knighthood because of the selfless actions of a handful of knights who vowed to protect pilgrims on their way to the Holy Land. In the beginning, these pious and valiant knights were so poor that they had to share the same horse and take turns riding it. Centuries later, when the Knights Templar had become the wealthiest and most powerful order in all of Europe, it was decided by church and state that the once godly Christian soldiers had acquired their earthly treasure and power by worshipping Satan and committing the most foul acts of desecration and blasphemy. The order of knights that had once served as the bulwark of Christianity during the Crusades to protect the Holy Land was ordered disbanded by papal decree, and its members tortured and burned at the stake. History has not yet determined the degree of their true guilt as heretics, but it is unlikely the Knights Templar deserved such an ignoble end.

While there was never any clear evidence to prove that the Knights Templar committed the acts of human sacrifice of which they were accused, the members of the Leopard Cult of Africa were responsible for many such ritual murders on their jungle altars and left hundreds of mutilated human corpses to prove their guilt. The Thuggee of India, who committed more murders than any other secret society, allegedly dedicated the lives of the thousands of victims which they strangled to death to their goddess Kali.

Of all the secret societies examined in this chapter, only the Tongs and the Freemasons remain in existence in the twenty-first century. While some contemporary metaphysical groups proclaim that their philosophical heritage may derive from the Knights Templar or the Rosicrucians, there is little to substantiate such claims other than an admiration for their precepts and ideals. On occasion, international law enforcement investigators may see elements suggestive of the Thuggee or the Assassins involved in certain murders or assassinations, but there is little evidence that these societies still exist as forces to be feared. On the other hand, there are those who insist that the Illuminati is working behind the scenes to

THE DEATH OF DIANA, PRINCESS OF WALES

Many conspiracy theories about the death of Diana, Princess of Wales (1961–1997), and her lover Dodi Al Fayed still abound. Among the most common allegations of August 31, 1997, are the following:

- Princess Diana was assassinated by angry international arms dealers because of her high-profile global campaign against the use of land mines.

- The men on motorcycles who caused the Fayed limousine to crash were not the paparazzi, but hired assassins who provoked the driver into dangerous speeds and precipitated an accident.

- Diana was murdered by British Intelligence on orders from the Royal Family. Queen Elizabeth and Prince Philip were upset by the business of Prince Charles and Princess Diana's divorce. Newspapers reported that the Royals discussed dire consequences with Diana if she continued the relationship. Conspiracy theorists maintain when rumors circulated that Diana might be pregnant with Dodi's child, the Royal Family ordered her death.

- Princess Diana paid the ultimate price for dabbling in the dark arts. It was well known that Princess Diana and Sarah Ferguson, ex-wife of Prince Andrew, sought the counsel of Spiritualist mediums and psychic-sensitives. Some conspiracy buffs have suggested that the death of Diana and Dodi was a result of occult practices that backfired on the princess and that curses she had directed against her enemies had somehow boomeranged and unleashed their energy upon Diana and her lover.

- Diana was killed because she had offended a powerful secret society. Some theorists insist that this secret society did not approve of the public and private actions of Princess Diana and carried out her death sentence before she further embarrassed the Royals.

SOURCES:

"Death of a Princess." *E! Online.*[Online] http://www.eonline.com/Features/Features/Diana/.

Princess Diana: The Conspiracy Theories.[Online] http://www.londonnet.co.uk/In/talk/news/diana_conspiracy_theories.html.

"Princess Diana: Murder Coverup." *Conspiracy Planet.* [Online] http://www.conspiracyplanet.com/channel.cfm?ChannelID' 41.

bring about a New World Order that will enslave most of the world population.

The most secret of all mystery groups remains the Rosicrucians, whose manifestos helped give birth to many of the most liberating ideals of the European Enlightenment. Although one may see advertisements in magazines inviting the reader to fill out a coupon and become a member of the ancient order of the Rosy Cross, the modern organization exists as a homage to the original anonymous followers of the mysterious Illumined Father Christian Rosencreutz, for no known member of the original group that surfaced in the early 1600s was ever identified.

✤ DELVING DEEPER

Daraul, Arkon. *A History of Secret Societies*. New York: Pocket Books, 1969.

Heckethorn, Charles William. *Secret Societies of All Ages and Countries*. Kila, Mont.: Kessinger Publishing, 1997.

Howard, Michael. *The Occult Conspiracy: Secret Societies—*

Their Influence and Power in World History. Rochester, Vt.: Inner Traditions, 1989.

THE ASSASSINS

Regarded as one of the most fearful of all secret societies, the Hashashin, the Assassins, seemed capable of penetrating any security, of striking down any victim regardless of the body of men who might guard him. They moved as if they were deadly shadows and struck with a fury that shattered the nerves and the resolve of their most stalwart foes. The very name of the secret society of killers has given the English language the words "assassin," one who kills for fanatical or monetary reasons; "assassinate," the act of killing suddenly and treacherously; and "assassination," the murder of a prominent person. The original appellation for the society, the Hashashin, is derived from the Arabic "hashish," a name for Indian hemp (*cannabis sativa*), and the accusation was made by European Crusaders and others that the Assassins made liberal use of the narcotic effects of hashish to achieve their fierce courage and to eliminate their fear of death.

Most of the early members of the secret society were followers of the Nizari branch of the Isma Iliyya sect of Shiite Muslims and were located primarily in Syria and Persia. In 1090, Hasan ibn Sabbah (1034–1124) seized the mountain citadel of Alamaut in northern Persia and made it his "Eagles' Nest," a center where he, as grand master, could live in relative safety and direct his forces throughout Asia. Hasan became known as the "old man of the mountains," and he set about creating a fanatical organization composed of devotees, known as *fedayeen*, who did whatever he commanded with blind obedience.

Hasan frequently bought boys from poverty-stricken parents and reared them in the camps where he had gathered young men to be trained as suicide commandos, leading them step by step to higher levels of combat proficiency. At the same time that he was shaping his men into fierce warriors, he also indoctrinated them spiritually, convincing them that as they advanced under his tutelage they would come closer to the sacred and ultimate mystery that only he could reveal. Hasan told them confidentially that the conventional teachings of Islam had misled them. Paradise could not be attained by following the preachings of Muhammad (c. 570–632), but only by complete obedience to Hasan Ibn Sabah, who was the true Incarnation of God on Earth.

Most sources citing the history of the Assassins state that in order to be certain that no doubts remained among the initiates that he was deity made flesh, Hasan supplied them with generous amounts of the drug hashish, then hypnotically guided them to the lavish gardens of heaven where they were allowed to witness the beauty of the afterlife. When the youths regained full consciousness, they were convinced that they had been allowed a glimpse of their future dwelling place in paradise. Although such stories have been widely circulated since the Crusades in the eleventh century, other sources have recently stated that such accusations of heavy drug use among the Assassins only reflected the fact that their contemporaries despised them as members of a minority and unfairly associated the sect with one of the more detestable vices of the time.

Whether or not Hasan ibn Sabbah's cruelty and ruthlessness has been exaggerated by time, one persistent illustration survives to depict the lengths to which he would go to gain dominance over his men. According to the account, on one occasion when Hasan sought to impress a group of young men to become his obedient fedayeen, he dug a hole in front of his throne deep enough to allow only a man's head to remain visible. Next, he commanded a fedayeen to lower himself into the hole and to place a tray with an opening in it around his neck. Once the hole was covered with a colorful rug and the loose dirt brushed aside, it appeared as though Hasan had decapitated a man and placed his head upon a tray. To make the illusion all the more convincing, he poured fresh blood around the supposed detached head of his assistant.

When an aide brought the potential recruits before his throne, Hasan informed them sternly that as God on Earth he had many fearful and wondrous powers. He would cause the decapitated head on the tray before them to speak to them of the glories in paradise that awaited those warriors who died in battle.

At this point, the loyal fedayeen with his head on the tray opened his eyes and testified to the marvels that his soul had witnessed in the hereafter. After the new men had been duly impressed and had sworn their allegiance to Hasan, they walked away speaking in hushed tones of the glory of serving God on Earth. And once the illusion had accomplished its desired end, Hasan had the fedayeen who had so ably assisted him decapitated and his head stuck on a pole so that all could see that he was truly quite dead.

Although the Hashashin came to be feared by Christian Crusaders, kings, princes, sheikhs, and sultans, their membership probably never numbered more than 2,000 fedayeen at any one time. Because Hasan had indoctrinated his warriors to the belief that death in the pursuit of orders guaranteed an immediate transference to paradise, they fought with a fury untouched by the normal fear of dying in combat. Masters of disguise and of many languages and dialects, the Assassins might one day appear as simple peasants working around a castle wall and the next emerge as highly capable warriors springing on their victims from the shadows. The Assassins inveigled themselves into the services of all the surrounding rulers, posing as loyal soldiers or servants, but always awaiting the bidding of their grand master to strike if ordered to do so. A powerful sultan who defied the orders of Hasan might suddenly find himself attacked by Assassins who for many years had been regarded as trusted servants but had only been hiding in his service until such time as the grand master ordered his assassination. As the power of Hasan's secret society became known throughout the East, a monarch never knew which of his seemingly faithful retinue was really an Assassin only awaiting orders to murder him.

BETWEEN 1090 and 1256, there were eight Grand Masters who ruled the society of Assassins

Between 1090 and 1256, there were eight grand masters who ruled the society of Assassins. In 1256 and 1258, the Mongols virtually destroyed the sect in Iran and in Syria. Although the Assassins scattered throughout the East and into Europe, in 1272, the Mamluk Sultan Baybars brought about their downfall as an organized sect.

❖ **DELVING DEEPER**

Heckethorn, Charles William. *Secret Societies of All Ages and Countries.* Kila, Mont.: Kessinger Publishing, 1997.

Howard, Michael. *The Occult Conspiracy: Secret Societies—Their Influence and Power in World History.* Rochester, Vt.: Inner Traditions, 1989.

Howarth, Stephen. *The Knights Templar.* New York: Barnes & Noble, 1993.

THE DECIDED ONES OF JUPITER

In the early nineteenth century, southern Italy suffered greatly from the raids of small gangs of bandits who would descend from their hideouts in the mountains of Calabria and Abruzzi to rob travelers and to loot the villages. The authorities seemed unable to squelch the bands of thieves and protect the people, and only the vendettas and feuds between gangs themselves prevented the outlaws from uniting as one force to wreak greater havoc. Then, in 1816, a man named Ciro Annunchiarico (d. 1818) became southern Italy's greatest nightmare when he claimed the power of Jupiter, father of the gods of Imperial Rome, and successfully brought the bandit gangs into a single striking force, leading them to rob, pillage, and burn under the banner of the skull and crossbones and the motto, "Sadness, Death, Terror, and Mourning."

By 1817, Annunchiarico commanded 20,000 members of the secret society of the Decided Ones of Jupiter the Thunderer. The men were divided into camps of 300 to 400 members, and squadrons of 40 to 60. The society was structured along military lines and strict discipline was enforced. If Ciro Annunchiarico had so desired, he could easily have led an open revolution against any state government in southern Italy. But Annunchiarico, who claimed that the might of the great god Jupiter flowed through his body, was more interested in personal aggrandizement than in political opportunities.

In 1816, a man named Ciro Annunchiarico became southern Italy's greatest nightmare.

Annunchiarico was the son of wealthy parents who had entered the priesthood and who had seemed destined for a fruitful career in the Roman Catholic Church. The many tasks faced by a common parish priest had little attraction for him, however, and he preferred the life of a country gentleman on the family estate. Neither did the young priest respect his vow of celibacy, and he seduced a young woman who was engaged to Giovanni Montolesi, the son of a wealthy merchant. When Montolesi learned of the affair, he sought out Annunchiarico and reproached him for bringing shame to the

priesthood and dishonor to his fiancee. Without a word in his defense, Annunchiarico drew a dagger from his belt and stabbed Montolesi in the heart. Then, from his bizarre perspective, Annunchiarico declared that the man whom he had murdered had insulted him and the entire Roman Catholic priesthood, so he swore a blood-feud against the entire Montolesi family, ambushing and murdering 13 of 14 members in the next few months. Understandably, Annunchiarico was eventually pursued by the authorities and fled with some friends into the mountains to become outlaws.

As a youth, Annunchiarico had gained a reputation for scholarship and high intelligence. As the leader of a small band of brigands who favored a life of luxury above that of living in spartan hideouts, he developed a plan to combine the people's love and respect of the priesthood with their fear of secret societies. Boldly summoning the other bandit chiefs in the mountains to a meeting, Annunchiarico eloquently convinced them that they should unite as one to resist the soldiers that were constantly being sent out to hunt them down. While the chiefs were deciding just who it was among them who should lead the newly united force, Annunchiarico appeared in the full regalia of the priesthood and announced that he would celebrate the Mass. As the chiefs all kneeled to receive his blessing, such an attitude of obeisance signaled their acquiescence to his leadership. And at the same time that he was celebrating the Mass of the Roman Catholic Church, Annunchiarico informed all of the assembled outlaws that the spirit of Jupiter, the ancient father of the gods, had passed into his person and commanded him to form a new order, the Decided Ones of Jupiter.

In a brief period of time, numerous independent bands of thieves and murderers became a single secret society. And when word spread of the alleged supernatural powers of their leader, Ciro Annunchiarico, now known as Jupiter the Thunderer, men flocked to the mountains to join the lodges of the Decided Ones. In order to facilitate the rapid dispersal of his legendary abilities, Annunchiarico secretly used men who resembled him to serve as his doubles, dressed in priestly robes exactly like his, so it would appear that Jupiter the

Thunderer could lead raids in several different places at the same time. He also had his personal bodyguard outfitted in devilish costumes, complete with horns and tails, to perpetuate the belief that he had the power to command and control demons. Neither any of his men nor any of the villagers dared to speak a word against Annunchiarico for fear that an invisible demon lurking nearby would report such an abuse and bring retribution upon them. And then there were reports of his terrible thunderbolts, which he was said to be able to hurtle at his enemies just as Jupiter had flung the deadly bolts in ancient times. When Annunchiarico informed the village clerics that he had now achieved divinity and that only he could celebrate Mass, they all immediately ceased their local celebrations lest they be struck down.

Small bands of soldiers sent against the Decided Ones were quickly annihilated. In 1818, a force of 1,000 regular troops under the command of General d'Octavio were sent into the mountains to arrest Annunchiarico and to destroy his band of outlaws. The superstitious recruits were so fearful of the mighty Jupiter that they permitted Annunchiarico to enter their camp at night and to place a dagger at the throat of their general. Annunchiarico decreed his mercy, but warned the general and the 1,000 men that if they ever dared again to violate his mountains, his thunderbolts would be certain to kill them all. General d'Octavio and his troops were gone at first light the next morning.

When the authorities realized that any army conscripted from southern Italy would hold Annunchiarico in the same kind of superstitious awe as the local populace, they hired a force of 1,200 German and Swiss mercenaries under the command of an Englishman, General Church. Strangely enough, the approach of these battle-hardened veterans of the Napoleonic wars affected Annunchiarico in ways that astonished his men. It became apparent that their god was visibly nervous, even frightened by the approach of the professional soldiers toward the mountains. Suddenly the person who harbored the spirit of Jupiter seemed like an ordinary mortal—and not even a very brave one at that. When word reached the camps of the Decided Ones that

the mercenaries were well-equipped and exceedingly experienced men of war, thousands of them deserted within hours. Within a few days, Annunchiarico had only a few hundred of his most loyal disciples remaining out of what had been a fearsome band of 20,000.

Annunchiarico and his remaining Decided Ones retreated to the small village of Santa Marzano, choosing its location because of the wall that encircled the town. Hoping that members of the local populace would join in their defense, Annunchiarico prepared for siege. But the citizens of Santa Marzano could also see that the mighty Jupiter the Thunderer was, after all, just another bandit, and nothing about his person convinced any of them to risk their lives defending him against the Swiss and German soldiers. Within a few days of siege, General Church's mercenaries entered the village and killed those Decided Ones who offered resistance and arrested the others. Annunchiarico and three of his lieutenants managed to escape but were captured four days later.

Even as he was being led to the firing squad, Annunchiarico boasted that he had killed 60 or 70 men with his own hands, and he mocked the priest who came to administer the last rites. Many of the common people who had gathered on the day of execution murmured that the Thunderer would call down one of Jupiter's thunderbolts and escape from the mercenaries who had captured him. Incredibly, after the command was given to the 21-member firing squad to fire a volley at Ciro Annunchiarico, he remained alive, and somehow managed to get to his knees to begin a prayer to Jupiter. The astonished General Church ordered that the Thunderer's own musket be loaded with a silver bullet and that a soldier discharge the weapon directly into Annunchiarico's head, making certain that the legendary leader of the secret society was truly dead.

✳ DELVING DEEPER

Daraul, Arkon. *A History of Secret Societies*. New York: Pocket Books, 1969.

Heckethorn, Charles William. *Secret Societies of All Ages and Countries*. Kila, Mont.: Kessinger Publishing, 1997.

Lefebure, Charles. *The Blood Cults*. New York: Ace Books, 1969.

Conspiracy theorists fear that within the first few years of the twenty-first century, all Americans will be forced to receive a programmable biochip implant somewhere in their body. The biochip will likely be implanted on the back of the right or the left hand to facilitate scanning. A number will be assigned to each individual for life.

Though the biochip's function will be described as primarily for purposes of identification, it will be linked to a massive supercomputer system, enabling government agencies to maintain surveillance of all citizens by ground sensors and satellites. Even worse, say the alarmists, once the system is in place, the biochips can transform everyone into a controlled slave, for these devices will make it possible for outside intelligences to influence a person's brain cells and to direct the individual's brain neurons. Through biochip brain implants, people can be forced to think and to act exactly as preprogrammed.

Furthermore, the conspiracy theorists allege, a U.S. Naval research laboratory, funded by intelligence agencies, has achieved the incredible breakthrough of uniting living brain cells with microchips. They contend that when such a chip is injected into a man's or a woman's brain, he or she instantly becomes a living vegetable and a subservient New World Order slave. And once this device is perfected, the biochip implant could easily be utilized as a "Frankenstein-type weapon," and the Defense Department can produce an army of killer zombies.

Various conspiracy journals recount the allegations of a couple in Palo Alto, California, who are convinced that their teenaged son's psychological problems are the result of a biochip that was implanted into his head by a CIA agent during a tonsillectomy. According to the young man and his parents, he is constantly receiving threats and negative thoughts through transmissions received by the biochip. They contend the device has shown up on X-rays, but that the evidence was destroyed by CIA agents.

Before his execution, former American soldier and convicted Oklahoma City Federal Building bomber

BIG BROTHER'S BIOCHIP IMPLANTS GUARANTEE SLAVERY FOR THE MASSES

Timothy McVeigh (1968–2002) frequently stated his contention that federal agents were able to track him during the 1990s because of an electronic monitoring device that had been placed in his leg. McVeigh and others believed that the U.S. Army secretly implanted such devices in the legs of American soldiers during the Gulf War.

SOURCES:
Conspiracy Journal. [Online] http://members.tripod.com/uforeview.
Conspiracy Planet. [Online] http://www.conspiracyplanet.com/.
"MKULTRA, Biochips, Microchip Implants." *Psychops.com.*
 [Online] http://www. psychops.com.

THE FREEMASONS

There are those who claim that the Freemasons constitute a powerful secret brotherhood of darkness that is planning to take over the world. According to some scholars of the occult, the Masons' "Supreme Architect of the Universe" is none other than Lucifer, who cloaks himself in Masonic literature under such names as Zoraster, Shiva, Abaddon, and other pagan-god disguises. The so-called "holy writings" of Freemasonry, as well as their secret rites, passwords, initiations, and handshakes have their origins in the Roman mystery religions, Egyptian rituals, and Babylonian paganism. Often linked to the **Illuminati**, Freemasonry is said to have exerted its influence on every aspect of American society—including its currency.

Of all of the above alarmist concerns, only the part about the currency may have some credence. On the front of a one-dollar bill, there is a portrait of George Washington (1732–1799), an avowed Mason, who donned his Masonic apron and presided over the dedication of the United States Capitol. The flip side of the bill displays the Great Seal of the United States. The front side of the seal depicts the spread eagle, arrows in one claw, olive branch in the other, and a banner proclaiming *E Pluribus Unum* in its beak. Opposite the spread eagle, the backside of the seal, is an incomplete pyramid with an eye floating in a glowing triangle where the capstone should be. Above the eye is the caption *Annuit Coeptis,* commonly translated as "He has favored our undertaking," and in a scroll beneath is the slogan *Novus Ordo Seclorum,* "a new order of the ages."

Congress first authorized the creation of a Great Seal of the United States in 1792, but no real effort was made to have anyone design one. Nearly 100 years later, in 1884, Congress once again authorized the task of designing a Great Seal for the nation. In 1892, funds were allocated in the hope that an appropriate seal would be finished in time for the Chicago's World Fair. At last both sides of the seal were finally completed, but at its premiere showing, the side that featured the pyramid with the all-seeing eye was turned to the wall because some viewers were

Masonic temple in Alexandria, Virginia. (CORBIS CORPORATION)

offended by the symbol's Masonic associations. The backside of the Great Seal, first authorized by Congress in 1792, was not seen by the American public until 1935 when President Franklin Delano Roosevelt (1882–1945), a 32nd-degree Mason, put it on the back of the one-dollar bill.

GEORGE *Washington was an avowed Mason.*

Most scholars agree that the pyramid represented on the bill is the Great Pyramid of Cheops at Giza, which, to a Mason, is emblematic of the continuity of the craft of Freemasonry from the dawn of civilization in Egypt. For Freemasons it is also a reminder of the legend that Egyptian civilization was founded by survivors from **Atlantis** and that the United States is the New Atlantis foretold by the great master Mason Sir Francis Bacon (1561–1626). The pyramid with the all-seeing eye represents the Great Architect of the Universe that guided the Founding Fathers of the United States to establish a nation that might one day reveal itself as the heir of the ancient mysteries of Atlantis and restore all humankind to the earthly paradise that existed in that Golden Age of old.

The central mythos of Freemasonry centers around the building of the great temple of King Solomon (tenth century B.C.E.) and Solomon's securing the services of the most accomplished architect in the world, Hiram Abiff, who was said to have designed the magnificent temple according to the precepts of the Great Architect of the Universe. Although Hiram is mentioned in biblical accounts as a master of the arts of construction, the rites of Freemasonry extend beyond the Bible and fashion a parallel myth, portraying Hiram as a primary figure in the creation of the temple. According to Masonic tradition, the ancient builders of Solomon's Temple created the rites still practiced in modern lodges, with the various degrees of initiation and their secret symbols and handshakes.

While the Free and Accepted Order of Freemasons is the oldest fraternity in the world, it doesn't really extend back to the stone masons working on Solomon's Temple—nor does it date even farther back to those who labored on the Egyptian pyramids,

as some Masons have claimed. Freemasonry did evolve from the guilds of the stonemasons who traveled from city to city in Europe of the fourteenth century looking for work on the great cathedrals being constructed at that time. The secret passwords and handshakes were unique ways by which a newcomer to a city might prove that he really was a true member of the guild. While there are references to Freemasonry as early as 1390, the fraternity did not come into being until 1717 when four London lodges united.

From its actual beginnings in the early 1700s, Freemasonry exerted a great deal of influence upon society. For one thing, in the midst of seemingly incessant quarreling over religion throughout the European nations, the Freemasons were nondenominational, asking only that its members recognized a Supreme Being and sought somehow to better humanity through the course of their own lives. Because men of low rank could become members and no religious philosophy was deemed

Officers of the New York Mecca Temple. (CORBIS CORPORATION)

superior to another, the lodges of Freemasonry became champions of the emerging concepts of democracy that were suffusing the Enlightenment. Such freedoms of thought and spirituality did not endear the Freemasons to many facets of established society, particularly the Roman Catholic Church, who condemned the fraternity as anti-Christian.

By the mid-1700s, Freemasonry had established its lodges throughout Europe and had been carried across the ocean to the New World by numerous immigrants. George Washington, Benjamin Franklin (1706–1790), John Hancock (1737–1793), Paul Revere (1735–1818), and many other of the Founding Fathers of the United States were openly proud of being Masons. A freed slave, Prince Hall, who was initiated into Masonry by a British soldier in Boston, later founded an African lodge, which became the still-extant Prince Hall Masons.

After the Revolution (1775–83), American Freemasonry became extremely powerful in the United States. Lodges were constructed in the smallest of villages, and it became an undeniable sign of prestige in any community to be a member of the Masons. For businessmen who wished to succeed, it was almost a requirement to join the Freemasons.

THE *Free and Accepted Order of Freemasons is the oldest fraternity in the world.*

At the same time, however, those individuals who were not privy to its secrets had begun to spread rumors about the bizarre rites and grim pledges that the members of the fraternity were sworn to uphold. Curiosity and concern that satanic rites might be held by supposedly upstanding businessmen who had sold their souls to the devil began to spread doubts about what was really going on behind the closed doors of its lodges. While the various oaths and rituals of the Masons would quite likely be judged as a bit overly dramatic and flamboyant by some, they were largely symbolic and representative of an earlier age—and far less dangerous to their initiates than many contemporary college fraternities or sororities.

It was the abducted and assumed tragic death of one of its members in 1826 that led to the near-annihilation of the Masons in the United States. William Morgan, a disillusioned Mason from Batavia, New York, let it be known that he was writing a book that would reveal all the secrets of Freemasonry to the world. The printer's shop that was going to publish his manuscript was torched, and a few days later, Morgan was arrested on charges that he was in arrears on a two-dollar debt. That night, a stranger arrived to pay Morgan's bail, and the dissident Mason was then seized by a group of his fellow lodge members and forced into a carriage. Neither Morgan nor his remains were ever found.

BY *1897, the Masons had about 750,000 members.*

One of the cornerstones of Masonry was its loyalty to its members, but the entire nation was offended by the manner in which the juries were stacked in favor of those Masons who were accused of having murdered William Morgan. The general population demanded justice, and they were shocked by the power of a secret society that could stonewall three special prosecutors. After 20 trials for murder and kidnapping, the local sheriff, who was a Mason, and who was obviously an integral element in Morgan's abduction and disappearance, received the most severe judgment of all the defendants when he was sentenced to 30 months in jail.

Not only did an anti-Mason sentiment swell within the country, but the Anti-Mason Party was founded that elected governors in Pennsylvania and Vermont and won seven electoral votes in the 1832 election. It was no longer prestigious to be a Mason. In state after state, lodges closed. Overall, the fraternity lost more than half of its members.

By 1845, Freemasonry began to revive in the United States, but it never again achieved the social status that it had once enjoyed. In 1872, two Masons formed a kind of parody of the Masons and named it the Ancient Arabic Order of the Nobles of the Mystic Shrine, aka, The Shriners. By 1897, the Masons had about 750,000 members, and numerous other fraternal organizations such as the Knights of Columbus, the Benevolent and Protective Order of Elks, the Odd Fellows, and the Loyal Order of Moose sprang into being. In the 1950s, the Masons reached their numerical peak in America with more than four million members.

In 2001, there were about two million Masons in the United States and their average age was well over 60. Younger men, it seems, are no longer attracted to an organization whose members receive such grandiose titles as Master of the Royal Secret, Knight of the Brazen Serpent, or Worshipful Master. As for being a secret society, Masonic Lodge telephone numbers are in the directory, and the texts of many of their oaths have been made public, i.e., "You agree to be a good man and true; you agree to conform to the laws of the country in which you reside; you promise not to be concerned in plots and conspiracies against the government."

❁ **DELVING DEEPER**

Carlson, Peter. "Fezzes, Sphinxes and Secret Handshakes," *The Washington Post*, November 25, 2001 [Online] http://www.washingtonpost.com/wp-dyn/articles/A61372-2001Nov20.html.

Goeringer, Conrad. "Freemasons—From the 700 Club to Art Bell, an Object of Conspiracy Thinking." *American Atheist*, May 1998 [Online] http://www.americanatheist.org/supplement/conspiracy.html.

Lomas, Robert, and Christopher Knight. *The Hiram Key: Pharaohs, Freemasons, and the Discovery of the Secret Scrolls of Jesus*. Boston: Element Books, 1999.

MaCoy, Robert. *A Dictionary of Freemasonry*. New York: Gramercy Books, 2000.

Seligmann, Kurt. *The History of Magic*. New York: Pantheon Books, 1948.

THE GARDUNA

The origins of the Garduna begin in a legend not dissimilar from that of El Cid (c. 1043–1099), the heroic knight who defended northern Spain from the invading Moors in the eleventh century, and the secret society continues to this day in a criminal organization akin to the Mafia. According to tradition, around 710 a holy man named Apollinario, who lived a hermitlike existence in the hills above Cordova, had a vision in which the Blessed Virgin Mary appointed him to be the savior of Spain and drive the Moors out of the land. At first the holy man was staggered by the very suggestion, regardless of the source from whence it had come. What remained of Gothic Spain had fallen into decay, deteriorating into a patchwork of petty princedoms, woefully ineffectual against the powerful Moors who had conquered most of the land and established their royal seat in Cordova. But when the apparition of Mary presented him with a button that she said had been taken from the robe of Christ, Apollinario knew that he had been given the power to raise a band of holy warriors. He followed her orders to gather an army from the simple countryfolk of Spain, even from the bandits who lived in the mountains, and to avoid the corrupt nobles and landed aristocracy.

The hermit from the hills above Cordova was blessed with a charisma that caused the common people to flock to his leadership. He told them that those who followed him in the Garduna, his sacred army, would be licensed by God and the Holy Virgin to destroy the invading heathens by any means. There would be open warfare, of course, but they would also be free to plot murders and practice any kind of secret treachery. Those who joined the Garduna would be absolved of all wrongdoing as long as their violence was committed only against non-Christians. Thousands joined the holy man in his crusade against the Moors, and his army of peasants, beggars, and bandits fought so fiercely under the standard of the Holy Virgin of Cordova that no Moorish force could repel them.

While the Garduna may have harassed the powerful Muslim armies and conducted a guerilla-type warfare against them, they by no means drove the invaders from Spain as legend told it. After about 714, the Gothic monarchy of Spain had been replaced by the institutions of the conquering Arabs, and a short time after

Spain had fallen to the Moors, it became the most prosperous and civilized country in the West. Within a few more years, the Arabs had extended their European empire north of the Pyrenees Mountains to the south of France and from the mouth of the Garonne to that of the Rhone. In 732, Charles Martel of France stemmed the Muslim tide of conquest at the Battle of Tours, and the Arabs retreated back to Spain where they retained a peaceful possession of the country for many centuries. Cordova became a highly respected seat of art and learning, and the Arab philosophers became the sages of the West.

THOSE *who followed Apollinario in the Garduna, would be licensed by God and the Holy Virgin to destroy the invading heathens.*

Over the centuries, the Garduna degenerated into a loosely knit criminal network controlled by the descendants of the mountain bandits who had followed Apollinario in his crusade against the Moors. Deception and murder were still practiced on a large scale by the Garduna, and they maintained the old dictum that only the blood of non-Christians was to be shed. Perhaps the Garduna would have vanished completely into legend if fifteenth-century Spain had not become a Christian nation and King Ferdinand V (1452–1516) and Queen Isabella I (1451–1504) had not so avidly supported the mission of the **Inquisition** and that of its chief heretic hunter in Spain, Tomas de Torquemada (1420–1498).

Until the Inquisition, Moors, Jews, and Christians had for centuries lived quite peacefully in Spain. The Moors and the Jews were respected for their learning and for their skill as craftsmen and merchants, and it was widely acknowledged that both groups of citizens had made considerable contributions to Spain's rise to power and its recent acquisitions in the New World. Ferdinand reasoned that the Moors and the Jews had grown too powerful and too rich, and that he could extend the

Spanish Empire farther if he were to acquire their wealth. He also considered them heretics because they were not Christians.

The slaughter of innocent people began in earnest with Muslim and Jewish shopkeepers and scholars condemned as heretics and witches. The terrible machinery of the Inquisition was quite effective in and of itself, but Ferdinand recalled the stories of the Garduna, who killed only heathens, and he summoned their leaders to meet with high officers of church and state.

For the bandit chiefs of the Garduna, it was as if they were given a license to kill and to loot. Church officials told them that they must once again become holy warriors and become a weapon of terror against all heretics. All their sins would be forgiven. All their crimes would be pardoned. They were to be a secret society of murderers with the full approval of church and state.

F⊙R *over 100 years, the Garduna murdered, raped, and looted on the orders of the Inquisition.*

For more than 100 years, the Garduna murdered, raped, and looted on the orders of the Inquisition. Their victims were always non-Christians or those suspected of being heretics.

By 1670, the Inquisition withdrew its support from the Garduna, but the holy warriors became a secret cult within the church and continued their attacks against all those deemed contrary to the teachings of Christianity. When the church itself withdrew its recognition of the Garduna, they became a secret society, maintaining always that everything they did was an expression of God's will and any alleged crime they might commit was free of the taint of any sin.

During the eighteenth century, the Garduna had expanded its parameters of potential victims to include Christians, as well as unbelievers, and they had begun selling their services of murder, kidnapping, robbery, and so forth to anyone who could afford them. They

had become so powerful and daring that if any member of the society should be caught and imprisoned, the others thought nothing of attacking the prison and freeing him.

At the height of its powers in the eighteenth century, the Garduna instituted ranks within the society which could only be attained by acts of merit. At the head of the Garduna was the great brother or grand master, who ruled the society from its headquarters in Seville. Following his orders were the commanders, the district chiefs, and the chiefs, the leaders of individual bands. Under the chiefs came the swordsmen, well-trained men who were responsible for planning the criminal operations of the Garduna. The true fighting men of the society were called the athletes, tough and ruthless individuals who were often escaped convicts, galley-slaves, and vicious criminals. Below the athletes in rank were the "bellows," elderly men who were regarded by their cities and villages as men of good character who acted as the disposers of stolen goods for the society. The lowest rank in the Garduna was held by the "goats," the new recruits who had yet to prove their abilities. There were also two female ranks: the sirens, young beautiful women whose task it was to seduce state officials; and the covers, whose assignment lay in luring unsuspecting victims into ambushes where they could be robbed or murdered.

In 1822, in an era of social reform, police entered the home of the grand master in Seville, arrested him, and confiscated all his documents. Remarkably, the Garduna had kept meticulous records of all of their various criminal activities from 1520 to that date. The grand master and 16 of his district chiefs were publicly hanged in the main square of the city. Members of the other ranks of the Garduna scattered and resumed a life of banditry in the mountains.

The Garduna gave evidence of their survival as a secret society throughout the Spanish Civil War (1936–39) when their battle cry of "Remember the Virgin of Cordova!" was frequently heard. It has been said that the Garduna have established their own church, blending their concept of unorthodox Catholicism with a kind of "holy socialism." With branches allegedly established in Portugal and South America, as well as Spain, the Garduna continues to flourish as a criminal secret society 1,200 years after its conception by the hermit Apollinario.

✣ DELVING DEEPER

Daraul, Arkon. *A History of Secret Societies*. New York: Pocket Books, 1969.

Heckethorn, Charles William. *Secret Societies of All Ages and Countries*. Kila, Mont.: Kessinger Publishing, 1997.

Lefebure, Charles. *The Blood Cults*. New York: Ace Books, 1969.

THE HOLY VEHM

In the middle of the thirteenth century, when outlaw bands and mercenaries roamed the lawless territory between the Rhine and the Weser rivers in Westphalia, Germany, the Chivalrous Order of the Holy Vehm (or Fehm), a secret vigilante society, was formed by free men and commoners to protect themselves from the marauders. In the beginning, the resistance group had the approval of both the church and the Holy Roman emperor, but as time passed the Holy Vehm became a law unto itself, passing judgment on all those whom they decided should receive a death sentence.

Because the society began with only a handful of members and violent retaliation could be expected from any gang of outlaws who might learn the identities of those commoners who dared to oppose them, an oath of secrecy was imposed upon all those with the courage to join the ranks of the Vehm. During the initiation ceremonies, candidates vowed to kill themselves and even their spouses and children, rather than permit any society secrets to be betrayed. Once the oath had been made, one of the Vehm's *Stuhlherren* or judges, would move his sword across the initiates' throats, drawing a few drops of blood to serve as a silent reminder of the fate that awaited all traitors to the society. After this ritual had been observed, the initiates kissed the cross that was formed by the space between the sword's blade and hilt. Below the *Stuhlherren* in rank were the deputy judges, the

Freischoffen, and the executioners, the *Frohnboten.* The deputy judges and the executioners carried out the various tasks of inquisitors, jury, and hangman.

THE *Holy Vehm was formed by free men and commoners to protect themselves from the marauders.*

The name "Vehm" or "Fehm" was a corruption of the Latin word "fama," a law founded upon a common or agreed upon opinion. However, "Fehm" could also mean something that was set apart, and the leaders of the Holy Vehm soon decided that their crusade against evildoers had set them apart and above the laws that governed others. Within a few decades of its formation, the Vehm had more than 200,000 free men and commoners in its ranks—each man sworn to uphold the Ten Commandments and to eliminate all heresies, heretics, perjurers, traitors, and servants of Satan. Once anyone was suspected of violating one or more of the Lord's commandments or laws, he or she was brought before one of the Holy Vehm's courts and was unlikely to escape the death sentence to be hanged.

Because of the great power that the Vehm acquired, it conducted trials of noted outlaws and thieves unopposed in public places, such as village squares or market places, in the full light of midday. As its numbers and influence grew, the Vehm had little reason to fear anyone speaking out against them, but the harsh and punitive secret courts conducted by the society, the *Heimliches Gericht,* were always held at midnight in order to create an even more sinister and frightening effect to their reading of the death sentence. Even less merciful to those suspected of witchcraft or heresy were the "forbidden court," *Verbotene Acht,* and the *Heimliches Acht,* the "secret tribunal," both of which were conducted by the Black Vehm, a splinter group of the Holy Vehm.

Once the outlaws, thieves, and other assorted brigands had been largely driven from Westphalia, the Vehm turned its attention to those men and women suspected of heresies or of betraying the commandments of God in a variety of sins. Before suspects came to court, they were served with three summonses, each of which gave them the opportunity of attending voluntarily. Each summons also gave the accused a period of consent of six weeks and three days. Because the tribunals of the Vehm had gained a reputation of pronouncing only death sentences, few people attended the courts of their own volition. Those who tried to escape were condemned without the usual pretense of a trial and Vehm executioners were assigned to hunt them down.

Because the tribunals of the Vehm were willing to accept the weakest of circumstantial evidence against any individual accused of a crime or an act of heresy, there appears to be no record of any of the secret courts ever finding anyone innocent. While no accurate records of their victims were ever kept, historians have estimated that thousands of men and women—the innocent along with the guilty—were dragged into the night to attend one of the Vehm's secret courts.

An entire population of sleeping villagers might be awakened by the thudding of swords' hilts on their doors and be summoned by torchlight to attend a midnight tribunal that accused one of their neighbors of some act of heresy—real or imagined. Regardless of the charges levied against those victims the Vehm accused, the sentence was always death. And if any spoke in defense of their friends, they were likely to be hanged as well, for giving false witness to defend a heretic or a traitor. On those rare occasions when the tribunal failed to convince even its own members of an accused individual's guilt, that unfortunate person was hanged to preserve the secrecy of the tribunal.

Eventually the Holy Vehm was condemned by the church and the German state, but the secret society remained active in a greatly diminished capacity. Toward the end of the nineteenth century, it went underground and seemingly ceased all acts of violence. In the 1930s, with the rise of the Nazis to power in Germany, for the first time in its 700-year history the Vehm came into the open, focusing its bigotry upon the Jewish people, judging them to be guilty of heresy. The Chivalrous Order of the Holy Vehm appears to have been destroyed along with their Nazi allies with the fall of the Third Reich in 1945.

❊ DELVING DEEPER

Angebert, Jean-Michel. *The Occult and the Third Reich*. New York: Macmillan, 1974.

Daraul, Arkon. *A History of Secret Societies*. New York: Pocket Books, 1969.

Heckethorn, Charles William. *Secret Societies of All Ages and Countries*. Kila, Mont.: Kessinger Publishing, 1997.

THE ILLUMINATI

For many conspiracy theorists, the Illuminati is the ultimate secret society, a group that stretches its tentacles of control to encompass the entire world. According to these theorists, the members of the Illuminati are the real rulers of the world, and they have been pulling the strings from behind the political scenes for centuries. They have infiltrated every government and every aspect of society around the planet—and some say that their ultimate goal is to accomplish a satanic New World Order, a one-world government, that will prepare Earth's citizens for the coming of the **Antichrist.**

Although such paranoid claims make for exciting reading, the Illuminati of history, rather than legend, was a secret society formed in Bavaria in 1776 with the political goal of encouraging rebellion of the people and the abolition of the established monarchies. Structuring the society along the lines of the classes and orders of the **Freemasons,** the Illuminati included levels of enlightenment that could be achieved by undergoing initiation through various mystical rites and ceremonies. Although the society's founder, a professor of religious law named Adam Weishaupt, sought to establish a new world order in the late eighteenth-century, the Illuminati was destroyed within 15 years of its founding.

The term "Illuminati" was first used by Spanish occultists toward the end of the fif-

Certain scholars who have studied the makeup of the Bilderbergers insist that the group is controlled by the 10-man Inner Circle of the Illuminati. According to their claims, this secret cabal has painstakingly prepared an agenda for the masses of humanity into the millennium. Such individuals as the Bilderbergers will become the world's masters, and the vast majority of the global population may look forward to a future existence as pawns, if not slaves, of the Illuminati.

According to certain sources who claim knowledge of the basic plan for world dominance set in motion by the Bilderbergers, the following goals are among their principal objectives:

The United States must promptly pay its debt to the United Nations. In addition, the United States will be asked to contribute billions of dollars to the International Monetary Fund. U.S. taxpayers will be bled almost dry by such expenditures.

The North Atlantic Treaty Organization (NATO) will be converted into a United Nations military force. U.S. troops will therefore come under the command of NATO's foreign officers.

"Corporate Governance" will dissolve national sovereignty and bring all of Earth's corporations under a single global order. Local control over businesses and corporations by nations and states will be terminated. The great giants of finance will be able to disregard the laws and dictates of all governments, including those of the United States.

As the twenty-first century dawns, a new system of fascism will emerge under the guise of free trade practices that will be guided by the Illuminati.

The Bilderbergers have approved the Red Chinese model of economics as the standard for the emerging European superstate and the United States. As in Red China, all dissidents will be dealt with severely and placed in work camps.

As soon as the program can be implemented, citizens in every nation will be issued the Universal Biometrics Identification Card.

Bilderbergers Plan for a New World Order

A Gestapo-like police state will be established to enforce the dictates of the Illuminati's New World Order.

Sources:

Bilderbergers Role in the New World Order.[Online] http://www.jeremiahproject.com/prophecy/nworder04.html.

New World Order: The Bilderbergs. [Online] http://conspiracies.about.com/newsissues/conspiracies/cs/thebilderbergs.

Vankin, Jonathan, and John Whalen. *The 60 Greatest Conspiracies of All Time.* New York: Barnes & Noble, 1996.

teenth century to signify those alchemists and magicians who appeared to possess the "light" of spiritual illumination from a higher source. The term may have originated in the **Gnostic** dualism of the forces of Light and Darkness, and many individuals who claimed to be Illuminati, those enlightened by a higher wisdom, joined the **Rosicrucians** and took refuge in France to escape the fires of the Spanish Inquisition.

THE *Illuminati of history, rather than legend, was a secret society formed in Bavaria in 1776.*

The secret society known as the Order of the Illuminati was founded in the city of Ingolstadt in the southern German monarchy of Bavaria on May 1, 1776 by Adam Weishaupt, a 28-year-old professor of religious law. Beginning with only five members, Weishaupt's order grew slowly, numbering about 60 in five cities by 1780. The professor deliberately blended mysticism into the workings of the brotherhood in order to make his agenda of republicanism appear to be more mysterious than a political reform group. He joined the Masons in Munich in 1777 and adopted many of their classes and orders and promised his initiates that they would receive a special communication of occult knowledge as they advanced higher in the ranks of the Illuminati.

Weishaupt's society had little effect on the German political structure until 1780 when he attracted the interest of Adolf Francis, the Baron Von Knigge, a master occultist and a man who had risen to the highest levels in many of the secret societies that preceded the Illuminati, including the Masons. Knigge had no problem melding his interest in the supernatural with Weishaupt's goal of political revolution, and the two men quickly established branches of the Illuminati throughout all of Germany. A few months after Knigge had joined Weishaupt's cause, membership in the Illuminati swelled to 300.

Weishaupt had taken great care to enlist as many young men of wealth and position as possible, maintaining that philanthropy, as well as mysticism, was a principal goal of the society. He had also managed to create around himself a great aura of mystery, permitting himself to be seen by none but those in the highest ranks of the society, encouraging the myth that he was an adept of such great power that he existed largely as an invisible presence. Initiates into the ranks of the Illuminati underwent secret rites, wore bizarre costumes, and participated in grotesque ceremonies that were designed to give complete obedience to Weishaupt. Soon the Illuminati became a force to be reckoned with behind the scenes in Germany's political life, and its members worked secretly to overthrow both church and state.

As their influence as a secret society grew, Weishaupt and Knigge became concerned that a good many authorities were beginning to take seriously the rumors of the existence of the Illuminati. If it should be proven that the society existed in fact, certain of the more powerful German princes would take immediate steps to suppress it. To hide the society even more completely from the scrutiny of public view, the leaders implemented Weishaupt's original plan of grafting the Illuminati onto the larger brotherhood of the Freemasons. The Illuminati were already utilizing the classes and grades of Freemasonry, so the initiates of the Illuminati would easily amalgamate with the more established society. To appear to become one with the Freemasons would allow Illuminism to spread more widely and rapidly, and Weishaupt and Knigge had great confidence that they would soon attain complete control over the blended organizations.

The hierarchy within the Freemasons were not long in discovering that the two interlopers had joined the fraternal brotherhood with less than honorable motives, and in 1782, a group within the Masons called the Strict Observance demanded that a council be held at Wilhelmsbad to examine the true beliefs of Weishaupt and the Illuminati. Knigge's powers of persuasion effectively blocked the attempt of the Strict Observance contingent to expel Illuminism from their society, and he managed to enroll almost all the members of the council in the Illuminati. By 1784, Illuminati membership had risen to 3,000, and the secret society appeared on the verge of assuming control of the entire Masonic establishment.

At the same time that their goals seemed within their grasp, Weishaupt and Knigge fell into a sharp disagreement about the correct manner of proceeding with their master plan; and in April 1784, Knigge withdrew from the Illuminati, leaving Weishaupt the supreme commander of the increasingly powerful society. Later in that same year, a number of initiates who had reached the highest level within the Illuminati became disillusioned when the special supernatural communication from a higher source that Weishaupt had promised had still not manifested after eight years of membership in the society. It now became obvious to them that Weishaupt had only sought to use them as blind instruments for the achievement of his political ambitions. The Illuminati was denounced as a subversive organization by many of its former members, some of whom informed the duchess dowager Maria Anna of Bavaria and the Bavarian monarch, Carl Theodore, that the society sought the overthrow of church and state.

In June 1784, Carl Theodore issued an edict outlawing all secret societies in his provinces. In March 1785, another edict specifically condemned the Illuminati. Weishaupt had already fled to a neighboring province in February, 1785, where he hoped to inspire the loyal members of the Illuminati to continue as a society. In 1787, the duke of Bavaria issued a final edit against the Order of the Illuminati, and Weishaupt apparently faded into obscurity. Although he never realized his goal of a German Republic and the overthrowing of the European monarchies, the sparks that he had ignited with the Illuminati would soon burst into the flames of the French Revolution in 1789.

⌖ DELVING DEEPER

Carroll, Robert Todd. "Illuminati, The New World Order & Paranoid Conspiracy Theorists," *The Skeptics Dictionary*. http://skepdic.com/ illuminati. html.

Roberts, J. *Mythology of the Secret Societies*. New York: MacMillan, 1972.

Vankin, Jonathan and John Whalen. *The Seventy Greatest Conspiracies of All Time: History's Biggest Mysteries, Coverups, and Cabals*. New York: Citadel, 1998.

Wilgus, Neal. *The Illuminoids*. New York: Pocket Books, 1978.

Wilson, Robert Anton. *Masks of the Illuminati*. New York: Pocket Books, 1981.

THE KNIGHTS TEMPLAR

The two principal orders of knighthood of the Crusades were established prior to the launching of the first crusade in 1096 and shortly before the second crusade began in 1146. The fundamental principle on which the new orders were based was the union of monasticism and chivalry. Before this time, a man could choose to devote himself to religion and become a monk, or he could elect to become a warrior and devote himself to defending God and country. The founding of the orders of knighthood permitted the vow of religion and the vow of war to be united in a single effort to free the Holy Land from the Muslims.

The oldest of the religio-chivalric orders was the Knights of Saint John of Jerusalem, also known as the Knights Hospitallers and subsequently as the Knights of Malta and the Knights of Rhodes, founded in 1048. By the middle of the twelfth century, the Hospitallers had become a powerful military factor in the East, and their membership included the most accomplished knights in Christendom. By 1153 they had become the pride of the Christians and the terror of the Saracens. Unfortunately, after a great number of victories for the cross, the moral and chivalric ideals of the order began to become corrupted by the enormous wealth that its warriors had accumulated. In 1187, the Hospitallers were almost annihilated in the disastrous battle of Tiberias, where the Saracen army under the generalship of Saladin (1137–1193), the sultan of Egypt and Syria, thoroughly defeated the Christians and reclaimed Jerusalem.

The second of the great orders of knighthood was founded in 1117 by two French knights and was originally known as the Knights of the Temple of Solomon and later as the Knights Templar or the Knights of the Red Cross. Hugues des Paiens and Geoffrey of Saint-Omer, two compassionate nobles, had

observed the hardships endured by Christian travelers en route to Jerusalem and decided to serve as guides and protectors for the defenseless pilgrims. The warrior guides soon gained a reputation for their service to the helpless wayfarers; they were joined by seven other knights who admired their principles. The nine men bound themselves by the traditional vows of obedience, chastity, and poverty, then added the oaths to defend the Holy Sepulcher and to protect those pilgrims who journeyed there. At first the Knights of Saint John, the Hospitallers, lent aid and encouragement to the new society of brothers. There could be no rivalry with this new order of knights who comprised only nine members and were known by others as the "Poor Soldiers of the Holy City." It was said that Hugues and Geof-

frey only had one horse between them when they first began their missions of benevolence.

Then, at the council of Troyes in 1127, St. Bernard of Clairvaux (1090–1153) drew up a code for the order and designed an appropriate uniform, consisting of a white tunic and mantle with a red cross on the left breast. Pope Honorius II (d. 1130) approved the following rules of conduct and discipline for the order in 1128:

- to recite vocal prayers at certain hours;

- to abstain from meat four days in the week; to cease hunting and hawking;

- to defend with their lives the mysteries of the Christian faith;

- to observe the seven sacraments of the church, the fourteen articles of faith, the creeds of the apostles and Athanasius;

- to uphold the doctrines of the Two Testaments, including the interpretations of the church fathers, the unity of God and the trinity of his persons, and the virginity of Mary both before and after the birth of Jesus;

- to go beyond the seas when called to do so in defense of the cause;

- to retreat not from the foe unless outnumbered three to one.

In addition to the rules of conduct and discipline, humility was one of the first principles of membership in the Knights Templar. The helmet of the Templar must bear no crest; his beard should never be cut; his personal behavior should be that of a servant of others; and his tunic should be girt with a linen cord as a symbol that he was bound in service.

There were four classes of members in the Templars—knights, squires, servitors, and priests—each with their individual list of duties and obligations. The presiding officer of the order was called the grand master and was assisted by a lieutenant, a steward, a marshal, and a treasurer. The states of Christendom were divided into provinces, and over each was set a grand master. The grand master of

Jerusalem was considered the head of the entire brotherhood, which grew in numbers, influence, and wealth to become one of the most powerful organizations in the medieval world. Counts, dukes, princes, and even kings sought to wear the red cross and white mantle of the Templar, an honor which was recognized throughout Europe.

THE *two principal Orders of Knighthood of the Crusades were established in 1096.*

In 1139, Pope Innocent II (d. 1143) granted the Templars an unprecedented mark of papal approval: the churches of the Templars were exempt from interdicts; their properties and revenues were free from taxation to either crown or Holy Mother Church. The Templars now had the prestige of being triumphant crusaders. They had the blessing of the pope. They had the gratitude of those whom they had protected on their pilgrimages. They had vast estates with mansions that could not be invaded by any civil officer. Thousands beseeched the order to allow them to become members of the Templars. In the course of time the Knights of the Temple became a sovereign body, pledging allegiance to no secular ruler. In spiritual matters, the pope was still recognized as supreme, but in all other matters, the grand master of Jerusalem was as independent and as wealthy as the greatest king in Europe.

What had begun as the mission of two poor knights with one horse who vowed to watch over Christian pilgrims on their way to Jerusalem had become a privileged order of opportunists bloated with wealth. And in their new quest for power and wealth, the protection of the pilgrims was often forgotten. Even St. Bernard issued a series of exhortations that the order was accepting into its membership too many knights who were but adventurers and outlaws and that a good number of the nobility who had joined the Templars were men who had been regarded as oppressors and scourges by their serfs.

THE *Knights Templars owed their allegiance only to the pope.*

There were three divisions of the Templars in the East—Jerusalem, Antioch, and Tripoli. In Europe, there were 16 provinces—France, Auvergne, Normandy, Aquitaine, Poitou, Provence, England, Germany, Upper and Lower Italy, Apulia, Sicily, Portugal, Castile, Leon, and Aragon. A majority of the Templars were French, and it was estimated by the middle of the thirteenth century that as many as 9,000 manors were held by the Templars in France.

The chief seat of the Templars had remained in Jerusalem from the origins of the order in 1118 to 1187, when it was moved to Antioch after the Christians' defeat by Saladin in the plain of Tiberias. The Hospitallers and the Templars had been slaughtered in battle and 230 captive knights had been beheaded when they refused the Muslims' offer to convert to the religion of the Prophet. The grand master established the Templar headquarters in Antioch for four years, then moved to Acre in 1191. A third transfer of the Templar seat was made in 1217 when the grand master moved to the Pilgrim's Castle near Cesarea. When the Muslims captured Acre in 1291 and overthrew the Christian kingdom, the Templars had bravely fought until they were exterminated almost to the man. The surviving Templars retreated to Cyprus, which they had purchased from King Richard the Lion-Hearted (1157–1199) for 35,000 marks.

Although defeated by the soldiers of the Prophet Muhammad and driven out of the Holy Land, the Knights Templar retained their many estates and their enormous wealth in Europe. However, especially in France, the Templars were becoming diminished in popularity, and the jealousies of the government had been aroused against them. Lords, dukes, and princes were not only envious of the order's burgeoning treasury, but they fumed over the Templars' exemption from the burdens of taxation imposed by church and state on others. The self-righteous among the rulers and the people were indignant over the knights' pride, arrogance, and licentiousness, and rumors began to spread that the order had acquired heretical practices during their time in the East.

In 1306, King Philip IV (1268–1314) of France, called Philip the Fair, sought refuge for himself and the royal treasury in the Templars' massive fortress in Paris. The unruly mobs were calling for his death, and he feared that the disloyal among his nobles would loot the nation's wealth. While Philip was in the process of entrusting the treasury of France to the Templars' protection, he also managed to gain sight of the incredible wealth that the Knights had accumulated. When he fully comprehended that this was only a portion of their immeasurable riches and that the Templars had forts and estates throughout France, each containing its own deposit of treasure, he was awed by the enormity of their riches.

When Philip sat more securely on his throne, he began to perceive the Templars as rivals for his kingdom. The Knights had more money and power than he, the king, and they owed their allegiance only to the pope. Philip met with Pope Clement V (c. 1260–1314) to seek his counsel on how the order might be exterminated. Although the Templars had enjoyed the blessing of the papacy for decades, the pope admitted that he had been made uneasy by accusations that the order had sought to protect their own interests by securing a separate treaty with the Mulis when the Christian kingdom in the East was falling. Clement, however, was reluctant to make any kind of move against the Knights. The king pressed his case with the pope—and made an issue of the fact that the papacy at that time was located at Avignon, which was one of Philip's territories.

Then Philip found the mysterious Esquire de Floyran, who claimed to have been a member of the Knights Templar. Floyran said that the order had deceived the church and the people for more than a hundred years. What had begun as a pious service to pilgrims and defenders of the cross against the infidels had degenerated into a monstrous blood cult. Principal among the demons they worshipped was Baphomet, the three-headed god of the **Assassins,** a heretical Muslim sect. Floyran swore that he had seen initiates into the order spitting upon crucifixes, participating in vile rites, even sacrificing babies to demons.

There has never been any conclusive evidence to prove whether de Floyran was a true member of the Knights Templar who had a personal grudge against the order or if he was an imposter on the king's own payroll, but armed with the supposed insider's sensational accounts, the backing of the highest church officials in France, and the endorsement of William of Paris, the Grand Inquisitor, King Philip demanded that the pope conduct an investigation into such charges against the Knights Templar. Whether or not Clement believed such stories, he gave his approval that a judicial inquiry be instituted, and the knights were charged with heresy and immorality.

On the night of October 13, 1307, all of the Templars' castles in France were surrounded by large bodies of men that were led by small parties of priests and noblemen. When the unsuspecting knights were ordered to open their gates in the name of the king, they immediately complied. Taken completely by surprise, about 900 knights were arrested, and all their property and holdings in France were seized. When word of the arrests reached other countries, other nobles and priests quickly followed suit and imprisoned the Templars wherever they might be found.

The Knights Templar were accused of infidelity, Muhammadanism, atheism, heresy, invoking Satan, worshipping demons, desecration of holy objects, and uncleanness. The prosecution had difficulty proving such charges, so they were often forced to resort to torturing the prisoners to obtain confessions. In Paris, the grand master of the Templars, Jacques de Molay (1243–1314), pleaded the innocence of the order against all such charges. In spite of his personal friendship with de Molay, who was the godfather of his younger son, Philip ordered the grand master and the 140 knights imprisoned with him to be starved, tortured, and kept in filthy dungeons.

Although the pope had little problem yielding to pressure and issuing a ban on the order, he hesitated to give his sanction to the extermination of the knights. Philip, however, was determined to see the Templars destroyed and their wealth distributed to the state. For two weeks, the knights imprisoned in Paris suffered the rack, the thumbscrew, the pincers, the branding iron, and the fire. Thirty-six died under torture without speaking. The rest confessed to every charge the Inquisition had leveled against them—the worship of Baphomet, a black cat, and a serpent; the sacrifice of babies and the murders of pious knights who opposed them.

A grand council was called in Paris on May 10, 1310, to review the confessions. But Philip's victory was sullied when 54 of the knights withdrew their confessions and appealed to government and church officials that they had been tortured. They swore that they had remained true to their vows and that they had never practiced any kind of **witchcraft** or **Satanism.** Philip silenced their pleas three days later when he ordered all 54 of the Templars burned at the stake in a field behind the alley of St. Antoine.

In 1312, the pope convened the Council of Venice to weigh the fate of the Templars. It was decided that the order should be abolished and its property confiscated, but Pope Clement chose to reserve final judgment concerning whether the knights were guilty of the heinous charges brought against them. In spite of 573 witnesses for their defense, Templars were tortured en masse, then burned at the stake. The landed possessions of the order were transferred to the Hospitallers, and their wealth was distributed to the sovereigns of various states. Everywhere in Christendom, except in Portugal, where the Templars assumed the name of the Knights of Christ, the order as an organization was suppressed.

In 1314, as he was being burned to death on a scaffold erected for the occasion in front of Notre Dame, the Knights Templar grand master, Jacques de Molay, recanted the confession that he gave under torture and proclaimed his innocence to Pope Clement V and King Philip—and he invited them to meet him at heaven's gate. When both dignitaries died soon after de Molay's execution, it was believed by the public at large that the grand master and the Knights Templar had been innocent of the charges of heresy.

Although the Order was officially dissolved by Papal Decree in 1312, the mystique of the Knights Templar still remains strong in the twenty-first century. There are groups claiming an association with the Templar Order around the world. Some only affirm that they are following the ideals of the Knights Templar. Others state that they can trace a historical connection with the original order.

The Militi Templi Scotia or the Scottish Knights Templar point out that the papal Order of Suppression issued in 1312 was not enforced in Scotland because the Scots believed the charges against the Knights were unproven. Under the excommunicated King, Robert the Bruce, Scotland provided a safe haven for any Knights Templar who were able to flee Europe and reach its shores. According to tradition, the Knights who sought refuge in Scotland fought side by side with Robert the Bruce to win independence from England. In turn, the king protected the Order and Temple lands in Scotland.

The Militi Templi Scotia remains active and emphasizes its historical connection to the original Order of Templar Knights. They make a point of proclaiming that they are not a secret society and have even expanded membership to include women. As with the original Order, however, all members must be professing Christians or individuals of "high ideals."

Another group in the United Kingdom also claims a historical continuity with the original Order because of Knights Templar who managed to reach England. The Supreme Military Order of Temple of Jerusalem of England, Wales, and Scotland states that it is not a secret society and that, as with the Militi Templi Scotia, it has no affiliation with the Freemasons. The order is open only to Christians according to the website http://theknightstemplar.org. Associated with the Supreme Military Order of Temple of Jerusalem is the North American Order of Poor Fellow Soldiers of Christ and the Temple of Solomon, Knights Templar and can be found at the website http://www.knights templar.org.

✤ **DELVING DEEPER**
Ahmed, Rollo. *The Black Art*. London: Arrow Books, 1966.

Baigent, Michael, and Richard Leigh. *The Temple and the Lodge*. New York: Arcade, 1989.

Clifton, Charles S. *Encyclopedia of Heresies and Heretics*. New York: Barnes & Noble, 1998.

Howarth, Stephen. *The Knights Templar*. New York: Barnes & Noble, 1993.

Vankin, Jonathan, and John Whalen. *The Seventy Greatest Conspiracies of All Time: History's Biggest Mysteries, Coverups, and Cabals*. New York: Citadel, 1998.

THE LEOPARD MEN

In ancient Egypt, the leopard was esteemed as an aspect of divinity and associated with the god Osiris, the judge of the dead. For many African tribes, the leopard is a powerful totem animal that is believed to guide the spirits of the dead to rest.

For many centuries a leopard cult has existed in West Africa, particularly in Nigeria and Sierra Leone, wherein its members kill as does the leopard, by slashing, gashing, and mauling their human prey with steel claws and knives. Later, during gory ceremonies, they drink the blood and eat the flesh of human victims. Those initiates who aspire to become members of the cult must return from a night's foray with a bottle of their victim's blood and drink it in the presence of the assembled members. The cultists believe that a magical elixir known as *borfima,* which they brew from their victim's intestines, grants them superhuman powers and enables them to transform themselves into leopards.

The members of the cult kill on the slightest pretext. Perhaps one of the members became ill or his crops failed. Such misfortunes as these would be sufficient to demand a human sacrifice. A likely victim would be chosen, the date and time of the killing agreed upon, and the executioner, known as the Bati Yeli, would be selected. The Bati Yeli wore the ritual leopard mask and a leopard skin robe. It was preferable that the sacrifice be performed at one of the leopard cult's jungle shrines, but if circumstances demanded a more immediate shedding of blood, the rite could be conducted with the ceremonial two-pronged steel claw anywhere at all.

The first really serious outbreak of leopard-cult murders in Sierra Leone and Nigeria occurred shortly after World War I (1914–18). At that time, it was believed the cult was suppressed by the region's white administrators because many of its members were captured and executed. However, in actual fact, the leopard men simply went underground, continuing to perform ritual murders sporadically every year over the next two decades.

In 1946, the leopard men became bold and there were 48 cases of murder and attempted murder committed by the leopard cult in that year alone. And it soon became obvious that, much like the **Mau-Mau** in Kenya, the leopard men had begun directing many of their attacks against white men as if to convince the native population that the cult had no fear of the police or of the white rulers. The trend continued during the first seven months of 1947, when there were 43 known ritual killings performed by the leopard cult.

Terry Wilson had been district officer of a province in Eastern Nigeria for only six months when, early in 1947, he discovered that the leopard men had begun operating in his jurisdiction, claiming mainly young women as their victims. When Wilson raided the house of a local chief named Nagogo, his men found a leopard mask, a leopard-skin robe, and a steel claw. Acting on a tip from an informer, Wilson ordered his police officers to dig near the chief's house, where they found the remains of 13 victims. The chief was put in prison to await trial, and Wilson set out on a determined mission to put an end to the leopard men's reign of terror.

But the local inhabitants were too terrified of the leopard cult to come forward. There were several more murders during the weeks that followed, including the wife and daughter of Nagogo, the imprisoned chieftain. A desperate Wilson hoped that the sight of the mutilated bodies of his family would anger Nagogo into betraying the cult members who had so obviously turned on him, but the shock proved too much for the chief. When he saw the bloodied corpses of his wife and daughter and realized how viciously his fellow leopard men had betrayed him, he collapsed and died of heart failure.

F☉R *many African tribes, the leopard is a powerful totem animal.*

Although Wilson received 200 additional police officers as reinforcements, the leopard men became increasingly bold in their nocturnal attacks. One night they even sacrificed a female victim inside the police compound and managed to get away without being seen. After that cruelly defiant gesture, the cult committed several murders in broad daylight. The native inhabitants of the region lost all confidence in the police and their ability to stop the slashings and killings of the powerful leopard men. Even some of Wilson's men began to believe that the cultists might truly have the ability to shapeshift into leopards and to fade unseen into the shadows.

One night in mid-August 1947, Wilson was awakened by the warning growl from his dog. When he rose to investigate, a four-foot-long, barbed arrow whistled by his head, narrowly missing him and embedding itself in the wall. The next morning at police headquarters, he learned that two of his officers had also barely escaped death that previous night.

Wilson knew that his men were becoming unnerved. They were trying to stop an enemy who was essentially invisible. They struck without warning after preselecting their victims by a process that evaded all attempts to define it. There was no way for Wilson and his officers to determine who the cult's next victims would be or to guess where they might strike. And the natives were far too intimidated to inform on the leopard men—if, in fact, they did know anything of importance to tell the officers.

The district officer decided to attempt to set a trap. On the path to a village where several slayings had already taken place, Wilson sent one of his best men, posing as the son of a native woman. The two walked side by side toward the village while Wilson and a dozen other officers concealed themselves in the bushes at the side of the path.

Suddenly, issuing the blood-curdling shriek of an attacking leopard, a tall man in leopard robes charged headlong at the couple, swinging a large club. The young police officer struggled with the leopard man, but before Wilson and the other men could arrive on the scene, the cultist had smashed in the officer's skull with the club and fled into the bushes.

Wilson had lost one of his best officers, but the knife that the young man still held in his hand was covered in blood. The police would now be able to search for a man with a severe knife wound.

The district officer was about to have some men take the constable's body to the compound when he had a sudden flash of intuition that the leopard man might return to the scene of the crime. While the other officers searched the neighboring villages, Wilson hid himself behind some bushes overlooking the trail.

Around midnight, just as Wilson was beginning to think about returning to the compound, a nightmarish figure crawling on all fours emerged from the jungle, pounced on the young officer's corpse, and began clawing at his face like a leopard. But rather than claws raking the body, Wilson caught the glint of a two-pronged steel claw in the moonlight. The killer had returned to complete the cult ritual of sacrifice. Wilson advanced on the leopard man, and the robed murderer snarled at him as if he were truly a big cat. When he came at him with the two-pronged claw, Wilson shot him in the chest.

With Wilson's act of courage, the natives of the region had been provided with proof that the leopard men were not supernatural beings that could not be stopped. The members of the cult did not have magic that could make them impervious to bullets. They were, after all, men of flesh and blood—savage, bestial, and vicious—but men, nonetheless. Once word had spread that the district officer had killed one of the leopard men, witnesses began to come forward in great numbers with clues to the identity of cult members and the possible location of a secret jungle shrine.

The shrine itself was discovered deep in the jungle, cunningly hidden and protected by a large boulder. The cult's altar was a flat stone slab that was covered with dark bloodstains. Human bones were strewn over the ground. A grotesque effigy of a half-leopard, half-man towered above the gory altar.

During February of 1948, 73 initiated members of the cult were arrested and sent to prison. Eventually, 39 of them were sentenced to death and hanged in Abak Prison, their executions witnessed by a number of local tribal chiefs who could testify to their villages that the leopard men were not immortal.

Interestingly, on January 10, 1948, just a month before the leopard men were hanged in Nigeria, three women and four men were executed for their part in the lion men murders in the Singida district in Tanganyika. The lion people had dressed in lion skins and murdered more than 40 natives in ritual slayings that left wounds on their victims that resembled the marks of a lion's claws.

✤ DELVING DEEPER

Daraul, Arkon. *A History of Secret Societies*. New York: Pocket Books, 1969.

NASA meddler Richard Hoagland insists that not only have the astronauts been to Mars, but they have been covering up the discovery of ruins and artifacts. Especially intrigued by the so-called Mars Face, a Sphinx-like object that appeared on numerous NASA photographs during the Viking I orbit in 1976, Hoagland has demanded the agency to divulge the discovery.

In April 1998, NASA's Mars Global Surveyor spacecraft traveled near Mars and sent back photos debunking theories that ancient civilizations constructed the face. The new pictures showed only an pile of rocks, completely devoid of the profile of the previous portraits of the Mars Face.

Within hours of NASA's statement, Hoagland's website declared, "Honey, I Shrunk the Face!" He insists NASA has been hiding the artifacts for decades. Hoagland unearthed a 1960 NASA-commissioned report recommending any future discoveries of alien life be kept from the public so as not to disturb the evolutionary flow of twentieth-century civilization.

NASA Covers Up Evidence of Alien Life on Mars

SOURCES:

Hoagland, Richard C. *The Enterprise Mission.* [Online] http://www.enterprisemission.com/.

———. *The Monuments of Mars: A City on the Edge of Forever.* Berkeley, Calif.: North Atlantic Books, 1987.

Vankin, Jonathan, and John Whalen. *The 60 Greatest Conspiracies of All Time.* New York: Barnes & Noble, 1996.

Eisler, Robert. *Man into Wolf.* London: Spring Books, n.d.

Lefebure, Charles. *The Blood Cults.* New York: Ace Books, 1969.

The Mau-Mau

It has been said that no one knows the real meaning of "Mau-Mau" other than a Kikuyu (also Gikuyu) tribesperson and that is because its name, like its origins, is shrouded in ancient African tribal mysteries and covered in blood. On the other hand, some authorities claim that the name was invented by European settlers and applied to the native insurrectionists in Kenya. At any rate, the name was first heard among the white population of Africa in 1948 when police officials in the British colony of Kenya

began to receive rumors of strange ceremonies being held late at night in the jungle. These midnight assemblies were said to be bestial rituals that mocked Christian rites and included the eating of human flesh and the drinking of blood. Then came the reports of native people being dragged from their beds at night, being beaten or maimed, and forced to swear oaths of initiation to a secret society. In each case, their assailants were said to be members of a secret society called the Mau-Mau.

In 1952, a state of emergency was declared in Kenya as the midnight rituals and beatings had escalated into the murder of Kikuyu policemen, whose bodies were found mutilated and bound with wire, floating in rivers. White farmers discovered their cattle disemboweled and the tendons in their legs severed so they could not walk. The secret society that

Mau-Mau being rounded up. (CORBIS CORPORATION)

had begun by practicing **black magic** and the administration of blood oaths had degenerated into the most violent sorts of barbarism.

THE *Mau-Mau weapon of choice was the machete.*

The Mau-Mau weapon of choice was the panga, the broad-bladed machete commonly used to hack a path through thick jungle vegetation. The society appeared to favor bloody and brutal attacks as a means of striking fear into the hearts and minds of all who might oppose them, but their choice of enemies seemed often difficult to comprehend. The first man to die at the hand of the Mau-Mau

was a Kikuyu chief who spoke out against the secret society that had chosen to resort to savagery and barbarism to achieve its political objectives. In October 1952, a lone white settler was killed and disemboweled. An elderly farmer was found dead in November; in January 1953, two men who worked a farm as partners were discovered murdered by the Mau-Mau. A vicious attack on January 24, 1953, claimed the Rucks, a family of English heritage, who had always been regarded as dealing with their black employees in a fair-minded and charitable manner, even to the extent of supporting a clinic at their own expense. The bodies of the husband, wife, and their six-year-old son were found so hacked and ripped as to be nearly unrecognizable as human beings.

Later it was learned that native men and women who had been in the Rucks' employ for many years had been foremost in the slaughter of the English family. What seemed particularly insidious to the white population was discovering to their horror that employees who had been loyal to them for decades were suddenly rising up and butchering them without warning. When the Mau-Mau demanded that blood be shed, long-standing associations and friendships between black and white were no longer considered something of value.

Such unprovoked butchery as that exhibited toward the Rucks had the white farmers watching their employees apprehensively and preparing for another brutal attack on their isolated homes. But the next violent raid occurred on March 26, 1953, against the police station at Naivasha. The station was overrun and guns and ammunition were taken away in a truck. Later that same night, the Mau-Mau bound the circular huts of the villages of Lari with cables so the doors could not be opened, poured gasoline over the thatched roofs, and set the homes on fire. Most of the men of the village were away serving in the Kikuyu Guard, an anti-Mau-Mau force, so the greatest number of the 90 bodies found in the charred remains were those of women and children. In addition, the Mau-Mau had mutilated more than1,000 of the villagers' cattle as further punishment for opposing them.

As nearly as it can be determined from the vantage point of an historical re-examination of events, the Mau-Mau was quite likely an ancient Kikuyu secret society that was reactivated. The Kikuyu tribe was the most populous and educated in Kenya, but their culture also permitted secret societies to flourish, and there were many such groups that had been in existence since long before the Europeans came to Africa. The Mau-Mau leaders invoked the old secret society in order to stir up the Kikuyu tribe to support their demands for independence and for the return of the Kikuyu land that the whites had stolen over the years. What was ignored by the society's leaders was the fact that the land occupied by the European settlers had long been designated a kind of buffer zone between the Kikuyu and their traditional enemies the Mazai tribe.

The ranks of the Mau-Mau increased when they began to force many unwilling individuals from other tribes into participating in their blood oaths. The oathing ceremonies began with the new members taking a vow to honor the old religion of their tribal ancestors. There were at least seven stages of oath-taking, which might take several days or weeks to complete and which included the drinking of blood, eating portions of human flesh, cohabiting with animals, and ingesting bits of brains from disinterred corpses. After the seventh stage of the oath-taking had been reached, the members had to repeat the cycle and reinforce their vows by beginning again. No man or woman was exempt from this requirement, not even the leaders of the society.

BY *the time the Mau Mau was disbanded, they had slaughtered over 2,000 African tribespeople.*

The Mau-Mau reign of terror was broken by groups of white settlers who joined the auxiliary police and army units who had combined forces with ex-terrorist Kikuyus. The former Mau-Mau members were provided with small arms and grenades, and they, in turn, taught the whites how to move silently through the thick underbrush. In May 1956, Dedan Kimathi, who was identified as the militant head of the Mau-Mau, was captured by a party of Kikuyu tribal police. Soon after Kimathi had been apprehended, the Mau-Mau society crumbled from lack of ammunition and arms, internal quarrels in the ranks, and disease brought about by the hardship of existing in the jungle under extremely difficult conditions. By the time the Mau-Mau was disbanded, they had slaughtered more than 2,000 African tribespeople and brutally maimed many thousands more native people. Although the murders of Kenyan civilians of European ancestry were brutal and bloody, the actual numbers of those killed at the hands of the Mau-Mau were greatly exaggerated by the media. Actual deaths of white settlers attributed to the Mau-Mau insurrectionists have been listed as low as 32 to 57, to as high as less than 100.

Dedan Kimathi was executed by the British in 1957 for having ordered atrocities and murders as the leader of the Mau-Mau. The Kikuyu Central Association, the political party that fronted for the secret activities of the Mau-Mau, was headed by Johnstone Kamau, better known as Jomo Kenyatta (1892–1978). Under his leadership, Kenya gained independence in 1963.

✤ DELVING DEEPER

Malboa, Wunyabari O. *Mau-Mau and Kenya: An Analysis of a Peasant Revolt* . Bloomington: Indiana University Press, 1998.

Roseberg, Carl G. *The Myth of Mau-Mau.* New York: Meridian, 1970.

Warwick, Mark. "Mau-Mau: Messengers of Misery." [Online] http://www. multiline.com. au/~markw/ maumau.html. 21 December 2002.

THE ROSICRUCIANS

The citizens of Paris awoke one morning in 1622 to find that their city had been ornamented with posters which the Brethren of the Rosy Cross (Rosicrucians) had scattered to announce that their secret order was now moving among the Parisians to save them from the error of death. In the seventeenth century, the Rosicrucians were rumored to have accomplished the transmutation of metals, the means of prolonging life, the knowledge to see and to hear what was occurring in distant places, and the ability to detect secret and hidden objects.

ROSICRUCIANS *were rumored to have accomplished the transmutation of metals.*

Such announcements were met with great excitement. It was a time of reformation and enlightenment, and all of Europe was looking forward to the new world that the **alchemists** and **magicians** promised was about to emerge from the ashes of the old. And leading such a movement of a new appreciation of the arts and sciences and humankind's true place in the universe was the Illumined Father and Brother Christian Rosencreutz (1378–1484),

a brilliant magus, who at the age of 16 had already gained secret wisdom teachings from the sages of Arabia and the Holy Land.

When Rosencreutz returned to Germany circa 1450, he became a recluse, for he could see that Europe was not yet ready for the complete reformation which he so yearned to present to it. For one thing, he claimed to have acquired the fabled philosopher's stone, which enabled him to produce all the gold and precious gems necessary to allow him to build a house where he could live peacefully and well. To share the power of the legendary stone of transmutation with the unwise, the worldly, and the greedy would be disastrous. Quietly, Rosencreutz accepted only a handful of carefully evaluated students to whom he imparted the knowledge that he had acquired in ancient Egypt and the connection that he had made with the mystery schools and the esoteric teachings of great masters. He was particularly enthusiastic about telling his students about **Pharaoh Amenhotep** and the monotheistic view of one God. At first there were only three disciples in attendance; then later, eight brothers, including Rosencreutz himself, swore to uphold the following precepts:

1. They would not profess any creed but the goal of healing the sick without reward;

2. They would affect no particular style of clothing;

3. They would meet once each year in the House of the Sainted Spirit;

4. Each brother would carefully choose his own successor;

5. The letters "R.C." would serve as their only seal and character;

6. The Brotherhood would remain secret for 100 years.

When Rosencreutz died in 1484 at the age of 106, the five brethren who had been chosen to travel throughout Europe performing charitable deeds had established a reputation for being selfless benefactors. Although Rosencreutz had been buried in secret, one of the brothers happened by chance to discover his burial chamber and read the promise inscribed above the entrance that Rosencreutz would return in 126 years. The discovery of the illumined father's prediction inspired the surviving brothers to work in earnest to spread the teachings of Christian Rosencreutz throughout the world.

Between 1604 and 1616, three manifestos were released in Germany by the secret brotherhood of the Rosicrucians (from the Latin, Rosae Crucis, "Rose Cross"). The first two pamphlets called upon the educated and influential to unite to bring about a reformation of the educational, moral, and scientific establishments of Europe. The German monk Martin Luther (1483–1546) had already set in motion a reformation in the spiritual sphere of life, the Rosicrucian Fraternity pointed out, but now it was time to educate the people of Europe to understand the true relationship of humankind to the universe and to perceive truly the distinctions between the material and the divine.

The manifestos condemned all those who contributed to the moral decay of Europe, and the brotherhood promised to help alleviate all suffering and to eradicate all ignorance. The Illumined Father Christian Rosencreutz possessed the wisdom and the wealth through the transmutation of base metals to elevate the common people of Europe.

The manifestos also shared some startling assertions, among them:

1. The end of the world was near, but those who had become enlightened by the new reformation would be initiated into a higher consciousness.

2. New stars had appeared in the constellations of Cygnus and Serpentarius that predicted the destruction of the Roman Catholic Church.

3. The Illumined Father divined the secret code that God placed in the universe in the beginning of time and blessed those who possess such magic.

4. The transmutation of base metals into gold and precious gems is a natural miracle that has been revealed to such magi as Christian Rosencreutz. Forget about the efforts of the pseudo-chemists.

5. The Rosicrucian Fellowship has wealth to distribute, but it does not wish a single coin from anyone.

The manifestos created great excitement in early seventeenth-century Europe. Royalty, common folk, merchants, mystics, alchemists—all clamored for more information about the mysterious secret brotherhood. Those who were ill wished healing. Those who were poor were eager to accept a portion of the wealth the brotherhood was willing to distribute. Those who were greedy wanted their turn with the philosopher's stone and their opportunity to transmute tons of base metals into tons of gold.

And perhaps most of all, people wanted to join the secret society and become Rosicrucians, but no one knew where any of their lodges were or where they might find the House of the Sainted Spirit. Desperate individuals placed their letters of application for the fraternity in public places where they hoped the Rosicrucians might find them and contact them.

It wasn't long before charlatans began posing as members of the secret fraternity and attempting to charge the gullible for admittance, but when the deceivers could not produce mounds of gold upon demand, the crooks were either imprisoned or pummeled. Nor had too much time passed before word spread among the religious that the Rosicrucians were satanists who sought only to delude Europe into sin.

In spite of entreaties, threats, and demands, no Rosicrucian stepped forward to identify himself, and the society remained secret—the most secret of all secret societies. It is interesting to speculate that the symbol of Martin Luther, the Protestant reformer and founder of the Lutheran Church, was a red rose and a cross, which remains the emblem of Lutheranism. Could Luther also have sought to reform the whole societal structure of Europe, as well as the Roman Catholic Church? Unlikely, for Luther would not have used the language of the alchemist and the magus. Another member, according to some, is the great Francis Bacon (1561–1626), whose unfinished manuscript, *The New Atlantis* (1627), describes an earthly utopian paradise, a secret brotherhood who wear the Rose Cross on their turbans, who heal people without charge, and who meet yearly in their temple. The philosopher Rene Descartes

(1596–1650) was once nearly arrested on the accusation that he was a member of the secret society, but he convinced his accusers that the Rosicrucians were invisible, while, he, it was plain to see, was not.

While the true identity of the Rosicrucians may never be known, nor whether such a man as Christian Rosencreutz ever really existed, the concepts expressed in their three manifestos pertaining to individual freedom, the separation of church and state, and the quest to determine humankind's true place in the universe became ideals that inspired the period of Enlightenment and have been carried over into modern times.

✤ DELVING DEEPER

McFadden, Ashley. "The Rosicrucians—A Brief Historical Overview." R.C. Times, summer 1994 [Online] http://www.arcgl.org/rosie.htm.

Spence, Lewis. An Encyclopedia of Occultism. New Hyde Park, N.Y.: University Books, 1960.

Yates, Frances A. The Rosicrucian Enlightenment. Boulder, Colo.: Shambhala, 1978.

THE THUGGEE

No organized cult of killers has ever murdered as many people as the Thuggee. In the 1830s this Indian secret society strangled upward of 30,000 native people and travelers as a sacrifice to their goddess Kali, the "Dark Mother," the Hindu Triple Goddess of creation, preservation, and destruction. The name Thuggee comes from the Sanskrit sthaga, "deceiver."

THE name Thuggee comes from the Sanskrit sthaga, "deceiver."

Although the Thuggee probably originated sometime in the sixteenth century, they were not uncovered by British authorities until about 1812. Great Britain was beginning to expand its territories in India, and the British administrators were becoming increasingly alarmed by reports of bands of stranglers that were roving the countryside murdering travelers. At first there appeared to be no connection between the bizarre killings, but then the bodies of 50 victims were found hidden in a series of wells in the Ganges area. Such large-scale mass murder could not have been kept secret for so long unless special pains had been taken to dispose of the victims' corpses. Examination of the bodies revealed that the murderers had broken all joints of their victims' limbs to speed up the process of decomposition and to prevent the swelling of the graves that would attract scavenging jackals and other wild animals. Such evidence convinced the authorities that they were dealing with one secret society, the Thuggee.

The murderous craft of the Thuggee was hereditary. Its practitioners were trained from earliest childhood to murder by the quick, quiet method of a strong cloth noose tightened about the neck of their victims. This weapon, the "Rumal," was worn knotted about the waist of each member of the Thuggee.

The Thuggee gloried in silent and efficient acts of murder above any other earthly accomplishment, and they traveled often in the guise of traders, pilgrims, and even as soldiers marching to or from service. On occasion, the more flamboyant would pretend to be a rajah with a large retinue of followers. Each band of Thuggee had a small unit of scouts and inveiglers who would loiter about hotels and market places gaining information regarding travelers and the weight of their coin purses. The inveiglers posed as travelers headed for the same destination as their intended victims. They would worm themselves into the confidences of their prey, pleading the old adage of safety in numbers.

The mass slaughters of large groups of merchants and travelers were usually committed when all were encamped. Working in groups of three, one Thuggee would loop the Rumal around the victim's neck, another would press his head forward, and the third would grab his legs and throw him to the ground. In the rare instance when an intended victim escaped the nooses in the death area, he would run into scouts posted at the edge of the jungle. One hundred percent mortality of their victims was the goal of the Thuggee.

In spite of what first appeared to be indiscriminate murder on a very large scale, the Thuggee had a peculiar code of ethics whose rules forbade the killing of fakirs, musicians, dancers, sweepers, oil vendors, carpenters, blacksmiths, maimed or leprous persons, Ganges water-carriers, and women. Despite the restriction against the murder of females, however, the presence of wives traveling with their husbands often necessitated the strangling of a woman to protect the secrecy of the society.

The strongest rule of the brotherhood was the one prohibiting the shedding of blood. According to Thuggee beliefs, the goddess Kali taught the fathers of thuggery to strangle with a noose and to kill without permitting the flow of blood. All victims of the Thuggee were sacrificed to Kali, and the members of the secret society would have been greatly incensed by an accusation that they killed only for booty.

With the exception of a small number of boys who may have been captured or spared during a raid, a man had to be born into the cult in order to become an initiate. The minimum age for initiation into the society was 10, and the young candidates were allowed to watch their elders at work from hidden points some distance from the site of the attack. At the age of 18, they were permitted to make their first human sacrifices to Kali.

The Thuggee had their female counterparts in a secret sect of Tantrists who held that it was only by a constant indulgence in passion that a human could ever achieve total union with Kali. Only indulgence in the five vices that corrupt the soul of humankind—wine, meat, fish, mystical gesticulations, and sexual indulgence—could drive the poisons out of the human body and purify the soul.

In 1822, William Sleeman, an officer in the Bengal Army who had transferred to civil service, was appointed by Governor General Lord Bentinck to rid India of the society of stranglers. Fluent in four Indian dialects, Sleeman had been the British official who had first confirmed the growing suspicion that the murders were committed throughout central India by the Thuggee. He was well aware that it would be no easy task putting a halt to such large-scale murders, for the members of the secret society were indistinguishable from any other of the many bands of outlaws who infested the country's roads. And what made the job of identifying the Thugs even more difficult was the fact that they were indistinguishable from any of the travelers and merchants who were their victims. As their name implied, they were master deceivers.

Finally, by meticulously marking the scene of each discovered attack site on a map and by maintaining careful records of the dates, Sleeman was able to begin to predict the areas where the next mass murders were likely to take place. When his agents and informants brought him word that known members of the Thuggee had been seen in a certain region, Sleeman sent his personally recruited police officers out disguised as merchants in order to ambush the Thugs who appeared to attack what they believed was a group of harmless travelers.

Between 1830 and 1841, Sleeman's police captured at least 3,700 Thugs, breaking forever the back of the infamous secret society. Of this total, only 50 received a pardon for supplying valuable information that had been utilized in destroying the secret society. The remainder of those apprehended were imprisoned for life and 500 were hanged. Without exception, the Thuggee condemned to be hanged went to their own deaths with the same lack of emotion with which they had murdered their victims. In many instances, their final request from the hangman was that they be permitted to place the noose around their own neck.

Trials of Thuggee brought out many ghastly facts about the deadly skills of some of its members. A band of 20 confessed that they had participated in 5,200 murders. An individual named Buhram, who had been a strangler for 40 years, had the highest lifetime score to his discredit—931. When asked if he experienced any feelings of remorse or guilt, he answered sharply that no man should ever feel compunction in following his trade.

Although isolated cases of a Thug's proficiency with a noose still exist in India and in other parts of the world, the stranglers of the goddess Kali no longer exist as a secret society. The designation of "thug," however, remains as a negative term applied to brutish criminals.

The violent chapter imprinted in India's history by the cult of the Thuggee has been portrayed quite often in motion pictures, notably *Gunga Din* (1939) with Cary Grant, Douglas Fairbanks, Jr., and Victor McLaglen; Terence Fisher's *Stranglers of Bombay* (1960); Steven Spielberg's *Indiana Jones and the Temple of Doom* (1984) with Harrison Ford and Kate Capshaw; and *The Deceivers* (1988) with Pierce Brosnan.

❋ Delving Deeper

Brantlinger, Patrick. *Confessions of a Thug.* Oxford: Oxford World Classics, 1998.

Daraul, Arkon. *A History of Secret Societies.* New York: Pocket Books, 1969.

Heckethorn, Charles William. *Secret Societies of All Ages and Countries.* Kila, Mont.: Kessinger Publishing, 1997.

Howard, Michael. *The Occult Conspiracy: Secret Societies—Their Influence and Power in World History.* Rochester, Vt.: Inner Traditions, 1989.

The Tongs

According to the Internet Movie Base, the Chinese Tongs have been an integral element of violence and mystery in 140 motion pictures in China and the United States. Interestingly, the first American film on the subject, *The War of the Tongs,* was released in 1917. In 1985, *Year of the Dragon* provoked a great deal of controversy in its portrayal of a racist white cop (Mickey Rourke) battling hordes of evil Chinese gang members. The greatest flaw in the motion picture was blending Chinese gangs, the Tongs, and the Triad into one massive "Chinese Mafia" kind of amalgamated crime organization. In actuality, although the gangs exist, they are separate from the Tongs, a survivor of the protective societies of ancient times, and the Triad, a recent element of organized crime that grew out of the Tongs.

The first Tong in America is believed to have originated in San Francisco in 1874.

Essentially, the Tong (which originally meant "parlor") was a merchants' protective association created to defend themselves against brutal treatment directed at them by the white inhabitants of the city. Eventually, the Tong became powerful enough to sell "protection" to the newer merchants and to establish illegal gambling halls. Success in extortion and gambling led to an extension of activities into opium distribution and prostitution.

Although in 1880 the Chinese population in New York City was only around 800, the first Tong was established there in that year. By 1890, a rush of immigration increased the total to 13,000 Chinese in the city, and the Tong was ready to exploit a population isolated by language, culture, and prejudice. In 1900, rival Tongs ignited a series of Tong wars that lasted intermittently until the 1930s. It was at that time that the larger American public became fully aware of the Tong warriors with their chain mail shirts and hatchets.

Like so many secret societies, the origins of the Triad Tong have been lost in the lore of legend. According to some students of the Tongs, in 1647 a community of monks who lived in the Fukien Province of China had become masters in the art of war. When a foreign prince invaded China, the emperor sent 138 of these monks to throw out the invading forces. After three months of bitter fighting, they routed the enemy and returned to their monastery laden with gifts and honors from the grateful emperor.

While the monks were content to resume their lives of contemplation, some of the emperor's ministers were jealous of the favors he had bestowed upon them and persuaded him that the monks were deceptively planning a rebellion. Fearful of their martial arts skills, the emperor decided to attack the monks without warning and sent a strong force of the Imperial Guard, armed with gunpowder, to destroy the monastery. It was said the flames ignited by the blasts soared up to heaven, where they were seen by the Immortals who, perceiving the injustice being dealt the monks, came down to Earth and pushed aside one of the monastery's huge walls, enabling 18 monks to escape. Most of them

The question of who killed U.S. President John F. Kennedy (1917–1963) on November 22, 1963, has been a subject of controversy. Conspiracy theorists dispute allegations that Lee Harvey Oswald was able to accurately hit a moving target at that distance with the bolt-action rifle allegedly in his possession. They insist one person could not have fired so many shots so quickly from this type of rifle.

In 1964, the Warren Commission, a group of government officials investigating the assassination, concluded that a single bullet passed through Kennedy's body and struck Texas governor John Connally. A fatal second shot hit the president in the head, and another bullet missed the presidential automobile altogether.

Conspiracy theorists dismiss the so-called "magic bullet" that passed through Kennedy and through the back, ribs, right wrist, and left leg of Connally. Governor and Nellie Connally believed that two bullets had struck the president and that a third and separate bullet had wounded the governor.

On July 3, 1997, former U.S. president Gerald Ford, the only surviving member of the Warren Commission, admitted he had altered the commission's description of the gunshot. According to Ford, the original text said that a bullet had entered Kennedy's back at a point slightly above the shoulder and to the right of the spine. Ford changed the bullet's entrance point from Kennedy's upper back to "the base of the back of the neck." Such a seemingly minor change would support the commission's single-assassin hypothesis that was based on the "magical" path of a single bullet that could pass through Kennedy's neck and leave another six wounds on his body before striking Texas governor John Connally's back, ribs, right wrist, and left leg. Ford told the Associated Press, "My changes were only an attempt to be more precise. I think our judgments have stood the test of time."

A poll conducted by the University of Ohio and Scripps Howard News Service in 1997 revealed that 51 percent of Americans dismissed the "magic bullet" theory. Twenty percent believed federal government

THE "MAGIC BULLET" THAT KILLED JFK?

agents killed Kennedy. Another 33 percent, while not accusing government agents, felt that a conspiracy was "somewhat likely."

SOURCES:

"Ford Faked JFK Report." *Tabloid News Services.* [Online] http://www.tabloid.net.

Lane, Mark. *Plausible Denial.* New York: Thunder's Mouth Press, 1991.

Summers, Anthony. *Conspiracy.* New York: Paragon House, 1989.

Vankin, Jonathan, and John Whalen. *The 60 Greatest Conspiracies of All Time.* New York: Barnes & Noble, 1996.

were so badly burned that they soon died, and the surviving five escaped from the Imperial troops by miraculous means.

After many ordeals the five monks came to a city in Fukien Province where they founded a Tong whose aim was to overthrow the emperor who had betrayed their loyalty. That Tong exists today as the Triad Tong, and the five monks who founded it, according to the legend, are known as the Five Ancestors. Although the revolt against the emperor failed, the survivors scattered throughout China and established five Provincial Grand Lodges, each led by one of the five monks.

THE *true name of the Tong was "I Ho Chuan," which means the Tong of "The Fists of Righteous Harmony."*

Initiation into the Triad Society is based on a blood ceremony. First, the ancient Five Heroes are invoked by an "Incense Master" who offers libations of tea and wine. The candidate for initiation is challenged at the entrance to the lodge by guards carrying razor-edged swords. He is allowed to enter only after answering a series of ritual questions as he crawls under crossed swords. Once inside the lodge, the initiate participates in a lengthy reenactment of the traditional ordeals of the Five Ancestors, swears 36 oaths, and learns his first secret signs. Then a rooster is brought in and beheaded, a warning to the initiate that he will suffer the same fate if he betrays the Tong. Finally, he drinks a mixture of blood, wine, cinnabar, and ashes. In times past, the blood used to be drawn from the initiate and other members of the lodge. Today the blood is generally that of the slaughtered rooster.

The blood oaths that were so favored by the Tongs originated with the Yellow Turbans, one of the earliest and most mystical societies in China. Founded in the middle of the second century in northeast China, the Yellow Turbans revered Chang Cheuh, a great healer and magician, as a savior of the nation against the despotic Han dynasty. Cheuh's society soon numbered so many thousands that he needed 36 generals to lead the rebellion that conquered the entire north of China within less than a month. Three of Chang Cheuh's disciples have been credited with taking the first blood oath when each of them slit open a vein, filled a vessel with blood, and drank the mixture of their vital fluid while vowing eternal brotherhood. This basic blood oath ceremony, with many variations, became an integral part of Tong ritual.

In the summer of 1900, the notorious Boxer Tong drove more than 3,000 people—mainly European missionaries, their families, and Chinese Christian converts—into the legation district of Peking. The siege had been provoked by the terror tactics of the Tong, which had been given almost a free hand by the Manchu government to free the nation from the foreign imperialists whom they accused of exploiting the Chinese people. "Boxer" was the Western name for this Tong, derived from its symbol of a clenched fist. The true name of the Tong was "I Ho Chuan," which means the Tong of "The Fists of Righteous Harmony."

The Boxers believed that they could achieve the righteousness of their cause by force, and they depended greatly on supernatural elements to aid them in achieving invulnerability. They employed rituals compounded of self-hypnotism, mass-hysteria, and drugs. At the height of their ceremonies, the initiates reached a state of frenzy wherein they would smash their clenched fists against unyielding surfaces until the blood flowed from broken knuckles. Then after a period of spasmodic twitching, foaming at the mouth and screaming hysterically, they would roll about on the ground until they became unconscious. At this point, they were led into the Inner Temple to be taught the magical secrets of the Tong and to receive their power of invulnerability against death at the hands of a foreigner. The imparting of invulnerability was followed by the blood oath of the Tong, in which each initiate drank a measure of blood.

Initially the violence of the Boxers was directed against small Christian missionary outposts, especially in the Shantung province. The Empress Dowager, who became a regent after forcing her nephew from the throne, had encouraged the attacks. On her orders, Imperial officers were ordered to assist the Tong during the 55-day siege against the foreign legations. However, even before the various nations whose citizens were under attack sent relief forces to capture the city and squelch the rebellion, many Imperial soldiers had already deserted the Boxers and were starting to fight against them from the ranks of other Tongs.

The Triad reached the United States with the mass of Chinese workers who immigrated to the west coast during the gold rush fever of the 1840s. Bewildered in a strange land and mercilessly exploited by people who had hired them as common laborers, the Chinese immigrants welcomed the protection provided by the Triads that sprang up among their communities, hiding behind the fronts of innocent social clubs. Among the first of the Triads to establish itself in the United States was the so-called "Five Companies," named after the five districts of China. Once it had established itself, it began to exploit the same Chinese population it had previously protected.

The main nerve-center of the Triad was—and remains—Hong Kong. There are seven main branches, each with its own area of influence and working independently of the others. Although its influence on the course of Chinese politics has been considerable, the Triad has never been unduly concerned about which government happens to be in power.

✤ Delving Deeper

"Boo How Doy: The Early History of Chinese Tongs in New York." *Organized Crime.* [Online] http://organizedcrime.about.com/library/weekly/aa062401a.htm.

Booth, Martin. *The Dragon Syndicates: The Global Phenomenon of the Triads.* New York: Carroll and Graf, 2001.

Chin, Ko-Lin. *Extortion, Enterprise, and Ethnicity.* Studies in Crime and Public Policy. New York: Oxford University Press, 1996.

Huston, Peter. *Tongs, Gangs, and Triads: Chinese Crime Groups in North America.* Boulder, Colo.: Paladin Press, 1995.

Making the Connection

blasphemy An irreverent utterance or action showing a disrespect for sacred things or for God.

chieftain The leader of a clan, tribe, or group.

conspiracy An evil, treacherous, or unlawful plan formulated in secret between two or more people to commit a subversive action or plot.

desecration When something sacred is treated in a profane or damaging manner.

fanatical Extreme enthusiasm, frenzy, or zeal about a particular belief, as in politics or religion.

heresy The willful, persistent act of adhering to an opinion or belief that rejects or contradicts established teachings or theories that are traditional in philosophy, religion, science, or politics.

heretic From the Greek *hairetikos*, meaning "able to choose." Someone who does not conform or whose opinions, theories, or beliefs contradict the conventional established teaching, doctrines, or principles, especially that of religion.

insurrectionist Someone who is in rebellion or revolt against an established authority, ruler, or government.

leprous From the Greek, *lepros*, meaning "scale." Something resembling the symptoms of or relating to the disease of leprosy, which covers a person's skin with scales or ulcerations.

magus A priest, wizard, or someone who is skilled or learned, especially in astrology, magic, sorcery, or the like.

metaphysical Relating to abstract thought or the philosophical study of the nature of existence and truth.

philanthropy From the Greek *philanthropos*, meaning "humane," and from *philos*, meaning "loving." An affection or desire to help improve the spiritual, social, or material welfare of humanity through acts of charity or benevolence.

shapeshift Someone or something that is able to change form or shape.

subversive To cause the ruin or downfall of something or to undermine or overthrow principles, an institution, or a government.

supernatural Relating to or pertaining to God or the characteristics of God; a deity or magic of something that is above and beyond what is normally explained by natural laws.

transmutation The act of transforming or changing from one nature, form, or state into another.

CHAPTER 6
MAGIC AND SORCERY

The earliest traces of magical practice are found in the European caves of the Paleolithic Age, c. 50,000 B.C.E., in which it seems clear that early humans sought by supernatural means to placate the spirits of the animals they killed for food, to dispel the restless spirits of the humans they had slain in territorial disputes, and to bring peace to the spirits of their deceased tribal kin. Throughout the evolving centuries to the present day, humankind continues to seek magical means of improving its lot in life, providing order to the chaos of the physical world, and winning the favor of the inhabitants of the unseen world.

INTRODUCTION

The practice of magic and sorcery began in Paleolithic times, at least 50,000 years ago, when early humans began to believe that there was supernatural power in a charm, a spell, or a ritual to work good or evil. As such beliefs progressed, certain tribal members were elevated in status to that of magician, sorcerer, priest, and priestess by their demonstrable abilities to influence the weather, to heal the sick, to communicate with the spirit worlds, and to interpret dreams. The four main principles behind early magic remained constant throughout the evolution of magical practices: 1.) A representation of a person or thing can be made to affect the person or thing it depicts. 2.) Once objects have been in touch with each other they continue to influence one another even at great distances. 3.) An unseen world of spirit forces may be invoked to fulfill the magician's will. 4.) As above, so it is below; as within, so it is without. There is nothing in heaven or in Earth that is not also in humankind.

Primitive animism, such as imitating the animal of the hunt through preparatory dance, cutting off a bit of an enemy's hair or clothing to be used in a charm against him, and invoking evil spirits to cause destruction to competing villages, eventually gained a higher level of sophistication and evolved into more formal religious practices and the rudiments of early science. The word "magic" comes from the Greek "magein," denoting the science and religion of the priests of Zoroaster (or according to some scholars from "megas," signifying the "great" secret science, i.e. knowledge). So it is that by the time of the historic period, the great civilizations of Egypt, Babylonia, and Persia had fully developed magical systems with entire hierarchies of sorcerers, priests, seers, and **magi.** Greece and Rome supported both a state religion of gods and goddesses and a loosely structured priestcraft as well as a healthy respect for those magicians who could prove their worth as dependable soothsayers. In addition, the **mystery schools** in Greece and Rome were popular with aristocrat and commoner alike and kept alive the mystical impulse in both cultures. Many researchers have drawn comparisons between certain of the mystery school traditions and the great festivals, the **Sabbats** of the witches as they gathered in the forests of Europe.

When Constantine the Great (d. 337) legally sanctioned Christianity throughout the Roman Empire, he in effect granted the early Church Fathers a kind of dominion over their constituents that they had not previously enjoyed. As the influence of the Christian clergy grew in the empire, many of them expressed their opinions that magic and sorcery were not harmonious with the teachings of Christ. At the Ecumenical Council of Laodicea held in 364, a canon was issued that forbade Christian priests to practice magic, astrology, or mathematics. By 525, with the influence of Christianity growing ever stronger, the Council of Oxia prohibited the parishioners from consulting sorcerers, diviners, or any kind of seer. A canon passed by the Council of Constantinople in 625 prescribed excommunication for a period of six years for anyone found practicing divination or who consulted with a diviner. The Council of Tours in 613 ordered all priests to teach their congregations that magical practices were ineffective methods by which to guarantee the health of humans and animals and were not to be employed as a means of bettering one's lot in life. With each subsequent church council issuing stronger canons and edicts against magic and sorcery, those who dared to continue practicing the occult arts were forced to go underground.

European magic remained a pastiche of older pagan practices and ancient rituals until the Crusades of the eleventh, twelfth, and thirteenth centuries. Warrior knights, nobles, and clerics returned from their encounters with the Muslim armies with a great appreciation of their science and their sophisticated levels of magic. Other crusaders remained after battles had been won or lost to explore the arts of the Eastern sorcerers and to learn for the first time of the alchemical works of the magi of old Persia and the scholars and magicians of the Byzantine Empire. Many Christian adventurers returned with the secrets of what they called "Constantinople magic" and began to experiment with the ancient teachings in hidden laboratories. By the twelfth century, a school of medieval magic built on the magical systems of the Spanish Moors and the Jewish Kabbalah had begun to achieve popularity among the intellectuals of Europe, who found in alchemy a perfect expression of their quest for God and for gold. The true alchemist sought the transcendent powers of the material and immaterial dominions that could transmute base metals into gold and transform the baser human instincts into a purity of spirit.

Although the church had issued many canons forbidding the clergy to practice magic and commanding them to teach their parishioners that the teachings of Christ were all that was necessary to achieve peace on Earth and salvation in heaven, it had taken little real action against those learned men practicing magic or the common folk practicing witchcraft other than an occasional excommunication or expulsion from the congregation. Organized persecution of magicians or witches was practically unknown. In 906, Abbot Regino of Prum recognized that earlier canon laws had done little to eradicate the practices of magic and wizardry, so he issued his *Canon Episcopi* to condemn as heretical any belief in witchcraft or the power of sorcerers. If anyone believed in such alleged powers, Satan was deceiving them, declared Abbot Regino. In 1000, Deacon Burchard, who would later become archbishop of Worms, published *Corrector*, which updated Regino's work and stressed that only God had the power to change one thing into another. Alchemists could not change base metals into gold, and witches could not shapeshift into animals.

Church punishment of those who persisted in practicing magic or witchcraft remained virtually nonexistent until exaggerated claims of the powers of the Cathar sect reached the ears of the papacy. According to startling reports, the Cathars were practicing foul sorceries, blasphemous heresies, and **black magick.** What was worse, they appeared to be prospering in their cities in southern France. In 1208, Pope Innocent III (1160 or 1161–1216) ordered a crusade launched against the Cathars, who were able to resist the armies sent against them until their central city of Montesegur fell in 1246. Hundreds of Cathars were burned at the stake as heretics, witches, and sorcerers, for by the time their besieged sect had fallen, the Holy Inquisition had been founded in 1233 to stamp out magic, sorcery, and witchcraft.

After it became quite apparent that the church and state had undergone a dramatic change in attitude toward the practice of magic, the alchemists/magicians and the magi became much more cautious in sharing the results of their experimentations. Because the practitioners of "higher magic," such as **Paracelsus, Agrippa, Roger Bacon, Albertus Magnus,** and others emphasized the mystical, the practical, and the appropriate religious imagery in their work, they did not suffer the severe persecutions directed toward the practitioners of so-called "lesser magic," the witches, the wizards, and the sorcerers who were condemned as black magicians. They were, however, kept under close scrutiny by the church and were subject to constant attacks by their more conventional peers in the medical and clerical professions. For any of them to have become too outspoken regarding their magical practices would have won them their own time of interrogation and torture at the hands of the Inquisition.

Paracelsus may well have expressed the credo of the alchemist of higher magic when he said that nature does not produce anything that is perfect in itself—it is humankind that must bring everything to perfection. It is the sincere alchemist-magician who fulfills nature. God, Paracelsus said, did not create objects made of iron. God created the metal that must be enjoined with fire in order to fashion useful items. Nothing has been created in its final state. Everything is first created in its primary state. It is the alchemist who must bring the fire of creativity to make art. Alchemy is the art that makes the impure into the pure. Higher magic can separate the useful from the useless and transmute it into its final substance and ultimate essence.

✦ DELVING DEEPER

Caron M., and S. Hutin. *The Alchemists.* Translated by Helen R. Lane. New York: Grove Press, 1961.

Seligmann, Kurt. *The History of Magic.* New York: Meridian Books, 1960.

Spence, Lewis. *An Encyclopedia of Occultism*. New Hyde Park, N.Y.: University Books, 1960.

Williams, Charles. *Witchcraft*. New York: Meridian Books, 1960.

ALCHEMY

The image of alchemists as defrocked wizards and full-time frauds is not quite accurate. Most of them were, in fact, highly spiritual men whose quest to transmute one substance into another was closer to mysticism than modern chemistry. The essence of alchemy lay in the belief that certain incantations and rituals could convince or command angelic beings to change base metals into precious ones.

According to ancient tradition, the mummy of **Hermes Trismegistus,** the master of alchemical philosophy, was found in an obscure chamber of the Great Pyramid of Giza, clutching an emerald tablet in its hands. The words contained on the tablet revealed the alchemical creed that "It is true and without falsehood and most real: that which is above is like that which is below, to perpetuate the miracles of one thing. And as all things have been derived from one, by the thought of one, so all things are born from this thing, by adoption." Within the secrets inscribed on the tablet was the "most powerful of all powers," the process by which the world was created and by which all "subtle things" might penetrate "every solid thing," and by which base material might be transformed into precious metals and gems.

ALCHEMY *was introduced to the Western world in the second century C.E.*

For centuries, the writings of Hermes Trismegistus were considered a precious legacy from the master of alchemy. The Hermetics believed that the nature of the cosmos was sacramental: "that which is above is like that which is below." In other words, the nature of the spiritual world could be discovered through the study of the material substance of Earth; and earthly humans, created of the dust of the ground, comprised the *prima materia* of the heavenly beings they would become, just as the base elements of Earth comprised the raw materials for gold. The alchemical adepts believed that the most perfect thing on the planet was gold and that it was linked with the sun. The sun was considered to be the lowest manifestation of the spiritual world and therefore provided the intermediary between God and humankind.

The science of alchemy was introduced to the Western world at the beginning of the second century of the common era. It was, however, 200 years before the practice of the craft reached its zenith, concurrent with the persecutions of the pagans by the Christians. Zosimus of Panapolis, self-appointed apologist of alchemy, cited a passage in Genesis as the origin of the arcane art: "The sons of God saw that the daughters of men were fair." To this scriptural reference, Zosimus added the tradition that in reward for their favors, the "sons of God," who were believed to be fallen angels, endowed these women with the knowledge of how to make jewels, colorful garments, and perfumes with which to enhance their earthly charms.

The seven principal angels whose favor the alchemist sought to obtain for their transformation were Michael, who was believed to transmute base metals into gold and to dissolve any enmity directed toward the alchemist; Gabriel, who fashioned silver and foresaw the future; Samuel, who protected against physical harm; and Raphael, Sachiel, Ansel, and Cassiel, who could create various gems and guard the alchemist from attack by demons. However, members of the clergy were skeptical that the alchemists were truly calling upon angels, rather than demons in disguise, and they recalled the words of the Church Father Tertullian (c. 155 or 160–after 220), who confirmed earlier beliefs that the "sons of God" referred to in Genesis were evil perverts who bequeathed their wisdom to mortals with the sole intention of seducing them to mundane pleasures.

While the Hermetic was akin to the mystic, a great deal more came out of those smoky laboratories than candidates for the torture chambers of the Inquisition. In the intellectual half-light of the Middle Ages, the brotherhood of alchemy, perhaps by accident as much as design, did produce a number of valuable chemical discoveries. Albert le Grand produced potassium lye; Raymond Lully (1235–1315) prepared biocarbonate of potassium; **Paracelsus** (1493–1541) was the first to describe zinc and chemical compounds to medicine; Blaise Vigenere (1523–1596) discovered benzoic acid. Discoveries increased during the Renaissance when such men as Basil Valentine (c. 1450–1492) discovered sulphuric acid, and Johann Friedrich Boetticher (1682–1719) became the first European to produce porcelain. Evidence has been disinterred from the musty alchemists' libraries in Europe that suggests that certain of the medieval and Renaissance alchemists conducted experiments with photography, radio transmission, phonography, and aerial flight, as well as the endless quest to transmute base metals into gold.

✸ DELVING DEEPER

Budge, E. A. Wallis. *Egyptian Magic*. New York: Dover Books, 1971.

Caron M. and S. Hutin. *The Alchemists*. Trans. by Helen R. Lane. New York: Grove Press, 1961.

Heer, Friedrich. *The Medieval World: Europe 1100 to 1350*. Translated by Janet Sondheimer. Cleveland, Ohio: World Books, 1961.

Meyer, Marvin, and Richard Smith, eds. *Ancient Christian Magic*. San Francisco: HarperSanFrancisco, 1994.

Seligmann, Kurt. *The History of Magic*. New York: Meridian Books, 1960.

Spence, Lewis. *An Encyclopedia of Occultism*. New Hyde Park, N.Y.: University Books, 1960.

Williams, Charles. *Witchcraft*. New York: Meridian Books, 1960.

VALENTINE ANDREAE (1586–1654)

Valentine Andreae (or Andreas) was a Lutheran pastor who held as his ideal not only Martin Luther (1483–1546), the powerful guiding force behind the Protestant Reformation, but also Christian Rosencreutz (1378–1484), legendary founder of the **Rosicrucian** mystical movement, and Paracelsus (1493–1541), the revered alchemist. Andreae was a brilliant scholar who

as a youth had traveled widely throughout Europe and had risen in the clerical ranks to become a chaplain at the Court of Wurtemberg, Germany. Embittered by the misery that had been brought to his fatherland as a result of the Thirty Years' War (1618–48), Andreae became an apologist for the Rosicrucians and wrote *The Hermetic Romance* or *The Chemical Wedding* (1616), an allegorical autobiography of Christian Rosencreutz the founder of the fraternity. Since the seal of the Rosicrucian Fraternity, the seal of Martin Luther, and the crest of the Andreae family all bear the image of the cross and the rose, understandable confusion has arisen from time to time regarding the "autobiography." Upon the book's initial publication, many scholars, aware that Rosencreutz had been dead for 130 years, speculated that his spirit had dictated the work. Later academic debates swirled around the question of whether or not Andreae and Rosencreutz were the same person and whether the Fraternity was actually founded in the seventeenth century, rather than the fifteenth.

Andreae admitted the work was his own and proclaimed it an allegorical novel written in tribute to Rosencreutz, as well as a symbolic depiction of the science of alchemy and Hermetic magic. Others identified the work as a comic romance, lightly depicting the most profound alchemical symbols in a fanciful manner. The royal wedding to which the hero Rosencreutz is invited is in reality the alchemical process itself in which the female and male principles are joined together. As the novel continues, the vast arcana of alchemical truths are represented by various animals, mythological beings, and human personalities.

In addition to being an advocate of alchemy and the process of contacting intermediary spirits to accomplish good for society, Andreae believed in becoming an active reformer of social ills, as well as supporting the reformation of the church. His treatises *The Tower of Babel* (1619) and *The Christianopolitan Republic* (1620) argue in favor of a general transformation of European society.

✸ DELVING DEEPER

Caron, M., and S. Hutin. *The Alchemists*. Translated by Helen R. Lane. New York: Grove Press, 1961.

De Givry, Emile Grillot. *Illustrated Anthology of Sorcery, Magic and Alchemy*. Trans. by J. Courtenay Locke. New York: Causeway Books, 1973.

Seligmann, Kurt. *The History of Magic*. New York: Meridian Books, 1960.

Spence, Lewis. *An Encyclopedia of Occultism*. New Hyde Park, N.Y.: University Books, 1960.

ROGER BACON (c. 1220–1292)

Roger Bacon, an English Franciscan friar, scientist, and philosopher, accepted what he termed the "natural magic" that occurred within mathematical and physical areas of experimentation, but he was resolutely against the use of incantations, the invocation of spirits, and the casting of spells. In his opinion, magicians were charlatans, reciting magical formulas even though they knew the effects they created were but the products of natural phenomena.

Bacon recognized that there were mysterious forces that appeared to be magical, such as those that moved the stars and the planets; but he argued that all knowledge that existed on Earth depended upon the power of mathematics. The friar also admitted the difficulties in discerning between the natural magic of science and the black arts. He was convinced, though, that natural magic was good and black magic was evil.

This thirteenth-century alchemist seemed to have powers of prediction when he told his contemporaries that physics, not magic, would produce huge vessels that would be able to navigate the oceans and rivers without sails or oars, cars without horses that would be able to move at tremendous speed, flying machines that would soar across the skies guided by a single man seated at centrally located controls, submarine machines that could dive to the bottom of the sea without danger to its crew, and great bridges without pillars that could span rivers. Bacon has been credited with dozens of inventions, such as the telescope, eye glasses, gunpowder—all derived through his science, rather than his magic.

In his medical practice, Bacon worked with certain alchemical formulas prized by specially gifted scientists since ancient times that could create a mysterious liquid known to prolong human life. He also employed the alchemical and homeopathic principles that "like produces like," that is, if one wishes to prolong one's life, he or she should eat the flesh of creatures that are long-lived, such as various reptiles.

Steadfastly arguing that all human knowledge depends upon a study of mathematics, Bacon insisted that the noblest expression of mathematics is **astrology.** At each person's birth the heavenly energies determine powerful physical, mental, and emotional factors that strongly affect that individual's destiny. The stars do not decide one's fate, Bacon conceded, for humans did have free will as a divine gift, but the celestial movements did most certainly dispose one toward one's fate. Therefore, he concluded, astrology should be utilized as a powerful tool in medicine, alchemy, and predicting the future of individuals and nations.

Friar Bacon was well aware that the church did not share his enthusiasm for astrology, but he argued that the Bible itself is the basic source of astrological knowledge and that a careful study of astrology would ultimately prove the claims of theology. Fellow clerics who opposed such a study, Bacon said, were merely ignorant.

In spite of such statements that seemed tinged with heresy, Bacon's religious views were essentially orthodox, and he sincerely believed that his studies would only serve to advance the power and the prestige of the church. He also drew upon scripture when he acknowledged the enormous power of the spoken word ("In the beginning was the Word, and the Word was with God, and the Word was God." John 1:1). Bacon stated that all miracles at the beginning of the world were the result of God's word. Therefore, when humans spoke with concentration and the proper intention and desire, their very words could accomplish powerful effects upon the self, upon others, and upon material things.

In his great determination to produce a work that would unify all learning, wisdom, and faith, Friar Bacon wrote *Opus Majus* (1268). Despite the fact that Bacon continued to attack superstition and reject the black arts, he remains widely known as a magician, rather than an early experimental scientist.

✤ DELVING DEEPER

Caron, M., and S. Hutin. *The Alchemists*. Trans. by Helen R. Lane. New York: Grove Press, 1961.

De Givry, Emile Grillot. *Illustrated Anthology of Sorcery, Magic and Alchemy*. Trans. by J. Courtenay Locke. New York: Causeway Books, 1973.

Heer, Friedrich. *The Medieval World: Europe 1100 to 1350*. Trans. by Janet Sondheimer. Cleveland, Ohio: World Books, 1961.

Seligmann, Kurt. *The History of Magic*. New York: Meridian Books, 1960.

Spence, Lewis. *An Encyclopedia of Occultism*. New Hyde Park, N.Y.: University Books, 1960.

HELVETIUS (1625–709)

While not a great deal is known about the life of John Fredrick Schweitzer, called Helvetius, his place in the history of alchemy is secure because, according to tradition, he witnessed a genuine transmutation of base metal into gold and later replicated the process in the presence of doubtful observers.

On December 27, 1666, when he was working in his study at the Hague, a stranger appeared and informed him that he would remove all Helvetius's doubts about the existence of the **philosopher's stone** that could serve as the catalyst to change base metals into gold because he possessed such magic. The stranger immediately drew from his pocket a small ivory box, containing three pieces of metal of the color of brimstone and, for their size, extremely heavy. With those three bits of metal, the man told Helvetius, he could make as much as 20 tons of gold.

Helvetius examined the pieces of metal, taking the opportunity of a moment's distraction to scrape off a small portion with his thumbnail. Returning the metal to his mysterious visitor, he asked that he perform the process of transmutation before him.

The stranger answered firmly that he was not allowed to do so. It was enough that he had verified the existence of the metal to Helvetius. It was his purpose only to offer encouragement to alchemical experiments.

After the man's departure, Helvetius procured a crucible and a portion of lead into which, when the metal was in a molten state, he threw the stolen grain he had secretly scraped from the stranger's philosopher's stone. The alchemist was disappointed when the grain evaporated and left the lead in its original state. Thinking that he had been made the fool by some mad burgher's whimsy, Helvetius returned to his own experiments, forgetting about the dream of a magical philosopher's stone.

Some weeks later, when he had almost forgotten the incident, Helvetius received another visit from the stranger. He impatiently told the man to perform a transmutation before his eyes or to leave.

This time the stranger surprised him by agreeing to prove that what he and his brother alchemists most desired truly did exist. He admonished Helvetius that one grain was sufficient for the process to be accomplished, but it was necessary to wrap it in a ball of wax before throwing it on the molten metal, otherwise its extreme volatility would cause it to vaporize. To the alchemist's astonishment and his great delight, the stranger transmuted several ounces of lead into gold. Then he permitted Helvetius to repeat the process by himself, allowing the alchemist to convert six ounces of lead into pure gold.

Helvetius found it impossible to keep a secret of such immense value and importance. Soon the word of his remarkably successful experiments spread throughout Holland, and Helvetius demonstrated the power of the philosopher's stone in the presence of the Duke of Orange and many other prestigious witnesses. The duke's own goldsmith assayed the gold and declared it to be of highest quality. The famous philosopher Baruch Spinoza (1632–1677) visited Helvetius in his laboratory and examined the crucible and gold for himself. He left the alchemist convinced that the transmutation had been authentic.

Soon, after repeated demands for such incredible demonstrations, Helvetius had exhausted the small supply of catalytic pieces that he had received from the mysterious stranger. Search as he might, Helvetius could not find the man in all of North Holland nor learn his name, and the stranger never again visited him.

❋ DELVING DEEPER

Caron, M., and S. Hutin. *The Alchemists*. Translated by Helen R. Lane. New York: Grove Press, 1961.

De Givry, Emile Grillot. *Illustrated Anthology of Sorcery, Magic and Alchemy*. Translated by J. Courtenay Locke. New York: Causeway Books, 1973.

Seligmann, Kurt. *The History of Magic*. New York: Meridian Books, 1960.

Spence, Lewis. *An Encyclopedia of Occultism*. New Hyde Park, N.Y.: University Books, 1960.

HERMES TRISMEGISTUS

In alchemical/magical tradition, powerful secrets of alchemy were found inscribed on an emerald tablet in the hands of the mummy of Hermes Trismegistus, the master magician and alchemist, who had been entombed in an obscure chamber of the Great Pyramid of Giza. The preamble to the key to transmuting base materials to precious metals and gems instructed the adept that "It is true, without falsehood, and most real: that which is above is like that which is below, to perpetrate the miracles of one thing." The writings of Hermes Trismegistus were considered by the alchemists as a legacy from the master of alchemy and were, therefore, precious to them.

As much as the thought of such a find may fire the imagination, the discovery of the Emerald Tablet at Giza is quite likely an allegory. The alchemists, who were concerned with the spiritual perfection of humankind as well as the transmutation of base metals into gold, commonly recorded their formulas and esoteric truths in allegorical form. Today it is known that there was no single personage named Hermes Trismegistus and that the Leyden Papyrus discovered in the tomb of the anonymous magician contains the oldest known copy of the inscription from the legendary Emerald Tablet, which is itself a description of the seven stages of gold-making.

Hermes, who is called Trismegistus, "three times the greatest," was a deity of a group of Greeks who once founded a colony in Egypt. This transplanted god drew his name from Hermes (Mercury to the Romans), the messenger of the Greek hierarchy of deities and the god who conducted the souls of the dead to the underworld kingdom of Hades. The Egyptians identified Hermes Trismegistus with Thoth, who, in their pantheon of gods, was the divine inventor of writing and the spoken word. These same Greek colonists developed an interest in the old Egyptian religion, then went on to combine elements of their hellenistic beliefs, add fragments of Judaism and other Eastern belief constructs, and set about creating a synthesis of the various theologies. A vast number of unknown authors worked at the great task of composing a series of esoteric writings, all of which were attributed to the mythical figure of Thoth-Hermes. Eventually, Thoth-Hermes became humanized into a legendary king, who supposedly wrote the amazing total of 36,525 volumes of metaphysical teachings. In the third century, Clement of Alexandria reduced the total to 42, which he said he saw in a vision being carried by adepts.

❋ DELVING DEEPER

Budge, E. A. Wallis. *Egyptian Magic*. New York: Dover Books, 1971.

Caron, M., and S. Hutin. *The Alchemists*. Translated by Helen R. Lane. New York: Grove Press, 1961.

Seligmann, Kurt. *The History of Magic*. New York: Meridian Books, 1960.

Spence, Lewis. *An Encyclopedia of Occultism.* New Hyde Park, N.Y.: University Books, 1960.

ALBERTUS MAGNUS (c. 1193–1280?)

Albertus Magnus, Bishop of Ratisbon, became interested in alchemy and is credited with some extraordinary accomplishments, including the invention of the pistol and the cannon. Albertus is said to be one of those magi who actually achieved the transmutation of base metals into gold by means of the **philosopher's stone.** In addition, some said that he was able to exert control over atmospheric conditions, once even transforming a cold winter day into a pleasant summer afternoon so he and his guests could dine comfortably outside. A prolific writer, Albertus produced 21 volumes containing directions for the neophyte-practicing alchemist. Certain witnesses to his laboratory credited him with the creation of an automaton that performed menial tasks and was capable of intelligent speech. The term "Magnus" (great) usually ascribed to him was not awarded to him as a result of his many accomplishments, but is simply the Latin equivalent of his family name, de Groot.

Born at Larvingen on the Danube in circa 1193, Albertus was thought as a child to be quite stupid, capable, it seemed, of understanding only basic religious ideals, rather than any kind of complex study. Then one night the boy claimed to have received a visitation from the Blessed Virgin, and his intelligence quotient soared thereafter. Feeling obliged to devote his life to the clergy when he completed his studies, Albertus did so well in the clerical profession that he was made Bishop of Ratisbon. He held the position only a brief time before he resigned and announced that he would devote his intellect and his energy to science.

Albertus's scientific discoveries and his studies in alchemy and magic were always conducted with complete loyalty to the church. In his estimation, magic should be used only for good, and from the modern perspective, Albertus was not so much an alchemist as he was one of the most brilliant of the early experimental chemists. It remains a matter of conjecture whether or not Albertus really did accomplish the ultimate alchemical feat of transmuting base metals into gold, but tradition has it that he bequeathed his philosopher's stone to his distinguished pupil, St. Thomas Aquinas (1224–1274). Once it was in his possession, according to the old legend, Aquinas destroyed the stone, fearful that the accusations of communing with Satan that had been levied at his mentor might be true.

Ever since he left the clergy, Albertus had lived in pleasant seclusion in his estate near Cologne. As he grew older, it is said that the dullness of mind that had characterized his youth returned, and Albertus Magnus died in relative obscurity.

❊ DELVING DEEPER

Caron, M., and S. Hutin. *The Alchemists.* Trans. by Helen R. Lane. New York: Grove Press, 1961.

Seligmann, Kurt. *The History of Magic.* New York: Meridian Books, 1960.

Spence, Lewis. *An Encyclopedia of Occultism.* New Hyde Park, N.Y.: University Books, 1960.

Summers, Montague. *The History of Witchcraft.* New York: University Books, 1956.

PARACELSUS (1493–1541)

The German physician Theophrastus Bombast von Hohenheim traveled throughout Europe, practicing medicine, occultism, and

Paracelsus (1493–1541).

alchemy under the name of Paracelsus. As with so many of the true alchemists, Paracelsus believed that it was far more important to contemplate nature and the majesty of God's handiworks than to spend all one's time studying the knowledge that could be found in books. If one could acquire the kind of purity of belief, such as Jesus (c. 6 B.C.E.–c. 30 C.E.) affirmed existed in the heart of a child, one could literally transform base substances into precious metals and gems, for the primary ingredient necessary for alchemical success lay in obtaining the *prima materia*, the essence of all substances, the primeval building blocks of the universe. In the view of Paracelsus, this essential substance was both visible and invisible, and it was the soul of the world from which all elements had sprung, and its power was accessible to all who had the purity of heart and the faith to attain it. For Paracelsus, as for many of his alchemical brotherhood, the gospels of Jesus and the writings of **Hermes Trismegistus** had much in common.

Paracelsus also excited the medical community and lay people alike with his wonder medicine, the alkahest. There was the spirit alkahest that fortified the body against diseases, and there was the metal alkahest that matured and perfected base metals into gold.

As a result of a series of chemical experiments, Paracelsus became the first to describe zinc, which had been unknown to science, and he introduced many practical curative compounds to the medical practitioners of his day. At the same time that he delivered these medicines into the hands of the doctors, he admonished them to remember always that the first doctor of humankind was God, the divine creator of all health.

Paracelsus believed firmly that the fully realized human was the one who lived a healthful life. In addition, those who sought divine harmony should study astrology in order to learn the harmony of the spheres, should become a theologian in order to comprehend the needs of the soul, and should practice alchemy in order to understand that there are universal substances to be found everywhere in the material world. Those many accomplishments should then be capped with the fully realized human becoming a mystic to perceive always that there exist things beyond logic.

✣ DELVING DEEPER

Caron, M., and S. Hutin. *The Alchemists.* Trans. by Helen R. Lane. New York: Grove Press, 1961.

Seligmann, Kurt. *The History of Magic.* New York: Meridian Books, 1960.

Spence, Lewis. *An Encyclopedia of Occultism.* New Hyde Park, N.Y.: University Books, 1960.

Summers, Montague. *The History of Witchcraft.* New York: University Books, 1956.

MAGICK

For thousands of generations, from the earliest days of the cave dweller to Star Wars technology, a belief in magick has served the human race. And its practitioners maintain that it will be as powerful and as meaningful in the New Age. Magick, spelled with a "k," is the use of rituals, chants, ceremonies, and affirmations designed to give the individual control of the supernatural forces that manipulate the universe. Magic spelled minus the "k" denotes trickery, sleight-of-hand, misdirection, the rabbit-out-of-the-hat stage magician.

According to those who practice magick, the supernatural forces could not care less by what names they are called. It does not matter to them if the magician or sorcerer ascribes to them the catch phrases of contemporary science or evokes the ancient names of the old gods and goddesses. What is important to these forces is that the magician acknowledges that they do exist…that they are there to be called upon and to act as powerful servants for those who have learned to control them.

Those who seriously practice the ancient rites and rituals of magick truly believe that they can master the ability to control unseen forces that can be made to produce whatever it is that they seek in life—peace, happiness, the secret of love, the pursuit of wealth—all these things can come easily to those who understand the power of true magick.

The practitioners devoted to the various belief systems have few problems weaving their particular school of magick into the fabric of contemporary living, no matter how complex a schedule they might have. Moments can be culled from the day's work and assembled before bedtime for ritual work. For the more complex ceremonies a greater amount of time is needed, but for certain elementary rituals they claim that 15 minutes to a half hour are all that is required. Absolute quiet is preferable, but the magician can acquire the ability to blot out extraneous sounds and perform the necessary rituals regardless of environmental distractions. The serious magicians keep a record of what works, what does not work, and what factors they think contributed to the success of a particular ritual.

It may be that true magick lies in the unlimited reach of the psyche: mind contacting mind through other than sensory means; mind influencing matter and other minds; mind elevating itself to a level of consciousness where past, present, and future become an Eternal Now. Although humans may clothe these experiences according to the cultural context in which they are most functional, these evidences of the non-physical capabilities of human beings are universal.

Prestidigitation, the-hand-is-quicker-than-the-eye kind of magic, may have been born when certain clever individuals began to use their brains in an attempt to mimic the transcendental qualities of their mind. Perhaps long ago, a canny young man, jealous of a master shaman's ability to move an object through **psychokinesis,** mind influencing matter, cleverly duplicated the feat by attaching one end of a long black hair to a pebble and the other to a finger. The shaman might have spent years acquiring the discipline necessary to a semi-controlled functioning of his psychic ability, but the crafty young magician with his trickery could guarantee results on every attempt.

MAGICK spelled with a "k" refers to rituals, chants, and ceremonies. Magick spelled minus the "k" alludes to trickery, sleight-of-hand, and misdirection

Throughout all of history, there have been sorcerers, **magi,** and magicians. Perhaps some were truly able to produce the genuine manifestation of some extraordinary psychic ability, but it is likely that the far greater numbers of wizards and miracle workers had only mastered an imitative exploitation based on the essence of the idea of supernatural powers.

❀ DELVING DEEPER

De Givry, Emile Grillot. *Illustrated Anthology of Sorcery, Magic and Alchemy.* Trans. by J. Courtenay Locke. New York: Causeway Books, 1973.

Heer, Friedrich. *The Medieval World: Europe 1100 to 1350.* Trans. by Janet Sondheimer. Cleveland, Ohio: World Books, 1961.

Seligmann, Kurt. *The History of Magic.* New York: Meridian Books, 1960.

Spence, Lewis. *An Encyclopedia of Occultism.* New Hyde Park, N.Y.: University Books, 1960.

ABRAMELIN MAGICK

The essence of Abramelin magick can be found in *The Sacred Magic of Abramelin the Mage,* which was translated by MacGregor Mathers from a manuscript written in French

Merlin, the **magus** who served as a tutor to young Arthur Pendragon before he became king, has become almost universally known as the mentor to all those youth seeking wisdom, spiritual values, and material prosperity. Although scholars tell those fascinated by the legend of Camelot that Merlin, Arthur, Guinevere, and Lancelot, are fictional creations, there are still those who seek out their graves.

Some scholars point to a sixth-century writer and seer named Myrrdin, who went mad and took refuge in the Forest of Celydon when his king Gwenddolau was defeated at the Battle of Arderydd in 573. Merlin first appears in the *History of the Kings of Britain*, (1135) a classic work by Geoffrey of Monmouth (c. 1100–1154).

Merlin became the prophet associated with the quest for the **Holy Grail.** Other accounts detail how Merlin became trapped in a hawthorn tree, where he dwells forever. Some scholars think, this version restores the story of Myrddin, trapped by his madness in the forest.

Merlin: Real or Fiction?

Sources:

Monroe, Douglas, ed. *The Lost Books of Merlyn: Druid Magic from the Age of Arthur.* St. Paul, Minn.: Llewellyn, 1998.

White, T. H. *The Book of Merlyn: The Unpublished Conclusion to the Once and Future King.* Austin: University of Texas Press, 1988.

in the eighteenth century. The work purports to be much older, however. It was dated 1458 and claims to be translated originally from Hebrew. The text reveals to the adept that the universe is teeming with hordes of angels and demons that interact with human beings on many levels. All the vast array of phenomena on Earth are produced by the demonic entities, who are under the control of the angels. Humans are somewhere midway between the angelic and the demonic intelligences on the spiritual scale, and each human entity has both a guardian angel and a malevolent demon that hover near him or her from birth until death.

Abramelin magick provides instruction to the initiates of the "Magic of Light" that will enable them to achieve mastery over the demons and place them under their control. Abramelin the great magus learned how to accomplish such a difficult task by undergoing a process of spiritual cleansing and the development of a powerful will. In addition to spiritual and mental exercises, Abramelin discovered words of power that can be arranged in magic squares and written on parchment. With the proper application of these magical squares, the magus can command the demons and order them to assist him in the acquisition of earthly knowledge and power. By applying such magic words as "abracadabra," Abramelin magicians claim they can gain the love of anyone they desire, discover hidden treasures, become invisible, invoke spirits to appear, fly through the air and travel great distances in a matter of minutes, and animate corpses to create zombies to serve them. Abramelin magicians believe they can heal illnesses or cause diseases, bring about peace or war, create prosperity or poverty. They claim to shapeshift into different animal or human forms.

The difficulty that most practitioners of Abramelin magick encounter is that there are few words in any language that are able to fulfill the requirements of such productive squares. The basic concept of the Abramelin school of magick as determined by MacGregor Mathers in his translation of the French manuscript dictates that the letters in the squares must form the word that represents the desired object and must read the same in all directions. Mathers achieved little success in translating the words provided by Abramelin or in forming others that were little more than collections of meaningless letters.

✤ Delving Deeper

Cavendish, Richard. *The Black Arts*. New York: Capricorn Books, 1968.

Meyer, Marvin, and Richard Smith, eds. *Ancient Christian Magic*. San Francisco: HarperSanFrancisco, 1994.

Seligmann, Kurt. *The History of Magic*. New York: Meridian Books, 1960.

Spence, Lewis. *An Encyclopedia of Occultism*. New Hyde Park, N.Y.: University Books, 1960.

Williams, Charles. *Witchcraft*. New York: Meridian Books, 1960.

Black Magick

Black magick is the use of supernatural knowledge and powers for the purpose of doing evil or for working evil upon another human being. Practitioners of black magick deliberately seek to invoke demonic entities in order to control their powers and to force them to obey their will. Black magick is, therefore, a perversion of the mystical sciences. Rather than attempting to be of service to one's fellow humans as do the practitioners of **white magick,** the black magicians seek to gain control over supernatural forces for the sole purpose of personal aggrandizement, the glorification of their baser appetites, and the sowing of discord, discontent, and disease.

The desire to use supernatural entities to wreak havoc upon one's enemy or to acquire material wealth and power was in play during the time of the ancient Egyptians and Persians. The Greeks and Hebrews adapted many of the rituals and incantations, transforming the gods of the earlier cultures into the

demons of their own time. This process of deity transmutation was continued into medieval times when the earlier gods of the Middle East became devils, the ancient mysteries and fertility rites became orgies, and the orders of worship for the old hierarchy of gods and goddesses became patterns for sorcery. By the Middle Ages, belief in black magick and the powers of evil became so intense that the world had become a dark and shadowy place of dread ruled by Satan.

The sorcerers of the Middle Ages who practiced black magick followed to the letter the instructions recorded in the **Great Grimoires,** books filled with rites, rituals, incantations, conjurations, and evocations of demonic entities. The deity most often invoked by the dark sorcerer of medieval times to the present day is Satanas, a direct descendant of the

Baphomet: The Sabbatic Goat from the 1896 edition of *Transcendental Magic*. (FORTEAN PICTURE LIBRARY)

Egyptian Set and an alias for the Persians' Ahriman, the Muslims' Iblis, the Hebrews' Asmodeus and Beelzebub, and Pan, the goat-footed nature god of the Greeks, who became the image of Satan in the common mind. In addition to Satan, the master creator of evil, there were many other ancient gods who had been transformed into demons and personified as vices who could be ordered to do the bidding of the black magicians of the Middle Ages: Moloch, who devours children; Belial, who forments rebellion; Astarte and Astaroth, who seduce men and women into debauchery; Baphomet, who plots murders, and so on.

BLACK *magick is the use of supernatural knowledge and powers for doing evil.*

✣ DELVING DEEPER

Cavendish, Richard. *The Black Arts*. New York: Capricorn Books, 1968.

LaVey, Anton Szandor. *The Satanic Bible*. New York: Avon Books, 1969.

Rhodes, H. T. F. *The Satanic Mass*. London: Arrow Books, 1965.

Seligmann, Kurt. *The History of Magic*. New York: Meridian Books, 1960.

ENOCHIAN MAGICK

The apocryphal book of Enoch told of the order of angels called "Watchers," or "The Sleepless Ones." The leader of the Watchers was called Semjaza (in other places, Azazel, the name of one of the Hebrews' principal demons), who led 200 Watchers down to Earth to take wives from among the daughters of men. It was from such a union that the Nephilim, the giants, the heroes of old, as well as the ancient practitioners of sorcery, were born. The fallen angels taught their wives to cast various spells and to practice the arts of enchantment. They imparted to the women the lore of plants and the properties of certain roots. Semjaza did not neglect human men, teaching them how to manufacture weapons and tools of destruction.

In Enochian magick, the practitioner employed words of power that allegedly had been passed down in an oral tradition from the times of Enoch. The actual evocation began with the chanting of the appropriate words, which varied from spirit to spirit. These words of power were said, by their very sounds, to exert a strong emotional effect. A famous example is: *Eca zodocare iad goho Torzodu odo kilale qaa! Zodacare od sodameranul Zodorje lape zodiredo ol noco mada dae iadapiel!* These words are supposedly from the Enochian language, believed by magicians and other occultists to pre-date Sanskrit. They were addressed to the angelic beings that the magi believed would assist them in their magick and they translate as follows: "Move, therefore, and show yourselves! Open the mysteries of your creation! Be friendly unto me, for I am servant of the same, your God, and I am a true worshipper of the Highest."

In all chanting, recitations, and litanies, the impact of a group is far more impressive than that of a single voice, and the Enochian practitioners always thought a group must be composed of individual seekers of like dedication. When properly performed, such rituals have a powerful impact on the emotions. This is heightened by a measured walking around the inside of a magic circle, and dancing.

✣ DELVING DEEPER

Meyer, Marvin, and Richard Smith, eds. *Ancient Christian Magic*. San Francisco: HarperSanFrancisco, 1994.

Seligmann, Kurt. *The History of Magic*. New York: Meridian Books, 1960.

Spence, Lewis. *An Encyclopedia of Occultism*. New Hyde Park, N.Y.: University Books, 1960.

Williams, Charles. *Witchcraft*. New York: Meridian Books, 1960.

VODUN/VODOUN/VOODOO

Vodun, voudoun, or, more popularly, voodoo, means "spirit" in the language of the West African Yoruba people. Vodun as a religion is a mixture of African beliefs and rites that may go back as many as 6,000 years with the teachings, saints, and rituals of Roman Catholicism. Early slaves, who were snatched from their homes and families on Africa's West Coast, brought their gods and religious practices with them to Haiti and other West

Among certain Hispanic and Native American cultures of the Southwest, the practice of Burjeria is feared as a manifestation of evil. Those who use rituals, spells, incantations, potions, and powders to work ill against others are known as brujas (witches), who are primarily female in number (the male witch is known as a brujo). All the negative facets of witchcraft feared by people throughout the world are practiced by the brujas: manifesting the evil eye, casting spells to cause physical or mental illness, bringing about bad luck, even death. The brujas create dolls in which they insert bits of the victim's hair, fingernail clippings, or pieces of clothing and focus their evil intent upon the miniature representative of the person to be cursed. If an Anglo doctor with modern medical techniques cannot cure someone who has fallen suddenly ill, a bruja is suspected as being the cause of the problem.

Brujas are also thought to be accomplished shapeshifters, possessing the supernatural ability to transform themselves into owls, coyotes, or cats. In the form of an animal, they may spy upon potential victims and may even administer a potion into their unsuspecting quarry's food or water or hide a bad-luck charm on his or her premises. There are certain amulets or rituals that offer some protection from the brujas, but the only sure way to rid oneself of their evil deeds is to employ the services of a **curandero.** Sometimes the curandero is able to contact the bruja through supernatural means and demand that the curse or spell be removed. In more severe cases, the curandero may have to direct a spell toward the bruja and defeat her on the spiritual level in order to force her to remove the evil directed toward the victim.

THE PRACTICE OF BRUJERIA

SOURCES:

"Curandismo." *The Handbook of Texas Online.* [Online] http://www.tsha.utexas.edu/handbook/online/articles/view/CC/sdc 1.html.

Middleton, John, ed. *Magic, Witchcraft and Curing.* Garden City, N.Y.: Natural History Press, 1967.

Simmons, Marc. *Witchcraft in the Southwest.* Flagstaff, Ariz.: Northland Press, 1974.

Villoldo, Alberto, and Stanley Krippner. *Healing States: A Journey into the World of Spiritual Healing and Shamanism.* New York: Simon & Schuster Inc. Fireside Book, 1987.

Indian islands. Plantation owners, who purchased the slaves for rigorous labor, were compelled by order of the lieutenant-general to baptize their slaves in the Catholic religion. The slave suffered no conflict of theology. They accepted the white man's "water" and quickly adopted Catholic saints into their family of nature gods and goddesses.

VOODOO *refers to "spirit."*

The connotations of evil and fear that are associated with vodun originated primarily from the white plantation owners' obsession with the threat of slave revolts, for they and their overseers were outnumbered 16 to 1 by the field hands whom they worked unmercifully in the broiling Haitian sun. As the black population increased and the white demand for slave labor remained unceasing, vodun

began to take on an anti-white liturgy. Several "messiahs" emerged among the slaves, who were subsequently put to death by the whites in the "big houses." A number of laws began to be passed forbidding any plantation owner to allow "night dances" among his Negroes.

In 1791, a slave revolt took place under the leadership of Toussaint L'Ouverture (1743–1803) which was to lead to Haiti's independence from France in 1804. Although L'Ouverture died in a Napoleonic prison, his generals had become sufficiently inspired by his example to continue the struggle for freedom until the myth of white supremacy was banished from the island.

After the Concordat of 1860, when relations were once again reestablished with France, the priests who came to Haiti found the vestiges of Catholicism kept alive in vodun. The clergy fulminated against vodun from the pulpits but did not actively campaign against their rival priesthood until 1896 when an impatient monseigneur tried to organize an anti-vodun league without success. It wasn't until 1940 that the

Catholic Church launched a violent campaign of renunciation directed at the adherents of vodun. The priests went about their methodic attack with such zeal that the government was forced to intercede and command them to temper the fires of their campaign.

Today there are more than 60 million people who practice vodun worldwide, largely where Haitian emigrants have settled in Benin, Dominican Republic, Ghana, Togo, various cities in the United States, and, of course, in Haiti. In South America, there are many religions similar to vodun, such as Umbanda, Quimbanda, or Candomble. A male priest of vodun is called a houngan or hungan; his female counterpart, a mambo. The place where one practices vodun is a series of buildings called a humfort or hounfou. A "congregation" is called a hunsi or hounsis, and the hungan cures, divines, and cares for them through the good graces of a loa, his guiding spirit.

The worship of the supernatural loa is the central purpose of vodun. They are the old gods of Africa, the local spirits of Haiti, who occupy a position to the fore of God, Christ, the Virgin, and the saints. From the beginning, the Haitians adamantly refused to accept the church's position that the loa are the "fallen angels" who rebelled against God. The loa do good and guide and protect humankind, the hungans argue. They, like the saints of Roman Catholicism, were once men and women who lived exemplary lives and who now are given a specific responsibility to assist human spirituality. Certainly there are those priests, the bokors, who perform acts of evil sorcery, the left-hand path of vodun, but rarely will a hungan resort to such practices.

The loa communicates with its faithful ones by possessing their bodies during a trance or by appearing to them in dreams. The possession usually takes place during ritual dancing in the humfort. Each participant eventually undergoes a personality change and adapts a trait of his or her particular loa. The adherents of vodun refer to this phenomenon of the invasion of the body by a supernatural agency as that of the loa mounting its "horse."

There is a great difference, the hungan maintains, between possession by a loa and possession by an evil spirit. An evil spirit would bring chaos to the dancing and perhaps great harm to the one possessed. The traditional dances of vodun are conducted on a serious plane with rhythm and suppleness but not with the orgiastic sensuality depicted in motion pictures about voodoo or in the displays performed for the tourist trade.

All vodun ceremonies must be climaxed with sacrifice to the loa. Chickens are most commonly offered to the loa, although the wealthy may offer a goat or a bull. The possessed usually drinks of the blood that is collected in a vessel, thereby satisfying the hunger of the loa. Other dancers may also partake of the blood, sometimes adding spices to the vital fluid. After the ceremony, the sacrificed animal is usually cooked and eaten.

A VOUDOUN *"congregation" is called a hunsi or hounsis.*

The traditional belief structure of the Yoruba envisioned a chief god named Olorun, who remains aloof and unknowable to humankind, but who permitted a lesser deity, Obatala, to create the earth and all its life forms. There are hundreds of minor spirits whose influence may be invoked by humankind, such as Ayza, the protector; Baron Samedi, guardian of the grave; Dambala, the serpent; Ezli, the female spirit of love; Ogou Balanjo, spirit of healing; and Mawu Lisa, spirit of creation. Each follower of vodun has his or her own "met tet," a guardian spirit that corresponds to a Catholic's special saint.

Vodun has a supernatural entity that is unique among the practitioners of sorcery—the zombi, those dread creatures of the undead who prowl about at night doing the bidding of those magicians who follow the left-hand path. Vodun lore actually has two types of zombi: the undead and those who died by violence. A Haitian is most cautious in his or her approach to a cemetery for it is there that one is most likely to meet one of the unfortunate wraiths who died without time for proper ritual. For the

Haitian peasant, zombies, the living dead, are to be feared as real instruments of hungan who have succumbed to the influence of evil and become sorcerers. The people of the villages believe that the sorcerer unearths a corpse and wafts under its nose a bottle containing its soul. Then, as if he were fanning a tiny spark of life in dry tinder, the sorcerer nurtures the spark of life in the corpse until he has fashioned a zombi. The deceased are often buried face downward by considerate relatives so the corpse cannot hear the call of the sorcerer. Some villagers take the precaution of providing their departed with a weapon, such as a machete, with which to ward off the evil hungan.

Haiti is filled with terrible tales of the zombi. There are eyewitness accounts from those who have allegedly discovered friends or relatives, supposedly long-dead, laboring in the field of some native sorcerer. Upon investigation, such zombi usually turn out to be mentally defective individuals who bear a strong resemblance to the deceased. Unfortunately, some unscrupulous hungan have been known to take advantage of mentally handicapped individuals and turn them into virtual beasts of burden. Then, too, it is quite likely that certain hungan have discovered the secret and utilization of many powerful jungle drugs. Modern science owes a heavy debt to native sorcery for some of its most effective painkillers and tranquilizers. It seems possible that a hungan who follows the left-hand path, seeking his own vengeance or that of another, could mix a powerful drug into the victim's food and induce a deep state of hypnotic lethargy in the person, transforming him or her into a blank-eyed, shuffling, obedient zombi.

There is also the matter of the voodoo doll and voodoo curses. Anthropologist Walter Cannon spent several years collecting examples of "voodoo death," instances in which men and women died as a result of being the recipient of a curse, an alleged supernatural visitation, or the breaking of some tribal or cultural taboo. The question that Cannon sought to answer was, "How can an ominous and persistent state of fear end the life of a human?"

Fear, one of the most powerful and deep-rooted of the emotions, has its effects mediated through the nervous system and the endocrine apparatus, the "sympathetic-adrenal system." Cannon has hypothesized that, "if these powerful emotions prevail and the bodily forces are fully mobilized for action, and if this state of extreme perturbation continues for an uncontrolled possession of the organism for a considerable period . . . dire results may ensue." Cannon has suggested, then, that "vodun death" may result from a state of shock due to a persistent and continuous outpouring of adrenalin and a depletion of the adrenal corticosteroid hormones. Such a constant agitation caused by an abiding sense of fear could consequently induce a fatal reduction in blood pressure. Cannon assessed voodoo death as a real phenomenon set in motion by "shocking emotional stress to obvious or repressed terror." Dr. J. C. Barker, in his collection of case histories of individuals who had willed others, or themselves, to death (*Scared to Death* [1969]), saw voodoolike death as resulting, "purely from extreme fear and exhaustion...essentially a psychosomatic phenomenon."

✦ DELVING DEEPER

Bach, Marcus. *Inside Voodoo*. New York: Signet, 1968.

Barker, J. C. *Scared to Death*. New York: Dell Books, 1969.

Brean, Joseph. "Scared to Death Isn't Just an Expression." *National Post with file from Agence France-Presse*, December 21, 2001. [Online] http://www.nationalpost.com/search/story.html?f'/stories/20011221/931884.html&qs'Jos.

Huxley, Francis. *The Invisibles: Voodoo Gods in Haiti*. New York: McGraw-Hill, 1969.

"Vodun." [Online] http://www.religioustolerance.org/voodoo.htm.

WHITE MAGICK

In the earliest of societies, the practitioner of white magick was the **shaman,** the medicine man, the herbalist—the individual sought out by the village when it was necessary to receive a proper potion to dissolve an illness or a proper charm to drive away an evil spirit. In these same early societies, the roles of priest and magician were often combined into a man or a woman who had the ability to enter a **trance state** and commune with the entities that dwelt in nature and the spirits who lived in the unseen world. The priest/magican knew how to appease angry entities whose sacred spaces were violated, how to eject an unwelcome possessing spirit from a human body, and where to find the herbs that could banish illness. All of these tasks were accomplished with the good of the tribal members as the priest/magician's primary objective.

By the Middle Ages in Europe, magic and religion remained intertwined for those who would practice white magick. Although **black magick** certainly existed as a power and claimed those dark magicians who succumbed to personal greed and were paid to use their craft against others, the practitioners of the higher magic attracted such gifted minds as that of **Eliphas Levi, Agrippa,** and **Paracelsus,** all of whom considered magic as the true road to communion with God and believed that the fruits of such communion should be expressed in service to their fellow humans. Levi believed that the white magicians who devoted themselves to faith and reason, science and belief would be able to endow themselves with a sovereign power that would make them masters over all spirits and the forces of the material world. Paracelsus proclaimed that the white magician did not need to draw magic circles, chant spells, or practice rituals. In his belief construct nothing was impossible to the human spirit that linked itself with God. All magic was possible to the human mind expressing itself through faith and imagination.

White magicians continue to practice their traditions on a high level of mystical ideals and devote themselves to transcendental magic, rather than the occult. While the darker applications of magic and sorcery receive the greater share of popular attention, those adepts of all traditions who practice white magick continue to do so quietly and secretly, serving humankind by working in the light, rather than the darkness.

❦ DELVING DEEPER

Meyer, Marvin, and Richard Smith, eds. *Ancient Christian Magic.* San Francisco: HarperSanFrancisco, 1994.

Seligmann, Kurt. *The History of Magic.* New York: Meridian Books, 1960.

Spence, Lewis. *An Encyclopedia of Occultism.* New Hyde Park, N.Y.: University Books, 1960.

MAGI

Everyone who knows the traditional story of Christmas has heard of the three magi who followed the star in the East and who traveled afar to worship at the manger wherein lay the baby Jesus (c. 6 B.C.E.–c. 30 C.E.). These magi were not kings, but "wise ones," astrologers and priests of ancient Persia, philosophers of Zoroastrian wisdom, and their title has provided the root for the words "magic," "magician," and so forth. Such men were the councilors of the Eastern empires, the possessors of occult secrets that guided royalty.

DURING *the Middle Ages, magi were men who accumulated occult wisdom and knowledge from the Kabbalah.*

In Europe during the Middle Ages, those who bore the title of magi were more likely to be men who had devoted their lives to the accumulation of occult wisdom and knowledge from the Kabbalah, the ancient Egyptians, the Arabs, and various pagan sources, and had thereby come under the scrutiny of the church and suspected of communicating with demons. Although these individuals valiantly clung to precious fragments of ancient lore and insisted that they were practitioners of good magic, the clergy saw few distinctions between the magi and the witches that the Inquisition sought to bring to trial for demonolatry and devil worship. It was not until the advent of the Renaissance that the magi and their forbidden knowledge began to gain a certain acceptance among the courts of Europe and the better educated members of the general populace.

Perhaps one of the greatest difficulties that the magi had with the orthodox clergy was their contention that angelic beings could be summoned to assist in the practice of white magick. There were seven major planetary spirits, or archangels, that the magi were interested in contacting: Raphael, Gabriel, Canael, Michael, Zadikel, Haniel, and Zaphkiel. One of the original sources of such instruction allegedly came from the great Egyptian magi and master of the occult, Hermes-Thoth, who described the revelation he had been given when he received a shimmering vision of a perfectly formed, colossal man of great beauty. Gently the being spoke to Hermes and identified itself as Pymander, the thought of the All-Powerful, who had come to give him strength because of his love of justice and his desire to seek the truth.

Pymander told Hermes that he might make a wish and it would be granted to him. Hermes-Thoth asked for a ray of the entity's divine knowledge. Pymander granted the wish, and Hermes was immediately inundated with wondrous visions, all beyond human comprehension and imagination. After the imagery had ceased, the blackness surrounding Hermes grew terrifying. A harsh and discordant voice boomed through the ether, creating a chaotic tempest of roaring winds and thunderous explosions. The mighty and terrible voice left Hermes filled with awe. Then from the All-Powerful came seven spirits who moved in seven circles; and in the circles were all the beings that composed the universe. The action of the seven spirits in their circles is called fate, and these circles themselves are enclosed in the divine Thought that permeates them eternally.

Hermes was given to comprehend that God had committed to the seven spirits the governing of the elements and the creation of their combined products. But because God created humans in his own image, and, pleased with this image, had given them power over terrestrial nature, God would grant the ability to command the seven spirits to those humans who could learn to know themselves, for they were and could come to conquer the duality of their earthly nature. They would truly become magi who learned to triumph over sensual temptations and to increase their mental faculties. God would give such adepts a measure of light in proportion to their merits, and they would be allowed to penetrate the most profound mysteries of nature. Assisting these magi in their work on Earth would be the seven superior spirits of the Egyptian system, acting as intermediaries between God and humans. These seven spirits were the same beings that the Brahmans of ancient India called the seven Devas, that in Persia were called the seven Amaschapands, that in Chaldea were called the seven Great Angels, that in Jewish Kabbalism are called the seven Archangels.

Later, various magi sought to reconcile the Christian hierarchy of celestial spirits with the traditions of Hermes by classifying the angels into three hierarchies, each subdivided into three orders:

- *The First Hierarchy:* Seraphim, Cherubim, and Thrones

- *The Second Hierarchy:* Dominions, Powers, and Authorities [Virtues]

- *The Third Hierarchy:* Principalities, Archangels, and Angels.

These spirits are considered more perfect in essence than humans, and they are thought to be on Earth to help. They work out the pattern of ordeals that each human being must pass through, and they give an account of human actions to God after one passes from the physical plane. They cannot, however, interfere in any way with human free will, which always must make the choice between good and evil. In their capacity to help, though, these angels can be called upon to assist humans in various ways.

It is these archangels, then, that the magi evoke in their ceremonies. Accompanying the concept of the planetary spirits, or archangels, was something the Egyptians called "hekau" or word of power. The word of power, when spoken, released a vibration capable of evoking spirits. The most powerful hekau for calling up a specific spirit in ceremonial magic is that spirit's name.

"To name is to define," cried **Count Cagliostro,** a famous occultist of the eighteenth century. And, to the magi of the Middle Ages, to know the name of a spirit was to be able to command its presence, thereby making them true miracle workers.

❖ DELVING DEEPER

Budge, E. A. Wallis. *Egyptian Magic*. New York: Dover Books, 1971.

Caron, M., and S. Hutin. *The Alchemists*. Translated by Helen R. Lane. New York: Grove Press, 1961.

Meyer, Marvin, and Richard Smith, eds. *Ancient Christian Magic*. San Francisco: HarperSanFrancisco, 1994.

Seligmann, Kurt. *The History of Magic*. New York: Meridian Books, 1960.

Spence, Lewis. *An Encyclopedia of Occultism*. New Hyde Park, N.Y.: University Books, 1960.

(Henry) Cornelius Agrippa (von Nettesheim) (1486–1535).
(FORTEAN PICTURE LIBRARY)

AGRIPPA (1486–1535)

Henry Cornelius Agrippa von Nettesheim, author of *The Occult Philosophy*, (1531) one of the most influential works in Western occultism, was an accomplished physician, soldier, and occultist who traveled widely throughout Europe. More commonly known as Agrippa, the versatile magus envisioned magic as a blend of scientific knowledge, religious doctrine, and occult secrets. While his intellect brought him fame, wealth, and political favor, the turbulent times in which he practiced his craft also brought him condemnation, poverty, and prison. Agrippa became immersed in the supernatural and the occult and sought to develop a synthesis that would unite various magical systems and religious traditions with the Kabbalah.

While in Paris on a mission for the Emperor Maximilian I (1459–1519), Agrippa formed a secret society with a group of like-minded scholars and noblemen. The pact they vowed to uphold envisioned a reformed world, and they pledged to come to one another's assistance whenever needed. Later, when their efforts to restore one of their members to his former position of power failed, the group was disbanded.

A humanist and feminist ahead of his time, Agrippa exalted the position of women far above the prevailing sentiment of the early sixteenth century. In 1509, he composed *The Nobility of the Female Sex* and *The Superiority of Women* while lecturing at the university at Dole. Agrippa annoyed a number of clerics

when he presented teachings from the Bible, the Church Fathers, and various works of philosophy to argue his praise of women. The paean to the fair sex was dedicated to Margaret of Austria, Maximilian's daughter, who was mistress of Dole and Burgundy, in the hope that he might obtain her patronage. Unfortunately for his cause, a Franciscan friar in Margaret's cabinet warned her that Agrippa was a heretic who taught the Kabbalah of the Jews and whose attentions were not to be trusted. Once the clergy saw that royal support would not be forthcoming for Agrippa, they also managed to squelch publication of his praise of women.

Discouraged by Margaret's rejection of his work, Agrippa went first to England, then to Cologne where he continued his lectures and his studies. In 1515, his military prowess while serving in Maximilian's campaign in Italy earned him a knighthood on the battlefield. Coincident with this honor, the Cardinal of St. Croix asked Agrippa to serve as representative to the council of Pope Leo X (1475–1521). Agrippa was pleased to do so, for he saw this as an opportunity to rectify matters with the church whose clergy he had offended in the past, but when the council was disbanded before he could state his defense, he abandoned both his military and ecclesiastical careers.

Agrippa returned to teaching, lecturing on **Hermes Trismegistus** at Turin and Pavia, and

Cornelius Agrippa's
magical square.
(FORTEAN PICTURE LIBRARY)

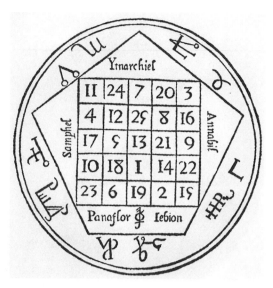

adding to his fame as a magus. In 1520, he left his position as a city official at Metz when he ran afoul of the inquisitor Savini from whom he rescued a woman unjustly accused of witchcraft. With the unforgiving Inquisition now keeping a close watch on his activities, Agrippa began practicing medicine in such cities as Cologne, Geneva, and Fribourg. In 1524, King Francis I (1494–1547) appointed him as personal physician to his mother, the Duchesse Louise of Savoy, and Agrippa was at last on a pension. Such security soon dissipated, however, when he rebuked the duchess for asking him to debase his talents by divining her future from the stars.

Agrippa continued his nomadic existence, moving from city to city, country to country. In 1529, he was summoned to provide counsel for Henry VIII of England (1491–1547), the chancellor of Germany, an Italian marquis, and Margaret of Austria, governor of the Netherlands. Twenty years after he had dedicated *The Superiority of Women* to her, Margaret finally granted her approval to the work and appointed Agrippa historiographer of her court.

It was at this time when destiny appeared at last to have smiled upon him that Agrippa confused follower and foe alike by publishing *On the Vanity of Arts and Sciences* (1529), which proclaimed that nothing was certain in either the arts or the sciences. The product of his disillusionment with the lack of material rewards that his scholarship and his alchemical practices had produced, Agrippa's work

advised that the only reliable source to which humans might turn was religious faith. As if such preachments were not baffling enough coming from a leading occultist of the day, a scholar known throughout all of Europe as the great champion of alchemy and magic, Agrippa's *Occult Philosophy*, which had been written when he was a youth but had remained in manuscript form, was published about a year later. In this monumental work, Agrippa declared that magi were able to perform miracles through the occult wisdom revealed to them by supernatural beings. With one book recanting the occult beliefs of the other, but still declaring that all human endeavors were uncertain acts of vanity, Agrippa found himself once again devoid of a stable audience and relieved of his pension as an imperial historiographer. He was jailed in Brussels for one year for his inability to pay his debts, and upon his release he sought refuge at Grenoble in the home of M. Allard, Receiver General of the Provence. Agrippa died there in 1535.

Before he died, Agrippa was seen everywhere with his large black dog, Monsieur. Because of his reputation among the people as a black magician, it was widely believed among the townsfolk of Grenoble that Monsieur was Agrippa's **familiar.** After Agrippa's death, the large dog seemed to vanish mysteriously, thereby convincing people that the magus had been in league with Satan all along. Although a friend testified that he had often walked Monsieur for the scholar and that the large black canine was simply a dog, the townspeople persisted in their belief that they had often witnessed the magus Agrippa in the company of his demonic familiar.

❈ **DELVING DEEPER**

Cavendish, Richard. *The Black Arts.* New York: Capricorn Books, 1968.

Caron, M., and S. Hutin. *The Alchemists.* Translated by Helen R. Lane. New York: Grove Press, 1961.

De Givry, Emile Grillot. *Illustrated Anthology of Sorcery, Magic and Alchemy.* Translated by J. Courtenay Locke. New York: Causeway Books, 1973.

Heer, Friedrich. *The Medieval World: Europe 1100 to 1350.* Translated by Janet Sondheimer. Cleveland, Ohio: World Books, 1961.

Meyer, Marvin, and Richard Smith, eds. *Ancient Christian Magic*. San Francisco: HarperSanFrancisco, 1994.

Seligmann, Kurt. *The History of Magic*. New York: Meridian Books, 1960.

Spence, Lewis. *An Encyclopedia of Occultism*. New Hyde Park, N.Y.: University Books, 1960.

COUNT ALLESANDRO CAGLIOSTRO (1743–1795)

Count Allesandro Cagliostro was widely known as the man who held the secret of the **philosopher's stone,** the alchemist who turned lowly metals into gold and in Strasburg produced alchemically a diamond which he presented to Cardinal Louis de Rohan. Cagliostro was said to have invented the "water of beauty," a virtual fountain of youth, and when the best doctors in Europe admitted their defeat in difficult cases, they summoned the count and his curative powers. Although most students of sorcery and magic regard Cagliostro as a charlatan, certain scholars of the occult still regard him as one of the greatest magi of all time.

By the time he was 14, Cagliostro (Peter Basalmo) was an assistant to an apothecary in Palermo, Italy, and had become an expert in the principles of chemistry and medicine. Driven to obtain less conventional knowledge, the teenager fell in with a group of vagabonds who were continually in trouble with the police. When he was 17, he had gained a reputation as one who could evoke the spirits of the dead, but he used this knowledge to fleece a wealthy citizen of Palermo and he fled to Messina, where he assumed the title and the identity of Count Cagliostro.

It was in Messina that the young man met the mysterious Althotas, a man of Asian appearance, dressed in caftan and robes, who upon their first encounter proceeded to reveal the events of Cagliostro's past. As they became better acquainted, Althotas said that he didn't believe in ordinary magic, but maintained that the physical laws were mutable and could be manipulated by the powers of mind. The two traveled together to Egypt where they visited the priests of many esoteric traditions and received much secret knowledge. From Egypt they went to Asia and began to pursue alchemical experiments.

When Althotas died on the island of Malta, Cagliostro returned to Italy with a considerable fortune accumulated from his work with various alchemical teachers. In 1770, when he was 26 years old, he met Lorenza Feliciani while in Rome, and he asked her to marry him. Lorenza's father was impressed by Cagliostro's apparent wealth and readily consented to the wedding. While some biographers believe his riches came from his successful alchemical experiments, others accuse the count of duping wealthy aristocrats out of their inheritances and of running disreputable gambling houses. His marriage to Lorenza is also clouded with charges of chicanery and deceit. Although most accounts depict her as an honest and good woman, she traveled throughout Europe and Great Britain with Cagliostro and appears to have been involved in his various schemes. By far the most important of Cagliostro's creations was the Egyptian Masonic rite, whose lodges admitted both sexes and whose main temple was presided over by the Grand Mistress Lorenza and the Grand Copt Cagliostro.

C⊙UПT *Allesandro Cagliostro was allegedly the one who held the secret of the philosopher's stone.*

In the lodges ruled by the Grand Mistress and the Grand Copt, women were so emancipated that they were encouraged to remove all of their clothing to be initiated into the mysteries of nature. Those women who received the magnetic powers bestowed upon them by the Grand Copt were promised the ability to make full use of their own occult force. In the Egyptian Masonic lodge, physical happiness was equivalent to spiritual peace.

Wealthy members of European royalty sought his magical elixir of regeneration, and Count Cagliostro is said to have cured thousands of people with his lotions and potions during his reign in Europe as a master conjurer. Today, researchers can only guess if these illnesses were linked to hysteria or psychosomatic delusions.

Although the church had chosen to ignore accusations of deception and charlatanism directed against Cagliostro, it could not overlook the formation of another Masonic lodge. And when the Grand Copt sought to establish a lodge within the boundaries of the papal states, he was arrested on September 27, 1789, by order of the Holy Inquisition and imprisoned in the Castle of Saint Angelo. Inquisitors examined Cagliostro for 18 months, and he was condemned to death on April 7, 1791. However, his sentence was commuted to perpetual imprisonment in the Castle of Saint Angelo. Unable to accept such a fate, Cagliostro attempted to escape. He was placed in solitary confinement in a cistern in the Castle of San Leo near Montefeltro where he suffered with little food, air, or movement. Sometime in 1795, the governor took pity on the prisoner and had him removed to a cell on ground level. It was here, around March 6, the unhappy magi died. Although the records are incomplete, it is thought that his wife, Lorenza, who had been sentenced to the Convent of St. Appolonia, a penitentiary for women in Rome, died in 1794.

❈ DELVING DEEPER

De Givry, Emile Grillot. *Illustrated Anthology of Sorcery, Magic and Alchemy.* Translated by J. Courtenay Locke. New York: Causeway Books, 1973.

Seligmann, Kurt. *The History of Magic.* New York: Meridian Books, 1960.

Spence, Lewis. *An Encyclopedia of Occultism.* New Hyde Park, N.Y.: University Books, 1960.

ALEISTER CROWLEY (1875–1947)

Aleister Crowley (Edward Alexander Crowley) is one of the most controversial figures in the annals of modern occultism. Along with the Freudians, Crowley believed that most of humankind's ills were caused by inhibition of the sexual impulses. Consequently, much of Crowley's magick drew its impetus from the release of psychic energy through sexual activity, including homosexuality and other practices that earned for Crowley the distinction of being named one of the most sinister figures of modern times. In his day, and for some time

afterward, the name of Aleister Crowley was almost synonymous with evil. Crowley's own mother, a fundamentalist Christian, dubbed him "The Great Beast 666," a diabolical image drawn from the Book of Revelation.

In Cairo, Egypt, in 1904 a being that called itself "Aiwass" suddenly took possession of Crowley's wife after she had uttered something to the effect that "they" wished to communicate with him. At the time, they were standing before the Stele of Revealing in the Cairo Museum. There followed three days of dictation by Aiwass to Crowley. The text of this dictation forms *The Book of the Law* (1904), which was supposed to herald the coming of the Age of Horus, the child.

Crowley won the distinction of being the "wickedest man in the world" while he was conducting an institution he called the Sacred Abbey of Thelema. Located on the island of Sicily, the abbey was dedicated to the practice of magic, uninhibited sex accompanied by liberal use of drugs, and worship of ancient Gnostic deities. Ritual intercourse, both hetero and homosexual in nature, was the chief form of worship.

Drawing upon ancient Gnostic magical texts, Crowley added to an old Graeco-Egyptian text and performed the rite of *Liber samekh,* celebrating sexual release and the passage of the spirit from a lower level of consciousness to a higher one. Crowley added his own contributions to the original Gnostic text, some of which were "High Supernatural Black Magic" and "Intercourse with the Demon." According to Crowley the ritual was the one to be employed by the Beast 666 for the attainment of knowledge and conversation with his holy guardian angel. In *The Black Arts* (1968) Richard Cavendish comments on the *Liber samekh:* "To know the angel and have intercourse with the demon . . . means to summon up and liberate the forces of the magician's unconscious. The performance of the ritual is accompanied by...the mounting frenzy with which the barbarous names of power are chanted...ending in a climax which is both physical and psychological and in which the magician's innermost powers are unleashed."

Crowley's life and career are illustrations of the two possibilities inherent in experimenting with altered states of consciousness. Whatever else might be said about him, Crowley was a powerful magician and a master of the art of ritual. Crowley's excesses and eventual decline probably were results of his reliance upon narcotics. His philosophy of life was summed up in an analysis by journalist Tom Driberg in the days when Crowley was beginning to be called the wickedest man in the world: "His basic commandment was 'Do what thou wilt.' Since his training in serious, formal magick (as he spelt it) was rigorous, he did not mean by this 'Follow each casual impulse.' He meant 'Discover your own true will and do it.' In other words, 'Know yourself and be yourself.'"

Before his death Crowley was rumored to have started a group on the American West Coast that included the study and practice of alchemy. The deaths of several persons as the results of mysterious explosions were connected with this practice; but if a Crowley cult ever existed, it had all but vanished within a few years after his death.

Aleister Crowley in 1934.
(AP/WIDE WORLD PHOTOS)

ALEISTER *Crowley was dubbed "The Great Beast 666."*

❖ DELVING DEEPER

Aleister Crowley Foundation. [Online] http://www. thelemicgoldendawn.org/acf/acfl.htm.

Cavendish, Richard. *The Black Arts*. New York: Capricorn Books, 1968.

Mannix, Daniel P. *The Beast*. New York: Ballantine Books, 1959.

Rhodes, H. T. F. *The Satanic Mass*. London: Arrow
Books, 1965.

JOHN DEE (1527–1608)

Although Dr. John Dee's reputation as a black
magician may be undeserved, he seems destined to remain so categorized in the history of
magic and the occult. Dee came from a family
of means, and he was admitted to St. John's
College, Cambridge, when he was only 15.
His application to his studies was intense, and
he soon distinguished himself as a scholar. He
slept only four hours per night, ate a light
meal, participated in various forms of recreation for two hours, then used the remaining
18 hours for study.

When he left Cambridge, he traveled to
Holland to study with Mercator (1512–1594)
and other learned men of his day. Returning
home, he was made a fellow of Trinity College, and he gained a wide reputation as an
astronomer.

Dee left England again soon after acquiring fame as an astrologer and an astronomer,

and he taught at many European universities.
In 1551, he was back in England and was
received by King Edward VI (1537–1553),
who awarded him a pension of 100 crowns per
annum. This stipend Dee later exchanged for
a rectory at Upton-upon-Severn.

During Queen Mary I's (1516–1558) reign
(1553–58), Dee was accused of trying to kill
her by "enchantments." He was seized, con-
fined, and tried. After a long trial that lasted
until 1555, he was at last acquitted.

When Elizabeth I (1533–1603) ascended
to the throne in 1558, she consulted with Dee
as to which day the stars deemed the most
propitious hours for her coronation. Pleased
with his pronouncements, she continued to
grant him the favor of her attention, and she
made many promises of preferment—none of
which were kept. Disillusioned by the
intrigues of the English Royal Court, Dee left
the country for Holland. In 1564 while residing in Antwerp, Dee published his greatest
work, *Monas Hieroglyphica*. After he had presented a copy to the Emperor Maximilian II

(1527–1576), Dee returned to England to produce more learned occult volumes.

In 1571, while residing once again on the Continent, Dee fell ill. When Elizabeth heard of it, she sent two of her best physicians to attend to him. The queen also conveyed additional proofs of her high regard for him and made further promises. When he recovered, Dee returned to England and settled at Mortlake in Surrey. Here he accumulated an extensive library of works on occultism and allied subjects, prompting his neighbors to decree that he was in league with the devil. While Dee insisted that he did not practice black magic, it seemed apparent that he knew a great deal about the subject.

After Elizabeth's death, James I (1566–1625) refused to extend patronage to Dee because of his troubled reputation as a practitioner of the dark arts. Dee returned to Mortlake, where he died in 1608 in a state of neglect and poverty. Dr. John Dee's globes, magic stone, and other items of his occult practices may be seen today in the British Museum.

John Dee (1572–1608).
(FORTEAN PICTURE LIBRARY)

✤ DELVING DEEPER

Caron, M., and S. Hutin. *The Alchemists*. Translated by Helen R. Lane. New York: Grove Press, 1961.

De Givry, Emile Grillot. *Illustrated Anthology of Sorcery, Magic and Alchemy*. Translated by J. Courtenay Locke. New York: Causeway Books, 1973.

Seligmann, Kurt. *The History of Magic*. New York: Meridian Books, 1960.

Spence, Lewis. *An Encyclopedia of Occultism*. New Hyde Park, N.Y.: University Books, 1960.

DR. FAUST (C. 1480–1540)

Although many assume that Dr. Faust was a fictional character created by Christopher Marlowe (1564–1593) for his famous play, *The Tragedy of Dr. Faustus* (1589), and utilized again later by Johannn Wolfgang von Goethe (1749–1832) for his masterwork *Faust* (1808), there actually was a magician named Georg Faust, who was born in Knittlingen, Wurttenburg, Germany, around 1480. Faust was a traveling magician, visiting town after town, performing feats of legerdemain, telling fortunes, and professing to have supernatural powers. While some contemporary scholars were impressed with his alleged abilities, others branded him as nothing more than an unscrupulous charlatan. At some point, Georg Faust became confused with an academic named Johann Faust, and he was mistakenly credited with many of the learned professor's scholastic achievements.

THE *first cinematic production of Dr. Faust was a French film in 1905.*

When Georg Faust died around 1540, he had become such a legendary magician in Germany that in 1558 Johann Speiss published a book entitled *The History of Dr. Johann Faust*, which listed his many feats and adventures. Speiss included his interpretation of how Faust had become a master magician by selling his soul to the devil in exchange for 24 years of limitless knowledge and power.

Over the course of time, the Faust story has been the subject of numerous plays, operas, and films. The first cinematic production of the ageless tale of Dr. Faust selling his soul to the devil for unlimited knowledge was a French film in 1905. The noted German actor Emil Jannings played the role in a classic

version of the story in 1926, and British actor Richard Burton enacted Dr. Faustus in 1968.

✤ DELVING DEEPER

De Givry, Emile Grillot. *Illustrated Anthology of Sorcery, Magic and Alchemy*. Translated by J. Courtenay Locke. New York: Causeway Books, 1973.

Seligmann, Kurt. *The History of Magic*. New York: Meridian Books, 1960.

Spence, Lewis. *An Encyclopedia of Occultism*. New Hyde Park, N.Y.: University Books, 1960.

MARIE LAVEAU (C. 1794–1881)

Marie Laveau succeeded Sanite Dede as the **voodoo** queen (high priestess) of New Orleans sometime around 1830. No one in the hierarchy of voodoo priests and priestesses disputed Laveau's rise to that position, for it was widely known that she was gifted with powers of sorcery and the ability to fashion charms of unfailing efficacy.

Laveau was a Creole freewoman, and by profession a hair dresser. Her prestige among the white establishment was assured when the son of a wealthy New Orleans merchant was arrested for a crime of which he was innocent, although there was much false evidence against him. His father appealed to the voodoo high priestess to put a spell on the judge to cause him to find the young man not guilty.

Laveau took three Guinea peppers and placed them in her mouth before she went to the cathedral to pray. Although she was the recognized voodoo priestess of New Orleans, she did not find her beliefs incompatible with Catholicism and Christian charity, and she attended Mass daily. On that particular day, she knelt at the altar for several hours, praying for the young man to be found innocent. Then, later, by a ruse, she managed to enter the courtroom and place the peppers under the judge's seat. The judge found the prisoner not guilty, and Marie Laveau was handsomely rewarded by the merchant.

Laveau greatly popularized voodoo by revising some of the rituals until they became her unique mixture of West Indian and African tribal religions and Roman Catholicism. She invited politicians and police officials to the public ceremonies that she con-

Tomb of Voodoo Queen Marie Laveau I (1783–1881). (CORBIS CORPORATION)

ducted on the banks of Bayou St. John on the night of June 23, St. John's Eve. On other occasions, she would hold voodoo rituals on the shore of Lake Pontchartrain and at her cottage, Maison Blanche. Hundreds of the most prominent families in New Orleans would be present at these public celebrations of voodoo, hoping to get a glimpse of Marie Laveau herself dancing with her large snake, Zombi, draped over her shoulders. For the white onlookers, the music and the dance provided exciting entertainment. For Marie Laveau's fellow worshippers, the rites were spiritual celebrations, and even Zombi was an agent of great voodoo powers. On other occasions in private places, the high priestess celebrated the authentic rites of voodoo for her devoted congregation, far from the critical eyes of the white establishment and clergy.

For many years, legend had it that Marie Laveau had discovered the secrets of immortality and that she lived to be nearly 200 years old. Some speak in hushed whispers that she is still alive, conducting voodoo rituals in the secret shadows of New Orleans. Such a legend quite likely began when Laveau cleverly passed the position of high priestess to her daughter, who greatly resembled her, at a strategic time when she had just begun to age. Laveau retired from public appearances to continue to conduct the intricate network of spies and informants she had built up while her daughter assumed the public persona of Marie Laveau, voodoo queen of New Orleans. Because she now appeared ageless and could sometimes be seen in more than one place at a time, her power and mystery grew ever stronger among her voodoo worshippers and the elite white community, as well. As far as it can be determined, Marie Laveau died in New Orleans on June 15, 1881.

MARIE *Laveau was the recognized voodoo priestess of New Orleans.*

✦ DELVING DEEPER

Arbury, David. "Marie Laveau." *Voodoo Dreams*. [Online] http://isa.hc.asu.edu/voodoodreams/ marie_laveau.asp. 3 March 2002.

Hollerman, Joe. "Mysterious, Spooky, and Sometimes Even a Little Scary." *St. Louis Post-Dispatch*, February 7, 2002. [Online] http://home.post-dispatch. com/channel/pedweb.nsf/text/86256A0E0068FE5 086256B9003E1. 3 March 2002.

"Marie Laveau." *Welcome to the Voodoo Museum*. [Online] http:// www.voodoomuseum.com/marie. html. 3 March 2002.

Metraux, Alfred. *Voodoo*. New York: Oxford University Press, 1959.

Steiger, Brad, and John Pendragon. *The Weird, the Wild, & the Wicked*. New York: Pyramid Books, 1969.

ELIPHAS LEVI (C. 1810–1875)

Eliphas Levi (Alphonse Louis Constant) was born in France about 1810, the son of a shoemaker. His parents soon decided that he

should be educated for the life of a parish priest. Constant became a deacon, took a vow of celibacy, and seemed destined for a quiet life in the clergy. But then his life suddenly assumed a different course when he upset members of the church hierarchy for espousing doctrines quite contrary to those endorsed by the papacy. For one thing, Father Constant felt that somewhere along the ages the theologians of the church had confused Lucifer, the bearer of light, with Satan, the Prince of Darkness, and had judged him unfairly. Such a liberal attitude to the angel who led the revolt in heaven did not sit at all well with his superiors, and Father Constant was expelled from the church.

For many years after his expulsion from the Roman Catholic Church, Father Constant appears to have traveled throughout France and other European nations rather anonymously, and little is known of those years in which he lived in obscurity, collecting his thoughts, forming his political and spiritual philosophies. In 1839, he published a pamphlet entitled *The Gospel of Liberty*, which, because of its socialistic leanings, earned him six months in prison in Paris.

Once he served his term in prison, he put aside his vow of celibacy and married a 16-year-old girl, whose parents soon had the union annulled. It was after his painful separation from his wife that Alphonse Louis Constant assumed the identity of Eliphas Levi and began to devote his time to an intensive study of alchemy and the occult. Often his focus was on the **Kabbalah** and the **tarot,** believing firmly that the ancient cards depicted a concise summary of all the revelations that had come down to humankind through the ages.

Levi saw in the symbolism of the tarot cards the key to the Egyptian hieroglyphs, the mysteries of Solomon, and the truths hidden in the apocryphal text of the Book of Enoch and the scrolls of **Hermes Trismesgistus.** To do a spread of the tarot cards, in Levi's opinion, was to establish communication with the spirit world. To seek within the tarot might bring the serious magician a clue to the manipulation of the natural and divine energy that permeated all of nature. The existence of such a force, Eliphas Levi believed, was to discover the Great Arcanum of Practical Magick.

His *Doctrine of Transcendental Magic* was published in 1855, followed by *Rituals of Transcendental Magic* in 1856. Other works of Eliphas Levi include *The Key of the Grand Mysteries* (1861) and *The Science of the Spirits* (1865). Eliphas Levi died in 1875, esteemed by many and hailed as the last of the alchemists. Others have criticized certain of his writings by suggesting that his imagination may have in some instances surpassed his actual knowledge of the arcane.

❈ DELVING DEEPER

De Givry, Emile Grillot. *Illustrated Anthology of Sorcery, Magic and Alchemy.* Translated by J. Courtenay Locke. New York: Causeway Books, 1973.

Seligmann, Kurt. *The History of Magic.* New York: Meridian Books, 1960.

Spence, Lewis. *An Encyclopedia of Occultism.* New Hyde Park, N.Y.: University Books, 1960.

SIMON MAGUS (C. FIRST CENTURY)

Several cults with widely differing beliefs all bearing the label of "Gnostic" arose in the first century, very strongly competing with the advent of Christianity. Many of the Gnostic sects blended elements of Christianity with the **Eleusianian mysteries,** combining them with Indian, Egyptian, and Babylonian magic, and bringing in aspects of the Jewish Kabbalah as well.

The first Gnostic of importance was Simon Magus, a Samarian sorcerer, a contemporary of the apostles, who was converted to Christianity by Philip. Although he had been a highly respected magus, Simon continued to be impressed by the remarkable powers of the apostles and their ability to heal and to manifest miracles. When he saw Peter and John baptizing people by the laying on of hands, he asked that he might be taught the power of transferring the Holy Spirit to others. Eagerly, Simon offered to pay the apostles a fee to teach him how to manifest the Holy Spirit. Peter strongly rebuked him for attempting to buy this profound spiritual gift (Acts 8:9–24). Simon accepted the rebuke and asked Peter to pray for his forgiveness. The term "simony" to

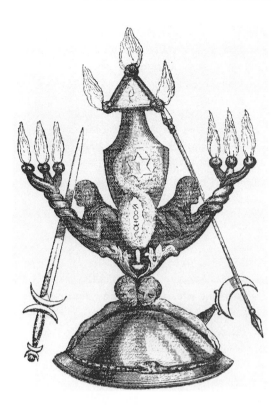

Eliphas Levi's magical instruments. (FORTEAN PICTURE LIBRARY)

describe the purchasing of ecclesiastic blessings has come down through the ages.

Simon apparently brooded over his inability to acquire the Holy Spirit from the apostles, and, according to legend, he fell back on his old ways of sorcery and began to traffic once again with demons. To prove his power, Simon announced to all of Rome that he would fly into the sky and ascend to the heavens, just as Jesus had done. Remarkably, Simon, supported by demons, began to fly upward. Peter, however, fearful that many innocents would be attracted to this false prophet, prayed that God would end Simon's flight. Frightened away by the apostle's prayers, the demons fled the artificial wings supporting Simon, and the magus crashed to the ground, breaking both legs.

The story of Simon Magus fueled the beliefs of generations of magi and alchemists that there was a secret oral tradition that had been passed down from Jesus that had much greater power and authority than the scriptures and epistles offered by the orthodox teachers of Christianity. The Gnostics, like the initiates of the Greek and Egyptian mysteries, sought direct experience with the divine and they believed that this communion could be achieved by uttering secret words of wisdom that God had granted to specially enlightened teachers.

✦ DELVING DEEPER

Meyer, Marvin, and Richard Smith, eds. *Ancient Christian Magic*. San Francisco: HarperSanFrancisco, 1994.

Seligmann, Kurt. *The History of Magic*. New York: Meridian Books, 1960.

PICO DELLA MIRANDOLA (1463–1494)

Born in 1463 in Mirandola castle, near Modena, Italy, Pico, the Count of Mirandola, was one of those precocious young geniuses who were gifted with a precise memory, a facility for language, and a talent for philosophy, mathematics, and theology. Early in his studies, Mirandola came to believe that the future could be predicted through a practiced interpretation of dreams, communication with benevolent spirits, and a careful analysis of the intestines of birds. He took a great deal of inspiration from the ancient Chaldean oracles and the old mystery schools of **Orpheus** and **Eleusis,** and he was greatly influenced by the teachings of the **Kabbalah.** For centuries, the Kabbalah had remained a mysterious esoteric philosophy that had been developed within the larger framework of the Jewish religion. Jealously guarded by various rabbis, the teachings of the Kabbalah remained largely unknown by medieval Christians until such magicians/scholars as Pico Mirandola brought the ancient mystery within the reach of European alchemists and magi by translating the Hebrew into Latin.

When he was 24, Mirandola became confident that he could prove the divinity of Christ through certain doctrines of the Kabbalah and esoteric magic, and armed with 900 theses for public debate on the matter, he set out for Rome. The young magician's proofs were not accepted warmly by the church, however, relying as they did upon such elements as nature spirits, pagan gods, and Jewish mysticism. Pope Innocent VIII (1432–1492), ever on the alert for the presence of witches in whatever disguise they may present themselves, appointed a commission to examine Count Mirandola's theses for any taint of heresy. Although his percentage of acceptable theses was quite high, the papal commission managed to discover four of Mirandola's arguments to be greatly heretical and another nine to be less so, but erroneous in their concepts.

In 1487, Pico Mirandola offered a defense of those 13 theses that had been judged heretical and accused those in the papal commission who had condemned them as being themselves heretics. They could hardly be considered worthy of judging him, he derided them, for they were essentially ignorant men who couldn't even speak or write acceptable Latin, the official language of the church.

Mirandola's intellectual snobbery was ill-advised, for he had offended bishops with power, two of whom had influence with the Inquisition. Mirandola fled Italy, but he was arrested in France and placed in a dungeon to await his trial for heresy. It was only through the intervention of such substantial members of the aristocracy as Lorenzo de Medici that he was allowed to return to Florence and be spared the certain tortures and likely death sentence at the hands of the inquisitors.

Innocent VIII remained unforgiving; but in 1493, one year before Pico Mirandola's death at the age of 31, Alexander VI (1431–1503) accepted his apology and removed at last the threat from the Inquisition that had pursued the young count for six years.

✦ DELVING DEEPER

De Givry, Emile Grillot. *Illustrated Anthology of Sorcery, Magic and Alchemy*. Translated by J. Courtenay Locke. New York: Causeway Books, 1973.

Seligmann, Kurt. *The History of Magic*. New York: Meridian Books, 1960.

Spence, Lewis. *An Encyclopedia of Occultism*. New Hyde Park, N.Y.: University Books, 1960.

PYTHAGORAS (C. 580–C. 500 B.C.E.)

Pythagoras, one of the greatest philosophers and mathematicians of the sixth century B.C.E., is said to have traveled the known world of his time, accumulating and absorbing wisdom and knowledge. According to the legends surrounding his life, he was taught by Zoroaster (c. 628–c. 551 B.C.E.), the Persian prophet, and the Brahmans of India; and he initiated into the **Orphic,** Egyptian, Judaic, Chaldean, and many other mystery schools.

Pythagoras is among those individuals given the status of becoming a myth in his own lifetime. The philosopher was said to have been born of the virgin Parthenis and fathered by the god Apollo. Pythagoras' human father, Mnesarchus, a ring merchant from Samos, and his mother consulted the **Delphic Oracle** and were told that he would be born in Sidon in Phoenicia and that he would produce works and wonders that would benefit all humankind. Wishing to please the gods, Mnesarchus demanded that his wife change her name from Parthenis to Pythasis, in order to honor the seeress at Delphi. When it was time for the child to be born, Mnesarchus devised "Pythagoras" to be a name in which each of the specially arranged letters held an individual sacred meaning.

After traveling the known world, Pythagoras formed his own school at Crotona in southern Italy. An unyielding taskmaster, he accepted only those students whom he assessed as already having established personal regimens of self-discipline. To further stress the seriousness of his study program, Pythagoras lectured while standing behind a curtain, thereby denying all personal contact with his students until they had achieved progress on a ladder of initiatory degrees that allowed them to reach the higher grades. While separated from them by the curtain, Pythagoras lectured his students on the basic principles of music, mathematics, astronomy, and philosophy.

Pythagoras called his disciples mathematicians, for he believed that the higher teachings began with the study of numbers. From his perspective, he had fashioned a rational theology. He believed the science of numbers lay in the living forces of divine faculties in action in the world, in universal macrocosm, and in the earthly microcosm of the human being. Numbers were transcendent entities, living virtues of the supreme "One," God, the source of universal harmony.

Devoted to his studies, his travels, and his school, Pythagoras did not marry until he was about 60. The young woman had been one of his disciples, and she bore him seven children. The legendary philosopher died when a rejected student led an angry mob against the school and burned down the house where Pythagoras and 40 students were gathered. Some accounts state that Pythagoras died in the fire; others have it that he died of grief, sorrowing over how difficult a task it was to elevate humanity.

PYTHAGORAS *was said to be fathered by the god Apollo.*

✾ DELVING DEEPER

Schure, Edouard. *The Great Initiates.* Translated by Gloria Rasberry. New York: Harper and Row, 1961.

Seligmann, Kurt. *The History of Magic.* New York: Meridian Books, 1960.

COUNT SAINT-GERMAIN

Frederick the Great (1712–1786) of Prussia called the Count of Saint-Germain the man who could not die, for according to the count, he had already lived 2,000 years by partaking of his discovery of a regenerative liquid that could prolong human life indefinitely.

Saint-Germain captivated the courts of Europe in the eighteenth century. He would refer to a pleasant chat with the Queen of Sheba and relay amusing anecdotes of Babylonian court gossip. He would speak with reverence of the miraculous event that he had witnessed at the marriage feast at Cana when the young rabbi Jesus (c. 6 B.C.E.–c. 30 C.E.) turned water into wine. Saint-Germain spoke and wrote Greek, Latin, Sanskrit, Arabic, Chinese, French, German, English, Italian, Portugese, and Spanish. He was also a talented painter and an accomplished virtuoso on the harpsichord and violin. The count was also a successful alchemist, and it was widely rumored that he had succeeded in transforming base metals into gold. It was believed that he could remove flaws from diamonds, and in this way improved one of the gems of King Louis XV (1710–1774). His chemical training far surpassed that of his contemporaries of the eighteenth century. His skill at mixing pigments was considered extraordinary, and famous painters begged in vain for the count to reveal his formulas.

MANY *occult groups claim Count Saint-Germain as their spirit guide.*

It was also claimed by many that Saint-Germain could render himself invisible—a remarkable accomplishment said to have been often witnessed. He was also a proficient hypnotist and could fall at will into a state of self-hypnosis. Members of Europe's royal courts also heard him speak often of an invention that would occur in the next century and which would unite people of all lands. He called it a steamboat, and he implied that it would be he who would be on hand in the future to help create the vessel.

Who was the Count of Saint-Germain and what was his true place of origin? The mystery has never been solved, and he remains one of history's most intriguing enigmas. Some scholars have conjected that the man was a clever spy on a secret mission who had deliberately shrouded his past with mystery. Why, these scholars ask, would the skeptical Prussian King Frederick promote such fantastic tales of the count unless he had some reason to do so?

Saint-Germain seems to betray himself as a diplomat with his astounding knowledge of the political past. Having gained access to secret court files, he could have studied European history methodically and with earnest purpose. His wide range of claimed artistic talents may have been amateurish, but wildly exaggerated by those who would stand to gain by the count's missions.

Old records show that Saint-Germain died in the arms of two chambermaids at the court of the Landgrave of Hessen-Cassel, a fervent alchemist. But in spite of his supposed death, there are many recorded instances of the reappearance of the count. Many believe that he only feigned death, just as he had done many times before, so that he could go on sipping of his elixir of life and observing world events from a more quiet perspective.

After the fall of the Bastille in July 1789, Marie Antoinette received a letter of warning that was allegedly signed by the Count of Saint-Germain. Madame Adhemar, Marie Antoinette's confident, kept a rendezvous with the count in a chapel. Saint-Germain, then supposedly dead for five years, told her that he had done everything that he could to prevent the Revolution, but that the great magician **Cagliostro,** a fervent antimonarchist, had taken control of the events. It was further said that the Count of Saint-Germain showed himself many times during the French Revolution. He was said to have been observed often near the guillotine, sadly shaking his head at the bloody work initiated by his pupil, Cagliostro.

Today, many occult groups claim the Count of Saint-Germain as their **spirit guide,** and he remains popular as a spiritual mentor from beyond. Others maintain that the Count of Saint-Germain still lives, periodically feigning death in whatever guise he continues to walk the earth, so that he might on occasion offer his counsel to those men and women in high political places.

✤ DELVING DEEPER

De Givry, Emile Grillot. *Illustrated Anthology of Sorcery, Magic and Alchemy.* Translated by J. Courtenay Locke. New York: Causeway Books, 1973.

Seligmann, Kurt. *The History of Magic.* New York: Meridian Books, 1960.

Skinner, Doug. "The Immortal Count." *Fortean Times,* June 2001, 40–44.

Spence, Lewis. *An Encyclopedia of Occultism.* New Hyde Park, N.Y.: University Books, 1960.

WICCA

According to the U.S. Census, the number of individuals professing to be Wiccans rose from the 8,000 reported in 1990 to 134,000 self-proclaimed witches in 2001. A study released in November 2001 by the Graduate Center of the City University of New York found that the number of adults who subscribe to a pagan religion was more than 140,000.

Since the Middle Ages, witchcraft, the "old religion," or Wicca, the "ancient craft of the wise," have been used interchangeably to name the followers of the same nature religion. While the interchangeability of the names remains true today, even those men and women who practice Wicca or witchcraft have difficulty reaching a consensus regarding what it is exactly that they believe and whether or not Wicca can truly be traced back to ancient times or whether it developed as a new natural religion in the early nineteenth century and gained momentum in the mid-twentieth century. As one practitioner of Wicca said, no Wiccan can decide for another what Wicca really is. One definite assertion that may be made about Wicca is that practitioners of the religion are not Satanists. They do not worship the devil or glory in the exaltation of evil. Worship of and agreements with the devil presuppose his existence, and the Wiccans do not believe in the Satan of Christianity.

Oberon Zell (formerly Tim Zell, primate of the neo-paganistic Church of All Worlds, St. Louis, Missouri, and publisher of *The Green Egg*) does not believe **Satanism** can be classed as a religion, but is merely a Christian heresy. According to Zell, a true pagan religion is one that originated in nature and is characterized by natural modes of expression, contrasted with those religions that owe their existence to a philosophy taught by one or more great prophets and formulated in various creeds and dogmas. Those who follow Wicca, the craft of the wise, maintain that their faith qualifies as a true pagan religion with its beliefs and practices rooted in the processes of nature.

Generally speaking, Wiccans believe that the sources of good and evil lie within each individual, thus universally agreeing with the eight words of the Wiccan Rede: "If it harm none, do what you will." The craft is therefore concerned with the properties of the human mind, including that little-known, little-used area of the psyche termed "the occult." Wiccans do not believe that there is anything supernatural about the manifestations and phenomena associated with this extrasensory

area of the mind. They believe that psychic powers lie dormant in everyone, to a greater or lesser degree, and the disciplines of Wicca are designed to develop these to the fullest.

Wicca is a polarized religion, embodying within its worship the male principle in the figure of the Horned God and the female in that of the goddess. Thus its adherents believe that Wicca presents a truer picture of the nature and workings of the universal creative principle than do those religions that overemphasize either the male or the female values and relegate the other to a subordinate status. Wicca incorporates both cognates of the universal creative principle.

WITCHCRAFT *is also referred to as the* "old religion."

In *Witchcraft Here and Now*, **Sybil Leek** defined witchcraft as a religion of a primitive and transcendent nature, "with overtones embodying the female in her most elevated octave" together with the "adoration of creative forces." In her view, such a religion provided "…the total aspect of godliness, in a god which has no name or a thousand different ones, one which has no sex but is both sexes and neutral as well."

Wiccans believe in good and evil as expressions of the same indestructible energy, which, like matter, is neither created nor destroyed but can be changed in form. Because Wiccans do not have a god or devil in the conventional sense of absolute good and absolute evil, they consider these qualities to be positive and negative expression of the same life-energy, neither of which are permanent forms but subject to change as situations and circumstances change.

Wicca conceives of spirit as part of the universal creative principle, existing as a thought form. In keeping with its transcendental nature, Wicca views spirit as the convenient expression for a certain kind of matter, which is thought to contain a dynamic energy of its own. This energy is capable of being transmitted by means of mental activity and can be used to transmute other forms of energy into matter.

Witchcraft/Wicca generally accepts the doctrines of reincarnation and karma but rejects the idea of original sin. Witches believe that the human spirit is at birth like a blank page upon which one's actions and experiences write the details of one's character. This is somewhat qualified by the belief that the ways in which individuals will react to their experiences during a particular incarnation is to a large extent determined by the karmic patterns inherited from past lives. Through a series of incarnations, the spirit seeks to perfect itself by learning to live to an ever-increasing extent in accord with nature's laws. The good is sought in those areas subject to human will. Evil, then, consists of the conscious rejection of the good and the conscious effort to embrace evil. This belief carries with it the idea that humans are free to choose good or evil but can lose this freedom through the constant and prolonged choice of one path or the other. On one side are what some religions would call "saints" and on the other, those who habitually choose evil, with the great majority of men and women falling somewhere in between the two extremes.

ACCORDING to the United States Census, the number of Wiccans rose to 134,000 in 2001.

At this point, one can see an important difference between Wicca and Satanism. Witches seek the good by willing the good, while those who practice **black magick** or who follow the "left-hand path" have yielded control of their thoughts and actions to the flesh, that part of human nature motivated solely by the search for satisfaction of instinctual and egotistical demands. That is not to say that witches believe the material aspect of humankind is evil, but, rather, that the striving for evil inherent in the instinctually

ordered flesh must be controlled and directed by the will in such a manner that its needs are satisfied, but not at the price of others' well-being and existence. Wicca seeks to be a polarized, or balanced, religion in which its adherents recognize that all emotions carried to an excess cause an imbalance.

The popular and enduring confusion of witchcraft and Satanism can be traced to two primary causes: the ignorance of those educators and journalists responsible for dissemination of public information and the practice of evangelical Christian clergy of linking the ancient craft of the wise with devil worship. Oberon Zell once observed that practitioners of the old religion/Wicca/neo-paganism often find themselves in the awkward position of having a public image that was not created by them, but by their persecutors. In Zell's thought, such an injustice would be much as if the Nazis had succeeded in eradicating Judaism to the extent that, generations later, the common opinion of what the Jewish faith was all about was derived solely from the anti-Semitic propaganda of the Third Reich—just as the opinion of what Wicca is all about has been largely derived from the tortured testimonies of those who were put on trial for witchcraft by the **Inquisition.** Zell's analogy makes the point that today's Wiccans may no longer be tortured or burned alive at the stake, but they still suffer from persecution of character at the hands of unknowing, indifferent, or biased journalists, clergypersons, and educators.

✳ DELVING DEEPER

Adler, Margot. *Drawing Down the Moon: Witches, Druids, Goddess-Worshippers and Other Pagans in America Today.* Boston: Beacon Press, 1986.

Buckland, Raymond. *Buckland's Complete Book of Witchcraft.* St. Paul, Minn.: Llewellyn Publications, 1987, 1997.

Cunningham, Scott. *Wicca: A Guide for the Solitary Practitioner.* St. Paul, Minn.: Llewellyn Publications, 1987.

Grimassi, Raven. *Encyclopedia of Wicca & Witchcraft.* St. Paul, Minn.: Llewellyn Publications, 2000.

Lewis, James R. *Magical Religion and Modern Witchcraft.* Albany: State University of New York Press, 1996.

PEOPLE OF WICCA

Those who follow the Wiccan path are a diverse group of individualists who pride themselves on being members of a religious philosophy that is flexible and adaptive to the needs of contemporary society. Athough there is the sometimes fiery debate as to the true historical roots of the faith, most Wiccans believe that none of them can dictate to any other just exactly what it is that they must believe. In other words, rather than one great book of Wiccan beliefs, an ancient *Book of Shadows* dogmatically outlining creeds and ecclesiasticisms, there are many books by many men and women who carefully explain the belief structures, rites, and rituals of their particular expression of the craft.

While there were no doubt hereditary witches who quietly practiced the old ways, there was little said publicly about witchcraft in Great Britain and Europe until the beginning of the twentieth century—perhaps because of the grim historical records of the **Inquisition** and its terrible trials for heresy and witchcraft that tormented the collective unconscious of the religiously minded. Texts about witchcraft were published by Christian scholars, and portrayed the craft as devil worship or demonic possession. Then, in 1897, Charles Godfrey Leland (1824–1903), an American who moved to England in 1870 to study gypsy love, published *Aradia: The Gospel of the Witches*, which detailed the rites and beliefs of the old religion that centered upon Diana, the goddess of the moon, and her daughter, Aradia. Although the book presented the Sabbats, rituals, spells, charms, and practices of witchcraft from the viewpoint of its ancient practitioners, the book went largely unnoticed by either scholars or the general public.

However, a little over 20 years later, Dr. Margaret Alice Murray (1863–1963), an Egyptologist on staff at the University College in London, began researching the thesis that witchcraft was actually the remnant of an ancient pre-Christian fertility religion that had nothing to do with the Christian concept of a devil that the witches had allegedly worshipped and brought upon them the wrath of

Zia Rose performing a Wicca ceremony. (ARCHIVES OF BRAD STEIGER)

the church during the time of the burning, the Inquisition. Although Murray's work underscored the research of Leland, she seemed to have been unaware of his groundbreaking studies. However, it was her book, *The Witch Cult in Western Europe* (1962), that established a doctrine that would be maintained for many years—Wiccans were members of an ancient pre-Christian religion that once thrived and flourished openly and had then survived underground for many centuries.

T⊙DAY'S *practitioners of Wicca come from a complete spectrum of men and women.*

Gerald Brosseau Gardner (1884–1964) is considered the father of all contemporary expressions of Wicca, and he became a well-known practitioner of the craft due to the many books that he published on the subject after the laws against practicing witchcraft were repealed in England in 1951. Gardner claimed to have been initiated into the famous New Forest Coven in 1939 by a traditional and hereditary witch named Dorothy

At the time of his death on March 10, 1985, Dr. Francis Israel Regardie was considered by many occultists to be the last living adept of the Hermetic Order of the Golden Dawn, a magical tradition that had numbered among its members William Butler Yeats (1865–1939), **Aleister Crowley** (1875–1947), and Dion Fortune. Regardie had demystified many esoteric mysteries surrounding the occult and presented understandable texts on practical magic.

By age 19, he began to correspond with Aleister Crowley. In 1928, he accepted the position of Crowley's personal secretary, hoping that the magician would tutor him in the mystic arts; however, Crowley left him to independently study magic. When Crowley's publisher declared bankruptcy, Regardie lost his job.

Although the Golden Dawn had ceased to exist as a functioning magical society as early as 1903, it continued to exist in various descendant orders, such as the Stella Matutina and the Alpha et Omega. In 1932, Regardie's distillation of the teachings of the Golden Dawn was published in *The Tree of Life,* and at once he was embroiled in controversy with those occultists who associated him with Crowley. While some demanded he never again dare to mention the name of the society, others, such as Dion Fortune, invited him to join the Order of Stella Matutina. In 1937 Regardie published four volumes entitled simply *The Golden Dawn.* It was Regardie's belief that the heritage of magic was the spiritual birthright of every man and woman and that the principles of such magical systems as the Golden Dawn should be made available to all who wished to pursue the ancient wisdom teachings.

Regardie's work *The Philosopher's Stone* (1937) was written from the perspective of Jungian symbolism. In 1941, he took up practice as a lay analyst, and in 1947, he relocated to California where he taught psychiatry. Regardie retired from practice in 1981 and moved to **Sedona, Arizona,** continuing to write until his death.

İsrael Regardie (1907–1985)

Sources:

Bonewits, P. E. I. *Real Magic.* New York: Coward, McCann & Georghegan, 1971.

Monnastre, Cris, and David Griffin. *Israel Regardie, Initiation, and Psychotherapy.* [Online] http://www.tarot.nu/gd/initiat.htm.

Regardie, Israel. *The Tree of Life: A Study in Magic.* New York: Samuel Weiser, 1972.

Clutterbuck. In 1954, Gardner published *Witchcraft Today*, which continued the thesis espoused by Margaret Murray that witchcraft had existed since pre-Christian times but had gone underground to escape persecution. According to many researchers, Gardner almost singlehandedly revived—some say reinvented—the worship of the Mother Goddess and combined it with elements from several other metaphysical schools. Gardnerian witchcraft influenced many practitioners, including the colorful **Sybil Leek** (1923–1983), who, like so many after her would do, modified Gardner's rituals and teachings to fit her own style of Wicca.

The person responsible for the introduction and growth of modern witchcraft in North America was **Raymond Buckland** (1934–   ), an Englishman who had emigrated to the United States in 1962. In 1963, Buckland traveled to Perth, Scotland, to be initiated into Wicca by Gardner's high priestess Lady Olwen and to meet Gardner. In 1966, Buckland established a museum of witchcraft in Long Island, New York. A prolific author of more than 30 books on Wicca and related subjects, Buckland founded Seax-Wica, a new branch of the craft, in 1973.

Gavin (1930–   ) and **Yvonne Frost** (1931–   ) formed the first Wiccan Church in 1968 and in 1972 gained federal recognition of witchcraft as a religion. In 1985, they convinced a federal appeals court that Wicca was a religion equal to any other.

Today's practitioners of Wicca are scientists, engineers, radio personalities, law enforcement officers, television stars, politicians, and the complete spectrum of active and productive men and women. There are associations, centers, festivals, gatherings, and hundreds of websites to satisfy both the serious and the curious regarding the practice of Wicca.

❊ DELVING DEEPER

Adler, Margot. *Drawing Down the Moon: Witches, Druids, Goddess-Worshippers and Other Pagans in America Today* Boston: Beacon Press, 1986.

Buckland, Raymond. *Buckland's Complete Book of Witchcraft*. St. Paul, Minn.: Llewellyn Publications, 1987, 1997.

Gardner, Gerald B. *The Meaning of Witchcraft*. New York: Samuel Weiser, 1959.

Leland, Charles G. *Aradia: The Gospel of the Witches*. Reprint, New York: Buckland Museum of Witchcraft and Magick, 1968.

Murray, Margaret Alice. *The Witch-Cult in Western Europe*. Oxford: Clarendon Press, 1962.

MARGOT ADLER (1946–   )

Margot Adler is the author of *Drawing Down the Moon: Witches, Druids, Goddess-Worshippers and Other Pagans in America Today* (1986) and *Heretic's Heart: A Journey through Spirit and Revolution* (1997). She received her B.A. from the University of California at Berkeley in 1968, has a master's degree from Columbia's Graduate School of Journalism, and was a Nieman Fellow at Harvard in 1982. In the early 1970s, Adler hosted three free-form radio shows on Pacifica Radio—*Hour of the Wolf, Unstuck in Time,* and *The Far Side of the Moon.* All merged cutting-edge ideas in science, psychology, feminism, ecology, parapsychology, and spirituality.

MARGOT *Adler is the granddaughter of reknown psychiatrist Alfred Adler.*

Granddaughter of reknowned psychiatrist Alfred Adler (1870–1937), Margot Adler is currently the New York Bureau Chief and Correspondent for National Public Radio, where she has been a reporter since 1979. Her pieces air on *All Things Considered, Weekend Edition,* and *Morning Edition.* She also hosts a debate show on the U.S. Constitution that takes place before a live audience in Philadelphia. The show, *Justice Talking,* airs on many public radio stations.

A practicing pagan since 1971, and a priestess of Wicca since 1973, Adler co-led a Gardnerian coven and a New York pagan group for many years. In the 1990s and into the new millennium, she has led ritual workshops around the country, and speaks frequently on earth-based spirituality and other topics related to paganism, Wicca, and Goddess spirituality. Many of her workshops involve ecstatic singing, chanting, and seasonal celebrations.

✤ DELVING DEEPER

Adler, Margot. *Drawing Down the Moon: Witches, Druids, Goddess-Worshippers and Other Pagans in America Today.* Boston: Beacon Press, 1986.

———.*Heretic's Heart: A Journey through Spirit and Revolution.* Boston: Beacon Press, 1997.

———. "A Time for Truth." *beliefnet*, [Online] http://www. beliefnet. com/story/40/story_4007.html.

Grimassi, Raven. *Encyclopedia of Wicca & Witchcraft.* St. Paul, Minn.: Llewellyn Publications, 2000.

PHILIP EMMONS (ISAAC) BONEWITS (1949–)

Philip Emmons (Isaac) Bonewits, priest, magician, scholar, author, bard, and activist, is best known for his leadership in modern Druidism and for his serious scholarship in the fields of the occult, metaphysics, and witchcraft. Born in Royal Oak, Michigan, the Bonewits family moved to Southern California when Isaac was nearly 12. His mother, a devout Roman Catholic, emphasized the importance of religion and hoped that Isaac might enter the priesthood. With an I.Q. tested at 200, Isaac went back and forth between parochial and public schools, largely due to the lack of programs for very bright students.

Bonewits's first exposure to real, rather than stage, magic came at age 13, when he met a young woman whose abilities as a practitioner of **voodoo** and as a diviner of the future convinced him that her abilities were genuine. After attending a Catholic high school seminary in ninth grade, Bonewits realized that he could not fulfill his mother's hope that he would become a Catholic priest. He graduated from public school a year early, spent a year in junior college, and enrolled at the University of California at Berkeley in 1966. It was at this time that he truly began practicing magic, creating his own rituals based on those that he was able to find in books.

Bonewits entered Berkeley as a psychology major but through the individual group study program was able to fashion his own course of study. Robert Larson, Bonewits's roommate, introduced him to Druidism and initiated him into the Reformed Druids of North America. Bonewits was ordained as a Druid priest in October 1969. In 1970 he graduated with a bachelor of arts degree in magic and thaumaturgy, the first person to do so at a Western educational institution. The media attention revolving around Bonewits's degree resulted in his obtaining a book contract, and in 1971 *Real Magic* was published, presenting his insights on magic, ritual, and psychic abilities.

In 1973 Bonewits moved to St. Paul, Minnesota, where he married folksinger Rusty Elliot, and where he assumed the editorship of *Gnostica,* a neopagan journal published by Carl Weschcke of Llewellyn Publications. The job lasted less than two years, but Bonewits remained in the Minneapolis/St. Paul area for about another year and established a Druid grove called the Schismatic Druids of North America. During this same period, Bonewits combined interests with a number of Jewish pagans and created the Hasidic Druids of North America.

In 1973 he stated publicly that the alleged antiquity of Wicca could not be supported by historical data. Bonewits asserted that the craft as it was practiced in the twentieth century did not go back beyond **Gerald B. Gardner** and **Doreen Valiente**—no earlier than the 1920s. Although such views were controversial at the time, by 1983 many scholars within the field began to acknowledge that neopagan Wicca may well be a new religion, rather than the continuation of an old one.

In 1974–75, Bonewits founded the Aquarian Anti-Defamation League (AADL), a civil liberties organization for members of minority and alternative belief systems. Bonewits and his wife divorced in 1976, and he decided to return to Berkeley, where he was elected archdruid of the Reformed Druids of North America. After disagreements with longtime members, Bonewits left the organization, and the Druidic publication that he had established, *The Druid Chronicler* (later *Pentalpha Journal*), soon folded without his involvement.

In 1979 he married Selene Kumin, but that relationship ended in 1982. In 1983 he

Neo druids gathered around Stonehenge. (ARCHIVE PHOTOS, INC.)

was initiated into the New Reformed Order of the Golden Dawn, and in that same year he married actress Sally Eaton. Bonewits and Eaton became heavily involved in the California revival of the Ordo Templi Orientis, or "O.T.O.," best known for its most important historical figure, **Aleister Crowley.** In 1986 Bonewits and Eaton separated.

Bonewits worked for a few months as a computer consultant in Kansas City, then moved to New York with his intended fourth wife, Deborah Lipp, a Wiccan high priestess, whom he married in 1988. The couple conducted a Gardnerian Wiccan "Pagan Way" group in New York and New Jersey, and in 1990 their son Arthur Shaffrey Lipp-Bonewits was born at their home in Dumont, New Jersey.

In that same year, Bonewits began showing symptoms of Eosinophilia Myalgia Syndrome. Bonewits became unable to work or to perform archdruidic duties, resulting in his loss of employment in 1992 and his assumption of the archdruid emeritus title on January 1, 1996. Although Bonewits began to recover from the

more debilitating effects of the disease in 1997, the long bouts of convalescence had caused damage to his marriage with Deborah, and in 1998 they separated. Bonewits has resumed a schedule of writing and lecturing and remains a potent force in the neopagan community.

❦ DELVING DEEPER

Bonewits, Isaac. *Real Magic*. New York: Coward, McCann & Georghegan, 1971.

Guiley, Rosemary. *The Encyclopedia of Witches and Witchcraft*. New York: Facts on File, 1989.

"Isaac Bonewits." [Online] http://www.neopagan.net. 12 February 2002.

RAYMOND BUCKLAND (1934–)

Born in London on August 31, 1934, Raymond Buckland emigrated from England to the United States in February 1962 and was responsible for the introduction of contemporary witchcraft into the United States at that time. Buckland's father was Stanley Thomas Buckland, married to Eileen Lizzie Wells. His father was a higher executive officer in the

Raymond Buckland.

from 1957 to 1959. His first job was as an engineering draftsman; then, after his stint in the R.A.F., he went to work for a London publishing firm. He taught himself to play the trombone and, for several years, led a Dixieland-style jazz band called "Count Rudolph's Syncopated Jazz Men," in his spare time playing regularly at the Piccadilly Jazz Club, Baker Street Jazz Club, and other venues.

In 1955 Buckland married Rosemary Moss and they had two sons—Robert and Regnauld. The family emigrated to the United States in 1962, settling in Brentwood, Long Island, New York. Buckland went to work for BOAC (now British Airways), which enabled him to travel extensively. He stayed with the airline for 10 years.

The Buckland family—nominally Church of England—was not particularly religious, but Buckland's reading drew him to witchcraft. He was greatly influenced by **Margaret Murray's** books *The Witch Cult in Western Europe* (1921) and *God of the Witches* (1952) and by **Gerald Gardner's** *Witchcraft Today* (1954) and *The Meaning of Witchcraft* (1959). Entering into a mail and telephone correspondence with Gardner, Buckland eventually was introduced to Gardner's high priestess, Lady Olwen (Monique Wilson), who initiated him into Wicca in Perth, Scotland, in December 1963. Buckland had finally got to meet Gardner just prior to that, before Gardner left for what was to be his final voyage to Lebanon. Buckland had become Gardner's spokesman in the United States, with Gardner forwarding to Buckland any mail he received from the U.S.

Buckland's craft name was Robat. With his wife, who became the Lady Rowen, they established the first contemporary witchcraft coven in the United States, building and expanding on it slowly and cautiously. With Gardner's books going out of print, Buckland took it upon himself to write his first book on the craft, *Witchcraft from the Inside*, which was published by Llewellyn Publications in 1971. Buckland then dedicated his life to straightening the misconceptions of witchcraft, speaking on the subject and writing articles. Initially he tried to remain anonymous but a newspaper reporter went back on her word and published

British Ministry of Health. In his spare time Stanley Buckland wrote, and had published, plays, short stories, poetry, and music, and he influenced and encouraged Raymond in the same pursuits.

At the age of 12, Buckland was introduced to Spiritualism by his father's brother, George, a Spiritualist. This led Buckland, an avid reader, to investigate that subject and to move on to such related subjects as **ghosts, ESP, magick, witchcraft, voodoo,** and the occult generally. Over time his interest focused on witchcraft.

Buckland was educated at Nottingham Boys High School, then at King's College School, Wimbledon. He holds a doctorate in anthropology from Brantridge Forest College, in Sussex. He served in the Royal Air Force his name and address. Despite the resulting physical and verbal attacks on him and his family, Buckland continued his work.

Inspired by Gerald Gardner's museum, Buckland gathered artifacts over the years and, in 1966, opened America's first museum of witchcraft and magic, first in the basement of his home, then in an old Victorian building in Bay Shore, Long Island. The museum was successful; being featured in numerous national magazine and newspaper articles, and was the subject of a television documentary. At various times a selection of artifacts was loaned to the Metropolitan Museum of Art and to other museums.

Buckland had his first article published when he was 12 years old. In 1969 *A Pocket Guide to the Supernatural,* his first book, was published by Ace Books. By the mid-1970s, with the breakup of his marriage to Rosemary, Buckland handed over leadership of the Gardnerian coven to a couple on Long Island and moved, with his museum, to Weirs Beach, New Hampshire. There he married his second wife, Joan Taylor.

By 1973 Buckland had determined that Gardnerian Wicca did not totally fulfill his religious requirements. He founded a new branch of the craft, taking nothing from Gardnerian (because of his oath to that tradition) but writing all new material. He based it on a Saxon background and called it Seax-Wica, or Saxon witchcraft. Contrary to reports by various misinformed writers, Seax-Wica was *not* started as a joke but as a serious branch of witchcraft—a branch to which Buckland then dedicated himself. Today the Seax-Wica tradition is found worldwide. Buckland moved from New Hampshire to Virginia Beach, Virginia. Aware that many people were unable to join the craft because of geographical location, among other reasons, Buckland started a correspondence course that he ran successfully for four years. The course was focused on Saxon witchcraft; a non-secret tradition.

In 1982 Buckland met Tara Cochran and, separating from Joan, married her in 1983. They lived for a couple of years in Charlottesville, Virginia, before moving to San Diego, California. The museum was placed in storage, where it remained until it was eventually passed on to Monte Plaisance, who reopened it in the French Quarter of New Orleans in 2001. In San Diego the correspondence course had to be phased out, since Buckland felt it took away too much of his writing time.

In 1992 the Bucklands moved to a small farm in Ohio and, after more than a quarter of a century of coven work, Buckland gave it up to work, with Tara, as solitaries. After 30 years of public activity, he retired from active involvement in the craft, settling for only occasional lectures, workshops, and book-signings. For his solitary practice, he drew mainly on Seax-Wica rites, together with aspects of PectiWita (a Scottish tradition inspired by Aidan Breac and developed by Buckland). In Ohio Buckland's writing developed to include novels, a number of divination decks, and saw a return to Spiritualism with the publication of *Doors to Other Worlds* (1993) and *The Truth about Spirit Communication* (1995).

In 1966 Raymond Buckland opened America's first museum of Witchcraft and Magic.

A prolific author, by 2001 Buckland had more than 30 books published, with more than a million copies in print and translated into 12 foreign languages. He has written a number of screenplays, numerous newspaper and magazine articles, and has appeared on many radio and television talk shows in the United States, Canada, England, and Italy. Buckland served as technical advisor for the Orson Welles movie *Necromancy* (1972) (*The Witching* on video), appeared in small character roles in movies, and has lectured at many colleges and universities across the United States. Among Buckland's best-known titles are *Practical Candleburning Rituals* (1970), *The Tree: Complete Book of Saxon Witchcraft* (1974), *Doors to Other Worlds* (1993), *Scottish Witchcraft* (1991), *The Witch Book* (2001), and the *Buckland Romani Tarot* (2001). Other books are *Advanced Candle*

Magic (1996), *Anatomy of the Occult* (1977), *The Book of African Divination* (1992), *Buckland Gypsies' Domino Divination Deck* (1995), *Coin Divination* (1999), *Gypsy Dream Dictionary* (1998), *Gypsy Fortunetelling Tarot Kit* (1998), *Here Is the Occult* (1974), *The Magick of Chant-O-Matics* (1978), *Mu Revealed* (pseudonym: Tony Earl; 1970), *Practical Color Magick* (1983), *Ray Buckland's Magic Cauldron* (1995), *Secrets of Gypsy Fortunetelling* (1988), *Secrets of Gypsy Love Magick* (1990), *The Truth about Spirit Communication* (1995), *Witchcraft from the Inside* (1971; 1995), *Witchcraft...the Religion* (1966), and two novels: *The Committee* (1993) and *Cardinal's Sin* (1996). He also produced the video *Witchcraft Yesterday and Today* (1990).

✴ DELVING DEEPER

Buckland, Raymond. *Amazing Secrets of the Psychic World*. New York: HC Publishing, 1975.

———. *Buckland's Complete Book of Witchcraft*. St. Paul, Minn.: Llewellyn Publications, 1986, 1997.

———. *A Pocket Guide to the Supernatural*. New York: Ace Books, 1969.

———. *Witchcraft Ancient and Modern*. (1970).

Grimassi, Raven. *Encyclopedia of Wicca & Witchcraft*. St. Paul, Minn.: Llewellyn Publications, 2000.

GAVIN FROST (1930–   ) AND YVONNE FROST (1931–   )

In 1968, Gavin and Yvonne Frost formed the first Wiccan church, the Church of Wicca, and continued lobbying for their cause until, in 1972, they gained federal recognition of witchcraft as a religion. In 1985, their persuasive arguments convinced a federal appeals court that Wicca was a religion equal to any other recognized as such in the United States. The Frosts' School of Wicca, also established in 1968, became the first craft correspondence school and continues to publish *Survival*, the longest-lived Wiccan newsletter in circulation. The School of Wicca has brought more than 200,000 people to the craft and has handled as many as one million requests for information in a single year. Authors of the controversial *Witches' Bible* (1975), the Frosts have coauthored 22 books and have appeared on hundreds of national television and radio shows to promote Wicca. Since 1972, Gavin and Yvonne have lived under a vow of poverty, turning over all their material possessions to the Church of Wicca.

It was in his final year at the University of London (King's College) shortly after the close of World War II that Gavin grew interested in the prehistoric peoples of the British Isles and in the reconstruction of their spiritual beliefs. At London University there were several people of the English upper middle class or lower aristocracy who wanted to form a witchcraft coven. Through contacts with Thomas Lethbridge, an authority on witchcraft who worked at the university, Frost and his friends got in touch with a group of witches in Penzance, who agreed to initiate a few students if they met certain conditions. Frost was among a group of four who were blindfolded and taken out to a place they later identified as Boskednan, a Nine-Maidens Circle. (The breath of nine maidens heats the celtic goddess Cerridwen's cauldron of inspiration.) They went through an initiation similar to the initiation that would appear many years later in *The Witch's Bible* and it was on that occasion when Frost got the scar on his wrist, the spirit-through-fire scar that is still visible. Roots of that coven's practice have always intrigued Frost because they seemed to owe nothing to **Gerald Gardner**'s work and because the order of service (the same as that shown later in Gavin and Yvonne Frosts' *The Good Witch's Bible*) did not resemble that of most other groups.

After earning an honors degree, Frost was requested to work for the Department of Atomic Energy and offered the opportunity to work on a doctorate in pure research. He completed his doctoral thesis on research into the separation of potassium and sodium ions by filtration, and moved on into research on the detection and classification of alpha waves. Then an old school friend contacted him and asked him to work on research in the infrared spectrum. Frost and his significant other, Dorothy Whitford, moved to de Havilland Aircraft in Hatfield near London. Here the research concentrated on investigation of long-wave infrared radiation for the British equivalent of the Sidewinder missile. Much of the testing of that missile was carried out on Salisbury Plain, and it was necessarily done at night. This gave Frost daytimes to explore nearby ancient monuments such as Stonehenge, and time to talk with local historians on what may be called the pagans of Stonehenge.

Gavin and Dorothy married and elected to emigrate to Montreal to work on the Canadian missile program. Upon arrival they learned they would immediately be assigned to Quebec City, site of the Canadian Missile Research Institute. Frost declined, joining instead Canadair's Training and Simulator group. His son Christopher was born in October 1954 in Montreal, and his daughter Sandra in April 1957, also in Montreal.

On one assignment Frost visited Chile when an F-86 had landed on a jungle strip near a remote mountain village, and its engine refused to start. The group needed about four days to locate the problem and get the plane flown out of there. In those four days in the village, Frost got his first taste of religion and healing as practiced by shamans. The villagers could not believe that an outsider, especially a Caucasian, would have any interest in their procedure or would be receptive toward it. But Frost saw many parallels in what they were doing to what he had been taught in the coven in England and had put on his mental shelf with the move to Canada.

When Frost moved to California, he became senior project engineer on the radar system in the F-104. This gave him the opportunity to travel extensively world-wide and achieve high-level contacts in many countries. When the opportunity arose to become the firm's European representative, Frost took it and moved his family to Munich, Germany.

Although the hours and work expectations were still high, there was more free time in Munich to investigate the fascinating subject of German sorcery. Gavin Frost studied for initiation with a group of German sorcerers in Geiselgasteig, the old Bohemian artists' colony south of Munich, but because Dorothy had no interest in the occult or in writing for a living, the family was beginning to fragment. Upon their return to the States, Gavin and Dorothy divorced.

It was here that Gavin Frost and Yvonne Wilson began the long process of establishing the spiritual path they called Wicca as a religion.

Yvonne Frost. (ARCHIVES OF BRAD STEIGER)

Yvonne's parents moved from rural Kentucky to California in 1930, and nine months later in March 1931 she was born in Los Angeles, the oldest of four siblings. She grew up in the hard-shell Baptist matrix, trying hard to conform and cause no trouble, but she felt bewildered inside. As the eldest of four children, she lived in silent obedience, wondering why she did not fit in. Qualifying for Mensa, the international high-IQ society, helped explain the feelings of alienation.

A 10-year marriage ended in divorce, and Yvonne began eight years of living as a self-supporting single woman. She enrolled part-time in a junior college and earned an Associate in Arts in 1962 with the highest GPA in her class. Yvonne also started to explore spiritual options. Buddhism was popular then, in the early 1960s, but she could not get comfortable with it. **Spiritualism** entered her awareness, with its dark-

Gavin Frost. (ARCHIVES OF BRAD STEIGER)

ened rooms, psychic development, **mediumship,** and Native American **spirit guides.**

In a Spiritualist seance in 1965, a voice came to her through the medium's trumpet: "Can I be your little girl?" Single as she was, Yvonne was taken aback. Still she managed to answer, "Yes. You come when it's time." Bronwyn Frost was born in 1969. In an **apport seance** Yvonne's spirit guide at that time, Dr. Alfred Russel Wallace, brought her a green cabochon stone. She had it set into a bracelet but has never been able to get it identified.

> THE Frosts *live under a vow of poverty, turning over all their material possessions to the Church of Wicca.*

Yvonne's career at that time was in aerospace, and Gavin Frost was her boss's boss. She formed her first impression of him when she saw how fellow workers yielded plenty of room to Dr. Frost as he strode the firm's halls. During Gavin's stint in Munich, he began work on a novel entitled *Pagans of Stonehenge* and asked her to edit it for him at long distance. Thus began Yvonne's career as a coauthor.

"One thing led to another," Yvonne Frost recalled. "We two became an item. I became interested in Gavin's path. The teachings of Spiritualism and Buddhism overlapped some aspects of the Craft, so learning the Craft was a natural step. After his divorce we moved together to St. Louis. There his work as international sales manager implied even more travel and longer hours away from home. I used my time to type all the School's lectures and the draft of *The Witch's Bible*." (1972)

Yvonne said that Gavin's witnessing Bronwyn's birth brought him an epiphany. He gave up his career in aerospace, though he worked intermittently for a year or so as a consultant, and committed his life and energies to the Craft. "No more gold credit cards, no more first-class flights world-wide, no more captain of industry and management matron for the two of us," Yvonne said. "We traded all this in for a vow of poverty and full-time commitment to living and teaching the Craft."

Continuing her remembrance, Yvonne observed, "In retrospect, our shared life begins to show a pattern. A couple of years remodeling a derelict building in St. Charles, Missouri; three years of raising pigs on unimproved rural Missouri acreage and an abandoned schoolhouse; 20 years in New Bern, North Carolina (site of the First Amendment guaranteeing religious freedom in this nation); all these chapters served to fill in gaps in our respective learning. What we did not already know about humility from the discomforts of rehabbing buildings and from raising pigs, we have learned well and thoroughly from the pagan/Wiccan community and the negativity of its reception. After the theological work, my greatest accomplishment is the establishment of the Church of Wicca as a federally recognized church, not only with regard to its tax-exempt status, but also in federal appeals court. The church's official letter of determination arrived from the IRS in 1972, making ours the first Wiccan Church (despite the resentful claims of others) to earn federal recognition. The key to such recognition of Wicca—the Craft— as a religion has been its well-defined theology."

✦ **DELVING DEEPER**

Frost, Gavin, and Yvonne Frost. *The Good Witch's Bible*. Hinton, W.Va.: Church and School of Wicca, 1996.

———. *The Magic Power of White Witchcraft*. New York: Prentice Hall, 1999.

———. *The Witch's Bible*. New York: Berkley Books, 1975.

———. *Witch's Book of Magic Ritual*. New York: Prentice Hall, 2002.

GERALD BROSSEAU GARDNER
(1884–1964)

Gerald Gardner is regarded as the founding father of all modern expressions of witchcraft/Wicca. Born in Lancashire, England, on June 13, 1884, Gardner spent a great deal of his adult life as a British civil servant and as a plantation manager in Southeast Asia. Although Gardner would later claim to have had an interest in the occult of great duration, he did not really begin to explore **Spiritualism** and the arcane until he had returned to England after his retirement shortly before World War II. There, in the autumn of 1939, he discovered witchcraft and, Dorothy Clutterbuck, a hereditary witch, high priestess of a New Forest coven, initiated him into a secret group of Wiccans. Throughout his writings, Gardner would always refer to the magical religion as Wica, rather than Wicca, as the word is spelled in common usage today.

In his book *The Meaning of Witchcraft* (1959), Gardner wrote that when he found Wicca, he knew that he had discovered something interesting, but he was nearly through the initiation when it struck him that the Old Religion did truly exist and that he had become a part of the great circle that had existed since time immemorial. To be a Gardnerian witch would thenceforth be to become a witch who had undergone an initiation that could hearken back to Gerald Gardner and through him to an unbroken lineage that had been hidden and kept secret by sacred oaths and the solemn practice of holy rituals.

At first, when Gardner published *High Magick's Aid* (1949), a fictional account of witches under the pseudonym of Scire, traditional witches became nervous and upset that he was beginning to reveal too much to the general public. Then, when the witchcraft laws were repealed in Great Britain in 1951 and Gardner wrote *Witchcraft Today* (1954), a

Dr. Gerald Brosseau Gardner (1884–1964). (RAYMOND BUCKLAND/FORTEAN PICTURE LIBRARY)

nonfictional treatment of modern witchcraft, he incurred the wrath of many traditional members of Wicca. Gardner argued that he did not reveal any secrets protected by the oath that he had taken during his initiation, but he feared that because so many of the traditional witches were growing very old, new members had to be encouraged to keep the craft alive. He announced his intentions to publish more books about Wicca and to become an outspoken spokesperson for witchcraft. From that time on, Gardner began to develop his own tradition that might be described as a combination of ritual and ceremonial magick, French Mediterranean witchcraft, and the incorporation of the concepts and ideas of such fellow witches as **Doreen Valiente.**

Gardner became the major spokesperson for contemporary witchcraft and the pagan community, and in 1960 he was invited as such to a reception at Buckingham Palace. He died on February 13, 1964, on the *S.S. Scottish Prince* while returning from a trip abroad.

⁜ DELVING DEEPER
Buckland, Raymond. *Buckland's Complete Book of Witchcraft*. St. Paul, Minn.: Llewellyn Publications, 1987, 1997.

Crowley, Vivianne. *Wicca: The Old Religion in the New Age*. London: Aquarian Press, 1989.

Gardner, Gerald. *The Meaning of Witchcraft*. London: Aquarian Press, 1982.

———. *Witchcraft Today*. 1954. Reprint, London: Rider, 1982.

SYBIL LEEK (1923–1983)

Sybil Leek was a witch, an astrologer, and a psychic who was born in England into a highly unusual family. Her maternal grandmother was a psychic lady and a follower of the Old Religion. Her father was an intellectual and well versed in metaphysics, but more inclined to a scientific investigation of a field of inquiry. Sybil's mother was a theosophist with an inborn affinity toward all children. Added to these were an assortment of aunts, cousins, and other extended family members.

Under the combined tutorial care of her family, Leek managed to escape the British public school system for many years. Each member of the family taught the child his or her particular specialty, as well as a diversity of other things. Leek learned about herbs, witchcraft, astrology, the general field of the occult, and the mystical Kabbalah. This unorthodox rearing was far from one-sided, however. Before the age of nine, young Sybil had "read through" the major classics. She had read the Bible, the works of Shakespeare, and many other volumes of Eastern religious and non-Western philosophies. Most of all, though, Leek learned from her grandmother, who taught her the Craft of the Wise. Once her preliminary instruction was completed, the young initiate journeyed to France, to the *Gorge du Loup* where Leek was initiated into the world's oldest religion.

S YBIL *Leek was the first person to be filmed in mediumistic trance.*

In her book *Diary of a Witch* (1969), Leek described briefly the oath of fidelity that every witch solemnly gives on the night of his or her initiation:

"It is accepted as being binding forever, and no initiate can take it lightly. She accepts wholeheartedly all the tenets of witchcraft—the acceptance of the Supreme Being, the knowledge that good and evil are equal parts of a human being, and that she must personally strive to outbalance evil with good. She must not debase the arts which she has been taught, and at all times she must be conscious of the need to be discreet, not only in her own life but with regard to any other members of the coven."

Shortly after Leek returned to England the family moved to the New Forest, a large area that roughly extends from Southampton northward to the borders of Salisbury and nearby Stonehenge, and westward to Dorset. It was in this area that Leek widened her lore of herbs, nature, and human psychology.

Since the age of 15, Sybil Leek had been in and out of various media jobs, and when she began moonlighting as a roving reporter for Southern Television it was her task to provide material for a series using the magazine format of small documentaries, interviews, and highlights of the day. The show's producers were particularly interested in Leek's contacts with the Gypsies of the New Forest, and she was able to present several interesting and informative vignettes about her nomadic friends.

It was in December of 1963 that Sybil Leek's media relationship caused her to be, probably, the first person to be filmed in mediumistic trance. The incident began when parapsychologist Bennison Herbert, who wished her to accompany him to a twelfth-century mansion that was allegedly haunted, contacted Leek. Almost immediately after the group entered the old house, Leek began to feel herself slipping away from the laughing joviality of the others. The group reached an upstairs room of the old stone building and settled around a large table. Within moments Leek was in a deep trance. Sights and sounds beyond the normal senses surrounded the entranced psychic. She felt someone come in through the door, then felt seized from behind. Leek, enraged, shouted at the image of the ghostly woman standing in the doorway. The struggle ceased as the heavy table at which the group was seated suddenly rose into the air and traversed the room. Then, with vented fury, the table repeatedly threw itself at the heavy stone wall, chipping the surface. A door slammed and something was heard running down the steps. Leek came out of her trance and was told what had happened by Herbert, who had taken notes on all the strange happenings.

At this point the BBC crew could no longer contain themselves. They hastily set up their lights and cameras, hoping to catch more of the same phenomena. The crew was not disappointed. The table began to move once more, traveling across the room to fling itself with renewed vigor at the ancient stonework. An incredulous solid man, weighing 220 pounds, tried to sit on the airborne table, only to be tossed off as if he were a featherweight. The table assaulted the wall with such force that it chipped a two-inch hole through the surface. The footage received wide distribution throughout the south of England and generated tremendous interest. The tables were shown in almost complete levitation and the mark on the wall was quite visible.

After achieving a great deal of fame as the Witch of New Forest, Sybil Leek came to the United States, where she teamed up with psychic investigator Hans Holzer (1920-   ) on a series of ghost-hunting expeditions. The two were often followed by an entourage of local, and sometimes international, media, eager to sniff out a good story. Frequently, movie cameras would roll while Leek was in a heavy trance state, but this never deterred the medium from obtaining solid material, which Holzer would then try to substantiate.

Leek never knew where their next jaunt was going to take them. Holzer usually investigated the cases brought to his attention, first affirming that the material represented a solid psychic case, worthy of being investigated. He would give Leek none of this information, to ensure that her trance information could never be accused of being the result of suggestion.

In addition to Leek's many talents as a psychic and her deep immersion in the Old Religion, she had yet another major field of interest that was with her all of her life. As she states in the opening lines of My Life in Astrology

(1972): "Astrology is my science; Witchcraft is my religion." For Sybil Leek, astrology lessons began when she was eight years old. From her grandmother, she learned the basics of astrology, with personality traits and psychology stressed; from her father, she learned the painstaking technical aspect of casting a chart.

In her younger days the world of astrology was a glamorous one. Every summer the family would vacation in the Riviera, and Leek's skills were in great demand among the celebrities and nobility that would gather on the beaches. Among her notable clients were the elder Aga Khan, Queen Marie of Rumania, and author Somerset Maugham. Although Leek had nostalgic feelings for that particular time, her later life was to show her an even more exciting use for her astrological skills.

Sybil Leek was determined to aid in the understanding of witchcraft. Unfortunately, she found some of the gravest misunderstandings in her adopted country of the United States. The press persistently confused witchcraft with black magick and Satanism, but Sybil Leek was instrumental in bringing a greater awareness of witchcraft to those persons who wished to form traditional covens, and she never ceased using her wit and celebrity to advance the truth about Wicca, the craft of the wise. She became a major force on the psychic scene, and her rich and varied life consistently led her to prove the deeper meanings and interrelationships between all areas of metaphysics, and her vast experience prepared her admirably for the research and study to which she devoted herself.

❖ DELVING DEEPER
Grimassi, Raven. Encyclopedia of Wicca & Witchcraft. St. Paul, Minn.: Llewellyn Publications, 2000.

Leek, Sybil. The Complete Art of Witchcraft. New York: New American Library, reissue 1991.

———. Diary of a Witch. New York: New American Library, 1969.

———. My Life in Astrology. Englewood Cliffs, N.J.: Prentice Hall, 1972.

MARGARET ALICE MURRAY (1863–1963)

For decades, Margaret Murray's The Witch-Cult in Western Europe (1921) was the definitive work on witchcraft and undoubtedly inspired such individuals as **Gerald Brosseau Gardner** to revive the Craft in the modern era. Murray's thesis was that witchcraft hearkened back to ancient, pre-Christian goddess worship and continued forward in unbroken lineage to contemporary times. The witch craze that seized Europe in the period from the fourteenth to the seventeenth centuries and that led to the persecution and deaths of thousands of those women who practiced witchcraft was nothing more or less than the attack of the patriarchal establishment on an ancient, woman-centered religion. In her opinion, based on her extensive research, the practice of witchcraft had nothing to do with the worship of Satan, an entity of evil that had been created by Christianity.

Although Murray shall probably always be known in the popular mind as the author of two seminal books on witchcraft, the aforementioned *The Witch-Cult in Western Europe* and *The God of the Witches* (1952), among her peers at the University College in London she was a respected scholar and specialist in Egyptian hieroglyphics. Because it was difficult in her day for a proper Englishwoman to become an archeologist, she first obtained a degree in linguistics, which led in turn to the study of Egyptian hieroglyphics and Egyptology. In the late 1890s, her work had been noticed by the eminent archeologist Sir Flinders Petrie (1853–1942), who permitted her to join him in his excavations at Abydos in Egypt. Because she distinguished herself on this expedition, she was invited to join the staff at the University College.

Murray was known as an ardent feminist, and her passion for the political advancement of women may well have influenced her interpretation of the European witchcraft trials as being organized campaigns of terror against those women who still practiced the old goddess-centered religions. Since her books on the history of witchcraft created little uproar among the academics of her day, there was no taint of sensationalism that prevented her from becoming a fellow of Britain's Royal Anthropological Institute in 1926. In 1931, Murray published *The Splendor That Was Egypt,* a book centered on Egyptology, her spe-

cial field of interest. From 1953 to 1955, she served as president of Britain's Folklore Society. Remarkably, in 1963, at the age of 100, Murray published her autobiography, *Centenary,* and *The Genesis of Religion* (1963).

✤ DELVING DEEPER

Franck, Irene M., and David M. Brownstone. *Women's World: A Timeline of Women in History.* San Francisco: HarperCollins Publishers, 1995.

Kass-Simon, G., and Patricia Farnes. *Women of Science: Righting the Record.* Bloomington: Indiana University Press, 1993.

Murray, Margaret Alice. *The Genesis of Religion.* New York: Philosophical Library, 1963.

———. *The God of the Witches.* London: Faber and Faber Unlimited, 1952.

———. *The Witch-Cult in Western Europe.* 1921. Reprint, Oxford: Clarendon Press, 1962.

M. MACHA NIGHTMARE

As her contribution to the emerging pagan culture, M. Macha NightMare (also known as Aline O'Brien), priestess and witch, chose to develop her skills as a collaborative ritualist and author. Early in her journey on the path of witchcraft, NightMare joined in the formation of Reclaiming Collective, a network of people who sought to bring together activism with earth-based spirituality and healing. She also participated with the collective in teaching the Craft and in performing public **sabbats** in San Francisco. The collective evolved into a Craft tradition, and eventually dissolved itself in 1997 and reemerged as a much larger and more inclusive entity.

With **Starhawk,** Macha NightMare coauthored *The Pagan Book of Living and Dying: Practical Rituals, Prayers, Blessings, and Meditations on Crossing Over* (1997), and she is the author of *Witchcraft and the Web: Weaving Pagan Traditions Online* (2001). In addition to her books, her articles have appeared in many periodicals, and she has spoken on behalf of the craft to electronic and print media.

NightMare holds elder and ministerial credentials through the Covenant of the Goddess (CoG), the oldest and largest nondenominational organization of witches in the United States. A member since 1981, she is a former national first officer and has served the covenant in many other capacities. She is on the teaching faculty of Cherry Hill [Pagan] Seminary in Bethel, Vermont, where she also serves on the Pagan Pastoral Counseling Advisory Panel.

Macha NightMare is a member of the Biodiversity Project Spirituality Working Group, which seeks to increase biodiversity awareness, preservation, and activism within religious communities. She also works with the Sacred Dying Foundation in educating funeral professionals and hospice workers about pagan beliefs and practices regarding death and dying. To keep current on pagan research, she participates in the Nature Religion Scholars Network.

Macha NightMare's matron is Kali Ma, and her magical practice, inspired by feminism and a concern for the health of the planet, is formed of Celtic, Hindu, and Tibetan practices, the sacred art of tantra, and the magic of enchantment. When the opportunity presents itself, NightMare travels the so-called "broomstick circuit," where she enjoys immersing herself in the diverse community that constitutes contemporary American witchcraft.

She resides in Marin County, California.

❋ DELVING DEEPER

M. Macha NightMare's website: [Online] http://www.machanightmare.com/bio.html. 27 February 2002.

NightMare, M. Macha. *Witchcraft and the Web: Weaving Pagan Traditions Online*. Montreal: ECW Press, 2001.

Starhawk, M. Macha NightMare, and the Reclaiming Collective. *The Pagan Book of Living and Dying: Practical Rituals, Prayers, Blessings, and Meditations on Crossing Over*. San Francisco: HarperSanFrancisco, 1997.

STARHAWK

A feminist and peace activist, Starhawk (also known as Miriam Simos) is one of the foremost voices of ecofeminism, and she travels widely in North America and Europe giving lectures and workshops, drawing on her 25 years of research and experience in the Goddess movement. Her book *The Spiral Dance: A Rebirth of the Ancient Religion of the Great God-dess* (1979, 1989) is currently regarded as the definitive work on modern, feminist witchcraft. Starhawk holds an M.A. in psychology from Antioch West University. She consulted on the films *Goddess Remembered* and *The Burning Times*, directed by Donna Read and produced by the National Film Board of Canada. She also cowrote the commentary for *Full Circle*, the third film in the same Women's Spirituality series. Many of Starhawk's works have been translated in German, Danish, Italian, Portuguese, and Japanese.

From organizing in her high school during the days of the Vietnam War, Starhawk has been active in social change movements for more than 30 years. She has participated in and helped with training and organizing antinuclear actions at Diablo Canyon, Livermore Weapons Lab, Vandenberg Airforce Base, and the Nevada Test Site, among others. She traveled to Nicaragua with Witness for Peace in 1984 and has made two trips to El Salvador to do ongoing support work for sustainability programs. She works on countless environmental and land use issues and was a founder of the Cazadero Hills Land Use Council in Western Sonoma County. Her focus in recent years has been the antiglobalization movement, training for and taking part in the anti-WTO action in Seattle, the anti-IMF/World Bank actions in Washington, D.C., and doing trainings in Europe for the actions in Prague.

STARHAWK *is one of the foremost voices of ecofeminism.*

Starhawk continues her collaboration with filmmaker Donna Read, working on an hour-long documentary on the life of archaeologist Marija Gimbutas. They have formed their own film company, Belili Productions.

Starhawk works with Reclaiming, a network of people who bring together activism with earth-based spirituality and healing, offering classes, intensives, public rituals, and training in the Goddess tradition of magical activism. She writes a regular column for the

Reclaiming Quarterly, and she is also a columnist on the Web for www.beliefnet.com and for www.znet.com.

She lives part-time in San Francisco, in a collective house with her partner and friends, and the rest of the time in a little hut in the woods where she practices the system of ecological design known as permaculture.

❋ Delving Deeper

Starhawk. *Dreaming the Dark: Magic, Sex, and Politics.* New York: Beacon, 1982.

————. *The Spiral Dance: A Rebirth of the Ancient Religion of the Great Goddess.* San Francisco: HarperSanFranciso, 1999.

————. *Truth or Dare: Encounters with Power, Authority and Mystery.* New York: Harper & Row, 1987.

Starhawk and Hilary Valentine. *The Twelve Wild Swans: Journies into Magic, Healing and Action.* San Francisco: HarperSanFrancisco, 2000.

Starhawk, M. Macha NightMare, and the Reclaiming Collective. *The Pagan Book of Living and Dying: Practical Rituals, Prayers, Blessings, and Meditations on Crossing Over.* San Francisco: HarperSanFrancisco, 1997.

Starhawk's website: [Online] http://www.starhawk. org. 26 February 2002.

Doreen Valiente (1922–1999)

One of the most influential individuals in the shaping of modern Wicca was born Doreen Edith Dominy in Mitcham, South London, on January 4, 1922, and spent her childhood in the west of England, an area noted for its rustic beauty and its connection to the folklore of the past. As an adult, she recalled that from a very young age she took to running about while riding on a broomstick. Although she did not consciously know why she had done so, she did remember that it upset her conventionally religious parents, who were opposed to any portrayal of witchcraft, whether or not it derived from childish display.

When Valiente was only seven, her first mystical experience happened one night while she was staring intently at the moon. She perceived at that time that what ordinary people embraced as the world of reality was but the facade behind which something much more real and potent lay waiting for those who would seek "the world of force beyond the world of form." At the age of 15, she walked out the door of the convent school to which she had been sent and refused to return.

At the age of 19, she married Joanis Vlachopoulos, a 32-year-old able seaman serving with the merchant navy. Six months later, in the summer of 1941, her husband was reported missing. Details are sketchy, but since World War II was in progress, it is assumed that Vlachopoulos was killed when his ship was destroyed by a Nazi torpedo. In 1944, Doreen married Casimiro Valiente.

In the summer of 1952, the year after the Witchcraft Act of 1735 was repealed, Doreen Valiente met a witch of the New Forest Coven who introduced her to **Gerald Brosseau Gardner.** On Midsummer's Eve 1953, she received the first degree of initiation into Wicca by Gardner, who at that time was operating a witchcraft museum on the Isle of Man. Although Gardner claimed that his *Book of Shadows* had been compiled by remnants of the Old Religion that he had pieced together for his Gardnerian tradition, the astute Doreen, whose witchcraft name was "Ameth," recognized passages from other works, such as **Aleister Crowley**'s *Gnostic Mass (1942)*.

Far from being humiliated or angered by his student's recognition that his *Book of Shadows* was much a pastiche of many traditions of witchcraft, with rites and rituals copied from ancient lore, as well as a few bits and pieces from **Freemasonry** and Crowley, Gardner invited her to improve, if she could, upon his fragments of the old and the new. Valiente accepted the challenge and replaced nearly all of the Crowley and Masonic excerpts with the thoughts and inspirations that she had received from her own mystical experiences since childhood. The reconstruction of the *Book of Shadows* achieved by Valiente gave the practitioners of Wicca a practical and workable system which has been followed by many witches ever since. Gardner and Valiente eventually parted company over his claim that his "Old Laws" should be heeded above her revisions, but Valiente continued to doubt the authenticity of some of the laws that Gardner claimed were derived from ancient traditions.

HEALING POWERS OF THE CURANDERO

The curandero works among the Hispanic people of California, Texas, Mexico, and many areas of South America as a master of the many skills involved in folk healing. Whether male or female, they acquire their abilities through two basic methods: By serving as an apprentice under the guidance of an experienced curandero or by receiving a spiritual vision that gives the knowledge upon them. To be a curandero is to have received a gift from God. The three common types of curanderos are the herbalist, the yerbero; the midwife, the partera; and the massage therapist, the sabador.

After serving an apprenticeship and proving themselves endowed with the requisite skills of healing, the curanderos treat a wide variety of illnesses brought to them by their patients. Among other native healers in the Hispanic culture, however, the curanderos are the only ones to have the skills necessary to remove illnesses or physical maladies inflicted by negative witchcraft.

SOURCES:

"Curandismo." *The Handbook of Texas Online.* [Online] http://www.tsha.utexas.edu/handbook/online/articles/view/CC/sdc1.html.

Middleton, John, ed. *Magic, Witchcraft and Curing.* Garden City, N.Y.: Natural History Press, 1967.

Villoldo, Alberto, and Stanley Krippner. *Healing States: A Journey into the World of Spiritual Healing and Shamanism.* New York: Simon & Schuster Inc. Fireside Book, 1987.

Although they later resumed their friendship, it was never again at the level which it had once attained.

When her husband passed away in 1972, Doreen Valiente began to devote herself to writing about witchcraft as she knew and understood it. After her *An ABC of Witchcraft* (1973) and *Natural Magic* (1975), she became recognized as an authority on magic and witchcraft. Her last days were spent in a nursing home, and after she had passed her magical legacy on to John Belham-Payne, she died on September 1, 1999.

⁜ **DELVING DEEPER**

"Biography of Doreen Valiente" [Online] http://www.doreenvaliente.com/ Biography.htm. 28 February 2002.

Grimassi, Raven. *Encyclopedia of Wicca & Witchcraft.* St. Paul, Minn.: Llewellyn Publications, 2000.

Valiente, Doreen. *An ABC of Witchcraft, Past and Present.* New York: St. Martin's Press, 1973.

———. *The Rebirth of Witchcraft.* Custer, Wash.: Robert Hale and Phoenix Publishing, 1989.

———. *Witchcraft for Tomorrow.* New York: St. Martin's Press, 1978.

WITCHCRAFT

Since the Middle Ages, witchcraft, the "Old Religion," or **Wicca,** the "ancient craft of the wise," all of which are different names for the same nature-based religion, has been unjustly, and for the most part purposely, interwoven with **Satanism** until, in popular thought, the two comprise a tapestry of confusion and misidentification. Wicca, in its contemporary expression, has evolved into what its followers term "neo-paganism," a concept reviewed in another section. The Old Religion, that which in the Middle Ages came to be known as witchcraft, is thought to have had its genesis in the later Paleolithic period, a time when early humans faced the elements and their environment with little more than their hands and a few crude tools of bone and stone to aid them in the struggle to survive. Like the other creatures around them, Stone Age humans had to adapt themselves constantly to changes in the weather, climate, and food supply. Having greater powers of perception, humankind's responses to these changes involved more than an instinctual change of habits or location. The human species could also wonder about the whys and wherefores of these things, and because of the remarkable facility of human imagination, these early men and women could ponder how these things might change for the better or worse in the future. As consciousness of humans increased, their world became more wonderful and more terrifying.

Primitive humans were primarily hunters. They needed the meat obtained from their prey, and they needed the animal skins for clothing. From the teeth and bones of the slaughtered animals, they fashioned simple tools and weapons. When the hunting was bad, they knew that their own existence was threatened. Why was the hunt successful at times and not at others? Perhaps there was a spirit who decided these things. If so, perhaps that spirit could be persuaded to control the hunt in favor of the human hunter.

In his classic work *The Golden Bough* (1890), Sir James George Frazer points out two factors influencing the nature of primitive religion:

1. the older concept of a "view of nature as a series of events occurring in an invariable order without the intervention of personal agency"; and

2. the later development that the "world is to a great extent worked by supernatural agents, that is, by personal beings acting on impulses and motives."

From the first concept arose the earliest rites of primitive religion consisting of sympa-

thetic magic, which is based on the belief that something that resembles something else is able to become or attract that which it resembles, or a given cause always produces a certain effect. An example of such rites is the shaman's lighting of the ceremonial fire each morning to ensure the sun's rising. If the shaman lights his fire each morning, then the god who lights the great fire in the heavens must see and follow suit.

By a similar process Stone Age humans sought to ensure the success of the hunt. In *Witchcraft from the Inside* (1997), **Raymond Buckland** writes:

> One man would represent the God and supervise the magick. As a God of Hunting, he was represented as being the animal being hunted. His representative, or priest, would therefore dress in an animal skin and wear a headdress of horns.

This God of the Hunt, then, is the Horned God pictured on the wall of the Caverne des Trois in southern France. At Le Tuc d'Audoubert, near the Caverne des Trois, archeologists found the clay figure of a bison. The figure shows a number of marks where spears were thrust into it during a ritual of sympathetic magic performed to ensure a successful hunt. According to Buckland: "A model of the animal to be hunted was made . . . and under the priest's direction, was attacked by the men of the tribe. Successful in 'killing' the clay animal, the men could thus go about after the real thing confident that the hunt would go exactly as acted before the God."

It is interesting to note the association of horns with divinity, a condition that finds expression in numerous strange and seemingly unassociated places. It is not difficult to associate the horned headdresses worn by the shamans of various tribal societies with the concept of a God of the Hunt. The headpieces of many ancient rulers, including the pharaohs of Egypt, include horns either of realistic or stylized design. Although the religion of the biblical Israelites was represented as distinctly antipagan, their sacrifices were offered on horned altars. The two bronze altars in Solomon's (10th century B.C.E.) tem-

Followers of the order of Italian witchcraft known as Stregeria claim that their tradition has maintained an unbroken lineage that goes back before the days of the Roman Empire.

According to the ways of the strege, the Goddess of the Old Religion, whether known as Diana, Aradia, or Demeter, has always been the benefactress of the outcast, the lonely, the people of the night. When the new religion of Christianity achieved dominance in Italy, the strege revered Mother Mary as an expression of the Goddess Diana.

Throughout Italy, Sicily, and Malta, there are many strege passing as devout church members, including a few Roman Catholic priests, who accept the Blessed Virgin Mary because they know she is just another incarnation of the Goddess Diana. One day, the strege believe religious tolerance will progress to the stage where they will once again have a public temple to the Goddess. More than one scholar of the mass conversions of the pagan populace of Europe during the Middle Ages has commented on the fact that the common folk simply went underground with their worship of Diana, or made the motions of giving reverence to the Virgin Mary, while secretly directing their true devotion to the Goddess.

"Christianization forced the Old Religionists underground in the twelfth century, but the sculptors paid tribute to their goddesses Demeter and Persephone by creating the Madonna and female Jesus. In ancient times people worshipped at the Temple of Demeter in Enna, Sicily, where they celebrated her daughter Persephone's resurrection from the underworld to become Goddess of souls and immortality. To this day the Sicilians worship the female deity more than the male, and every city has its sainted patroness."

STREGERIA: OLD RELIGION OR NEW?

SOURCES:

Grimassi, Raven. *Encyclopedia of Wicca & Witchcraft.* St. Paul, Minn.: Llewellyn Publications, 2000.

Machia, Arawn. "Ways of the Strega: An Introduction." [Online] http://www.monmouth.com/~equinoxbook/strega.html.

Steiger, Brad. *Revelation: The Divine Fire.* Englewood Cliffs, N.J.: Prentice-Hall, 1973.

ple were equipped with horns, as was the altar at the shrine of the **Ark of the Covenant** in Jerusalem before Solomon. Most curious of all, however, is Michaelangelo's (1475–1564) famous statue of Moses (14th–13th century B.C.E.), which depicts him with horns, thereby causing his head and face to bear a remarkable resemblance to Cerrnunos, as the Celts named the Horned God.

Because of the importance of human and animal fertility, the Horned God was soon joined by a goddess, whose purpose it was to ensure the success of all reproductive activities. She was also the goddess who oversaw the birth of human and animal progeny. At a later date, when primitive religious thought had evolved to the point of belief in some form of continuation after death, the goddess oversaw human and animal death as well.

WITH the advent of agriculture, the goddess was called upon to ensure crop fertility.

With the advent of agriculture, the goddess was called upon to extend her powers to ensure fertility of the crops. From this point on, the figure of the goddess began to overshadow that of the Horned God. A population that did not have to keep on the move increased rapidly, and soon a portion of the human tribes began to move out of the Tigris-Euphrates valley, the so-called cradle of civilization, and spread northward to what is now Europe and Asia. To the west, the fertile valley of the Nile proved an attractive site to agricultural peoples. And as humankind moved, their gods moved with them.

The population of medieval Europe had descended from the central Asian plateau. Centuries ago, they had strained against the barriers that the Roman legions had set against them until they had finally broken through and flooded the continent. Christianity and "civilized" ways were unknown to them at first, and they brought their own gods, customs, and rituals into the land. At the dis-

solution of the Roman Empire, the civilizing force in Europe became the Roman Catholic Church, and even though the ecclesiastical institution made great inroads into the pagan culture, it could not completely wash away the old rituals and nature worship.

Surviving the Roman Empire socially in the Middle Ages was the oppressive feudal system. Once-proud warriors were reduced to the role of serf farmers, and although they resented such a docile status, they were forced by necessity to accept it. Partially because of the frustrations of the common people and partially because of the tenacity of long-conditioned customs, the celebration of nature worship and various adaptations of the ancient **mystery religions** came to be practiced in secret. On those occasions when such seasonal nature celebrations were witnessed by members of the Christian clergy, the gatherings were condemned as expressions of witchcraft and were named "black sabbats," to distinguish the ceremonies as the complete opposite of the true and holy Sabbath days. The Horned God was deemed to be Satan, and the goddess believed to be Diana, goddess of the moon and the hunt.

For the serfs, the observance of the old nature worship was an expression of their conscious or unconscious yen to throw off the yoke of feudalism. The rulers had imposed the Christian God and the Christian ethic. The nobility and high church officials realized that such celebrations could only lead eventually to a rebellious and uncontrollable populace. The popularity of the pagan celebrations rose to its greatest height in the period of 1200 to the Renaissance. During this period, Europe was devastated and depopulated by famines, the ill-fated Crusades, and the black death.

Raymond Buckland feels that it is the naturalness and simplicity of the Old Religion that continues to hold great appeal for the individual who has become alienated by the pomp and ceremony and exclusivity of orthodox religion, as well as the small size of the "congregation." A coven of witches consists of no more than 12 members, the high priest or high priestess bringing the number up to the traditional 13.

"Witchcraft is very much a religion of participation," Buckland said. "Rather than being a spectator sitting in a pew at the back of a church, you are right there in the middle of things, participating."

It was in their enjoyment of the excitement and vigor of the Old Religion that the peasants could allow themselves the luxury of experiencing pleasure without the interference of the church, which sought to control and repress even human emotions. But it was that same expression of seeing the divine in all of the creator's works that brought the wrath of the church down upon the witches in the terrible form of the Inquisition.

❋ Delving Deeper

Buckland, Raymond. *Witchcraft from the Inside*. St. Paul: Llewellyn Publications, 1995.

Frazer, Sir James George. *The New Golden Bough*. Edited by Theodor H. Gaster. New York: Criterion Books, 1959.

Grimassi, Raven. *Encyclopedia of Wicca & Witchcraft*. St. Paul: Llewellyn Publications, 2000.

Michelet, Jules. *Satanism and Witchcraft*. New York: Citadel Press, 1960.

Russell, Jeffrey Burton. *Witchcraft in the Middle Ages*. Ithaca, N.Y.: Cornell University Press, 1972.

Seligmann, Kurt. *The History of Magic*. New York: Pantheon Books, 1948.

Trevor-Roper, H. R. *The European Witch-Craze*. New York: Harper & Row, 1967.

Familiars

The concept of certain spirit beings who assist a magician or a witch undoubtedly hearkens back to the totem animal guides that attended the ancient **shamans,** for the familiars express themselves most often in animal forms. The black cat, for instance, has become synonymous in popular folklore as the traditional companion of the witch. Attendant upon such a sorcerer as the legendary Cornelius **Agrippa** is the image of the black dog or the dark-haired wolf.

The ancient Greeks called upon the *predrii,* spirit beings who were ever at hand to provide assistance to the physicians or magicians. In Rome, the seers and soothsayers asked their familiars or *magistelli* to provide

supernatural assistance in their performance of magic and predictions. In many lands where the Christian missionaries planted their faith, various saints provided an acceptable substitute for the ancient practice of asking favors or help from the witches' familiar. Interestingly, many of the saints of Christendom are identified by an animal symbol, for example, the dog with St. Bernard; the lion with St. Mark; the stag with St. Eustace; and the crow with St. Anthony. However, in those regions where the country folk and rural residents persisted in calling upon their familiars, the church decreed the spirit beings to be demons sent by Satan to undermine the work of the clergy. All those accused of possessing a familiar or relying on it for guidance or assistance were forced to recant such a devilish partnership or be in danger of the torture chamber and the stake. While the much-loved St. Francis of Assisi was often represented symbolically by a wolf, if any of the common folk identified the wolf as their personal totem or guide, such a declaration would be taken as proof that they were witches who had the ability to shapeshift into a werewolf.

❋ Delving Deeper

Grimassi, Raven. *Encyclopedia of Wicca & Witchcraft*. St. Paul: Llewellyn Publications, 2000.

Michelet, Jules. *Satanism and Witchcraft*. New York: Citadel Press, 1960.

Russell, Jeffrey Burton. *Witchcraft in the Middle Ages*. Ithaca, N.Y.: Cornell University Press, 1972.

Seligmann, Kurt. *The History of Magic*. New York: Pantheon Books, 1948.

Walker, Barbara G. *The Woman's Dictionary of Symbols and Sacred Objects*. Edison, N.J.: Castle Books, 1988.

The Inquisition—The Time of the Burning

The Inquisition came into existence in 1231 with the *Excommunicamus* of Pope Gregory IX (c. 1170–1241), who at first urged local bishops to become more vigorous in ridding Europe of heretics, then lessened their responsibility for determining orthodoxy by establishing inquisitors under the special jurisdiction of the papacy. The office of inquisitor was entrusted primarily to the Franciscans and the Dominicans, because of their reputation for superior knowledge of theology and their declared freedom from worldly ambition. Each tribunal was ordered to include two inquisitors of equal authority, who would be assisted by notaries, police, and counselors. Because they had the power to excommunicate even members of royal houses, the inquisitors were formidable figures with whom to reckon. In 1257, the church officially sanctioned torture as a means of forcing witches, sorcerers, shapeshifters, and other heretics to confess their alliance with Satan.

THE *Inquisition came into existence in 1231.*

The Inquisition became a kind of hideous industry. It employed judges, jailers, torturers, exorcists, woodchoppers, and experts to destroy the evil ones who were threatening the ruling powers. "Witch persecutors…were craftsmen with a professional pride," Kurt Seligmann wrote in *The History of Magic* (1948). "A hangman grew melancholic when a witch resisted him unduly. That was akin to a personal offense. In order to save face he let the accused die under the torture, and thus his honor was not impaired, for the blame for the killing would then rest on the devil.…The business became so prosperous that the hangmen's wives arrayed themselves in silk robes.…For every witch burned, the hangman received an honorarium. He was not allowed to follow any other profession, therefore he had to make the best of his craft."

It was not long before the torturers had discovered a foolproof method for perpetuating their gory profession. Under torture, nearly any witch could be forced to name a long string of her "fellow witches," thereby turning the trial of a single individual into an ordeal for more than a hundred. One inquisitor boasted: "Give me a bishop, and I would soon have him confessing to being a wizard!" Another declared that the Holy Inquisition was the only alchemy that really worked, for the inquisitors had found the secret of transmuting human blood into gold.

The Jesuit Friedrich von Spee (1591–1635) became an opponent of the witchcraft trials in 1630 when the wise Duke of Brunswick brought him and a fellow priest into a torture chamber. As the duke and the two fathers, champions of the cause of the Inquisition, stood beside a confessed witch, who was being tortured further for her increased good of soul, the German nobleman asked the priests if, in their consciences, they could say that the Holy Tribunals were doing God's work. When the Jesuits answered loudly in the affirmative, the duke asked the poor woman on the rack to look carefully at his companions. "I suspect them of being witches," he said. With this, he indicated that the wretch be stretched another notch on the rack. At once she began screaming that the two devout fathers were agents of Satan, that she had seen them copulating with succubi and serpents and had dined with them on roasted baby at the last Sabbat.

Later, in an anti-Inquisition work, Father Spree declared: "Often I have thought that the only reason why we are not all wizards is due to the fact that we have not all been tortured. And there is truth in what an inquisitor dared to boast, that if he could reach the Pope, he would make him confess that he was a wizard."

By the late sixteenth century, the power of the Inquisition was beginning to wane. In 1563, Johann Weyer (Weir) (1515–1588), a critic of the Inquisition, managed to publish *De praestigus daemonum* in which he argued that while Satan does seek to ensnare and destroy human beings, the charges that accused witches, werewolves, and vampires possessed supernatural powers were false. Such abilities existed only in their minds and imaginations. However, as if to provide an antidote to Weyer's call for a rational approach to dealing with accusations of witchcraft, in 1580 the respected intellectual **Jean Bodin,** often referred to as the Aristotle of the sixteenth century, wrote *De La demonomanie des sorciers*, a book that argued that witches truly possessed demonic powers and caused the flames once again to burn high around thousands of heretics' stakes.

With the spread of Protestantism through Europe, Pope Paul III (1468–1549) established the Congregation of the Inquisition (also known as the Roman Inquisition and the Holy Office) in 1542 which consisted of six cardinals, including the reformer Gian Pietro Cardinal Carafa (1475–1559). Although their powers extended to the whole church, the Holy Office was less concerned about heresies and false beliefs of church members than they were with misstatements of orthodoxy in the academic writings of its theologians. When Carafa became Pope Paul IV in 1555, he approved the first *Index of Forbidden Books* (1559) and vigorously sought out any academics who were prompting any thought that offended church doctrine or favored Protestantism.

Although organized **witchcraft trials** continued to be held throughout Europe and even the American colonies until the late seventeenth century, they were most often civil affairs and the Inquisition had little part in such ordeals. However, the Holy Office continued to serve as the instrument by which the papal government regulated church order and doctrine, and it did try and condemn Galileo (1564–1642) in 1633. In 1965, Pope Paul VI (1897–1978) reorganized the Holy Office and renamed it the Congregation for the Doctrine of the Faith.

For many years and in dozens of books and articles on witches and Wicca, the number of innocent people executed for the practice of witchcraft during the four centuries of active persecution has been estimated as high as nine million. In 1999, Jenny Gibbons released the results of her research in the autumn issue of *PanGaia* in which she verified that overall, approximately 75 percent to 80 percent of those accused of witchcraft were women, but to date (circa 1999) an examination of the official trial records of the witchcraft trials indicate that less than 15,000 definite executions occurred in all of Europe and America combined. The period of the heaviest persecutions of witches occurred during the 100 years between 1550 and 1650, Gibbons reported, and the total number of men and women accused of witchcraft who were actually hanged or burned probably did not exceed 40,000.

Wiccan author and scholar **Margot Adler** has noted that the source of the oft-quoted

nine million witches put to death was first used by a German historian in the late eighteenth century who took the number of people killed in a witch hunt in his own German state and multiplied by the number of years various penal statutes existed, then reconfigured the number to correspond to the population of Europe. "It serves no end to perpetuate the miscalculation," Adler commented. "It's time to put away the exaggerated numbers forever."

B Y *the late sixteenth century, the power of the Inquisition was beginning to wane.*

❖ DELVING DEEPER

Adler, Margot. "A Time for Truth: Wiccans Struggle with Information that Revises Their History." *beliefnet.* [Online] http://www.beliefnet.com/story/40/story_4007.html.

Gibbons, Jenny. "A New Look at the Great European Witch Hunt" (excerpted from "The Great European Witch Hunt," published in the Autumn 1999 issue of *PanGaia*). *beliefnet* [Online] http://www.beliefnet.com/story/17/story_1744_1.html.

Lea, Henry Charles. *The Inquisition of the Middle Ages.* New York: Citadel Press, 1963.

Netanyahu, B. *The Origins of the Inquisition.* New York: Random House, 1995.

Russell, Jeffrey Burton. *Witchcraft in the Middle Ages.* Ithaca, N.Y.: Cornell University Press, 1972.

Seligmann, Kurt. *The History of Magic.* New York: Pantheon Books, 1948.

Trevor-Roper, H. R. *The European Witch-Craze.* New York: Harper & Row, 1967.

SABBATS

The Sabbat is a day of ascendancy for witches. In the European countrysides during the Middle Ages, the eight festival observances took on immense importance as thousands of peasants, common people, and members of the lesser nobility attended the seasonal celebrations. The Sabbats mark the passage of the year as it moves through its seasons: Samhain begins the year for those who follow the ways of witchcraft, and it occurs near October 31.

B efore gathering in the forest for a **Sabbat,** many witches applied "flying ointment" on their bodies. According to ancient lore, this ointment enables the witch to fly through the air, often accompanying the goddess Diana through the night sky. This ointment was made from atropa belladonna, commonly known as deadly nightshade and contains certain alkaloids, which produce vivid hallucinations.

Unfortunately individuals accused of witchcraft were arrested by the Inquisition and tortured. The priests and witch-hunters were not satisfied with accounts of merely flying to the gatherings in the forests. They wanted to hear how the witches encountered the devil, sold their souls to him, and plotted evil against all god-fearing villagers.

In his *The Black Arts* (1967) Richard Cavendish repeated the account of a woman who wished to test a recipe for witches' flying ointment. She rubbed on the ointment, uttered the appropriate spells, and in front of several witnesses, fell into a disturbed sleep.

FLYING HIGH WITH THE WITCHES

When she awakened, she insisted that she had been with Lady Venus and the goddess Diana, although she had not left the room.

SOURCES:

Ahmed, Rollo. *The Black Art.* London: Arrow Books, 1966.
Cavendish, Richard. *The Black Arts.* New York: Capricorn Books, 1967.

Yule marks the Winter Solstice and is celebrated near December 21, the longest, darkest night of the year. Candlemas, observed on February 2, is the festival of the Goddess Brigid. The Spring Equinox happens around March 21 and is a powerful time of magic. Beltane, May 1, celebrates love and oneness. The Summer Solstice, occurring around June 21, is also a time of power and strength of the deities of nature. August 1 recognizes Lammas, a time when fruit ripens and there are signs that harvest is near. The Fall Equinox, near or on September 21, celebrates a balance between light and dark, night and day.

In the Middle Ages, the Christian influence, so visible during the day, seemed to vanish at night as great groups of people gathered around a statue of the Horned God and began professing their allegiance to the great deities of nature. To staunch Christians, this horned image was an obscene representation of Satan, a black, grotesque figure that was fiendishly lit by the roaring fire in front of it. In the flickering light, the torso of the figure appeared to be human while the head, hands, and feet were shaped like those of a goat and covered with coarse, black hair. The altar beneath the image of the Horned God was constructed of stones, and the ceremony performed was intricate.

Although there was plenty of food and beer, many scholars of witchcraft believe that the high priests and priestesses took advantage of the entranced state of most of the worshippers and spiked the drinks with belladonna or other drugs. The crowd was then easily whipped into an intoxicated frenzy, which tended to free the inhibitions of the celebrants. At the peak of the collective emotions, the crowd acted as a single person and began almost automatically to dance the hypnotic witches' round. As the dance continued, the cathartic influence of the entire celebration magnified the energy of each individual until all of them forgot their own personality in expression of worship of the Horned God and the Goddess.

The Sabbat dance, or, as it is commonly known, the witches' round, was performed with the dancers moving in a back-to-back position with their hands clasped and their heads turned so that they might see each other. A wild dance such as this, which was essentially circular in movement, would need little help from the drugged drinks to bring about a condition of vertigo in the most hearty of dancers. The celebration lasted the entire night, and the crowd did not disperse until the crowing of the cock the following morning.

Reports of regular celebrations of the various Sabbats came from all over Europe. An estimated 25,000 attended such rituals in the countrysides of southern France and around the Black Forest region of Germany. As rumors of even larger gatherings spread throughout the land, the nobility and the churchmen decided to squelch such expressions out of existence with the use of the hideous machinery of the Inquisition. Even the most innocent amusements of the serfs were taken away. In the face of such large-scale persecutions, the mass meeting celebrations of the Sabbat were made impossible. But even though great pressure was brought to bear on such outward manifestations of the rituals, the Sabbats were still performed in modified versions in the private fields, orchards, and cellars of the peasants.

❈ DELVING DEEPER

Buckland, Raymond. *Witchcraft from the Inside*. St. Paul: Llewellyn Publications, 1995.

Grimassi, Raven. *Encyclopedia of Wicca & Witchcraft*. St. Paul: Llewellyn Publications, 2000.

Michelet, Jules. *Satanism and Witchcraft*. New York: Citadel Press, 1960.

Murray, Margaret. *The God of the Witches*. Garden City, N.Y.: Doubleday, 1960.

Russell, Jeffrey Burton. *Witchcraft in the Middle Ages*. Ithaca, N.Y.: Cornell University Press, 1972.

Seligmann, Kurt. *The History of Magic*. New York: Pantheon Books, 1948.

Trevor-Roper, H. R. *The European Witch-Craze*. New York: Harper & Row, 1967.

WITCHCRAFT TRIALS

In the period from about 1450 to 1750, somewhere around 40,000 to 60,000 individuals were tried as witches and condemned to death in central Europe. Of that number, as high as three-quarters of the victims were women.

Numerous scholars have pointed out that beginning in the fourteenth century, the close of the Middle Ages, the Christian establishment of Europe was forced to deal with an onset of social, economic, and religious changes. It was also during this time (1347–49) that the Black Death, the bubonic plague, nearly decimated the populations of the European nations and greatly encouraged rumors of devil-worshippers who conspired with other heretics, such as Jews and Muslims, to invoke Satan to bring about a pestilence that would destroy Christianity and the West. During most of the Middle Ages, those who practiced the Old Religion and worked with herbs and charms were largely ignored by the church and the **Inquisition.** After the scourge of the Black Death, witchcraft trials began to increase steadily throughout the fourteenth and fifteenth centuries.

The first major witch-hunt occurred in Switzerland in 1427; and in 1428, in Valais, there was a mass burning of 100 witches. In 1486, the infamous "hammer for witches," *Malleus Maleficarum*, the official textbook for trying and testing witches written by the monks Sprenger and Kramer, was published.

THE *first major witch-hunt occurred in Switzerland in 1427.*

In the early decades of the sixteenth century, when the Protestant Reformation began to restructure nearly all of Europe politically as well as religiously, witches were largely overlooked by the rulers of church and state who now struggled with the larger issues of the great division within Christianity. Then, after a time of relatively little persecution, the period of the great witchcraft craze or hysteria that many practicing witches and students of witchcraft today refer to as the "Burning Times," occurred from about 1550 to 1650.

Although organized witchcraft trials continued to be held throughout Europe and even the English colonies in North America until the late seventeenth century, they were most often civil affairs. About 40 people were executed in the English colonies between 1650 and 1710, and half of these victims perished as a result of the **Salem trials** of 1692. Persecution of witches and the trials held to punish them had been almost completely abolished in Europe by 1680. One last wave of the witch craze swept over Poland and other eastern European countries in the early eighteenth century, but it had dissipated by 1740. The last legal execution of a witch occurred in 1782 in Glarus, Switzerland—not far from where the witch craze had begun in 1428. The last known witch-burning in Europe took place in Poland in 1793, but it was an illegal act, for witch trials were abolished in that country in 1782.

THE *last legal execution of a witch occurred in 1782 in Glarus, Switzerland.*

The Inquisition or the Church itself had little part in any witchcraft trials after the latter part of the seventeenth century, but the Holy Office continued to serve as the instrument by which the papal government regulated church order and doctrine.

✣ DELVING DEEPER

Adler, Margot. "A Time for Truth: Wiccans Struggle with Information that Revises Their History." *beliefnet*. [Online] http://www.beliefnet.com/story/40/story_4007.html. 25 February 2002.

Gibbons, Jenny. "A New Look at the Great European Witch Hunt" (excerpted from "The Great European Witch Hunt," published in the autumn 1999 issue of *PanGaia*). *beliefnet* [Online] http://www.beliefnet.com/story/17/story_1744_1.html. 25 February 2002.

Lea, Henry Charles. *The Inquisition of the Middle Ages*. New York: Citadel Press, 1963.

Netanyahu, B. *The Origins of the Inquisition*. New York: Random House, 1995.

Russell, Jeffrey Burton. *Witchcraft in the Middle Ages*. Ithaca, N.Y.: Cornell University Press, 1972.

Seligmann, Kurt. *The History of Magic*. New York: Pantheon Books, 1948.

Trevor-Roper, H. R. *The European Witch-Craze*. New York: Harper & Row, 1967.

ENGLAND

The first record of a witch being burned at the stake in the British Isles was the execution of Petronilla de Meath at Killkenny, Ireland, on November 3, 1324. But from that time until the witch craze ended in the eighteenth century, Ireland would neither try nor burn any more witches. England did not really succumb to the witch craze that seized Central Europe. There was no law against witchcraft in England until 1542—and that law was repealed in 1547. Perhaps because the nation had a strong central government, as opposed to the independent city states which at that time created constant political turmoil within so many of the European countries, England did not tolerate wholesale witch burnings. The few burnings that did occur took place on the borders where different religious faiths were in conflict and the people were more disposed to see Satan in the other person's manner of worship.

The first recorded execution of a person associated with witchcraft occurred in 1441, but the convicted woman, Margaret Jourdemaine of London, was put to death not because she was a witch, but because she had been found guilty of murder. In 1563, perhaps in reaction to the witch craze in Europe, a new law against witchcraft was passed, and a 63-year-old widow named Agnes Waterhouse was condemned to death in 1566 for bewitching a man to death.

Torture could not be used against accused witches in England; therefore, only about 20 percent of those suspected of dealing with the devil were executed. The single period during which something approaching the witch hysteria on the European continent blighted England occurred during the English Civil War during the 1640s when the central government's power collapsed and opposing factions struggling for dominance were more likely to accuse their opponents of trafficking with the devil.

The last witches executed in England—Temperance Lloyd, Susanna Edwards, and Mary Trembles, all of Bideford, Devon—were all hanged on August 25, 1682. The death penalty of witches in England was abolished in 1736. Estimates of the number of witches put to death in England are about 400, and approximately 90 percent of those condemned were women.

Alleged murders by witchcraft and subsequent trials for witchcraft have not disappeared from the world scene, and the fear of cursing, hexing, and causing death by witchcraft remains very powerful in many nations.

In 1998, in scenes reminiscent of the Salem witch hunts, mobs in Indonesia attacked and killed 153 people who were accused of practicing sorcery. In an eight-year-period, from 1990 to 1998, more than 2,000 cases of witchcraft-related violence, including 577 murders, were recorded in the northern corner of South Africa.

In June 2001, the London *Sunday Times* reported that the president of Zimbabwe, Robert Mugabe, feared that he and his government had become the victims of black magic directed at them by powerful *Sangomas* (witchdoctors). In August 2001, a teenaged girl in Nigeria confessed to taking part in the ritual killing of 48 people after being initiated into a secret witchcraft cult. Three men were arrested by police in that African nation after they were found in possession of a human skull that they were using in Black Magick rituals.

The Washington Post reported on November 28, 2001, that Black Magic murders in the state of Maranhao in northeastern Brazil had claimed the lives of at least 26 boys. Although as many as one in six Brazilians practice a form of religion that combines Roman Catholicism with the ancient beliefs of African and Amazonian magic, such as Tambo de Mina, Umbanda, and **Macumba,** the priests of those religions denied any part of the mutilation deaths of the young boys. Authori-

ties remained convinced that Black Magic witchcraft was somehow behind the murders.

In December 2001, the Romanian Parliament announced that it was passing new laws to regulate the thousands of witches practicing in their country. It was suggested that politicians be given special advice on how to deal with the witches after the finance minister sufferred a broken leg the day after he introduced a special tax on witches.

THE *law against witchcraft in England was repealed in 1547.*

Although the widespread horror of the Inquisition being visited upon innocent individuals and hauling accused men and women into torture chambers has receded into a shameful chapter in human history, trials for witchcraft have by no means been relegated to the Middle Ages.

❋ DELVING DEEPER
"Case Study: The European Witch-Hunts, c. 1450–1750," *Gendercide Watch*. [Online] http://www.gendercide.org/case_witchhunts. html.

Faiola, Anthony. "Witchcraft Murders Cast a Gruesome Spell," November 28, 2001. [Online] http://www.washingtonpost.com/wp-dyn/articles/A25297-2001Nov27.html. 25 February 2002.

Johnson, R. W. "Mugabe's Men on the Run from Witchcraft," June 2, 2001. [Online] http://www.sunday-times.co.uk.

Notestein, Wallace. *A History of Witchcraft in England.* New York: Thomas Y. Crowell, 1968.

Russell, Jeffrey Burton. *Witchcraft in the Middle Ages.* Ithaca, N.Y.: Cornell University Press, 1972.

Trevor-Roper, H. R. *The European Witch-Craze.* New York: Harper & Row, 1967.

Summers, Montague. *The History of Witchcraft.* New York: University Books, 1956.

FRANCE

When an overview of the witchcraft trials in France is made in an effort to derive an accurate picture of the extent of the persecutions of those alleged to be witches, the issue becomes clouded because of two great heretic hunts that had far-reaching repercussions. The first was the crusade launched against the heretical Cathars in the south of France in 1208, and the second was the trial of the Knights Templar for heresy and witchcraft in 1312. From the beginning of the thirteenth century to the end of the seventeenth century, neither the church or civil courts nor the common people were able to make clear distinctions between Cathars, heretics, and witches.

In 1246, Montsegur, the center of the Albigensian (as the Cathars were also known) resistance fell, and hundreds of the sect who had for so many years withstood the only crusade ever launched against fellow Christians were burned at the stake. In that same year, the headquarters of the Inquisition was established in Toulouse. In 1252, Pope Innocent IV (d. 1254) issued a papal bull that placed the inquisitors above the law and demanded that every Christian—from the aristocracy to the peasantry—assist in the work of seeking out witches and heretics or face excommunication. In 1257, the church officially sanctioned torture as a means of forcing witches and heretics to confess to their evil ways.

In 1305, the Knights Templar, who had for centuries been the bulwark of Christianity against those who would destroy or defame it, were themselves accused of invoking Satan, consorting with female demons, and worshipping black cats. While many clergy, including the pope himself, were reluctant to believe such charges against the Knights Templar, it soon became apparent that the order had become too wealthy and powerful to fit suitably into the emerging political structure of France and the aspirations of its king, Philip the Fair (1268–1314).

After years of persecution, many knights scattered and went into hiding throughout Europe and England. Those valiant Templars who insisted upon presenting a defense were finally brought to trial in 1312; and in spite of 573 witnesses for their defense, at least 54 knights were tortured en masse, burned at the stake, and their order was disbanded by Pope Clement V (c. 1260–1314).

Perhaps because of such large numbers of Cathars having been executed at Montsegur and other cities in the Albi region of southern France, along with reports of the mass burning of the Knights Templar, exaggerated accounts of mass executions of witches passed into the literature of the witch craze in Europe and remained there for centuries. For example, there are many reference books that document the burning of several hundred witches in Toulouse between 1320 and 1350. In one single terrible day during that time, according to the old texts, 400 women were burned at the stake. Historians have since determined that such mass executions of witches at Toulouse never occurred. Such claims are exaggerations or fictions.

The old records also reveal that the witchhunters in France were not as gender biased as their counterparts in other European nations. Of the 1,300 witches whose appeals were heard by the French parliament, just over half were men. Also, contrary to popular supposition, in countries such as France, where the Catholic Church was firmly entrenched, the inquisitorial church courts were much more lenient than the civil courts in handing out death sentences to accused witches. Overall, in such Catholic nations as France, Italy, and Spain, the church courts executed far fewer people than the local community-based courts or the national courts. According to some statistics, in the period from 1550 to 1682, omitting the numbers of Cathars and Knights Templar executed, France sentenced approximately 1,500 accused witches to death.

⁂ **DELVING DEEPER**

"Case Study: The European Witch-Hunts, c. 1450–1750." *Gendercide Watch.* [Online] http://www.gendercide.org/case_witchhunts.html. 25 February 2002.

Russell, Jeffrey Burton. *Witchcraft in the Middle Ages.* Ithaca, N.Y.: Cornell University Press, 1972.

Trevor-Roper, H. R. *The European Witch-Craze.* New York: Harper & Row, 1967.

Summers, Montague. *The History of Witchcraft.* New York: University Books, 1956.

GERMANY

From the perspecive of the papacy, it seemed that witchcraft had become particularly virulent in Germany, and in 1484, Pope Innocent VIII (1432–1492) became so distressed with conditions in that country that he issued the papal bull *Summis Desiderantes Affectibus*. As an additional antidote to demonism, the pope authorized two Dominican inquisitors Henrich Institoris (also known as Kramer) (1430–1505) and Jacob Sprenger (1436–1495) to prepare a kind of guide book for those witchhunters who sought to battle Satan in the Rhineland. Their collaborative work, *Malleus Maleficarum*, "A Hammer for Witches" (1486), soon became the official handbook for those who conducted witchcraft trials throughout nearly all of Europe. While some members of the laity, the civil courts, and even the clergy had begun to question the actual power of witches, *Malleus Maleficarum* strongly refuted those arguments that suggested that the reality of the hellish works of those individuals who claimed an alliance with Satan existed only in troubled human minds.

According to *Malleus*, those angels who fell from heaven were intent upon destroying the human race—and anyone who believed otherwise believed contrary to the true faith. Therefore, any person who had consorted with demons and who had become witches must recant their evil ways or die.

The country that gave birth to the Protestant Reformation was also the center of the witchcraft trials in Europe, condemning to the stake 48 percent of all those who were accused of consorting with demons, perhaps as many as 26,000 victims. Oddly enough, although much political and religious restructuring was occurring in Germany, the country was not tolerant toward divergent ideas and beliefs. In southwestern Germany alone, more than 3,000 witches were executed between 1560 and 1680. Perhaps the reasons for such heavy persecution of suspected witches lay in the distrust that the warring Christian factions—the Roman Catholics and the newly emerging Protestant sects—had toward one another, and their religious zeal prompted them to accuse a variety of scapegoats as servants of Satan.

In 1630, Prince-Bishop Johann Georg II Fuchs von Dornheim, the infamous *Hexenbischof* (Witch Bishop), constructed a special torture chamber which he decorated with appropriate passages from scripture. He burned at least 600 heretics and witches, including a fellow bishop he suspected of being too lenient.

THE *witchcraft trials in Germany ended in 1684.*

While the Protestant states in Germany abandoned the persecution of witches a generation before those states under Roman Catholic dominance, the uncompromising nature of the Lutheran and Calvinist doctrines contributed to the continuation of the witchcraft trials until around 1660. The witchcraft trials in Germany ended in 1684. Of the approximately 26,000 accused witches condemned to death from around 1550 to 1684, 82 percent were women.

✷ DELVING DEEPER

"Case Study: The European Witch-Hunts, c. 1450–1750." *Gendercide Watch*. [Online] http://www.gendercide.org/case_witchhunts.html. 25 February 2002.

Russell, Jeffrey Burton. *Witchcraft in the Middle Ages*. Ithaca, N.Y.: Cornell University Press, 1972.

Trevor-Roper, H. R. *The European Witch-Craze*. New York: Harper & Row, 1967.

Summers, Montague. *The History of Witchcraft*. New York: University Books, 1956.

SALEM, MASSACHUSETTS

The Salem, Massachusetts, witchcraft trials of 1692 provide a classic example of what scholars mean when they refer to the "witch craze" or "witch hysteria" that swept through Europe in the sixteenth and seventeenth centuries. Because of the accusations of a small circle of prepubescent girls, an entire community became crazed and caught up in the fear that many of their neighbors were serving Satan in secret. The witch hysteria in Salem village resulted in the deaths of 24 men and women, who were hanged, were crushed to death, or died in prison.

The reign of terror that seized the village of Salem in Massachusetts Bay Colony in

1692 remains perhaps the single most celebrated of all witch hunts. Playwright Arthur
Miller's (1915–   ) moving stage treatment of
the nightmare at Salem, *The Crucible* (1953),
receives periodic revivals on Broadway, and in
1996 Miller wrote the screenplay for the
motion picture version, starring Winona
Ryder, Daniel Day-Lewis, Paul Scofield, and
Joan Allen. In her study of the witchcraft trials *The Devil in Massachusetts* (1961), Marion
L. Starkey made the following observation:
"No definitive history of the Salem witchcraft
trials has ever been written or is likely to be,
for it would take a lifetime and would be ency-
clopedic in dimension."

The madness began innocently enough in
the home of the Rev. Samuel Parris when his
slave Tituba began telling stories of **voodoo**
and restless spirits to his nine-year-old daughter Betty and her cousin Abigail Williams, 11.
While it is certain that the Puritan preacher
would have either scolded or beaten Tituba for

filling the girls' heads with such spooky tales,
Abigail and Betty cherished these secret times
with the slave woman and kept quiet about
the nature of their conversation. Soon the
exciting storytelling sessions in the Parris
household were attracting older girls, such as
16-year-old Mary Walcott and 18-year-old
Susanna Sheldon, who wanted Tituba to tell
their fortunes and predict their future husbands, as well as tell them ghost stories.
Although Rev. Parris and the other preachers
fulminated from the pulpits about the dangers
of seeking occult knowledge, the girls of
Salem ignored such warnings in favor of having a thrilling pastime that could help them
through a long, cold winter.

Then came the fateful afternoon when
Ann Putnam, a fragile, highly strung 12-year-
old, joined the circle in the company of the
Putnams' maid, 19-year-old Mercy Lewis. Ann
was much more widely read than the other
girls and was blessed with a quick wit, a high

intelligence, and a lively imagination. She soon became Tituba's most avid and apt pupil. Together with her literate mother, Ann had read far more than the other girls in the circle, and she was quite familiar with the imagery in the Book of Revelation with its dragons, horned beasts, devils, and damnation. It seems that while part of Ann's psyche was thrilled with the forbidden knowledge Tituba shared with them, another aspect was conflicted with guilt that they were flirting with devilish enchantment.

Undoubtedly most of the other girls were also conflicted with conscience and the fear of discovery. As the days passed, little Betty seemed distracted from her chores, subject to sudden fits of weeping, often noted to be staring blankly at the wall. Shortly thereafter, Abigail went far beyond weeping and blank stares. She got down on all fours and began barking like a dog or braying like a donkey. Mary Walcott and Susanna Sheldon fell into convulsions. Ann Putnam and the family maid, Mercy Lewis, also began to suffer seizures. Something evil seemed to have come to Salem.

About four years previously in the north end of Boston, four children in the John Godwin family had fallen into such fits, babbling blasphemies, ignoring the prayers of the clergy. It took the famous preacher Cotton Mather (1663–1728) to quiet the work of an alleged witch, an Irish washerwoman named Glover, and restore the children to normalcy. The memories of this horrid event, including the hanging of Witch Glover, were much alive in the minds of the Salem clergy when they began to ask the girls who it was who was tormenting them.

To no one's surprise, Tituba was the first name from the possessed childrens' lips. Nor did anyone doubt the naming of Sarah Good, considered by the townsfolk to be a bit of a tramp with a foul-smelling pipe, who had been suspected of spreading smallpox through witchcraft. But when the children named Sarah Osburne a witch, the village was shocked. Osburne was a property owner, who lived in one of the most substantial homes in Salem. Nevertheless, warrants were issued for all three women.

And from such a dramatic beginning, the list of names of the devil's disciples who were tormenting the girls grew steadily longer. The wealthy merchant Philip English; Goodwife Proctor, the wife of successful farmer and tavern keeper, John Proctor; Martha Cory, the wife of another prosperous farmer, Giles Cory. Sarah Good's four-year-old daughter, Dorcas, was also put in chains as an accused witch. Two magistrates, John Hathorne and Jonathan Corwin, were sent out from the General Court of Massachusetts Colony to hear testimony that described tales of talking animals, dark shapes, red cats, and a tall man, who was undoubtedly the devil himself.

When 71-year-old Rebecca Nurse was arrested for witchcraft against her neighbors, the townsfolk realized that if she could be named as a witch, no one was safe from such accusations. Nurse was considered a veritable saint by the village, a woman noted for her piety and simplicity of heart. Although the jury initially acquitted her, the judge ordered the jury to reconsider and she was found guilty. She was hanged on Gallows Hill on July 19, 1692.

In 1711, the Massachusetts legislature passed a general amnesty that exonerated all but six of the accused witches.

Several hundred people in and around Salem were accused of witchcraft, even the wife of Massachusetts governor William Phips. Such an absurdity provoked Phips into taking a stand against any further imprisonments and he forbade any more executions for witchcraft in Salem. Because of the governor's actions, the nearly 150 men and women who were still chained to prison walls were set free and many who had been convicted of witchcraft were pardoned.

In 1711, the Massachusetts legislature passed a general amnesty that exonerated all but six of the accused witches. In 1957, the state legislature passed a resolution exonerating Ann Pudeator, who had been hanged.

Finally, on November 1, 2001, acting Massachusetts governor Jane Swift approved a bill that cleared all the accused witches hanged in Salem in 1692 and 1693. The bill exonerated the final five who had not been cleared by the previous amnesty resolutions—Susannah Martin, Bridget Bishop, Alice Parker, Margaret Scott, and Wilmot Redd.

✤ DELVING DEEPER

Hansen, Chadwick. *Witchcraft at Salem*. New York: New American Library, 1970.

Noble, Christopher. "Relatives Cheer Bill Clearing Salem Witches." [Online] http://dailynews.yahoo. com/htx/nm/20011102/od/life_witches_dc_1.html. 4 March 2002.

Starkey, Marion L. *The Devil in Massachusetts: A Modern Enquiry into the Salem Witch Trials*. Garden City, N.Y.: Dolphin/Doubleday, 1961.

"A Village Possessed: A True Story of Witchcraft." *Discovery Online*. [Online] http://www.discovery. com/stories/history/witches/trials.html. 4 March 2002.

SCOTLAND

Although torture was forbidden to be used as an instrument to obtain confessions from witches in England, it was allowed in Scotland where half of all those accused of witchcraft from 1537 to 1722 were burned at the stake, a total of 1,350 to 1,739 victims—at least three times as many as were hanged in England—with women comprising 86 percent of that number.

In 1583 The Discovery of Witchcraft *was written.*

The first recorded execution of a witch in Scotland occurred in July 1537 when Janet Douglas, also known as Lady Glamis, was burned at the stake in Edinburgh. Lady Glamis died not because she was the victim of a trial inspired by the witch craze of Europe, but because she had been found guilty of using her abilities as a witch to murder.

In 1583, Englishman Reginald Scot (1538–1599) wrote *The Discovery of Witch-*

craft, which was his answer to the *Malleus Maleficarum* (1486) and what he considered the abuses being conducted against accused witches in Scotland, where torture was freely used to wring confessions out of those unfortunate enough to have gone to trial. Scot considered the witch-hunters to be sexually obsessed madmen who took delight in inflicting sadistic tortures on their victims. A person being put to torture could be made to confess to any charge, Scot argued. And if the witches were really so powerful, he questioned why had they not enslaved the human race centuries ago?

Scot's book so infuriated King James VI of Scotland (1566–1625) that he himself wrote a treatise on the reality of demon worship and the power of witches entitled *Demonologie* to refute *The Discovery of Witchcraft*. A few years later, when he ascended the throne of England, one of King James' first official acts was to order the public burning of Scot's book.

The last witch in the whole of the British Isles to be executed was Jenny Horn of Sutherland, Scotland, who was burned at the stake in 1722. Horn had been tried together with her daughter, who, the jury decided, was a victim of her mother's witchcraft, rather than an accomplice.

✤ DELVING DEEPER

"Case Study: The European Witch-Hunts, c. 1450–1750." *Gendercide Watch*. [Online] http://www. gendercide.org/case_witchhunts. html. 25 February 2002.

Notestein, Wallace. *A History of Witchcraft in England*. New York: Thomas Y. Crowell, 1968.

Russell, Jeffrey Burton. *Witchcraft in the Middle Ages*. Ithaca, N.Y.: Cornell University Press, 1972.

Summers, Montague. *The History of Witchcraft*. New York: University Books, 1956.

Trevor-Roper, H. R. *The European Witch-Craze*. New York: Harper & Row, 1967.

SPAIN

In 1478, at the request of King Ferdinand V (1452–1516) and Queen Isabella I (1451–1504), papal permission was granted to establish the Spanish Inquisition and to maintain it separate from the Inquisition that extended its jurisdiction over all the rest of Europe. The

Grimoires are books of ceremonies, rituals, and spells that are to be used in ceremonial magic composed in Europe from the fifteenth to the sixteenth centuries. The texts provide rules regarding symbols, chants, and spells, and describe how to utilize them to perform effective magical effects.

The most famous of all Grimoires is the *Key of Solomon,* allegedly prepared by the king himself. In the first century C.E. the historian Josephus (c. 37–c. 100) refers to a book of incantations for summoning spirits written by Solomon. Black magicians circulated the text throughout Europe in the twelfth century; the Inquisition condemned it as a dangerous text in 1559.

THE POWER OF THE GRIMOIRES

SOURCES:

Cavendish, Richard. *The Black Arts.* New York: Capricorn Books, 1967.

Grimassi, Raven. *Encyclopedia of Wicca & Witchcraft.* St. Paul, Minn.: Llewellyn Publications, 2000.

Spence, Lewis. *An Encyclopedia of Occultism.* New Hyde Park, N.Y.: University Books, 1960.

Spanish Inquisition was always more interested in persecuting heretics than those suspected of witchcraft. It has been estimated that of the 5,000 men and women accused of being witches, less than 1 percent were condemned to death. The Spanish Inquisition was concerned with trying the Marranos or conversos, those Jews suspected of insincerely converting to Christianity; the converts from Islam, similarly thought to be insincere in practicing the Christian faith; and, in the 1520s, those individuals who were believed to have converted to Protestantism. The support of Spain's royal house enabled Tomas de Torquemada (1420–1498) to become the single grand inquisitor whose name has become synonymous with the Inquisition's most cruel acts and excesses. Torquemada is known to have ordered the deaths by torture and burning of thousands of heretics and witches.

The Spanish Inquisition seemed to take special delight in the pomp and ceremony of the *auto-de-fe,* during which hundreds of heretics might be burned at one time. If an *auto-de-fe* could not be made to coincide with some great festival day, it was at least held on a Sunday so that the populace could make plans to attend the burnings.

The ghastly event began with a procession of the penitents led by Dominican friars. Behind them marched the wretched victims of the Inquisition, barefooted, stumbling, hollow-eyed with the pain and nightmare of their ordeal.

As in Spain, the same lack of concern regarding the practice of the Old Religion and the folk customs of the herbalists and *strega* (witches) was also the prevailing attitude in Italy, another nation in which the Roman

Catholic Church was strong and was not weakened by the Protestant Reformation. The clerical tribunals in either nation levied few death sentences toward witches, but many scholars have estimated that the neighbors had killed many men and women suspected of witchcraft. Some researchers have stated that as many as 25 percent of those executed for witchcraft in those countries were lynched by mobs who carried out the fatal sentences that they felt the Inquisition had failed to deliver.

❖ DELVING DEEPER

Lea, Henry Charles. *The Inquisition of the Middle Ages*. New York: Citadel Press, 1963.

Netanyahu, B. *The Origins of the Inquisition*. New York: Random House, 1995.

Russell, Jeffrey Burton. *Witchcraft in the Middle Ages*. Ithaca, N.Y.: Cornell University Press, 1972.

Swain, John. *The History of Torture*. New York: Award Books, 1969.

WITCHHUNTERS

In 1484, Pope Innocent VIII (1432–1492) so deplored the spread of witchcraft in Germany that he issued the papal bull *Summis Desiderantes Affectibus* and authorized two trusted Dominican inquistors, Henrich Institoris (Kramer) (c. 1430–1505) and Jacob Sprenger (c. 1436–1495), to squelch the power of Satan in the Rhineland. In 1486, Sprenger and Kramer published their *Malleus Maleficarum*, "A Hammer for Witches," which quickly became the "bible," the official handbook, of professional witch hunters. *Malleus Maleficarum* strongly refuted all those who claimed that the works of demons exist only in troubled human minds. The Bible clearly told the account of how certain angels fell from heaven and sought to bewitch and seduce humans, and Sprenger and Kramer issued a strict warning that to believe otherwise was to believe contrary to the true faith. Therefore, any persons who consorted with demons and became witches must recant their evil ways or be put to death.

In his *Witchcraft* (1960), Charles Williams wrote that if one were to judge *Malleus Maleficarum* as an intellectual achievement, the work of Sprenger and Kramer is almost of the first order. While one might suspect a book that detailed horrible tortures to be administered to unfortunate men and women to be the efforts of half-mad, sexually obsessed individuals, Williams said that "there is no sign that they were particularly interested in sex. They were interested in the Catholic faith and its perpetuation, and they were, also and therefore, interested in the great effort which it seemed to them was then in existence to destroy and eradicate the Catholic faith."

Williams believed that Sprenger and Kramer proceeded with great care in the *Malleus Maleficarum* to examine the nature of witchcraft and to analyze the best methods of operating against its menace. The two devout Dominican priests took extreme measures to correct error, to instruct against ignorance, and to direct cautious action.

The judges of the great tribunals examined, tried, and tortured female witches at a ratio of 10–1, 100–1, or 10,000–1, depending upon the authority cited. Only in the Scandinavian countries were men accused of being witches and sorcerers at an equal or larger percentage than women.

Once an accused woman found herself in prison through the testimony of someone who had allegedly seen her evil powers at work, she might well be as good as dead. At the height of the witchcraft mania in the fifteenth and sixteenth centuries, an accusation was equivalent to guilt in the eyes of many judges. Sadly, a neighbor woman jealous of the "witch's" youth and beauty, a suitor angered by her rejection, or a relative who sought her inheritance, may have brought the accusation of witchcraft. And no lawyer would dare defend such an accused witch for fear that he would himself be accused of heresy if he pled her case too well.

The common justice of the Inquisition demanded that a witch should not be condemned to death unless she convict herself by her own confession. Therefore, the judges would order her torture to force her to confess so that she might be put to death. In a vicious and most perplexing paradox of justice, the learned men held that even though the accusation of nearly anyone was enough to land a woman in prison as a witch—and if she got as far as prison she was thereby considered guilty—all the testimony counted for naught unless the witch confessed her guilt. No one, under common justice, could be put to death for witchcraft on the evidence of another's testimony. What is more, the witch must confess without torture by the court. Therefore, in order to fully comply with the law, the judges turned the accused witches over to the black-hooded torturers so they, themselves, would not be the ones torturing the accused. Once the witch had confessed, she was now eligible to be reconciled to the church, absolved of sin, and burned at the stake. Confession or not, of course, the accused witch found her way to the flaming pyres. The difference, in the eyes of Mother Church, was whether the woman went as guilty but penitent or guilty and impenitent.

Although recent scholarship has argued that the oft-cited figure of nine million innocent women and men condemned to torture and death for witchcraft durng the Inquisition should be lowered more reasonably to a maximum of 40,000, that number is still frighteningly representative of a ghastly miscarriage of justice toward human beings who were persecuted and killed in the name of religion.

Sometime in the 1550s, a highly respected doctor, Johann Weyer (Weir) (1515–1588), who believed in the power of Satan to deceive Earth's mortals, became a critic of the Inquisition and its claims that mere humans could really attain such supernatural powers as those which the tribunals ascribed to witches. Perhaps, he argued, Satan had tricked these unfortunate individuals into believing that they could work such magic in order to cause them to worship the dark forces, rather than God. In 1563, against strong opposition, Weyer published *De praestigus daemonum* in which he presented his arguments that while Satan sought always to ensnare human souls, the supernatural powers attributed to witches existed only in their minds and imaginations.

In 1583 Reginald Scot (1538–1599) wrote *The Discovery of Witchcraft*, which serves as a kind of answer or rebuttal to Sprenger's and Kramer's "Hammer for Witches." He said if witches were really as all-powerful and malig-

Pope Innocent VIII (1432–1492). (CORBIS CORPORATION)

nant as the Inquisitors claimed, why had they not enslaved or exterminated the human race long ago?

Unfortunately for many decades, the voices of Weyer and Scot were those of only a few sane men, desperately crying out in the wilderness of the incredible sexual mania that provided the fuel for the witchcraft persecutions. The reign of terror conducted by the witchhunters in Europe and Great Britain continued until the early part of the seventeenth century.

✷ **DELVING DEEPER**

Lea, Henry Charles. *The Inquisition of the Middle Ages*. New York: Citadel Press, 1963.

O'Keefe, Daniel Lawrence. *Stolen Lightning: The Social Theory of Magic*. New York: Vintage Books, 1983.

Russell, Jeffrey Burton. *Witchcraft in the Middle Ages*. Ithaca, N.Y.: Cornell University Press, 1972.

Seligmann, Kurt. *The History of Magic*. New York: Pantheon Books, 1948.

Trevor-Roper, H. R. *The European Witch-Craze*. New York: Harper & Row, 1967.

Williams, Charles. *Witchcraft*. New York: Meridian Books, 1960.

JEAN BODIN (C. 1529/30–1596)

Before he became obsessed with ridding the world of the evils of witchcraft, the brilliant Jean Bodin (Baudin or Bodinus) had been hailed as the Aristotle of the sixteenth century. When he was but a youth, Bodin was noticed by academics as rising young intellectual, and soon he was known throughout Europe as a formidable scholar of history, political theory, and the philosophy of law. Bodin became a celebrated jurisconsult and a leading member of the Parliament of Paris. In 1576, he wrote *The Six Books of the Republic*, a work that remains studied in the twenty-first century. Bodin portrayed a kind of ideal society in which humankind was governed by natural laws, a moral code given through conscience and God. In general, Bodin idealized the potential of humankind as becoming steadily noble and less beastlike. Scholars ponder what became of the utopian politician when Bodin sat down to write *Demonomanie des Sorciers* and became one of the men most responsible for keeping the fires of the **Inquisition** burning brightly.

The *Demonomanie* was first published in Paris in 1581 and again in 1616, 20 years after Bodin's death, as *Fleau des demons et des Sorciers*. In the first and second volumes of this monumental work, Bodin offered his proofs that spirits communicate with humankind, and he itemized the various means by which the righteous might distinguish the good spirits from their evil counterparts. Those men and women who seek to enter pacts with Satan in order to achieve diabolical prophecy, the ability to fly through the air, and the power to shapeshift into animal forms are dealing with evil spirits. Bodin acknowledged that he was well aware of spells by which one might summon incubi or succubi for carnal pleasure.

The third volume details methods by which the work of sorcerers and witches might be destroyed, and the fourth volume lists the characteristics by which witches, shapeshifters, and other servants of Satan might be identified. The massive work concludes with a refutation of Johann Weyer (1515–1588), a medical doctor and author of *De praestigiis daemonum* (1563), who, Bodin determined was in grave danger of committing heresy by arguing that those men and women who claimed to be witches and shapeshifters were merely people with unsound minds.

✤ DELVING DEEPER

Lea, Henry Charles. *The Inquisition of the Middle Ages*. New York: Citadel Press, 1963.

Netanyahu, B. *The Origins of the Inquisition*. New York: Random House, 1995.

Russell, Jeffrey Burton. *Witchcraft in the Middle Ages*. Ithaca, N.Y.: Cornell University Press, 1972.

Seligmann, Kurt. *The History of Magic*. New York: Pantheon Books, 1948.

Trevor-Roper, H. R. *The European Witch-Craze*. New York: Harper & Row, 1967.

HENRI BOGUET (1550–1619)

When he presided at witchcraft trials, Henri Boguet, an eminent judge of Saint-Claude in the Jura Mountains, was known for his cruelty, especially toward children. He had no doubt that Satan gifted witches with the ability to change shape into a variety of animal forms, especially the wolf, so that they might devour humans, and the cat, so they might better prowl by night. The craze of witch-hunting may have been first formulated by the clergy, but by 1600 such jurists as Boguet, **Jean Bodin,** and **Pierre de Lancre** had eagerly assumed the mantles of determined inquisitors.

In his book *Discours des Sorciers* (1610), Boguet recounted his official investigation of a family of werewolves and his observation of them while they were in prison in 1584. According to his testimony, the members of the Gandillon family walked on all fours and howled like wolves. Their eyes turned red and gleaming; their hair sprouted; their teeth became long and sharp; their fingernails turned horny and clawlike. In another case recounted in his book, Boguet told of eight-year-old Louise Maillat, who in the summer of 1598 was possessed by five **demons,** who identified themselves as Wolf, Cat, Dog, Jolly, and Griffon. In addition, the little girl was accused of shapeshifting into the form of a wolf.

Boguet devoted a chapter in his *Discours des Sorciers* to the carnal connection of demons with witches and sorcerers and expressed his conviction that the devil could become either a man or a woman to deceive people into his fold. Under his interrogations, Pierre and his son George, of the Gandillon family of werewolves, also confessed to having sexual liaisons with the devil. Boguet was also fascinated by the accounts that witches gave under torture concerning the festivals of the Black Sabbats and condemned them as mocking the high Christian festivals. In his records, Boguet noted that such Sabbats most often occurred on Thursday nights at the stroke of midnight and lasted until cock-crow. He also managed to wring confessions out of witches that they did, indeed, fly to such Sabbats astride sticks and brooms. He also got witches to confess that the Sabbats began always with the adoration of Satan, who appeared sometimes in the shape of a tall, dark man and at other times in the form of a goat.

The eminent jurisconsult, judge of the province of Burgundy and president of the Tribunal of St. Claude, was dreaded by all those who might one day find themselves standing before his judgment. He was fanatical, cruel, and implacable in his sessions of interrogation, and his *Discours des Sorciers* ran into 11 editions and became for a time the authoritative text for French bailiwicks. Boguet pronounced or ratified about 600 death sentences against witches. And while this learned man's wisdom was relied upon to determine the remarkable powers of witches and sorcerers, the level of his scientific acumen in other matters might be evaluated by his understanding that rotten sticks eventually turned into snakes.

✤ DELVING DEEPER

Lea, Henry Charles. *The Inquisition of the Middle Ages.* New York: Citadel Press, 1963.

Russell, Jeffrey Burton. *Witchcraft in the Middle Ages.* Ithaca, N.Y.: Cornell University Press, 1972.

Seligmann, Kurt. *The History of Magic.* New York: Pantheon Books, 1948.

Trevor-Roper, H. R. *The European Witch-Craze.* New York: Harper & Row, 1967.

MATTHEW HOPKINS (16??–1647)

It was once suggested that Matthew Hopkins, the witch-finder general, had become infallible in his ability to track down witches because he himself had employed a bit of sorcery and managed to steal one of Satan's address books so that he might copy down the names of the devil's disciples. Although Hopkins served England in the self-appointed capacity of "witch-finder" for a period of only two years, his name remains synonymous with the overzealous persecution of those men and women suspected of witchcraft. From 1645 to 1647, Hopkins and his two eager assistants, John Sterne and Mary Phillips, scoured the counties of eastern England searching for those who had Satan's mark upon them.

Little is known of the early life of Hopkins until he appeared on the scene as one who received payment for finding witches on behalf of various villages whose townspeople suspected evidence of Satan's disciples in their community. He was the son of James Hopkins, a minister of Wenham in Suffolk, and there are records to indicate that he became an unsuccessful lawyer in Ipswich. After moving to Manningtree circa 1644, he apparently appointed himself to the position of a witch finder and added the title "general" for its prestige value. Records suggest that Hopkins may have owned or been shown associated with the Thorn Inn in the adjacent parish of Mistley, and it is here in the inn that he began holding his first witchcraft trials. With his knowledge of English law and his earnest belief in the power of witchcraft to work evil on the simple and unsuspecting Christian villagers, Hopkins undoubtedly felt that he had all the qualifications necessary to become a professional witch-hunter. It is known that both Hopkins and his assistant Stearne were Puritans, and those who knew them stated that they were men of deep religious convictions.

E ITHER *guilty or innocent, of course, the accused witch was eliminated as a real or a potential emissary of Satan on Earth.*

Hopkins seemed to have a general knowledge of some of the European literature on witchcraft—enough, at least, to have become convinced that all witches received a **familiar,** an imp often disguised as a cat or some other

Matthew Hopkins, Witch Finder General. (CORBIS CORPORATION)

animal, after they had signed a pact with Satan. Hopkins believed the familiar sustained itself by feeding upon the witch's blood, and if such an act of unholy nourishment could be observed, it would immediately prove the guilt of a suspected witch.

Because torture as an aid to interrogation was forbidden in England, Hopkins devised a system of watching, searching, and swimming to test those individuals who had been accused of practicing witchcraft. The suspect would be stripped naked, covered with a loose-fitting gown, and forced to sit on a chair in the middle of a bare room. Then witnesses would watch the accused witch for hours, day and night, for several days if necessary. All this time, the alleged witch must be kept awake, sitting on the stool, forbidden to lie down, so the witnesses could detect a familiar if it should creep up to feed on its host. If the accused should begin to slump forward in sleep, he or she was immediately pushed erect and walked around the room to force him or her to remain awake. Since this process would often be continued for days, the suspect's feet might become bloody and bruised from the walking. While such an exhaustive and cruel regimen might not technically have been considered torture, its brutal effects produced the same results from its hapless victims.

In *The Discovery of Witches*, a pamphlet Hopkins published in 1647, he wrote that on one occasion he and Stearne witnessed six imps attempting to sneak into the room where a witch was being watched. One was a whitish thing, not quite as large as a cat; another was something like a dog with sandy spots; and a third resembled a greyhound with long legs. It seemed the other three got away before the two witch-hunters got a good look at them. On this particular occasion, six townspeople whom Hopkins had gathered as volunteers in the watching part of the ordeal swore that they, too, had seen the imps approaching the witch, and their testimony was often used by Hopkins to silence those skeptics who might doubt the reality of demonic familiars.

The "swimming" part of Hopkins's three-part test was a foolproof method of determining the guilt or innocence of a witch. Hopkins would have the witches bound in a painful position with their right thumb to their left big toe and their left thumb to their right big toe, then he would order them thrown into a river or a deep pond. If the witches sunk and drowned, they were innocent. It was clear that they possessed no supernatural powers, after all. If they somehow managed to stay afloat, however, they were judged guilty of witchcraft and men with long poles would push them under the water until they drowned. Either guilty or innocent, of course, the accused witch was eliminated as a real or a potential emissary of Satan on Earth.

Hopkins died on August 12, 1647. John Stearne attempted to carry on in the witch finder's footsteps for about another year, but the witchcraft craze was dying out in England.

DELVING DEEPER

"Matthew Hopkins—The Witchfinder General." [Online] http://www.rci.rutgers. edu/~jup/witches/bunn/matthew_hopkins.html.

Notestein, Wallace. *A History of Witchcraft in England*. New York: Thomas Y. Crowell, 1968.

Seligmann, Kurt. *The History of Magic*. New York: Pantheon Books, 1948.

Trevor-Roper, H. R. *The European Witch-Craze*. New York: Harper & Row, 1967.

POPE INNOCENT III (1160 OR 1161–1216)

Alarmed with the growing perceived influence of Satan in the Europe of the Middle Ages, Pope Innocent III actively began to chastise heretics as soon as he ascended to the papacy in 1198. The first burnings for heresy may have taken place in about the year 1000 in Ravenna, but the first actual recorded burning occurred at Orleans in 1022, followed by others at Monforte in 1028. Such executions for heresy by burning at the stake were sporadic and few until 1197 when Pedro II of Aragon (c. 1184–1213) ordered the burning of heretics who had relapsed in their promises to repent of their sins of doubt and questioning. In 1198, Pope Innocent declared such individuals as traitors against Christ and condemned them to death by burning.

In 1208, the Cathar sect—also known as the Albigensians—had become so popular among the people in Europe that Pope Innocent III considered them a greater threat to Christianity than the Islamic warriors who were pummeling the Christian knights on the Crusades. To satisfy his concern, he ordered the only crusade ever launched against fellow Christians by attacking the Cathars who resided in the Albi region of southern France.

In the opinion of Pope Innocent III and many of the church hierarchy, the Cathars were teaching the rudiments of witchcraft. Although the Cathars centered their faith in Christ, they perceived him as pure spirit that had descended from heaven on the instructions of the God of Good to liberate humankind from the world of matter. According to the Cathars, because Christ was pure spirit, he did not die on the cross and the teachings of the church were false. The Cathars rejected all the Catholic sacraments, and they taught that the God of the Old Testament was the lord of matter, the prince of this world—all terms which the Catholic Church reserved for Satan. Not only did the Cathars believe that the God revered as the Creator by the Church was really the devil, the Cathars instructed their followers that most of the patriarchs and prophets mentioned in the Old Testament were really demons.

The Cathars somehow managed to hold out against the armies massed against them until Montsegur, their final stronghold, fell in 1246. Hundreds of the remaining Cathars were burned at the stake—men, women, and children—but Innocent III did not live to see his triumph over the heretics, for he died in 1216. Before he died, however, Innocent III enacted a papal bull that allowed a judge to try a suspected witch or heretic even when there was no accuser and granted the judge the power to be both judge and prosecutor.

THE *Cathars rejected all the Catholic sacraments.*

✤ DELVING DEEPER

Lea, Henry Charles. *The Inquisition of the Middle Ages*. New York: Citadel Press, 1963.

Russell, Jeffrey Burton. *Witchcraft in the Middle Ages*. Ithaca, N.Y.: Cornell University Press, 1972.

Summers, Montague. *The History of Witchcraft*. New York: University Books, 1956.

Trevor-Roper, H. R. *The European Witch-Craze*. New York: Harper & Row, 1967.

PIERRE DE LANCRE (1553–1631)

By his own boast, witch trial judge Pierre de Lancre tortured and burned more than 600 men and women accused of consorting with demons. In his books *Tableau de l'Inconstance des mauvais Anges* (1613) and *L'Incredulite et Mescreance du Sortilege* (1622), de Lancre defended the belief in demons, black magic, and witchcraft. In his considered opinion, even to deny the possibility of witchcraft was heresy, for God himself in the Holy Bible had condemned magicians and sorcerers. De Lancre, however, was not a member of the clergy, and his concerns were social, rather than theological. He believed that sorcerers and witches were a well-organized anti-social force that sought to overthrow the established order.

It was customary for the judges of the witchcraft trials to denounce Jews as heretics and sorcerers. De Lancre was no exception, once stating that God had withdrawn his grace and promises from the Jewish people. He claimed also to have it on great authority that many Jews were powerful magicians who had the ability to shapeshift into wolves by night.

De Lancre, as so many of the trial judges, became rather fixated on the details that the witches provided of their carnal encounters with demons. The more questions he asked about these sexual matters and the more torture the witches suffered, the more lurid the accounts became. De Lancre decided that Incubi and Succubi, those demonic seducers of men and women, had as their mission the infliction of a double injury to their victims, attacking them in both their body and their soul.

When men or women accused of being sorcerers protested that the devil had not picked them up and flown them anywhere, Judge de Lancre decreed that those sorcerers who walked to the Sabbats held in the forests were just as guilty as those who were carried to such sites by Satan. De Lancre warned his fellow members of the tribunals to be wary of toads, for they could likely be **familiars** of the witches. One witch whom he tried and who confessed at length, described a number of toads that had attended a Sabbat in the Basses-Pyrenees region dressed in black and scarlet velvet with little bells attached to their coats and trousers.

In 1609, the Parliament of Bordeaux sent de Lancre to Labourd in the Bayonne district to administer punishment to the sorcerers who had infested the region. In short order, de Lancre deduced that Satan deceived a number of Roman Catholic priests into administering Black Masses to the witches in the area. Two priests, an elderly man of 70 and a young man of 27, were executed almost immediately upon de Lancre's arrival. The horrified bishop of Bayonne arranged for his five clergy members accused of sorcery to escape prison. He also interfered with the judge's orders of imprisonment for three other priests and arranged for them to escape and flee the countryside.

When he was not sentencing men and women to their horrible deaths, de Lancre was known to his Christian contemporaries as a sensitive and talented writer of idyllic pastoral accounts of country living. When he at last retired to his country estate, he turned all of his attention to writing and the construction of chapels, fountains, and grottos to beautify his lavish grounds.

✤ DELVING DEEPER

Lea, Henry Charles. *The Inquisition of the Middle Ages.* New York: Citadel Press, 1963.

Russell, Jeffrey Burton. *Witchcraft in the Middle Ages.* Ithaca, N.Y.: Cornell University Press, 1972.

Trevor-Roper, H. R. *The European Witch-Craze.* New York: Harper & Row, 1967.

MAKING THE CONNECTION

alchemy From Greek, *khemeia* to Arabic, *alkimiya* via medieval Latin: *alchimia* and Old French, fourteenth century: *alquemie,* meaning "the chemistry." A predecessor of chemistry practiced in the Middle Ages and Renaissance principally concerned with seeking methods of transforming base metals into gold and the "elixir of life."

apothacary From the Greek *apotheke* meaning "storehouse." A pharmacist or druggist who is licensed to prescribe, prepare and sell drugs and other medicines, or a pharmacy—where drugs and medicines are sold.

charlatan From the Italian *ciarlatano,* via seventeenth-century French *ciarlare,* meaning "to babble or patter" or "empty talk." Someone who makes elaborate claims or who pretends to have more skill or knowledge than is factual, such as a fraud or quack.

conjurations The act of reciting a name, words or particular phrases with the intent of summoning or invoking a supernatural force or occurrence.

enchantments Things or conditions which possess a charming or bewitching quality such as a magical spell.

enigma From Greek *ainigma* "to speak in riddles" and *ainos,* meaning "fables." Somebody or something that is ambiguous, puzzling or not easily understood and might have a hidden meaning or riddle.

evocation The act of calling forth, drawing out or summoning an event or memory from the past, as in recreating.

Gnostic From the Greek, *gnostikos*, meaning "concerning knowledge." A believer in Gnosticism, or relating to or possessing spiritual or intellectual knowledge or wisdom.

incantation From fourteenth-century French, *cantare*, meaning "to sing" via Latin—*incantare*—"to chant." The chanting, recitation or uttering of words supposed to produce a magical effect or power.

Inquisition Fourteenth century, from Latin *inquirere* via Old French *inquisicion*, meaning "to inquire." In the thirteenth century, Roman Catholicism appointed a special tribunal or committee whose chief function was to combat, suppress and punish heresy against the church. Remaining active until the modern era, the official investigations were often harsh and unfair.

loa A spirit that is thought to enter the devotee of the Haitian voodoo, during a trance state, and believed to be a protector and guide that could be a local deity, a deified ancestor or even a saint of the Roman Catholic Church.

neo-paganism Someone who believes in a contemporary or modernized version of the religions which existed before Christianity, especially those with a reverence for nature over the worship of a divine or supreme being.

rite Originally from an Indo-European base meaning "to fit together" and was the ancestor of the English words *arithmetic* and *rhyme* via, the Latin *ritus*. A formal act or observance as a community custom, such as the rite of courtship. Often has a solemn, religious or ceremonial meaning, such as the rite of baptism.

shape-shifter A supposed fictional being, spirit or something that is capable of changing its appearance or form.

wizard A variant of the fifteenth century word *wisard*, meaning "wise." Someone who professes to have magical powers as a magician or sorcerer, or a male witch. In general, someone who is extremely knowledgeable and clever.

CHAPTER 7
PROPHECY AND DIVINATION

Since the beginning of human history, men and women have sought out glimpses into the future. Soothsayers and seers have attempted to predict the destiny of their clients by interpreting signs in the entrails of animals, the movements of the stars in the heavens, the reflections in a crystal ball, the spread of a deck of cards, and even messages from the dead. All of these ancient practices are still utilized today by prophets and diviners who seek to answer the demands of those who wish foreknowledge of their earthly destiny.

INTRODUCTION

The desire to foresee the future quite likely began when early humans began to perceive that they were a part of nature, subject to its limitations and laws, and that they were seemingly powerless to alter those laws. Unlike the beasts around them, however, humans lived most of their lives in the knowledge that one day they would die, and that accidents and awful circumstances could snuff them out at any time. In addition, under certain circumstances, an unforeseen financial loss could be nearly as dreadful as a mortal wound. It was humanity's attempts to alleviate these fundamental anxieties regarding a fearful future that caused it to seek foreknowledge of tomorrow from the earliest times.

Divination, the method of obtaining knowledge of the unknown or the future by means of omens, has been practiced in all societies—barbarous and civilized. Ancient humans lived in a world of dualism, an arena of constant combat between positive and negative forces. Humans, the only creatures who react to their environment emotionally as well as physically, felt themselves surrounded by powerful and mysterious forces over which they had no control. Hoping to influence the supernatural beings whom they believed controlled their destiny, or at least to appease the beings' wrath, humans sought to know the will of the gods.

The ancient Chaldeans read the machinations of the gods in the star-filled heavens, as well as in the bloody livers of sacrificed fowl. When the king of Babylon went forth to war, he wrote the names of cities on his arrows, put them back into the quiver, and shook them. He then removed an arrow and attacked first the city whose name was written thereon. The children of Israel sought the word of the Lord in the jewels of the Ephod; and Jonah deemed it a just verdict when the casting of lots decreed that it was he who was the cause of the storm. Pharaoh elevated Joseph from his prison cell to the office of chief minister of Egypt and staked the survival of his kingdom on Joseph's interpretation of his dreams. In the same land of Egypt, priests of Isis and Ra listened as those deities spoke through the unmoving lips of the stone Sphinx.

The writings of **Hermes Trismegistus** were considered by the alchemists as a legacy from the master of alchemy and were, therefore, most precious to them. The alchemists, who were concerned with the spiritual perfection of humans as well as the transmutation of base metals into gold, recorded their formulas and esoteric truths in allegorical form. The Hermetics believed that the nature of the cosmos was sacramental, and Hermes' dictum that "that which is above is like that which is below" was the essence of universal truth. In other words, the nature of the spiritual world could be discovered through the study of the material, and earthly humans, created of the "dust of the ground," comprised the prima materia of the heavenly, just as the base elements of the earth comprised the raw materials for gold.

In Greece, where the world of matter was held in subjugation to the powers of mind, arithmetic was used as a means of divination. Numbers were assigned to the gods and goddesses, and when the right number was evoked, the corresponding deity answered.

The Roman emperors, considered somewhat divine themselves, could consult the gods, but it was generally forbidden for commoners to do so. Although up until the fourth century most of the Roman emperors were openly opposed to magic and divination, prescience was widely known in the land of the Tiber. Astrologers, both native and from Chaldea, were much in demand, and other diviners practiced augury utilizing the entrails of slaughtered animals. Although diviners and soothsayers were sometimes banished and sometimes executed, it was usually because they had failed to see what Caesar wanted them to see or because they had seen more than Caesar wanted them to see, not merely for the practice of their art.

It remained for the emperors who were converts to the new religion, Christianity, to declare the *religio paganorum* (the religion of the country people) to be forbidden practices and to pave the way for full-scale persecution. Although pagan temples were destroyed and images and books of the adepts burned, magicians continued to meet in secret and to perform their rites of divination.

Although the practice of occult arts was suppressed by Christianity, it was never completely excised. The mystical Neoplatonists put together a system of magic whose workings were attributed to supernatural agencies and beings, which were carefully differentiated from the demons Christianity sought to banish from the minds of men and women. Because intellectual activity was thought to be bound up with the influence of these demons, Europe descended into an abyss of ignorance and religious absurdity that history accurately terms the Dark Ages (about 476 to 1000).

But the tree of forbidden knowledge was not so easily cut down. In the East, where the Crescent overshadowed the influence of the Cross, Arab intellectuals preserved knowledge of the occult as well as significant portions of other classical thought and ancient lore. From Muslim-dominated Spain, this knowledge trickled back into Europe, where it was combined with alchemy and the Hermetic Mysteries.

The objects of divination may change, but not their function. Many of the ancient forms of divination are alive and flourishing in the Western world today. Many of them will be examined in this chapter along with examples of how they might be experienced. Instructions of some of the methods of divination and prophecies are included to encourage understanding of the techniques, not belief in their powers.

ASTROLOGY

The earliest humans soon learned that the fertility of the soil was dependent upon the favor of the Sun, as well as that of the rains, both of which were bestowed from the heavens. On the other hand were the adverse effects of lightning, wind, and hail, as well as floods. These phenomena were quite mysterious, as well as wonderful or dreadful, as the case might be. Then, as now, people felt themselves at the mercy of these powers; and, since these good and bad energies all seemed

to originate in the skies above, it was most logical that they should come to regard the heavens as the seat of the great gods. From this conviction evolved a theory of complete accord between phenomena observed in the heavens and occurrences observed on Earth.

ANCIENTS held the celestial bodies in great regard.

There is no doubt that the ancients held the celestial bodies in great regard, perhaps even in veneration. The Book of Job in the Old Testament affirms that "the morning stars sang together" when the foundation of Earth was laid. Later, Job was asked, "Do you know the ordinances of the heavens? Can you establish their rule on Earth?" (38:33). It is clear, also, that the ancients believed that the stars influenced the turn of events here on Earth. In Judges (5:9) it is recorded that Barak, commander of the Israelite army that was faced with a decisive battle with the Canaanite forces under Sisera, took heart when he was told by the prophetess Deborah, "From heaven fought the stars, from their courses they fought against Sisera." Deborah was not the only seer who had knowledge of the stars. Amos (5:8) speaks of God as "He who made the Pleiades and Orion, and turns deep darkness into morning." In Malachi 4:2, the righteous are promised that the "sun of righteousness shall rise, with healing in its wings (rays)."

Babylonian priests developed and perfected a system of interpreting the phenomena observed in the heavens for the purpose of determining the will of the powers of heaven. The Greeks enlarged the scope of astrology to include all the known sciences.

Empedocles, a Greek philosopher of about 450 B.C.E., developed the idea that the universe is composed of four basic elements: fire, water, air, and earth. Following the conquest of Babylonia by Alexander the Great (356–323 B.C.E.), it was found that Chaldean astrologers had divided the signs of the zodiac into four triangles of three each and called the

Astrological signs of the zodiac. (CORBIS CORPORATION)

groupings by the same names as were Empedocles's four elements. Aries, Sagittarius, and Leo were termed fire signs; Cancer, Scorpio, and Pisces, water; Libra, Aquarius, and Gemini, air; and Capricorn, Taurus, and Virgo comprised the signs of earth.

In essence, astrology deals with the relationship between the positions of the Sun, Moon, and planets and the life of an individual. Astrology has its philosophical root in the premise that each individual is a universe in miniature and mirrors within himself or herself the astrological pattern found in the heavens at the time of the individual's birth. From the standpoint of astrology, this means that the nature or personality of all individuals is determined by the pattern of the heavens at the time of their birth, plus their reactions to the stimuli found in their environment during growth and maturity.

The quality of personality that determines how individuals react to their environment is called temperament. Hippocrates (c. 460–c. 377 B.C.E.) described four kinds of temperament: sanguine, choleric, phlegmatic, and melancholic. The four temperaments of Hippocrates were symbolized by linking choleric to fire and sanguine to air. Water was the symbol of the phlegmatic temperament, and earth was that of the melancholic. The choleric and sanguine modes of reaction were characterized by easy excitability and quick alteration of interest, the interests being feeble in the former and intense in the latter. Conversely, the phlegmatic and melancholic temperaments were characterized by persistent but slow excitability of interest, the interest being feeble in the phlegmatic and in the melancholic, intense. (In usage today, only the negative aspect of these temperaments are common. Thus choleric today means easy to anger; melancholic, depressed; sanguine, over optimistic; and phlegmatic, too slow.)

Although different schools of astrology may designate different calendar dates for some of the signs, there is seldom a difference of more than a day or two. The interpretations of the mental, emotional, physical, and spiritual characteristics of the individual signs may also vary widely, but there are some general observations regarding the personalities of individuals born under the various Sun signs:

Aries, the Ram, March 21 to April 20, is a fire sign. The name comes from the Greek god of war. Individuals born under this sign have some aggressive traits about them that makes them dominant in friendship, partnership, and marriage. If they are deprived of their desire to dominate, they are liable to become discontented and difficult to get along with. Their views about life are definite, and they have little use for airs and graces. Aries people are a robust lot with a strong resistance to disease of any kind. However, once they do succumb to illness, they are inclined to run high temperatures. Neuralgia and migraines may also hinder them.

Taurus, the Bull, April 21 to May 21, is an earth sign. The word comes from the Latin meaning "bull." Taurus people like to have things their own way, but they are not quite as aggressive and as dominant as those under the

Aries sign. They are passionate in nature, and love means much to them. They also make splendid mothers or fathers. Taureans are generally not bookish types; they prefer life itself to fiction. Although Taureans are inclined to be generous, they will fly into a rage if they learn that they have been deceived.

Gemini, the Twins, May 22 to June 21, is an air sign. According to the ancient Romans, the sign of Gemini represents the twin sons, Castor and Pollux, who were born to Leda, the queen of Sparta, after Jupiter seduced her, the king of the gods. The twins were high-spirited, strong, and inseparable. Geminis are among the most intelligent citizens of the Zodiac; but they have a dual nature, and they frequently have difficulty in choosing between two courses of action. They are active, and they love freedom, change, and variety. In matters of health, nerves are liable to plague Geminis, and they often prefer to live close to meadows and woods where they are able to gain vigor from the wind and the rains.

THE *four kinds of temperament are sanguine, choleric, phlegmatic, and melancholic.*

Cancer, the Crab, June 22 to July 22, is a water sign. The ancient Chaldeans named Cancer after the crab, because of its backward or oblique movement, which brought to their mind the sun's immobility during the summer solstice as it enters this sign. Cancers have great imaginations, and they glory in fantasies of love and romance. Cancers hate to be flustered, and they like to take their time over important decisions. Cancer people usually strive to be cheerful and avoid depressions. Because of their natural affinity for water, whenever possible they make their homes on the coast or close to a lake or a large body of water.

Leo, the Lion, July 23 to August 23, is a fire sign. Leo, the fifth sign of the Zodiac, represents the lion, king of beasts, and according to Roman astrologers, the savage lion of Nemea, slain by Hercules. The typical Leo is a rather impressive person who dearly loves to

Astrological chart.

(CORBIS CORPORATION)

be in the limelight. Leo people generally have plenty of energy and strongwill power, and they make trustworthy and loyal friends. Leos cherish high ideals and love means a great deal to them. Because they tend to be adaptable, they make good marriage partners. Leo people are excellent and convivial hosts, who love to entertain others with big parties.

Virgo, the Virgin, August 24 to September 22, is an earth sign. Virgo was named in honor of the Greek goddess of Astraea, goddess of innocence and purity, who was placed among the stars. A typical Virgo is cool, calm, and collected and never loses his or her head in emotional matters. Virgo people belong to the intellectual class of individuals, and it is not an easy task for anyone to sway them once they have made a decision. On the negative side, they tend to be overly critical of others. They are quick to give vent to their

opinions, and they can indulge in biting sarcasm if so moved.

Libra, the Scales, September 23 to October 23, is an air sign. Libra is the only symbol of the zodiac that does not represent either an animal or a human. Long associated with harvest time and the fair measurement of crops, the scales may hearken back to ancient Egypt and the belief that the god Anubis weighed the souls of the dead to determine their worthiness. Libra people are often attractive and conform to the idealistic picture of the model man or woman. However, Libras tend to be rather moody and thin-skinned, and they hate anything painful or ugly. Luxury has a great attraction for them; and with their tendency to avoid the unpleasant aspects of life, many Librans live to a ripe old age, having the ability to recuperate from illness more quickly than those born under other signs.

Scorpio, the Scorpion, October 24 to November 22, is a water sign. Diana, the moon-goddess of the Romans, commanded Scorpio to kill the hunter Orion when Eos, goddess of the dawn, fell in love with him. After his death, Jupiter set the scorpion and Orion, still armed with his armor and sword, in the stars. Scorpios are definitely possessed of a passionate nature, and they are highly successful in winning the affections of those whom they desire. Scorpio people do not tolerate contradiction, and they can become exceedingly bitter once they are aroused to fury. On the other hand, they can be devoted friends and marriage partners once they have been made to feel secure. Scorpios are blessed with great reserves of strength, which they may draw upon in emergency situations.

Sagittarius, the Archer, November 23 to December 21, is a fire sign. Sagittarius is represented by Chiron, the wise centaur, a half-human, half-horse creature, who taught the ancient Greeks and Romans philosophy, music, and medicine. Freedom and change are the watchwords of Sagittarius people. They often find their minds divided, and they hate to have to make a choice between two courses—thus they usually end by trying to get the best of both. Impulsiveness is second nature to them, and movement and change are essential to their peace of mind. Sagittarians are often able to retain their physical youth into advanced maturity, and they are relatively free of health problems as well.

Capricorn, the Goat, December 22 to January 20, is an earth sign. Capricorn was named first in honor of the ancient Babylonian god, Ea, a part-goat, part fish entity, who emerged from the sea to bring learning and culture to the valley of Mesopotamia. The Romans transformed Ea to Pan, a half-goat, half-human god who ruled the woodlands and the fields. Capricorns are individuals of deeply rooted habits who tend to become industrious and economical individuals with great powers of endurance. Although generally kind, Capricorn people tend to be somewhat moody, often brooding over imagined slights and injuries. Capricorns are liable to feel sorry for themselves, and they may develop into super pessimists unless they are care-ful. A Capricorn needs to keep things carefree and light.

Aquarius, the Water Bearer, January 21 to February 19, is an air sign. Aquarius hearkens back to ancient Egypt and the god Hap, who represented the Nile River, the sustainer of all life. Aquarians are difficult to describe, for they are often moody, untidy, and rather eccentric—while at the same time being highly gifted and intellectual men and women, who contribute much to art, literature, and allied subjects. Aquarians do not fit into the general concept of conventional living, and they make for most interesting, albeit unusual, friends and companions. Aquarians must be free of mental and emotional tensions if they are to be healthy.

Pisces, the Fish, February 20 to March 20, is a water sign. Pisces, the fishes swimming in opposite directions, has been known by that designation since the astrologers of Babylonia named the constellation Two Fishes as long ago as 2000 B.C.E. Although Pisces people are industrious workers, they do not possess a great deal of stamina. It seems that fate often picks on Pisceans, and they are more liable to come into contact with suffering. For this reason, nursing, social work, medicine, and missionary work tend to attract Pisceans, and they are generally willing to make sacrifices for other people. Pisceans must always try to keep their own emotional life on an even keel in order not to disturb their health.

While many people associate astrology only with the brief summaries of the zodiacal signs in their daily newspapers and probably don't affix a great deal of serious attention to the advice provided by astrology columns, there are millions of men and women today who still regard the celestial bodies with the same veneration as did the ancients. Zolar, once described as "the dean of American astrologers," wrote in the preface to his book *It's All in the Stars* (New York: Zolar Publishing, 1962): "Astrology, in its purity, though forming a system of divination, is totally unconnected with either fortune telling or mediumship. It is a divine science of correspondences, in the study and application of which the intellect and intuition become blended in a natural, harmonious manner. They commence to vibrate in unison. When this union becomes complete, the ignorant man becomes the prophetic sage."

Joseph Goodavage, author of *Astrology: The Space Age Science* (1966), began his book with the following declaration: "Over many thousands of years astrologers have deduced a connection between the motions of the planets and positions of the stars with every kind of terrestrial activity. Their ability to predict future trends—even actual events—has been repeatedly demonstrated."

The "Star Gospel," outlined in *The History of Creation and Origin of Species* (1967) by Reuben Luther Katter, attaches religious interpretations to the 12 signs of the zodiac. Katter stated that the Star Gospel, also called Adamic Theology, antedates the Old Testament by 2,500 years. The Star Gospel uses the same 12 zodiacal signs as does astrology, but begins with Virgo and ends with Leo. Katter stated that, according to tradition, Jacob and his 12 sons carried zodiacal tablets and banners into Egypt and carried them out in the exodus. Like astrology, the Star Gospel holds that the 12 signs stand for 12 positions of the Sun in relation to Earth.

THE Chinese zodiac is comprised of a 12-year cycle.

While Western astrology evolved from the Egyptians, Babylonians, Chaldeans, and Greeks, Chinese astrology developed independently of outside influences and was formed around the belief that the emperor was divine. Some scholars of astrology place the beginning of Chinese astrology during the reign of Emperor Fu Hsi around 2800 B.C.E. and attribute the naming of the 12 signs of the Chinese zodiac to a legendary Emperor Yao.

The figures of the Chinese zodiac bear no similarity to those of the West. Each sign is represented by a different animal and is composed of a 12-year cycle. The interpretations of these signs emphasize different animal characteristics from those typical of classic Western stereotypes. For example, while a rat fills a European with revulsion, the Chinese zodiac sees the rodent as hard-working and industrious. In addition, there are five elements—wood, fire, earth, metal, and water—rather than the four of Western astrology—earth, air, fire, and water. The animals of the Chinese zodiac are the rat, ox, tiger, rabbit, dragon, snake, horse, ram, monkey, rooster, dog, and boar. According to tradition, when the Buddha (c. 563–c. 483 B.C.E.) lay dying, he called upon the animals to come to bid him farewell. The first 12 to arrive were the ones who are immortalized in the Chinese zodiac.

Astrology has been an integral aspect of daily life in China for centuries and remains so today. Although Communist doctrine and its rationalistic leaders have attempted to stamp out the influence of astrology and to depict its tenets as nothing more than superstition, the average man or woman in China will still make major decisions based on the guidance received from astrology.

Throughout Western history astrologers have claimed an association with the movements of the planets, comets, and eclipses with every important event that has taken place. Among the more familiar are the appearance of comets at the birth and death of Julius Caesar (c. 100–44 B.C.E.); the advent of World War I (1914) heralded by solar and lunar eclipses; and the birth and death of Mark Twain (1835–1910) coincident with the appearance of Halley's comet. In addition, astrologers have proclaimed the influence of the "stars" on the lives of everyone from Alexander the Great (356–323 B.C.E.) to President George W. Bush (1946–   ).

Many of the great philosophers who shaped the ideals and concepts of the West employed astrology as an aid in developing their thoughts. Individuals such as Pythagoras (c. 580–c. 500 B.C.E.), Aristotle (384–322 B.C.E.), and Ptolemy (127–151) were all astrologers. Nicolaus Copernicus (1473–1543), who gave science its first rational view of the universe, was a doctor, theologian, astronomer, and astrologer.

In the Middle Ages, **magi, alchemists,** scholars, and even the papacy embraced astrology. Pope Julius II (1443–1513) trusted his astrologers to set the date for his coronation; Pope Paul III (1468–1549) was guided throughout life by his horoscope; and Pope Leo X (1475–1521) established a chair of astrology at a major university. Church scholars began to associate the signs of the zodiac with the 12 apostles, and cathedrals throughout Europe were decorated with zodiacal symbols.

Danish astronomer Tycho Brahe (1546–1601), who built the first astronomical observatory in the Western world, practiced and defended astrology. Brahe's exact planetary figures allowed his pupil Johannes Kepler (1571–1630) to work out his great Laws of Motion. Sir Isaac Newton (1642–1727), who followed in Kepler's footsteps, used an eclectic mix of science and astrology to arrive at many of his theories.

Admiral George Dewey (1837–1917) and President Grover Cleveland (1837–1908)consulted astrologers throughout their lives. Psychiatrist Dr. Carl Jung (1875–1961) used astrology charts to assist him in diagnosis and treatment of his patients. John J. O'Neill, science editor of the New York *Herald Tribune*, the first science writer to win a Pulitzer Prize, began as a skeptic and ended up a believer in astrology. Astronomer Gustaf Stromberg (1882–1962) of the Mount Wilson Observatory believed in the charts of astrology as well as the science of astronomy. French psychologist and statistician Michael Gauquelin (d. 1991) spent more than 30 years investigating astrology, exhaustive research that led him to give verification to the importance of the planetary positions at a person's birth. British astronomer and Fellow of the Royal Astronomical Society Percy Seymour (1901–1980) set forth his theory that astrology is neither magical nor mystical—but in fact—magnetic.

During World War II (1939–1945), Allied intelligence knew that Adolf Hitler (1889–1945) and a number of his inner circle of the Nazi High Command, such as his deputy Rudolf Hess (1894–1987) and S.S. chief Heinrich Himmler (1900–1945), took a keen interest in astrology. During the dark days of the

Ptolemy I.

blitz of London, someone in Great Britain's newly established Psychological Research Bureau (PRB) decided that if they had an astrologer in Britain who could make the same calculations that the Nazi astrologers would make, the Allies might be able to ascertain what Hitler intended to do next. Louis de Wohl (1903–1961), the son of an officer in the Royal Hungarian Army, a novelist by profession, was known to be an expert in the field of astrology who had studied the subject for more than 20 years. De Wohl was solicited by the PRB to chart a course in the stars that would help bring about the downfall of the Third Reich. His known opponents on the Nazi side were astrologer Karl Ernst Krafft (1900–1945), graphologist/astrologer Elsbeth Ebertin (1880–1944), and Wilhelm Wulff (1893–1984), Himmler's personal astrologer for the SS.

While de Wohl made some startling hits, such as predicting the date that Germany would invade Holland in 1940, overall he scored only an average number of accurate predictions. However, for whatever astrological accuracy he may have lacked, he more than compensated when he devised the ingenious plan of forging 50 astrological quatrains allegedly from the pen of **Nostradamus**

(1503–1566) in which the great seer predicted the downfall of the Third Reich. These astrological leaflets were then dropped over Germany with the desired demoralizing effect. De Wohl had done such a superb job of imitating the old French seer's unique style in the "newly discovered quatrains" that even Joseph Goebbels (1897–1945), Hitler's propaganda minister who earlier had employed a similar deceit to predict Nazi triumph, was fooled.

Former President Ronald Reagan (1911–   ) and First Lady Nancy Reagan (1921–   ) were devotees of astrology long before their tenure in the White House, as were other actors of their Hollywood set, such as Tyrone Power (1913–1958), Susan Hayward (1918–1975), Marlene Dietrich (1901–1992), Ronald Colman (1891–1958), and Robert Cummings (1908–   ). The Reagans continued to confer with astrologist Joan Quigley regarding important dates and meetings while in office. While some Americans were shocked to learn that their first lady was using the advice obtained from an astrologer to plan her husband's day-to-day schedule, citizens of India seemed to accept calmly the fact that Indira Gandhi (1917–1984), prime minister from 1966 to 1977 and 1980 to 1984, used astrology to assist in decision-making until her death by assassination in 1984.

CHURCH *scholars associated the signs of the zodiac with the 12 apostles.*

Many astrologers feel that the figure of a ship upon the ocean, with no visible paths to follow, no clearly defined turns or alternative routes, and with no landmarks on which to guide itself, is appropriate to describe the methods by which they may assist an individual in a situation that requires decision-making, for, in the majority of decision situations, there can be more than one alternative. The astrological diagram of the zodiac places each individual facing a moment of decision in the center of destiny, represented by a circle, universally known as the symbol of infinity, as

well as perfection. The astrologer then draws radial lines from the individual's position to the circumference, or, poetically, the perimeter of eternity, thus symbolizing the unperceived number of possibilities accessible to him or her. Even if the individual is aware of only 12 of these, as might be illustrated by the houses of the zodiac, it is enough to cause him or her to wish for some sort of "navigator" to help interpret any directional signs that may be present. The art (or science) of astrology, as practiced by a competent astrologist, may serve as one star to be used in making a fix on the chart of destiny.

The astrologer and the celestial navigator have a number of things in common. Both look to the heavens for their points of reference; both make use of charts and tables developed during centuries of observation and recording. Both arrive at their conclusions through mathematical computation. The navigator charts a course, but does not establish a destination. The astrologer casts a horoscope, but does not determine character or destiny.

The role of astrology, so say the astrologers, is comparable to a ship's compass. The compass points the way to a predetermined destination, but it does not establish that destination. As a helmsman turns the ship's wheel to bring the vessel into accord with the compass, so the individual's free will must bring the vessel of his or her life into accord with the findings of astrology, if he or she is to benefit from them. By placing each individual at the center of the zodiac, astrology affirms that person's rightful place at the hub of the wheel of life, and it maintains that there is more in heaven and Earth than is conceived of through various philosophies of the five senses.

Modern astrology recognizes that human beings were not created to be mindless marionettes able to move and act only through the remote direction of forces they cannot comprehend, much less influence. At the same time astrology requires its adherents to accept responsibility for themselves and for their actions. In one sense it imposes an even greater responsibility, for having been made aware of their greatest potentials, according to the best knowledge and techniques available, those who steer their lives by the stars can no longer plead their failures due to blind chance and the fickleness of fate.

According to the astrologer, free will includes the prerogative of individuals to avail themselves of the best advice and direction from any and all sources they deem creditable before embarking on any course, before setting foot on any path, before making any decision, great or small, and to follow through once he or she has decided. Astrology, as practiced today, not only affirms the pre-eminence of free will, but insists upon it; and, according to its adherents, astrology, rightly used, serves as a dependable compass, pointing the way across time.

✤ Delving Deeper

Adams, Evangeline. *Astrology for Everyone*. New York: Dell Books, 1971.

Forrest, Steven. *The Inner Sky: Dynamic New Astrology for Everyone*. New York: Bantam Books, 1984.

Goodavage, Joseph. *Astrology: The Space Age Science*. New York: Signet Books, 1966.

Goodman, Linda. *Linda Goodman's Sun Signs*. New York: Bantam Books, 1985.

Lee, Dal. *Dictionary of Astrology*. New York: Paperback Library, 1968.

Quigley, Joan. *Astrology for Adults*. New York: Holt, Rinehart, Winston, 1978.

Woolfolk, Joanna Martine. *The Only Astrology Book You'll Ever Need*. New York: Madison Books, 2001.

Automatic Writing

On the evening of July 8, 1913, "Patience Worth," who claimed to be the spirit of a seventeenth-century Englishwoman, became a **spirit control** for Pearl Leonore Curran, a young woman in St. Louis, Missouri. Curran was not a practicing **medium,** nor did she have any interest in **Spiritualism,** yet during a period of three years, Patience Worth dictated through the process of automatic writing a stream of proverbs, lyric poetry, and plays, and a number of intricately constructed novels.

Curran's formal education had ended with the eighth grade. She seldom read, had never traveled, and was completely unfamiliar with literary people or people of a scholarly bent. At no time in her life had she ever given any indication of a latent creative gift. Yet, of one of the spirit-dictated novels, a reviewer for the *New York Times* wrote that the plot was fashioned with such skill, deftness, and ingenuity that such talent would be envied by many a novelist "in the flesh." In an anthology of the "best" poetry for the year 1917, Patience Worth had five poems selected, as against three of Amy Lowell's (1874–1925), three of Vachel Lindsay's (1879–1931), and one by Edgar Lee Masters (1869–1950)—all highly respected American poets, critics, and novelists.

Was Patience Worth a spirit or a secondary personality of Curran's? Whoever she was, the large body of literary works that bears her name was transmitted through the process of automatic writing, wherein a medium produces a script without the control of the conscious self—but allegedly under the control of a spirit entity.

The vast majority of those men and women who practice automatic writing on a regular basis do so because they believe that they receive spiritual and material guidance from intelligences in the spirit world or from a higher aspect of their own mind. Most of these individuals cherish this information as highly personal and seldom to be shared with others. Few practitioners of automatic writing seek to channel another "Patience Worth" and produce extensive literary works.

Those who practice automatic writing seat themselves comfortably at a table, a piece of paper before them, a pen or pencil held in their hand in the manner in which they normally write. The tip of the pen or pencil rests lightly on the paper. The writer's wrist and arm are kept loose, the wrist preferably in such a position that it does not touch the table at all. No direct light is allowed to shine on the paper. If necessary, it will be shielded with a piece of cardboard or something similar.

Automatic writers must learn to wait quietly and patiently and then give in to the slightest impulse to move the pen or pencil, keeping the paper smooth with the free hand. It is not necessary—and not even desirable—

Stella Horrocks in an automatic writing session. (FORTEAN PICTURE LIBRARY)

that the writers concentrate on their hand and what it is doing. If the writers do not wish to keep their eyes closed, they may even read a book while experimenting, just to keep their thoughts occupied.

With practice and patience, messages begin coming through. Those individuals who are successful at automatic writing say that it usually takes three or four sittings before the first intelligent results are achieved. They advise beginners that the length of the sittings should not be prolonged unduly, even after meaningful messages have begun to appear.

❀ DELVING DEEPER

Ahmed, Rollo. *The Black Art*. London: Arrow Books, 1966.

Petrie, Jodra. *Tell Fortunes and Predict the Future*. New York: Award Books, 1968.

Post, Eric G. *Communicating with the Beyond*. New York: Atlantic Publishing, 1946.

CARTOMANCY/TAROT

Seeking to foretell the future through a deck of cards (cartomancy) is an old and time-honored practice and a favorite of many professional, as well as amateur, psychics and seers. The exact time and place in which playing cards originated is unknown. However, it is certain that the cards were originally used as tools of divining the future, not for playing games. Some authorities attribute the popularity of using cards to predict the future to the

Gypsies, but it is difficult to separate such an assertion from the many stereotypes of the occult and the mysterious that have been visited upon these nomadic people.

Whether or not the origin of card reading can be attributed to the Gypsies, there is a loose consensus that it was wandering tribes of gypsies who brought the prototype of what is today considered a deck of cards to Europe some time in the fourteenth century. Although it is thought that the Gypsies came west from India by way of Persia, they often claimed that they were originally from Egypt. To make such an association with the ancient mysteries of the Nile added to their status with the Europeans and also increased the aura of the mysterious that they sought to create around themselves. Portraying themselves as diviners in the magical traditions of Egypt, the Gypsies began reading fortunes with picture cards called *atouts* that were popular in Persia. When the deck underwent a transformation in Europe, it was called *tarots*. These decks were similar to modern packs, but there were 78, rather than 52, cards, and the suits were not the familiar diamonds, spades, clubs, and hearts, but swords, cups, coins, and rods. Rather than king, queen, and jack, the tarot deck had 22 picture cards, and the king, queen, knight, and knave (or page) joined the "spot" cards from 10 down to one for each suit.

The theory perhaps closest to the true origin of the tarot cards as they appear today dates from the Renaissance (14th–17th century). Prior to this time, **Gnostics,** who are believed to have introduced the tarot into southern Europe, had to take their faith underground in order to escape persecution. To preserve their teachings, they recorded the fundamentals of their beliefs on a set of 22 plates that depicted the spiritual growth of humankind. Each plate, or card, in the 22 major mysteries (the Major Arcana) told the story of a single aspect of an individual initiate's inner spiritual progress to the state of complete perfection.

The Major Arcana follow humankind's spiritual pilgrimage toward the state of final perfection. The Minor Arcana trace humanity's journey through time. Essential to the understanding of the tarot is the doctrine of reincarnation, which teaches that each soul must experience birth into both sexes and all five races before it can attain final perfection.

The tarot, which some authorities describe as one of the world's oldest books disguised as a pack of playing cards, has remained a popular method of divining the future. Combining esoteric wisdom with the Hebrew system of numbers, many individuals maintain that it is likely that the philosophy of the ancient **Kabbalah** was the spiritual ancestor of the philosophy of the tarot. Enthusiasts in the New Age Movement have rediscovered and embraced the teachings of the Kabbalah and the ancient Egyptian wisdoms believed to be instilled in the cards. Although many authorities have suggested that the tarot cards were adapted from the pages of the legendary Egyptian book of magic, the Book of Thoth—and certain of the imagery on the cards encourages these perceptions—such an assertion cannot be proved. What does appear to be authentic lore in regard to the tarot cards is the fact that the Gnostics, during a period of persecution, recorded the fundamentals of their beliefs on plates similar to the cards of the tarot's Major Arcana. Adepts of the Kabbalah formalized the figures and established 22 allegories to correspond to the 22 letters of the Hebrew alphabet, maintaining that each letter was itself a divine being with occult powers of its own.

In the tarot, the two constituents of the world, or the system of worldly things, are duly represented. The 22 cards of the Major Arcana are concerned directly with the individual. The trump cards allegorize the traits and qualities that combine into personality, the relative conditions of good and evil that constitute a concept of conventional morality, and the substances expressed by the ancients as the four elements comprising a human's physical organism. The tarot is established on the premise that each human being is his or her own macrocosm. Although comprising a distinctive universe in miniature, the individual still functions as a component of the cosmic macrocosm. In the world, humans must have a society, with institutions to perform collectively for them the functions they can-

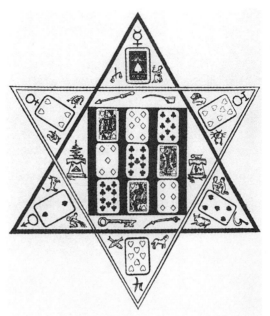

Cartomancy in hexagram used for predictions in the 1893 edition of *The Mystic Test Book*. (FORTEAN PICTURE LIBRARY)

not accomplish as individuals. Again, the situation is the same in the realm of the tarot.

I T is likely the Kabballah was the spiritual ancestor of the philosophy of the tarot.

Seeking to foretell the future through the tarot cards is an extremely ancient means of divination. Each card in the deck has acquired a traditional interpretation over the centuries, and the reader—or person telling the fortune—must become familiar with these meanings in order to give an accurate reading for the querent, the person seeking the foretelling of his or her future. There are many methods of placing or laying out the cards in the course of the reading. The reader may have the querent select a card at random to represent him or her in the reading and the resultant spread may revolve around that particular card. The reader may discover a particular spread or layout of the cards that seems to stimulate his or her psychic awareness and increase the ability to "tune in to" the querent. Some readers prefer to lay out the cards in the pattern of a cross, a circle, or several rows of cards placed in various representations of what the reader

French tarot cards.

(CORBIS CORPORATION)

perceives as best providing him or her with a window to the querent's future.

Here are some basic meanings of the individual cards in the Major Arcana:

The Juggler or Magician (arcanum one) stands with one hand raised to heaven and the other pointing to Earth, thereby confirming the teaching of **Hermes Trismegistus** that what is in heaven is like what is below, that the little world (microcosm) within a human being contains the elements of the universe (macrocosm), and that the study of humankind can lead the adept to an understanding of all creation. The number one signifies the first principle, unity, and in every religion it is the number representing the Divine Being. One is also the number of the soul of nature, the soul of the elements, and the active, causative and creative force of the unseen universe.

The High Priestess (arcanum two) is the most holy card in the tarot deck. It represents humankind's innate ability to interpret the word of God, the highest form of intellectual activity. The High Priestess symbolizes the knowledge hidden in the subconscious of every human being, and her image offers the wisdom that in order to tap the wellspring of occult knowledge, one must search one's own subconscious. Number two stands for the

mother principle and represents the expression of unity through woman (one and one).

The Empress (arcanum three) is the symbol of feminine instinct, a thought or solution that arises directly from the subconscious. The number three is the key that unlocks the door to intuition and is the driving energy that unites positive and negative, male and female. On the material level, the Empress card represents the human aspect of love and symbolizes the sexual conjunction of male and female.

The Emperor (arcanum four) warns that no one can compromise with his or her conscience. The Emperor of wisdom is activated by the fire of the vital force within all humans and regenerated by the alchemical slogan that all nature is regenerated by fire. The number four represents the primordial substance that is the origin of all the universe and is the numerical constituent of all manifestations in the third dimension.

The Hierophant, or Pope (arcanum five), stands for the search for truth and represents all organized religions, education, schooling, and any other kind of formal learning processes. The Pope, the interpreter of sacred mysteries, points the way to the pathways of silence and watchfulness and enables seekers to discover the inherent power of creative ability that lies dormant within them. Number five stands for the universal power of faith over human imagination, the faith to be creatively new.

The Lovers (arcanum six) represents marriage, the love of sibling for sibling, of parent for child, or the mystical bond that unites all those who are alike in soul. Number six signifies spiritual development, charity, and divine love and represents the duality of every problem in terms of both attraction and repulsion.

The Chariot (arcanum seven) driven by the king—its horses and wheels seemingly pulling away from each other, yet drawing the same vehicle—is an allegory of the struggle of the negative and positive forces that operate in all people during their journey toward the spiritual life. The Chariot symbolizes the victory of the inwardly united individual over the obstacles of life. Number seven represents the Fatherhood of God and divine realization.

Justice (arcantun eight), as it is expressed in the tarot's imagery, is not blindfolded. The ancients pictured Justice as a woman of mature age with large, open eyes; it is modern culture that has pictured Justice as blind. Justice also represents self-initiation into life's adversities, during which one looks inwardly and without bias at one's true self. The number eight signifies dualism, positive and negative, and the actions of unseen forces on matter.

The Hermit (arcanum nine) stands for every spiritual seeker in search of himself or herself. The Hermit pursues the lonely path of the awakened soul in his search for truth, guided by his lantern and protected by his staff. In essence, this card represents the experience of self-initiation and signifies wisdom and silence. Nine symbolizes astral light, the matrix of all visible forms of life.

The Wheel of Fortune (arcanum ten) is the card of victory, the sign of obstacles overcome by good fortune and by the active participation of the individual in the activities of the microcosm. The Wheel, or circle, is the symbol of completion, as every human is a closed system within himself or herself. A blind virgin cranked the Wheel, as all humans are controlled by unperceived psychic powers. Humans must learn to use their psychic abilities to control their life, rather than allow their life to be buffeted about in a blind manner.

The Force (arcanum eleven) symbolizes the inner strength by which one may overcome obstacles placed in the path of spiritual progress. Eleven is the number of the Aquarian Age, and represents universal energy—prana. Eleven also symbolizes spiritual will power, vitality, and/or intense strength.

The Hanged Man (arcanum twelve) represents taking on the new and giving up the old. This card allegorizes the prudent adept of arcanum nine (The Hermit), who has now freed himself from the Wheel of Life and Rebirth of arcanum ten. The adept has been elevated to glory through the equation and harmony between the higher and lower selves. Number 12 symbolizes sacrifice and signifies immortality and the elixir of life.

Death (arcanum thirteen) is interpreted as the giving up of old ways, the complete sever-

Female tarot card reader displaying a prediction. (CORBIS CORPORATION)

ance with the past, and the ending of friendships or close associations. Tarot card 13 also signifies discarding old ideas and modes of action. Death's sickle is a symbol of reaping, allegorizing the harvest of what humankind has endured in the physical state. The number 13 is neither lucky nor unlucky when considered by itself, and the number most often signifies a change for the better, a new birth.

Temperance or Patience (arcanum fourteen) signifies a time of waiting, a time for putting aside petty squabbles, a time for learning patience and understanding. Temperance, the Angel of Time, symbolizes hermetic harmony and equilibrium, the working unity of the male and female principles of nature and of humankind; and in humanity, the merger of soul and spirit. The number 14 symbolizes the descent of spirit into matter and represents the activity of humankind in the round of the seasons.

The Devil (arcanum fifteen) represents trouble. Being an individualist, the Devil upset the commandments of heaven, which enforced moral conduct, and so brought turmoil to the masses. He is the symbol of bad luck and of destruction, the antithesis of good. Fifteen signifies destiny and represents the immense force or power in the mind of humankind.

The Tower of Destruction (arcanum sixteen), the Lightning-Struck Tower, depicts pandemonium, bedlam, and disruption. The struck tower symbolizes the dark night of the soul when the spiritually untested and immature seekers are confronted by a dramatic test of their faith. In this respect, the Tower of Destruction has also been referred to as the "Fall of the Angels." The number 16 symbolizes an ending, a move, or a change; therefore, this card can also signify the breaking up of a romance or a love affair.

The Stars (arcanum seventeen) represents good luck or hope. The seven small stars on the card symbolize the universe along with the charity and hope represented by the number seven. The water in the stream before which the woman kneels symbolizes patience, utilized in overcoming obstacles. Above the kneeling woman's head are seven stars, symbols of solar energy directing beneficent rays on the enlightened adept. Directly above the woman's head, the top star—the star of the **Magi**—indicates the challenge presented by youth in its attempt to revitalize the earth. The number 17 represents wisdom and immortality.

The Moon (arcanum eighteen) is the representation of unknown facts, of knowledge obscured, and an interference with the search for hidden knowledge. The Moon's magnetism preserves and generates life, and the dog pictured on the card undoubtedly belongs to Hecate, the goddess of the Moon's darker aspect, or to Diana, goddess of the chase. The Moon itself symbolizes the reflected rays of the subconscious, and the light falling from the Moon signifies the descent of spirit into matter. The number 18 is a sign of trouble, anxiety, failure, and hidden dangers in general.

The Sun (arcanum nineteen) stands for good luck. The Moon (arcanum eighteen) gives insufficient light to illuminate hidden subconscious knowledge, but the Sun brings clarity, resulting in understanding, comprehension, and happiness. It enables adepts to see the essence of their acquired knowledge and fosters further enlightenment. The Sun card symbolizes complete identification with life here and now, and the hope and possibility of a life, or lives, yet to come in a higher state of being.

On *The Judgment* (arcanum twenty), Gabriel's trumpet summons the adept to newness of life, to change. The Judgment is a positive card, bringing portents of goodness and happiness. The man pictured rising from the depths of the earth represents self-consciousness. The woman rising with him symbolizes the subconscious, and the figure of their child represents the regenerated personality of the adept made manifest. The card does not refer to a final or universal judgment, for the earth traveler is summoned to judgment many times by the cyclical workings of karma.

The World (arcanum twenty-one) is the last numbered card of the Major Arcana and presents an allegory of transmutation completed. The adept has reached the ultimate end of his or her journey and has achieved an innate knowledge of all that is good in the universe, which is symbolized by the wreath that surrounds the Virgin. The World card represents honesty and truth, as well as success, harmony, and attainment.

The figure of *The Fool* (arcanum 0), stands for an individual who becomes so involved in the occult sciences that he or she misses the path to spiritual development. The Fool also reminds everyone that they learn from their mistakes. It carries a small pack on a stick, symbolizing the karmic debts which all men and women must carry through life. The Fool warns the wise that the more they know the less they really know, once they have become aware of the vast unknown.

The 56 cards of the Minor Arcana symbolize the four basic component groups of medieval society. The pip cards, therefore, are divided into four suits, each bearing a symbol representing one of these groups. Batons, also known as rods, which once represented the peasant or serf class, have come to be the symbol of money and financial interests. Coins, the card of the merchant or tradesman class, symbolize enterprise and worldly glory. Cups, the symbol of love and happiness, is the tarot representative of the clergy, while swords stand for the medieval nobility and allegorize hatred and misfortune.

Each of the four suits of the Minor Arcana has its own royal family. These are the king, queen, cavalier (knight), and knave (page, young male or female servant). In the world, a king is a man who rules a major territorial unit, one who holds a preeminent position and is a chief among competitors. It is the same in the tarot. The kings of batons, coins, cups, and swords each stand for a powerful male person with superior qualities, knowledge, and abilities in the category represented by his symbol. A queen, in the world and in the tarot, is the female counterpart of a king, and the same may be said for the queen of each respective suit with respect for gender. A cavalier, or knight, is a man upon whom a corresponding dignity has been conferred by a monarch, and in the tarot, represents a young man with qualities much like those of his parents, the king and queen of the same suit. All royal families have servants, and so it is with the rulers of the Minor Arcana suits. The knave in each suit represents either a young man or woman of humbler station than the cavalier, who is at times tricky, even deceitful.

Coins. Coins, or money, is the symbol of enterprise and worldly glory. The king of coins represents a man of refinement, wise in the ways of the marketplace. If the king of coins turns up in an inverted position, he will bring the negative qualities of doubt, fear, and danger.

The queen of money represents the hope of acquiring the ability to overcome obstacles. If inverted, she becomes a sign of evil.

The cavalier of coins symbolizes omens of disunion, discord, or quarrels. If this card turns up with the knight's head downward, its significance is reversed.

The knave, or servant of the house of coins, brings good news. If the knave is dealt upside down, he becomes a bearer of ill tidings.

The "spot" or numbered cards of the suit of coins are interpreted as follows: Ten brings the qualities of confidence, security, and honor. Nine signifies order, discipline, and an ability to plan. Eight is a sign of understanding. Seven promises success in life, gain for one's

enterprises, and a general condition of advantage and profit. Six is read as a sign of a promising undertaking. The five of coins points to gain and riches. Card four predicts a successful enterprise. The three also points to a prosperous enterprise. Two is a happy omen of good fortune. The one signifies a beginning.

Cups. Of more vital concern than money in the lives of most people are love and happiness. The king of cups represents a just man of fair play. Likewise, the queen of cups evokes the image of a well-loved, motherly woman. The knight of cups symbolizes a fair young man who possesses the same qualities as the king and queen. The page symbolizes similar qualities of love and happiness. If any of these cards are dealt inverted, their meaning signifies aspects of distrust and unhappiness.

The ten of cups represents satisfaction in personal accomplishments. The nine means triumph. Eight insures the forthcoming fulfillment of a wish. Seven indicates the presence of fresh concepts or images. The six of cups reveals thoughts of past loves. Five portends a union, possibly marriage. Four indicates displeasure over a relationship. Three is a happy card, promising success. The two of cups symbolizes love, the result of one added to one. The one-spot alludes celebrations and good cheer.

Swords. The tarot cards bearing swords bring associations of power, authority, hatred, and misfortune. The king of swords represents a man of authority, one used to issuing orders and seeing to their execution even if they bring about grief and fear. The queen of swords allegorizes a woman who is malicious, spiteful, selfishly domineering. The knight of swords brings to mind the same dark thoughts as the king and queen. The valet of this ominous suit can be seen as a spiteful, malicious, and prying young man or woman. Inverted, these cards suggest more positive applications of wealth and power.

The ten of swords foreshadows tears, afflictions, and sorrow. The nine is a card of hope. The eight relates to general calamities, such as sickness or injury. The seven reverses the ill omens of its predecessor, with an upsurge of hope and confidence. Six denotes a voyage. Five is a card of sadness and mourning. The four mirrors thoughts of stillness and periods of solitude. The three of swords is the card of severance and removal. The two stands for friendship. The ace is a herald of triumph.

Batons. The batons, also called rods or clubs, are symbols of the peasants or serfs of medieval society. The king of batons epitomizes the self-made man, a symbol of success through hard work. The queen of clubs is a loving woman, but very reserved. The knight of clubs indicates the presence of a helpful person. The valet who attends the royal family of finance is a man or woman of extremely sensitive nature. If any of these cards are inverted, they indicate individuals who may cause severe problems.

The ten of batons depicts gambling for high stakes. Nine indicates a loss of money. Eight brings good luck. The seven is a happy card of profit and gain. The six of batons is a portent of gifts, of gratification of desires. The five reveals thoughts permeated by avarice and greed. Four symbolizes gaiety and the pleasures money can buy. Three is a noble card, representing dignity transcending frivolous, impulsive actions. The two of clubs indicates a loss of money. The ace reveals a state of perfect contentment and triumph.

It is essential to remember that the meaning of any card of the tarot is colored by the interpretation the reader gets clairvoyantly. Although it may often appear that cosmic forces rule the tarot, and that the sequence of a shuffled and cut deck is not accidental, the cards must still be regarded as a device to free the reader's psychically sensitive subconscious and to serve as a generator of spontaneous thought. Its legendary powers exist within, not without, the human psyche.

TELLING FORTUNES WITH MODERN PLAYING CARDS

As with the tarot, each card in the modern deck of playing cards has acquired a traditional interpretation over the centuries, and the reader—or person telling the fortune—has become familiar with these meanings. The next step in the process is to interpret the drawing or placing of each card by the querent (or questioner)—the person seeking the for-

tune—in terms of certain of the cards next to which it appears in the layout or draw.

There are about as many methods of placing or laying out the cards as there are card readers. The reader may have the querent select a card at random to represent him or her in the reading and the resultant spread may revolve around that particular card. The reader may also through the process of trial and error develop a spread or layout that seems to stimulate his or her psychic awareness and increase the ability to "tune in to" the querent. Some readers prefer to draw—or allow the querent to draw—one card at a time and do a free-flowing interpretation. Others like the pattern of a cross, a circle, or several rows of cards placed in various representations of what the reader perceives as best providing a window to the querent's future.

Listed are some basic meanings of the individual cards in the traditional deck—minus the Joker (some readers use this card to represent the querent):

DIAMONDS: Diamonds represent the practical, material side of life, especially money. They can also stand for difficulties that will arise if insufficient energy is expended in the desire to accomplish financial goals.

The ace of diamonds signifies a beginning or an important message that brings money or a gift to the recipient. The king of diamonds represents a man who has achieved material wealth and success. The queen of diamonds is a woman who is noted for her flirtatious nature and her tendency to gossip about others. The jack of diamonds symbolizes a jealous friend or relative.

Regarding the "spot" or numbered cards of the suit of diamonds: Ten brings money—or possibly a journey that will result in financial success. Nine signifies a wish to wander and explore. Eight is a sign of financial success or a marriage that will take place. Seven warns of ill fortune in a financial enterprise. Six is read as an early marriage that is likely to fail. The five of diamonds points to gain and prosperity in business and in marriage. Four predicts that quarrels and disagreements lie ahead. The three points to disputes, quarrels, and potential lawsuits. Two is a happy card of good fortune in both love and business.

HEARTS: Hearts symbolize a strong emotional force that can nullify evil and indicate success in business, as well as in love.

The ace of hearts alludes to happiness in the home. The king of hearts is a just man, remembered for his fair play and his generosity. The queen of hearts evokes the image of a well-loved woman, a mother, faithful wife, or one's true love. The jack symbolizes a reliable and trustworthy friend or relative.

The ten of hearts promises success and good fortune in any project. The nine represents triumph, fulfillment, and success. When the eight turns up, it insures a happy occasion. Seven indicates false hopes. The six reveals a weakness to be overly generous and trusting. Five is a card of indecision. The four of hearts is the card of the bachelor or the spinster. The three is a card of cautions against becoming impetuous or easily angered. The two of hearts symbolizes success in love and in business.

SPADES: Although they have a reputation for being all bad, spades often signify warnings and cautions, rather than predicting actual dire consequences. Generally, though, when spades appear in a spread, they indicate bad luck, financial loss, illness, separation, divorce, even death.

The ace of spades is the card of misfortune, sometimes dramatically named the "death card." The ace may also signal the end of a relationship or a business situation. The king of spades represents a man whose unchecked ambitions may cause him to prove to be a danger. The queen of spades allegorizes a woman who is malicious, spiteful, selfishly domineering. The jack of spades can be seen as a spiteful and prying young man or woman, who only pretends to be a friend.

The ten of spades is an unlucky card that foreshadows tears, afflictions, and sorrows. The nine of spades is regarded as the absolute worst card in the pack and indicates forthcoming illness, loss of money, the infidelity of a loved one, or the failure of a business. The eight warns about false friends. The seven cautions one to avoid misunderstandings with friends and relatives. Six of spades is associated with discouragements, but the card also offers the hope of overcoming troubles through perseverance. Five is a lucky card representing business success and a happy marriage. The four of spades indicates a brief illness, temporary financial reverses, and warns against the petty jealousy of others. The three of spades is an unhappy card of severance and separation in love or marriage. The two indicates a complete separation from loved ones, the loss of a home, or a death.

CLUBS: While clubs most often symbolize friendship, they also warn of hypocrisy and treachery. Although clubs are generally good cards, they may advise caution in any life situation that involves placing too much trust in fair-weather friends.

The ace of clubs reveals a state of perfect contentment and triumph. It is a card of wealth, fame, and success in a chosen profession. The king of clubs represents a man who, though sometimes a rival, is a valuable friend. The queen of clubs is a woman who is occasionally temperamental, but who can always be relied upon to be loyal in love or in friendship. The jack signifies a generous, sincere, and constant friend whose devotion is never in question.

The ten of clubs is a strong good luck card. Nine indicates a loss of money and a variety of other troubles, including serious disputes with friends or family members. Eight of clubs warns against incurring bad debts. The seven is a happy card of profit and gain. The six of clubs is the partnership card, a sure portent of success based on a trustworthy friendship. The five is a marriage card, usually representing a happy future for both parties. Four symbolizes danger or a sudden misfortune or failure. Three is a sign of a second marriage and possibly a third. The two of clubs is an unwelcome card, indicating a loss of money or friendship.

How often may the cards be consulted by the querent? Most card readers answer that question by saying as often as the client wishes. Generally, repeat deals or readings should only be done to clarify questions left unanswered or unclear.

Delving Deeper

Cirlot, J. E. *A Dictionary of Symbols*. New York: Barnes & Noble, 1993.

Water divining instruments. (CORBIS CORPORATION)

Gibson, Walter B., and Litzka R. Gibson. *The Complete Illustrated Book of the Psychic Sciences*. Garden City, N.Y.: Doubleday & Co., 1966.

Karcher, Stephen. *The Illustrated Encyclopedia of Divination*. Rockport, Mass.: Element Books, 1997.

Louis, Anthony. *Tarot Plain and Simple*. St. Paul, Minn.: Llewellyn Publications, 1996.

Petrie, Jodra. *Tell Fortunes and Predict the Future*. New York: Award Books, 1968.

Waite, Arthur E. *A Manual of Cartomancy and Occult Divination*. Kessinger Publishing, 1997.

Dowsing

Dowsing, scientifically known as radioesthesia, is the interaction of the mind of the dowser and the energy of the object of interest. Most dowsing is used to find water and minerals. It has been used to find lost objects, even people. The ability to find people, artifacts, or substances by use of maps, pictures, or physically being in a place are currently the most popular applications of dowsing.

DOWSING, *or radioesthesia, is used to find water and minerals.*

The method of dowsers seldom varies. They grasp the ends of a forked twig (peach, apple, maple traditionally work best, though some modernists say a bent metal coat hanger works just as well) with palms upward. As they begin their search for water, they carry the butt of the stick pointed upward. When they near water, they can feel the pull as the butt end begins to dip downward. When the dowsers are over the water, the twig has been bent straight down, having turned through an arc of 180 degrees. A stick of brittle wood will break under the grip of a dowser as the butt moves downward. Pliable twigs will twist themselves downward despite an effort to hold them straight.

Few manifestations of so-called psychic ability have been more hotly debated than that of dowsing. On the one hand is the pronouncement of the scientific community which declares that locating water by means of a forked stick is utter nonsense, and on the other side of the argument are those men and women who go ahead and locate water with their forked maple twigs, completely impervious to the ridicule visited upon them by the skeptics. They could not care less whether or not a laboratory technician believes that water cannot be found in such a manner. All they know is that it works and that they have been finding water in just that way for years.

Novelist Kenneth Roberts stated in his book, *Henry Gross and His Dowsing Rod* (1951): "Not all the derision of all the geologists in the world can in any way alter the unfailing accuracy of the dowsing rod in Henry Gross's hands. Not all the cries of 'hokum,' 'fanciful delusion,' 'hoax,' 'pseudoscience' can destroy or even lessen the value of Henry's dowsing...."

In 1953, UNESCO sponsored a committee of prominent European scientists in their study of radioesthiesa. Their carefully considered consensus was that "there can be no doubt that it is a fact." The Academie des Sciences of Paris has commented that "it is impossible to deny the existence of the power, although its nature cannot be determined." Five Nobel Prize winners have endorsed dowsing, and so has the Institute of Technical Physics of the Dutch National Research Council.

In Germany in 1987 and 1988, more than 500 dowsers participated in more than 10,000 double-blind tests conducted by physicists in a barn near Munich. The researchers who held the so-called "Barn" experiments claimed that they had empirically proved that dowsing was a real phenomenon. However, subsequent analysis of the data by other scientists raise the argument that the results could reasonably be attributed to chance, rather than any kind of unknown psychic ability to find water or hidden objects.

✤ DELVING DEEPER

Baum, Joseph. *Beginners Handbook of Dowsing*. New York: Random House, 1974.

Bird, Christopher. *Divining Hand: The 500-Year-Old Mystery of Dowsing*. Atglen, Pa.: Whitford Press, 1993.

Carroll, Robert Todd. "Dowsing (a.k.a. water witching)." *The Skeptic's Dictionary*. [Online] http://skepdic.com/dowsing.html. 8 March 2002.

Graves, Tom. *Diviner's Handbook: A Guide to the Timeless Art of Dowsing*. Rochester, Vt.: Inner Traditions, 1990.

Roberts, Kenneth. *Henry Gross and His Dowsing Rod*. Garden City, N.Y.: Doubleday & Co., 1951.

Webster, Richard. *Dowsing for Beginners: The Art of Discovering Water, Treasure, Gold, Oil, Artifacts*. St. Paul, Minn.: Llewellyn Publications, 1996.

GRAPHOLOGY

Graphology or handwriting analysis is based upon the interpretation of certain signs and symbols to be found in a specimen of handwriting. In the view of a graphologist, the complicated mental, physical, and psychic machinery known as human beings betray so much detail about themselves in their handwriting because the actual process of handwriting begins in the mind, with thought. All handwriting is first an idea that becomes a desire to communicate that thought to paper. Graphologists perceive handwriting analysis as a doorway to the subconscious. As such, not only conscious but subconsciously formed habit patterns and personality traits show up in an individual's handwriting.

Because handwriting reveals the inner person through his or her subconscious, graphologists believe that there are universal symbols that are evident in handwriting, beginning as early as a child's first attempts at writing. For

King Faria, a water witch, holds a divining rod made of weeping willow. (CORBIS CORPORATION)

example, if in a child's handwriting analysts were to observe angular patterns formed like the points of arrows or spears, they would have little difficulty recognizing such formations as likely symbols of aggression. There has been some conflict within the ranks of graphology on the question of whether or not pre-writing scribbles may indicate personality traits in children. A scribble, as defined by graphologists, is a spontaneous discharge of energy. It is not meant to convey a message, and children make them for the sheer joy of it. To children, scribbling is simply a means of expression. They leave on the paper, therefore, a record of their prevailing mood, whether joy or unhappiness. Likewise, if they are angry, they may sit down and make motions on a piece of paper resembling the slashing actions of a knife.

HANDWRITING analysis is perceived as a doorway to the subconscious.

Graphologists are convinced that handwriting analysis can reveal an individual's innermost thoughts, motivations, and desires. The handwriting of individuals with an advanced psychosis and extreme neurosis would differ from that of an "average" person. In psychosis, the analyst would see traits that are considered normal, but they would be exaggerated, amplified, carried to such lengths that they would become, then, undesirable traits. For example, in the case of a schizophrenic, where the personality has separated itself from the everyday world and formed another world of its own, a graphologist would expect to see the handwriting symbols for imagination exaggerated to a tremendous degree. In the case of the extreme neurotic, the differences are again quantitative, rather than qualitative, dealing with a blown-up effect on one trait, and perhaps, a diminished, or totally absent, symbol trait which could balance the overemphasized qualities of the other.

Normal handwriting would, therefore, have to show the balance missing in neurotic or psychotic handwriting. A balanced handwriting would be the outward manifestation of a balanced mind. Leftward movement of the handwriting indicates a writer who has a tendency to live in the past and to be of a passive disposition. Rightward movement usually reveals a writer who is future-minded and somewhat aggressive.

The degree to which individuals have balanced their tendencies and personality traits is an invaluable clue to a prospective employer, and many companies and businesses have begun employing a graphologist on their staff. Graphologists maintain that an employer can get an indication as to how an individual will react under stress and determine whether or not a person in their employ would act in a violent, antisocial manner in moments of excitement in dealing with customers. To illustrate the above point, graphologists have shown how prospective embezzlers would give themselves away by their handwriting. The oval letters—the "o," the "a," and in certain cases, the oval formations on the small letters "p" and "d"—would be opened up at the bottom. It would appear as though someone had come along and erased the bottom of these letters, suggesting that the embezzlers want to fill up the holes with some money.

The above signs constitute a general rule and should not be regarded as universal or absolute. A cautious and discreet graphologist would be careful never to make a definite finding on the basis of only a few signs, but many handwriting analysts believe that company executives in charge of hiring could gain helpful information about prospective employees by looking for such signs as the following.

Small writing shows either the ability or the potential for a high degree of concentration. Narrow, peaked connecting strokes between words are an expression of withdrawal.

Introverted people are likely to sign their names far to the left of the main body of a piece of writing, continuing a general leftward trend.

Graphologists believe that even a glance at the white spaces to the left and right and above and below the written matter provides instant insight into the writer's personality. For example, if a left margin starts out narrow and widens as the lines of writing proceed down the page, the body of the writing should normally reveal, among other things, indications of enthusiasm, optimism, and generous spending habits. The left margin represents the beginning point for the writer's activities. If the lines of writing are begun far to the right of the page's left edge, the writer's pen had to make a considerable "leap" before tracing the first word. Individuals who begin writing in this way are also prone to "leap" enthusiastically into their undertakings.

If the left margin of the writing is overly wide, the writer may have erected a facade to conceal true feelings.

Since the hand must travel from left to right to execute a line of writing, a narrow left margin indicates a reluctance to move into the realm of action. The complete absence of a left margin may symbolize the writer's subconscious desire to return to an infantile state of dependency.

Individuals who set themselves apart from others because of snobbishness or pride leave inordinately wide left margins, but the graphologist must be careful, for such margins are also characteristic of the writing of shy persons.

If the left margin widens as the writing proceeds down the page, it is a sign of haste and a nervous nature. If, on the other hand, the left margin narrows as the lines descend, it shows that the writer suffers from fatigue, physical weakness, or perhaps, illness. Such a margin is also the sign of psychological or physiological depression.

The right margin symbolizes destinations reached, goals achieved, and the writer's attitude toward the future. In contrast to the left margin, which corresponds to the false front individuals may use to hide their feelings, the right margin reveals a genuine desire to be close or distant to the other people they contact in the course of living life. A wide right margin shows that the writer actually prefers to remain distant, while a narrow right margin shows a genuine desire for close relationships.

The idea of graphotherapeutics began in the early part of the twentieth century when a number of psychologists, psychiatrists, doctors of medicine, and graphologists cooperated in a study of the reciprocal effects of personality and handwriting. They interpreted symbols in handwriting as having been formed by a sort of feedback process. Not only does the mind influence or shape handwriting, but handwriting can also shape the mind. The flow of electrical energy in the form of nerve impulses throughout the nerves and various nerve endings also returns to the mind along other neural pathways. Working under this premise, when people see what they know to be an undesirable trait appearing in their handwriting, they can change the trait by changing their handwriting.

When handwriting experts in police laboratories examine a suspected forger's signature or an alleged note left by a suicide victim, the first problem they face is to determine the writer's special characteristics. Even skilled forgers may not be able to see the subtle marks, pressures, slanting, and shading that an expert graphologist will perceive almost at a glance. The FBI Laboratory and laboratories of state and city police departments keep on file all extortion and ransom notes, all threatening and defamatory letters, and all messages that threaten bombings, arson, or personal attacks on individuals. As strange as it may seem, criminals of all kinds who once put their demands or threats in writing will most often do so again.

A famous case that demonstrates how graphology can be effective in solving crimes

occurred on July 4, 1956, when Mrs. Morris Weinberger, a young mother of two, left her 33-day-old baby, Peter, in his carriage on the patio in the backyard of their home in Westbury, Long Island. Although she had been gone for only 15 minutes, when she returned she found the carriage empty and a ransom note that stated a demand for $2,000 and was signed, "Your Baby Sitter." In spite of her broadcast pleas for the return of their child, no further demands were issued by the kidnapper until July 10, when the Weinbergers received a telephone call and a second note.

Under the law at that time, the FBI could not enter a kidnapping case until seven days had passed. Once that time period had been observed, experts began immediately to study the kidnapper's notes. It was decided that the ransom notes had been written on a piece of paper that appeared to have come from a lined tablet designed for use in writing public records. Among distinctive aspects of the kidnapper's writing, there was a peculiarly looped capital "P," a rounded "A" with a short tail, and a capital "Y" that was strangely bold.

Six weeks after little Peter Weinberger had been taken from his carriage, a group of handwriting analysts managed to match the handwriting on the ransom note to that of a signature by a man who had received a suspended sentence. It was the 1,974,544th document that had been studied during the desperate search for baby Peter.

Tragically, the kidnapper, Angelo John LaMarca, who lived five miles from the Weinbergers, had thought he could solve his money problems by snatching a rich family's child. LaMarca had panicked on August 23rd and left the baby in a dense thicket to die. The kidnapper was found guilty of murder and died in the electric chair.

Although handwriting analysis may provide valuable leads that in some cases may lead to the discovery of the perpetrator of a crime and that person's subsequent arrest, the testimony of graphology by itself has not been accepted by appellate courts in the United States. In spite of the claims made by graphologists, the courts have ruled that it does not meet the requirements of the kind of science

Woman consulting with the book *I Ching* and using fortune sticks.
(FORTEAN PICTURE LIBRARY)

that may be relied upon in a court of law. In those instances where a person's employment may have hinged upon a graphoanalytical evaluation, plaintiffs may sue an employer who used graphology in an employment decision.

❋ DELVING DEEPER

"The Legal Implications of Graphology." *Washington University Law Quarterly.* [Online] http://ls.wustl.edu/WULQ/75-3/753-6.html. 20 May 2002.

Loth, David. *Crime Lab.* New York: Julian Messner, 1964.

Lowe, Sheila R. *The Complete Idiot's Guide to Handwriting Analysis.* New York: Alpha Books, 1999.

McNichol, Andrea. *Handwriting Analysis: Putting It to Work for You.* New York: McGraw Hill, 1994.

Santoy, Claude. *The ABC's of Handwriting Analysis: A Guide to Techniques and Interpretations.* New York: Marlowe & Co., 2001.

I CHING

The I Ching or Book of Changes has been used as a method of divination for more than 5,000 years, and in spite of its venerable age, modern enthusiasts insist that it is the most sophisticated method of predicting future events ever devised. Querents approach the I Ching with such questions as "What does the future hold for me?" "Should I marry now?" and throw coins. Each coin is assigned a number, so the results of the tosses are totaled to find the corresponding hexagram to learn the answers to the inquiries. The "book" consists of 64 hexagrams, each comprising six broken or unbroken lines. Although the text accompanying the I Ching does not refer to the two primal cosmic principles—the yin and the yang—in essence, the philosophical premise of the I Ching does hold that the broken line and the unbroken line can represent any pair of polar opposites, such as male/female, light/dark, and so forth.

Those who believe in the wisdom of I Ching maintain that within the 64 sections there exist teachings for every possible situation that anyone will encounter throughout his or her life. Within the hexagrams are represented numerous archetypal situations in catergories such as "The Rise to Power," "Proper Relationships," "Negativity," and so forth. The hidden meanings of the hexagrams were divined by ancient Chinese sages who were in tune with the philosophy of the Tao, which views human beings as creatures of nature and teaches that instincts, feelings, and imagination should be allowed to have free reign. Taoism is in sharp contrast to Confucianism, which envisions humankind as rational and moral creatures who have responsibilities to their society. The essential philosophy of Taoism is that the natural world and the Tao are one.

Those who rely on the I Ching as their dependable window to the future explain that they find this method of divination to be superior to all others because, as its name implies, it recognizes the difficulty of focusing on events that have not yet occurred and it takes into account the likelihood of changes that may most certainly occur. In fact, the basic premise of I Ching is that every situation in the panorama of human events has within its context an inherent tendency to change. While some may despair and complain that the only thing constant in life is change, those who rely on I Ching agree—but remain confident that changes occur within cycles and that these cycles may be observed, predicted, and acted upon.

❋ DELVING DEEPER

Carroll, Robert Todd. "I Ching." In *The Skeptic's Dictionary.*[Online] http: //skepdic.com/iching.html. 9 March 2002.

Dening, Sarah. *The Everyday I Ching.* New York: St. Martin's Press, 1997.

Seabrook, Myles. *I Ching for Everyone.* New York: Barnes & Noble, 1998.

Wilhelm, Helmut, Richard Helmut, and Irene Eber. *Understanding the I Ching.* Princeton: Princeton University Press, 1995.

KABBALAH

The Kabbalah (also Cabala, Kabala, Kaballah, Qaballah, etc.) is a mystical Jewish tradition that teaches that the elect of God shall know both Him and the universe and will be raised above common knowledge to a spiritual level where they will understand the secrets of Holy Writ and creation through symbolic interpretation. Kabbalists affirm that the elect shall discover in the ancient texts whatever they choose, and they have the right to assert that the things they discover had been in the sacred scriptures from the beginning.

THE *Kabbalah emerged as a text of power and influence in the thirteenth century.*

Letters and numbers, the Kabbalah teaches, are not merely signs invented by humans to record things, events, and thoughts, but are in themselves reservoirs of divine power. Hebrew, in the Kabbalistic sense, is a universal language, capable of restoring to humankind the universal understanding that existed before the confusion of tongues at the Tower of Babel. It is interesting to note that the Greek school of neo-Pythagorean philosophers also understood numbers and letters to be divine things endowed with supernatural powers.

The Kabbalah began to emerge as a text of power and influence in Spain and southern France in the thirteenth century. Many of its teachers proclaimed that the Kabbalah (Hebrew for "received tradition") had been given by God to Moses (14th–13th century B.C.E.) on Mt. Sinai along with the Torah, and generations of **magi, alchemists,** and magicians believed this claim to be true and revered the ancient texts as a legacy of the Creator to humankind, the apex of His creation. Contemporary scholarship suggests that rather than a divinely authored text, the Kabbalah was a product of the earlier mystical tradition of the Maaseh Bereshit and Maaseh Merkavah, both of which would only be taught to one stu-

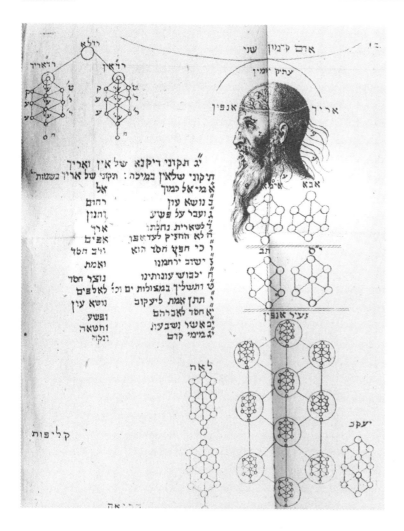

אדם קדמין שני

עתיק ימין

אנפין

אריך

יג תקוני דיקנא של אין ואריך
תיקוני שלאין במילה : תקוני של אריך בשמות
אל מי-אל כמוך
רחום נושא עון
וחנון ועבר על פשע
ארך לשארית נחלתו
אפים לא החזיק לעד אפו
ורב חסד כי חפץ חסד הוא
ואמת ישוב ירחמנו
נוצר חסד יכבוש עוונותינו
לאלפים ותשליך במצולות ים וכי
נושא עון תתן אמת ליעקב
ופשע חסד לאברהם
וחטאה אשר נשבעת
ונקה מימי קדם

אבא

חב

געיא אנפין

לאה

יעקב

קליפות

אור

Engraving from *Kabbala Dnudata Seu Dotrina Hebraeorum Transcendentalis et Metaphysica Atove Theologica* **by** Christian Knorr von Rosenroth, 1677. (FORTEAN PICTURE LIBRARY)

dent at a time. The Maaseh Bereshit (Hebrew for "work of creation") dealt with the divine utterances that brought the universe into being and how control of these sounds or letters would grant great magical powers over the material substance of the world. Maaseh Merkavah (Hebrew for "work of the chariot") attempted to utilize the mystical practices of heavenly ascent achieved by Ezekial in his vision of the fiery chariot and the throne of glory in heaven. After a period of intense preparation, including fasting, meditation, chanting, and the recitation of certain letter combinations and the names of angels, the adept of Maaseh Merkavah sought to attain a vision of the divine throne of God and to become transformed from human to angel.

Combined with the Maaseh Merkavah and the Maaseh Bereshit to form the Bible of the Kabbalists was the Zohar (Hebrew for "splendor"), which was ascribed to the follow-

ers of Simeon Bar Yochai, who was said to have recorded the mystical teachings of Elijah during the years the prophet spent hiding in a cave. Moses De Leon who claimed to possess a copy of the ancient manuscript, published The Zohar in the thirteenth century. After De Leon's death, however, his wife admitted that he had attributed his own writings to Simeon Bar Yochai in order to assure sales to those interested in such ancient magical texts. Modern scholars concede that while the Zohar splendidly depicts the spiritual reality that lies behind everyday experience in the material world, there are many passages that betray the influence of Spanish culture of the thirteenth century and were likely written at that time by De Leon.

The influence of the Kabbalah on mystical Judaism, as well the European alchemists, scholars, and philosophers of the Middle Ages, was powerful and all pervasive, and the text remained a source of strength and inspiration to seekers of enlightenment for many centuries. As the influence of the Christian Church grew stronger throughout all of Europe, the Kabbalah and those who taught its mysteries retreated into the shadows of universities and libraries; and for many scholars, the text was regarded as one of the esoteric and sometimes forbidden hidden works of ancient wisdom. In the twentieth century, Carl G. Jung (1875–1961) introduced the Kabbalah to the psychotherapeutic community and spoke highly of its value in achieving a sense of wholeness with the universe.

Study of the Kabbalah underwent a dramatic rebirth of interest in the 1960s when there was both a resurgence of Jewish spirituality and an interest in the mystic teachings of the Kabbalah by many individuals in the New Age Movement. The appeal of the Kabbalistic teachings to those seekers in the New Age lay to a great extent in the understanding that God's essence may emanate through various realms of existence and that each human may draw from that supreme power to help bring the act of creation to its final perfect state. Many Kabbalistic groups sprang up around the country utilizing the ancient teachings to assist their members to achieve deeper states of meditation, to accomplish healings of

Will the Red Heifer Bring About Armageddon?

◆ In March 2002, a red heifer was born in Israel that some Jewish traditionalists, as well as Christian and Muslim fundamentalists, believe could bring about the end of the world in 2005. According to ancient Jewish teachings, it was only the ashes of a flawless red heifer that could purify worshippers who went into the Temple in Jerusalem. The First Temple was destroyed by Nebuchadnezzar in 586 B.C.E.; the Romans demolished the Second Temple in 70C.E. Without a flawless red heifer to sacrifice to purify the Temple Mount, the Third Temple could not be rebuilt and the Messiah could not come.

Fundamentalist Christians shared the excitement of the birth because they believe that after Jesus Christ (c. 6 B.C.E.–c. 30 C.E.) has returned and defeated the forces of evil at the battle of **Armageddon,** he will begin his millennial reign from the Third Temple—which could not be rebuilt until the Temple Mount had been purified by the ashes of the red heifer.

The genetically engineered red heifer born in 1996 created a great deal of tension in Jerusalem, for Muslim leaders were concerned that fundamentalist Jews and Christians might use the sign of the calf's arrival as a signal to take over the Temple Mount, which the Muslims have occupied since 1967. Muslims revere the Temple Mount as the place where Muhammad (c. 570–632) ascended into heaven; and in 685, followers of the Prophet began constructing the 35-acre site known as the Noble Sanctuary, which today includes the Dome of the Rock and the al Aqsa mosque.

Once again, traditional rabbinical scholars insist that the three-year waiting period be observed, which means in their religious belief, that if no hairs of any other color have appeared in the heifer, it is of divine origin and may be sacrificed to purify the Temple Mount and construction on the Third Temple may begin. As Rod Dreher writing in the *National Review Online* put it: "You don't have to believe that a rust-colored calf could bring about the end of the world…but there are many people who do, and are prepared to act on that belief."

Sources:

Dreher, Rod. "Red-Heifer Days." *National Review Online,* April 11, 2002. [Online] http://www.nationalreview.com/script/printpage.asp?ref′dreher/ dreher041102.asp.

Unterman, Alan. *Dictionary of Jewish Lore and Legend.* London: Thames and Hudson, 1991.

themselves and others, and to reach higher levels of mystical insight.

✦ DELVING DEEPER

Berg, Yehuda. *The Power of Kabbalah*. San Diego, Calif.: Jodere Group, 2002.

Kaplan, Aryeh. *Meditation and Kabbalah*. New York: Weiser, 1989.

Scholem, Gershom. *Kabbalah*. New York: Penguin Group, 1978.

Spence, Lewis. *Encyclopedia of Occultism*. New Hyde Park, N.Y.: University Books, 1960.

Unterman, Alan. *Dictionary of Jewish Lore and Legend*. New York: Thams and Hudson, 1991.

NECROMANCY

Necromancy involves the evocation of spirits of deceased individuals for the purpose of divination. Some magicians believed that spirits could only be summoned during the first year of that person's death. Necromancy was forbidden by the Laws of Moses, but even the great king Saul (11th century B.C.E.) sought the advice of the prophet Samuel through the **mediumship** of the **Witch of Endor.** The Christian clergy also condemned the practice since the earliest days of the church. None of these warnings and proclamations have prevented sorcerers and **magi** from attempting to evoke the spirits of the dead through a variety of rituals.

A spirit could not be called without the magician first taking steps to protect himself. Should he not do this, his soul would be in danger. Protection took the form of **talismans,** seals, special powdered concoctions, and, most importantly, the magic circle. As long as the magician stood within the magic circle, he was invulnerable to whatever spirit entity he managed to call up.

A variety of circles were used. Sometimes a triple circle was drawn, the diameter of each concentric circle being six inches less than the one surrounding it. The outermost circle was marked at four equidistant points for north, south, east, and west. Magical words were written at each point: "Agial" at the eastern, "Tzabaoth" at the southern, "Jhvh" at

the western, and "Adhby" at the northern. Between each of these points a pentacle, or five-pointed star, was drawn.

The magician placed his brazier of lighted charcoal at the eastern point, in the smallest circle. Then his altar, its center plumb with the center of the brazier, was equipped. Upon the altar were the ritual tools, including salt water, incense, candles, and herbs appropriate to his specific undertaking. Lighted candles would also be placed around the outside circle. Each tool was carefully consecrated and wrapped in white linen.

In the circle with him, the magician would have prepared the proper talismans. Inscribed also within the circle were the seals of the spirits to be evoked. Next, a triangle was drawn to the side of the magic circle, and it was in this triangle that the spirit would manifest. The magician then commenced with the conjuration, the first order of business being the evocation of the magician's own guardian spirit. This was a further assurance of protection. Then the evocation of the planetary spirit was attempted.

Still other rites demanded that the magician draw a circle containing Solomon's seal (Star of David) with a rectangle superimposed over it, a cross within the center diamond formed by the seal. Solomon's seal was especially recommended for summoning air spirits. According to Peter of Abano (an occult author who lived from 1250 to 1318), this summoning should take place when the moon is waxing. Abano also recommended the inscription of four concentric circles for the invocation of good spirits. This should be done in the first hour of a Sunday in springtime. The names inscribed in the circles were Varcan, the Lord's king-angel of the air, and Tus, Andas, and Cynabel, who are the Lord's holy ministers. The highest angels of Sunday, according to Abano, are Michael, Dardiel, and Huratapal. The north wind carries these angels, and they can be invoked by magical ceremonies employing incense made of red sanders.

✦ DELVING DEEPER

Ahmed, Rollo. *The Black Art*. London: Arrow Books, 1966.

De Grivy, Emile Grillot. *A Pictorial Anthology of Witchcraft, Magic & Alchemy*. New Hyde Park, N.Y.: University Books, 1960.

Levi, Eliphas. *Transcendental Magic*. London: Rider & Co, 1958.

Waite, Arthur Edward. *The Book of Ceremonial Magic*. New Hyde Park, N.Y.: University Books, 1960.

Numerology

According to numerologists, each number possesses a certain power that exists in the occult connection between the relations of things and the principles in nature which they express. All that humans are capable of experiencing can be reduced to the digits one through nine. These single numbers are derived from the simplification of all combinations of numbers to their basic essence. This essence then vibrates through the single digit.

Because numerology became popular among New Age diviners in the 1970s, many people who have been introduced to the technique for the first time believe that it is of recent origin. On the contrary, numerology is among the oldest of the psychic sciences, and numerological divination and number charms are found in India, Greece, Egypt, China, and Europe.

Pythagoras (c. 580–c. 500 B.C.E.), the great Greek mathematician and mystic, proclaimed that the very world is built upon the magical power of numbers. According to his doctrines, numbers contained within them the essence of all that is in the natural and the spiritual worlds. For those who followed the teachings of Pythagoras, the number one symbolized unity and therefore the Creator-God. Two represented the duality of good and evil and stood for the devil. Four, symbolizing balance, was considered by Pythagoreans as their most holy and sacred number, and their most solemn oaths were sworn on four. Pythagoreans also used numbers to represent various planets and elements. For example, five stood for fire; six, earth; eight, air; twelve, water.

In addition to the teachings of Pythagoras, Cornelius Agrippa's (1486–1535) work *Occult Philosophy* (1533) quite likely furnished the basis for much of the belief in numerology practiced in the Western world. Agrippa also emphasized the powers inherent in numbers and even prescribed certain numbers as tools in banishing evil, promoting healing, and summoning benign spirits. The energy found in the number five, for instance, could exorcise demons and serve as an antidote to poisons.

Numerology *is among the oldest of the psychic sciences.*

Contemporary numerologists use their various systems to produce assessments of an individual's personality traits, behavior patterns, and to describe compatibility and a possible course of future events for their clients. Depending upon the numerological system, the first and most important number derives from one's birth date and is determined by reducing the numbers of that date into single digits. Beyond this cycle of nine, though, are the two Master Numbers 11 and 22. These never are reduced to single digits. Take the following birthdate for purposes of illustration:

March 29, 1985
3 11 23
3 + 11 + 5 = 19
1 + 9 = 10

The number has been found in this manner: March, the third month, provides the number 3. The day gives 2 + 9 = 11. 1 + 9 + 8 + 5 = 23. Three reduces no further. Eleven does not reduce, being a Master Number. Twenty three (2 + 3) reduces to 5; 3 + 11 + 5 = 19, 1 + 9 = 10 reduces to 1.

The number one, then, is the most important number in this person's life. It is his or her destiny, which cannot be changed, but which he or she does have the ability to direct. From this number, individuals may determine their potential; their hidden aptitudes, talents, and desires; and their specific mission in life.

According to numerology, there are specific meanings for each number, with both positive and negative aspects. Interpretations of the nine numbers may vary with the individual numerologist, but here, briefly, are some basic meanings for each number:

1—Number one people are independent and need to be, as they tend to be the oak that shelters multitudes. They must control and direct their body, mind, and spirit to the utmost efficiency. They should accept no limitations, yet they must learn to cooperate without losing their individuality. The negative aspect of the number one lies in the danger of emphasizing the needs of self over others.

2—People of the number two will naturally follow the lead of others. Those with this number become excellent diplomats, peacemakers, and go-betweens. Here, as opposed to the number one, the attraction is to groups, to communities. The number two is a perfect wife or husband, for all other numbers are compatible with them. The negative aspect of number two lies in the hazard of withdrawing from others and becoming extremely self-effacing.

NUMEROLOGISTS assessed personality traits, behavior patterns, and describe compatibility and a possible course of future events.

3—Those on this path through life have discovered the joy of living. They will tend to find their opportunities on the lighter side of life, in circulating and socializing. An artistic environment is best for the three personalities as they are always seeking expression through writing, speaking, or art. The negative polarity for the number three personality is to become superficial.

4—These people are the builders, those who start with a firm foundation and build something of lasting importance. People who are "fours" serve patiently and dependably and are capable of great achievements. They do the job at hand, striving to perfect the form of the task before them. The opposite polarity for the four personality is to become distant and removed from others.

5— Those with the number five as their destiny must be prepared for frequent, unexpected change and variety. Five personalities do a lot of traveling and learn to understand all classes and conditions of people, and they are generally without racial prejudice. Five people always are seeking the new and progressive. Number five personalities must guard against becoming self-indulgent.

6—Because six is the number of devotional, impersonal love, these people serve quietly, cheerfully, and efficiently, applying the law of balance to adjust inharmonious conditions. People often come to six personalities for material or spiritual aid, and they must always be ready to give it. Some persons with a six life-path are musically endowed, but their real love is for the home and the harmony therein. The opposite polarity for the six personality is to become tyrannical.

7—Seven is a cosmic number related to the seven planets, seven days of the week, seven colors, and seven notes on the musical scale. Things and opportunities are brought to the seven persons, without their actively seeking them. Those with this number should use their mental abilities to probe the deep mysteries and hidden truths of the universe. They are potential mystics; and with their extreme sensitivity, the seven personalities must guard against their tendency to wish to withdraw from the larger society in which they find themselves.

8—Those bearing the number eight in their life-path are the practical people of the material world. They usually desire and achieve love, power, and success. Eight is the number associated with large corporations and organizations. It is a powerful number, and those bearing the responsibilities of the number eight may succumb to the negative polarity of becoming demanding individuals.

9—Nine is the number representing humanitarianism. Those under this vibration must be prepared to give up all personal desire and ambitions. Number nine operates under the Law of Fulfillment, and its appeal is to the all-inclusive, to the many. The negative polarity of the number nine personality is to become egocentric.

11—A Master Number: This is the number of the dreamers, the visionaries, the ones who receive their ideals intuitively. Their destiny is to reveal something new and uplifting to the world. Number 11 is the messenger, the spokesman or broadcaster. The negative polarity for revelators is to become fanatical and judgmental in their beliefs.

22—A Master Number: This is the practical idealist who is concerned with the benefit and progress of humankind. A 22 readily conceives philanthropic plans and seeks to help the masses with their improvement, expansion, and growth. The negative vibrations that accrue around the 22 personalities may lead them to become self-promoters, rather than idealists who work for the general good of the many.

According to the precepts of numerology, one's name is very important, as it is concerned with sound, a direct manifestation of vibration. Therefore, since each letter of every alphabet has its distinctive sound, it follows that each letter would have its own distinctive number. Using the one to nine cycle it is imperative to establish the essence of the number.

The graph that follows, with a name given as an example, shows how to arrive at the number vibration.

1	2	3	4	5	6	7	8	9
A	B	C	D	E	F	G	H	I
J	K	L	M	N	O	P	Q	R
S	T	U	V	W	X	Y	Z	

Example:

M	A	R	Y	J	O	H	A	Y	E	S
4	1	9	7	1	6	8	1	7	5	1

21   7   22

3   7   4

14 (1+4)= 5

The five is the number of this person's name, and according to numerology such a number relates to the person's character and personality. Referring back to the basic explanation of the number vibration, a five would make Mary a progressively minded who must be prepared for much travel and many changes in her life.

Numerologists claim that numbers hold the key to determining many aspects of one's life and destiny. Some who practice numerology even believe that totaling the number of the vowels of one's name can identify the essence of a person's inner self and the soul. Using Mary's name again, we get the numbers 1 + 6 + 1 + 5. By totaling and simplifying these we arrive at the final digit of four. This number represents Mary's inner self. It expresses her real potential, longings, and hidden talents. As a four, her expression is to serve others patiently and dependably and to create something of lasting importance.

❋ DELVING DEEPER

Cirlot, J. E. A Dictionary of Symbols. New York: Barnes & Noble, 1993.

Gibson, Walter B., and Litzka R. Gibson. The Complete Illustrated Book of the Psychic Sciences. Garden City, N.Y.: Doubleday and Co., 1966.

Karcher, Stephen. The Illustrated Encyclopedia of Divination. Rockport, Mass.: Element Books, 1997.

Lagerquist, Kay, and Lisa Lenard. The Complete Idiot's Guide to Numerology. New York: Alpha Books, 1999.

Petrie, Jodra. Tell Fortunes and Predict the Future. New York: Award Books, 1968.

Spence, Lewis. An Encyclopedia of Occultism. New Hyde Park, N.Y.: University Books, 1960.

Woodruff, Maurice. The Secrets of Foretelling Your Own Future. New York: Signet, 1969.

PALMISTRY

Palmistry, most often associated with carnival fortune-telling booths and gypsy caravans, has been a popular means of divination for centuries. Some traditions state that the Brahmins of ancient India practiced the occult science as a means of determining the potential of their students. An old story has it that Aristotle (384–322 B.C.E.) discovered a treatise on the subject of palmistry that was written in letters of gold, which he then presented to Alexander the Great (356–323 B.C.E.), who took great interest in examining the character of his officers by analyzing the lines on their hands. Many years later, this magical volume was translated into Latin and found its way to Arabian **magi** and to magicians in Europe.

Essentially, those who read palms envision the human hand as a microcosm on which the

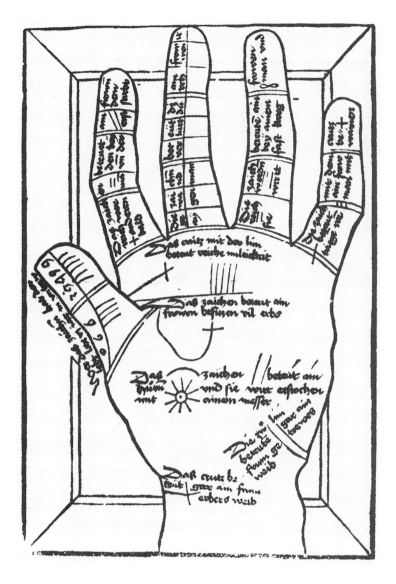

the left hand represents future potential, whereas the right hand depicts the actuality of their personality as it presently exists. For a left-handed person, this would be reversed. Other schools of palmistry state that in a right-handed person the subjective hand, the left, should be read first, for it indicates the natural inclinations and abilities of the subject. The right hand, the objective hand, predicts how far the individual will follow the pattern of life indicated by the subjective hand. In left-handed people, the right hand is subjective and the left is the objective.

For a palmist, each part of the hand is associated with a planetary spirit. The mount or mound of Jupiter is located at the base of the finger of Jupiter, the forefinger. The mount of Saturn is located at the base of the finger of Saturn, the second finger. The mount of the Sun is found at the base of the finger of the Sun, the third finger. The mount of Mercury rests at the base of the little finger, the finger of Mercury. The mount of Venus is the fleshy part of the palm at the base of the thumb. The mount of the Moon is located in the thicker part of the side of the hand, directly beneath the mount of Mercury below the little finger.

The major lines of the palm are the Life, Head, and Heart, which describe the basic personality traits as laid out in the palm. The Life line is the prominent line that begins at the base of the thumb (the mount of Venus) and runs up toward the finger of Jupiter—or, in other terms, the line that starts about halfway between the thumb and the forefinger and curves around the area of the thumb, ending usually near the base of the thumb, nearly at the wrist.

The Head line begins at the start of the Life line, and the two lines should be joined together, just touching. Once palmists locate the beginning of the Head line about midway between forefinger and thumb, they trace its course across the palm toward the outside of the hand.

The Heart line begins in the area of the mount of Jupiter at the base of the forefinger, then runs across the base of the other mounts to the edge of the hand. It is the first horizontal line in the palm.

individual's life path can be foreseen on the lines that crisscross the palm. Palmistry is subdivided into three parts: chirosophy, the determination of the mystical significance of the various lines; chirogonmy, analyzing the overall shape of the hand itself; and cheiromancy, divining the future and/or past from the form of the hand and fingers and the lines and markings thereon. Some palmists concentrate on reading only the lines of the hand. Others include the fleshy mounts, fingernails, fingers, and even the wrist lines for clues to an individual's life patterns.

There are a variety of opinions regarding which hand to read, left or right. Most commonly, the right hand is read in a right-handed person, and the left for a left-handed person. Traditionally, in a right-handed person,

Palm reading at the Festival of Mind, Body, and Spirit. (GUY LYON PLAYFAIR/FORTEAN PICTURE LIBRARY)

The line of Mercury, found beneath the little finger, is not present in many people's hands. The line of the Sun is located underneath the third (ring) finger. The line of Saturn, the so-called Fate line, is only found in about 40 percent of the population. This vertical line (s) runs from the wrist up towards the middle finger. The Girdle of Venus is composed of curved lines that will appear underneath the middle and ring fingers. The line of Intuition is a curved, crescent-like line that extends from the lowest part of the mount of the Moon to the mount of Mercury, located directly below the little finger. The lines of Affection or Marriage are located on the side of the hand under the little finger in the area called the mount of Mercury.

The longer one spends studying the human palm, the more lines and markings one is likely to discover. There are "bars," short lines that cross major lines, indicating warnings of serious interference. There are "crosses" that represent periods of ill health, unhappiness, or problems at work. There are even small "stars" consisting of several little crosslines that reveal something extremely rare or unusual. One may also see "triangles" (ingenuity), "squares," or "rectangles" (signs of protection).

Although few scientists have taken palm reading seriously, on December 9, 2001, the *Ananova* Internet News Service reported that researchers at Barcelona University in Spain had announced the preliminary results of extensive research that indicated that intelligence can be predicted by palm reading. According to these scientists, people with learning disabilities have distinctive patterns of lines on their palms. Other research indicated that the lines on the palm can reveal a person's susceptibility to heart disease, autism, anxiety, and schizophrenia.

⁂ **DELVING DEEPER**

Fairchild, Dennis. *Palm Reading: A Little Guide to Life's Secrets.* Philadlephia: Running Press, 1995.

Gibson, Walter B., and Litzka R. Gibson. *The Complete Illustrated Book of the Psychic Sciences.* Garden City, N.Y.: Doubleday & Co., 1966.

Hazel, Peter. *Palmistry Quick & Easy*. St. Paul, Minn.: Llewellyn Publications, 2001.

Karcher, Stephen. *The Illustrated Encyclopedia of Divination*. Rockport, Mass.: Element Books, 1997.

"Palm Reading Shows Intelligence: Research." *Ananova*, December 9, 2001. [Online] http://www.ananova.com/news/story/sm_469117.html. 9 March 2002.

Petrie, Joda. *7 Ways to Tell Fortunes & Predict the Future*. New York: Award Books, 1968.

Spence, Lewis. *An Encyclopedia of Occultism*. New Hyde Park, N.Y.: University Books, 1960.

PROPHETS AND DIVINERS

Thousands of years before the contemporary era, wise men and women listened while murmuring springs and streams spoke to them of what was to be, and they looked through the brilliance of precious stones into the world of tomorrow. Trees spoke to these early mediators between the gods and humans, as did the wise serpent, the wolf, and the birds that flew overhead.

Many centuries later, Chaldean priests contemplated the night sky and conceived the idea of a supreme spirit from whom sprang a familiar host of lesser deities. In the aftermath of this modification of the traditional order of things, a caste of priests arose, vested with all knowledge of the occult. Subsequently these priests became adept in the practice of divination, finding signs in the organs and intestines of sacrificed animals and translating dancing shapes of flames and swirls of smoke into images of future events. When the gods spoke directly to individuals in the symbolic language of dreams, the priests were there to interpret. In these and other ways, the will of the cosmic rulers was revealed to their earthbound subjects.

The children of Israel, even though they spurned the hordes of good and evil spirits recognized throughout the ancient world, practiced divination in several forms. The book of Genesis records that Laban, the father of Rachel, who became the wife of Isaac, possessed Teraphim—instruments of divination whose oracles were held to be of the highest truth.

Although the practice of sorcery and divination was forbidden to the Hebrews, the high priests of Israel inquired of the Lord regarding the future by means of the high priests' jeweled Ephod and the Urim and Thummim. When the Lord failed to speak to him through the Ephod, Saul (11th century B.C.E.), first king of Israel, resorted to **necromancy,** or divination through the spirits of the dead. Saul entreated the fabled **Witch of Endor** to call up the spirit of the great prophet Samuel, only to hear his own death foretold. According to tradition, Solomon (10th century B.C.E.), wisest of all the Hebrew monarchs, foretold the future by consulting demons, which he summoned with his magic lamp and great seal.

The **Sphinx,** the guardian of Egyptian magic, served as an oracle for diviners of that land. According to Plutarch, such thinkers as Solon, Thales, **Pythagoras** (c. 580–c. 500 B.C.E.), and Lycurgus traveled to Egypt to converse with priests who heard the voice of the Sphinx. Ancient **magi** solemnly testified that the statues of Egypt spoke, and when these oracles of hewn stone uttered their pronouncements, scribes wrote their words on rolls of papyrus while priests listened.

The Greeks saw in numbers the mystical keys to the Great Mind of the cosmos; and the fates of kingdoms, commerce, and human lives hung on the enigmatic utterances of the Delphic oracle. A Greek sect called the psychagogues conjured the spirits of the dead, who brought petitions for their survivors as well as prophetic messages. With so many deities to keep track of, it is no wonder that the Greeks were ever on the alert for omens, even in such simple phenomena as birds in flight and the sequence in which a fowl picked up kernels of grain. Socrates (c. 470–399 B.C.E.) foretold the future with the aid of his own familiar spirit, which replied to yes-and-no questions with sneezes to the right or to the left.

The Roman emperors, while officially forbidding divination, rewarded Chaldean astrologers with drachmas when their readings were favorable and with death or exile when they found adverse omens in the stars. Even the early Christian Church, which persecuted magicians and soothsayers, found that the use of crosses, beads, and relics and bones of the saints were useful aids in bringing the faithful

PHRENOLOGY

Austrian physician Franz Joseph Gall (1758–1828) speculated that different mental functions are located in specific parts of the brain, therefore becoming the first person to complete the theory of cerebral localization. In his book *The Anatomy and Physiology of the Nervous System in General and the Brain in Particular,* a four-volume set published between 1810 and 1819, Gall set down the principles that focused on the contours and measurements of the human head as the basis of his doctrine on cranioscopy or phrenology. (The word phrenology stems from *phrenos,* or mind, and *logos,* meaning study.)

Gall believed it possible to establish individual behavior, personality, character, and strengths and weaknesses by studying the contours or bumps on the head. Complete with topographical maps depicting and illustrating his findings, his book and theories caused a sensation that still continues today. Many either embraced and hailed phrenology as a new science, or shunned or scorned it at best, as a "pseudoscience." Even today, there are some doctors, practitioners, societies, and websites advocating the authenticity and accuracy of phrenology.

Perhaps because it appeared so logical, with easy-to-follow maps and interpretations of them, phrenology provided a relatively simple diagnostic technique, and caught on as a raving sensation throughout parts of Europe and the United States. The supposed scientific, medical application of phrenology soon found its way into the hands of self-taught and self-styled "experts" who exploited it. Phrenology became the basis for many things, from the selection of marriage partners to employees for the workplace; as a diagnostic tool for mental illness to a way of determining personality profiles— but mainly to generate money. Phrenology parlors were everywhere between 1820 and 1842, giving rise to many inventions. Phrenology machines made it possible for a person to get a detailed interpretation of their personality by allowing a helmet to descend upon his or her head and measure and read the bumps on the skull. Some of these machines and their history are preserved and on display in the Museum of Questionable Medical Devices, in Minneapolis, Minnesota.

SOURCES:

Cooper, Helen, and Peter Cooper *Heads, or the Art of Phrenology.* London: London Phrenology Co. Ltd., 1983.

Gall and Phrenology. [Online] http://human-nature.com/mba/chap1.html. 22 November 2002.

Hedderly, Frances. *Phrenology, A Study of Mind.* London: L. N. Fowler & Co. Ltd., 1970.

into a state of mind in which the voice of the Holy Spirit might be heard.

All human cultures throughout history have given great attention to their prophets and seers. Perhaps the quintessential prophet is **Nostradamus** (1503–1566), whose name has become synonymous with prophecy and who is better known to the general public than any of the Old Testament prophets. The French seer has inspired numerous books, countless articles, and a number of television specials. Although his visions of the future were written in poetic verse and read like gibberish to the skeptics, those who believe firmly in Nostradamus's gift of prophecy quote his predictions as if they were Holy Writ. The claim that Nostradamus had predicted the tragedy of the World Trade Center terrorist attack on September 11, 2001, was widely circulated on the Internet and on talk radio. The alleged prediction was soon exposed as a hoax, but not before thousands of books on Nostradamus were sold.

THE *practice of sorcery and divination was forbidden to the Hebrews.*

The twentieth century produced a number of prophets who gathered their believers and provoked their disbelievers, but none received the mass attention of **Edgar Cayce** (1877–1945), the famous "sleeping prophet" of Virginia Beach, and **Jeane Dixon** (1918–1997), Washington, D.C.'s "window on the world." Although there will always be seers who will produce an occasional startling prophecy that comes to pass and attract transient devotees until the next prophet comes along with an even more startling prediction, the trend at the onset of the twenty-first century appears to be individuals relying upon their own powers of prophecy and the insights gained from utilizing their own methods of divination.

❋ DELVING DEEPER

Cotterell, Arthur, ed. *Encyclopedia of World Mythology*. London: Dempsey Parr Books, 1999.

Gaskell, G. A. *Dictionary of All Scriptures & Myths*. Avenel, N.J.: Gramercy Books, 1981.

Seligmann, Kurt. *The History of Magic*. New York: Pantheon Books, 1960.

Spence, Lewis. *An Encyclopedia of Occultism*. New Hyde Park, N.Y.: University Books, 1960.

EDGAR CAYCE (1877–1945)

According to many, Edgar Cayce was one of the greatest clairvoyants of all time. Before his death at the age of 67 in 1945, the "Seer of Virginia Beach" went under self-induced hypnosis twice per day and gave more than 30,000 trance readings—9,000 of them medical diagnoses. In his lifetime, Cayce earned the gratitude of thousands of men, women, and children whose lives he had saved or improved through his diagnoses of illnesses that had escaped the examinations of highly trained medical personnel.

Always a controversial figure, Cayce was derided by cynics who asked how a man whose formal education had terminated with the ninth grade could become a greater healer than professional medical men with years of training behind them. His defenders were quick to point out that Edgar Cayce did not heal patients who sought his help, he merely diagnosed their ailments—often with a cooperating family physician standing at their side.

The skeptical German scholar Dr. Hugo Munsterberg investigated Cayce in 1910 with the announced intention of exposing him. Weeks later he left the seer to prepare an endorsement, rather than an expose, of Cayce's work. In 1929 Dr. William Moseley Brown, head of the psychology department at Washington and Lee University, declared, after an extensive investigation, that if ever there were such a thing as an authentic clairvoyant, that individual was Edgar Cayce. The authenticated cures attributed to Cayce's diagnoses number in the thousands.

Cayce's son, Hugh Lynn Cayce, once commented that his father had said that everyone was psychic, "but for many people manifestation of this ability can be very disturbing, upsetting, and in fact, it can even destroy the personality if it runs rampant in the person's life. This can be damaging if the individual does not use these abilities constructively. If he takes ego trips with it, or begins to fake it, the result can be destructive to the personality, particularly that of young children."

In 1931, the **Association for Research and Enlightenment (ARE)** was chartered in the state of Virginia as a nonprofit organization to conduct scientific and psychical research based on the Cayce readings. In 1947, two years after his death, the Edgar Cayce Foundation was established. The original ARE has become the membership arm of the Cayce programs. The foundation is the custodian of the original Cayce readings, and the memorabilia of the great contemporary seer's life and career. Both are headquartered in Virginia Beach, Virginia, and there are more than 1,500 ARE study groups around the world.

The ARE maintains an extensive library of information concerning the entire field of psychical research and metaphysics, as well as the Cayce materials. It also sponsors regular seminars, publishes a journal, and established Atlantic University as an environment in which various psychic attributes can be examined and developed. Since the establishment of the ARE, thousands of people from every corner of the nation, as well as from around the world, have journeyed to Virginia Beach to attend lectures and conferences and to investigate the information in the Cayce readings. Among these have been Jess Stern, author of *Edgar Cayce—The Sleeping Prophet* (1967) and Thomas Sugrue, author of *There Is a River* (1942), both of which are important books about the life and work of Edgar Cayce.

Astonishing tales of clairvoyant feats such as the location of missing persons, objects, and criminals have filled many books by a number of authors. Equally intriguing are the "life readings" that the seer gave regarding the past incarnations of individuals. Others speak of the series of trances in which Cayce gave a detailed recreation of everyday life in ancient **Atlantis,** and spoke of the Great Crystal that powered their society. According to his clairvoyant insights, Cayce perceived a secret room in the **Sphinx,** a veritable Hall of Records that would reveal many remarkable facts about the evolution of humankind on Earth. He also put forward a number of prophecies about the future.

In the period 1958 to 1998, Cayce foresaw a number of dramatic geographic changes. He predicted a shifting of the poles, which would be caused by the eruption of volcanoes in the torrid zones. Open waters would appear north of Greenland, and new islands would rise in the Caribbean Sea. He also stated South America would be shaken by a violent earthquake. While these cataclysmic events have not yet occurred, many of Cayce's followers believe that there are definite signs that such geographic changes are in the process of manifesting.

Long before his death in 1945, Cayce appeared to envision the racial strife that lay ahead. "He [the African American] is thy brother!" Cayce said while in trance. "Those who caused or brought servitude to him without thought or purpose have created that which must be met within their own principles, within their own selves....For He hath made of one blood the nations of the earth!...Raise not democracy above the brotherhood of man, the fatherhood of God."

As early as 1938, Cayce foresaw difficulty for Russia as long as its people were denied freedom of speech and the right to worship. Then, in a provocative vision, he declared, "...through Russia comes the hope of the world—not in respect to that which is sometimes termed Communism or Bolshevism—no! But freedom! That each man will live for his fellowman."

Hugh Lynn Cayce died on July 4, 1982, in Virginia Beach. Posthumously, a collection of his speeches concerning Edgar Cayce's teachings on Jesus and Christianity was published under the title *The Jesus I Knew.* Hugh Lynn's son Charles Thomas Cayce became the president of the ARE in 1976 after his father suffered a heart attack, and he still serves the organization in that position.

❋ **DELVING DEEPER**

Boltan, Brett, ed. *Edgar Cayce Speaks.* New York: Avon Books, 1969.

Carroll, Robert Todd. "Edgar Cayce." In *The Skeptic's Dictionary.* [Online] http://skepdic.com/cayce.html.

Cayce, Hugh Lynn. *Venture Inward.* New York: Paperback Library, 1966.

Cerminara, Gina. *Many Mansions*. New York: William Morrow, 1950.

Stearn, Jess. *Edgar Cayce—The Sleeping Prophet*. New York: Doubleday, 1967.

Sugrue, Thomas. *There Is a River: The Story of Edgar Cayce*. New York: H. Holt and Co., 1942.

Painting depicting Aegeus of Athens consulting the Oracle of Delphi. (FORTEAN PICTURE LIBRARY)

DELPHIC ORACLES

The famed Oracle of Delphi on the slopes of Mt. Parnassos in Greece made known the will of the gods to rulers, philosophers, generals, politicians, and anyone else of reasonably high status who was anxious to hear a favorable word from the gods. For centuries, the Temple of Apollo at Delphi in central Greece contained the most prestigious oracle in the Graeco-Roman world, a favorite of public officials and individuals alike. At various times throughout its long history, the oracle was said to relay prophetic messages and words of counsel from Python, the wise serpent son of the Mother-goddess Delphyne or from the Moon-goddess Artemis through their priestess daughters, the Pythonesses or Pythia. Then, according to myth, the god Apollo murdered Delphyne and claimed the shrine and the Pythia for himself, imprisoning the serpent seer in the recesses of a cave beneath the temple. The name of Delphi means "womb," and suggests the journey that the seekers of prophetic knowledge had to take as they entered the cave of the Pythoness and descended deeper into the mystical recesses of the oracle, deeper into the womb of Mother Earth.

The Pythia would await the seekers while seated upon a three-legged seat, or tripod, and it was from such a perch that she would issue her prophetic utterances. The many tripods scattered throughout the cave were, in essence, individual altars for her sister priestesses, the three legs symbolizing the connection between them and the triadic spirit of prophecy.

In the summer of 2001, Jelle de Boer of Wesleyan University in Connecticut and coworkers discovered a previously unknown geological fault that passes through the sanctuary of the Temple of Apollo. Such a crossing makes the bitumen-rich limestone found there much more permeable to gases and groundwater. The researchers went on to speculate that seismic activity on the faults could have heated such deposits, releasing light hydrocarbon gases, such as ethylene, a sweet-smelling gas that was once used in certain medical procedures as an anesthetic. Although fatal if inhaled in large quantities for too long a period of time, in small doses ethylene stimulates the central nervous system and produces a sensation of euphoria and a floating feeling conducive to an oracle's visions.

✳ DELVING DEEPER

Cotterell, Arthur, ed. *Encyclopedia of World Mythology*. London: Dempsey Parr Books, 1999.

De Boer, J. Z., J. R. Hale, and J. Chanton. "New Evidence of the Geological Origins of the Ancient Delphic Oracle." *Geology* 29 (2001): 707–710.

Gaskell, G. A. *Dictionary of All Scriptures & Myths*. Avenel, N.J.: Gramercy Books, 1981.

Piccardi, L. "Active Faulting at Delphi, Greece: Seismotectonic Remarks and a Hypothesis for the Geologic Environment of a Myth." *Geology* 28 (2001): 651–54.

Seligmann, Kurt. *The History of Magic*. New York: Pantheon Books, 1960.

Psychic Jean Dixon (1918–1997). (CORBIS CORPORATION)

JEANE DIXON (1918–1997)

According to a popular story concerning the remarkable abilities of the seeress Jeane Dixon, President Franklin D. Roosevelt (1882–1945) took the time one day in 1944 to clear his desk so that he might give undivided attention to her predictions concerning those terrible days during World War II (1939–45). After she had answered his questions about the efforts on the various military fronts, he asked her directly how much longer he would have to carry out the tasks that he had set before himself.

As if she had expected the question, she warned him as compassionately as she could that he would have very little time. The president was not satisfied. He wanted a more specific answer. She told him, then, that he would have no longer than the middle of the following year.

According to those who hold that Jeane Dixon was the most famous and accurate seer of political events in the twentieth century, she correctly predicted the results of every presidential election, foretold the deaths of U.N. Secretary-General Dag Hammarskjold (1905–1961) and President John F. Kennedy (1917–1963), predicted that the Russians would win the race into space, and in general foresaw events on both personal and international scales too numerous to mention. A devout Roman Catholic who faithfully attended Mass each morning, Dixon was convinced that the gift of prophecy that she possessed was closely associated with the power of God, and she claimed to be cautious that she did not abuse this ability. In the 1960s, when she was hailed as "Washington's Window to the Future," she ran a profitable real estate concern in Washington, D.C., with her husband, James L. Dixon.

There seemed to be no standard procedure to this seer's prophetic insights. They came to her at various times, in various places, and in various emotional states. In the book *The Call to Glory* (1971), she envisioned herself as a prophet who issued predictions in order to fulfill the mission that God had given her. The book's acknowledgements named Rev. Stephen Hartdegen, a Roman Catholic priest, as her "personal religious consultant" for the book. Dixon appeared to believe firmly that it was her God-given mission to predict the change in the top leadership positions of Soviet Russia while in front of television cameras, or while under a beautician's hair drier, to warn the woman sitting next to her to avoid an approaching airline disaster.

JEANE *Dixon foretold the death of U.S. President John F. Kennedy.*

In 1956, for an interview in *Parade* magazine, Dixon was asked to predict the results of the 1960 presidential election. She foretold that the election would be won by a Democrat, but that he would either be assassinated or die in office. In the 1960 presidential election many friends remembered her prediction. Even though Richard Nixon (1913–1994), the Republican candidate, would have more votes than Kennedy, the candidate on the Democrat's ticket, Kennedy would become president and, tragically, die while in office. Although the account of Dixon's famous Kennedy prediction was recalled in Ruth Montgomery's three million-copy bestseller *A Gift of Prophecy: The Phenomenal Jeane Dixon* (1966), many skeptics have pointed out that

Montgomery neglected to include the seeress's 1960 prediction that John F. Kennedy would definitely fail to win the presidency.

In spite of those who were skeptical of the true accuracy of her predictions, Jeane Dixon's many supporters insisted that her prophetic powers extended beyond the political sphere. According to numerous accounts, with but the barest knowledge of the people involved, she was been able to predict murders, suicides, the results of horse races, fires, and accidents. Once she was able to foresee the number that would win a raffle and purchased the corresponding ticket for her husband. He won a car.

After the death of Josef Stalin (1879–1953), world interest focused on Russia's next prime minister. When Georgy Malenkov (1902–1988) was finally elevated to the position, Jeane Dixon was asked before a national television audience how long Malenkov would be prime minister of the Soviet Union. The question was asked by the former U.S. ambassador to the Soviet Union, Joseph Davies, and he was obviously dubious about Dixon's prophetic power.

Using a crystal ball to focus her attention, Jeane Dixon said that Malenkov would be premier for less than two years. Ambassador Davies disagreed with Dixon in a tone that approached open mockery. He was sure that no premier of the Soviet Union would ever be replaced. It seemed in the nature of Russian politics that the leader would either be assassinated or die a natural death before another man could take over.

But Dixon stood firm. While smoothly acknowledging the ambassador's superior knowledge of the Russian situation, she nonetheless predicted that Malenkov's replacement would be a portly military man with wavy hair, green eyes, and a goatee. Davies had been in Russia for many years and said that he knew of no such man. Ignoring his apparent skepticism, Dixon went on to predict that not only would the Russians win the race into space, they would also dictate the terms of world peace.

Premier Malenkov was replaced by Nikolai Bulganin (1895–1975). Malenkov was not killed, and the new premier was exactly as Dixon had described him: ". . . a portly military man with wavy hair, green eyes, and a goatee," a comparatively unknown figure to the West. In 1957 Russia launched the first successful artificial Earth satellite, but Dixon was incorrect when she predicted that the Soviets would beat the United States to the moon. And, of course, far from dictating the terms of world peace, the Soviet Union collapsed in 1991.

Dixon's popularity enabled her to write a column on astrology that was nationally syndicated and to write a series of books, including *My Life and Prophecies* (1968), *Yesterday, Today and Forever* (1976), *Jeane Dixon's Astrological Cookbook* (1976), and *A Gift of Prayer* (1995). In 1962, she told Ronald Reagan (1911–   ) one day he would be president, and for a number of years, she served as the Reagans' astrological advisor.

Dixon's list of annual predictions inspired many recordkeepers doubtful of her gift of prophecy to maintain a tally of her hits and misses. Skeptic Robert Todd Carroll declared most of her predictions to have been "equivocal, vague, or mere possibility claims." John Allen Paulos, a mathematician at Temple University, coined the term "the Jeane Dixon effect" to describe the manner in which the media and a believing public would loudly proclaim a few accurate predictions and overlook the much larger number of incorrect forecasts.

When Jeane Dixon died from cardiopulmonary arrest on January 25, 1997, she remained a remarkable prophet in the eyes of her admirers, a spiritually devout woman who fulfilled her mission from God by sharing with the public her gifts of prophecy.

❖ DELVING DEEPER

Bringle, Mary. *Jeane Dixon: Prophet or Fraud?* New York: Tower Books, 1970.

Carroll, Robert Todd. "Jeane Dixon and the Jeane Dixon Effect." In *The Skeptic's Dictionary*, [Online] http://skepdic.com/dixon.html. 20 May 2002.

Delfano, M. M. *The Living Prophets.* New York: Dell Books, 1972.

Montgomery, Ruth. *A Gift of Prophecy: The Phenomenal Jeane Dixon.* New York: Bantam Books, 1966.

"Psychic Jeane Dixon Dies—'Astrologer to Stars' Had Legions of Believers." *CNN Interactive*, January 26, 1997. [Online] http://www.cnn.com/SHOWBIZ/9701/26/dixon/index.html. 20 May 2002.

Irene Hughes. (ARCHIVES OF BRAD STEIGER)

IRENE HUGHES (C. 1926–   )

In 1966 with her vision of the exact dates for a great Chicago blizzard, Irene Hughes soon became known widely as the "Chicago Seeress." She has foretold deaths, assassinations, marriages, divorces, winning teams in sports, major weather disasters, and the outcome of elections. Notarized statements, personal letters of affirmation, and newspaper records, have validated her predictions. She has predicted the following: In 1966, the Middle Eastern War of June 1967; in January 1967 President Lyndon B. Johnson (1908–1973) would not seek another term, which he announced in April of that year; in November 1967, the assassination of Robert Kennedy (1925–1968), which occurred in June 1968; in 1969, a "tragedy for Senator Kennedy, in or around water" prior to Edward "Ted" Kennedy's (1932–   ) crisis at Chappaquidick when the automobile that he was driving went into the water, drowning one of his campaign workers. In 1987 she published her prediction of a plummeting stock market and told a group of millionaires that the market would drop "400 points" on the following Monday. On "Black Monday," the market dropped 500 points. Two weeks before Princess Diana's (1961–1997) death in 1997, Hughes told her radio audience that the princess was in a death cycle and that her death would occur soon.

An area in which she has devoted particular attention has been that of offering psychic assistance to criminal investigators. In all cases, the police solicited Hughes's help.

Hughes's experience with the law and her own research into all phases of psychic phenomena has given her time to give thought to the matter of psychics and possible legal conflicts. "It should be stressed that the information a psychic gives to police officers should be for their use alone to check out and turn into factual evidence," she said. "No psychic information should ever be used in court without the police having first checked it out and proved it to be accurate."

❋ DELVING DEEPER

Hughes, Irene. *ESPecially, Irene: A Guide to Psychic Awareness*. Blavelt, N.Y.: Rudolf Steiner Publications, 1972.

Irene Hughes. [Online] http://www.irene-psychic.com. 29 May 2002.

Steiger, Brad. *Know the Future Today*. New York: Paperback Library, 1970.

OLOF JONSSON (1918–1998)

In February 1971 all the media was abuzz with rumors that one of the astronauts on the Apollo 14 mission was conducting a Moon-to-Earth ESP experiment with a psychic-sensitive somewhere on Earth. On February 26, *Life* magazine was revealed that Chicago-based Olof Jonsson was the psychic who had been chosen to participate with astronaut Edgar Mitchell in the experiment. Jonsson was considered the most tested, tried, laboratory-evaluated psychic-sensitive in the United States and Scandinavia.

In March 1952, Jonsson's psychic detective work led to a murderer responsible for the deaths of 13 victims. In each instance, the man attempted to destroy evidence by torching the home of his victim. The murderer turned out to be the police officer assigned to work closely with Jonsson on the investigation. When the officer realized the investigation was directed toward him, he committed suicide.

Jonsson came to the United States in 1953 to be investigated by the well-known parapsychologist Dr. **J. B. Rhine.** For the next 14 years Jonsson submitted to testing at various ESP testing laboratories. He would sit guessing Zener cards—the classic testing deck consisting of the symbols cross, square, wavy line, circle, and star—by the hundreds or the thousands.

In 1978, Olof Jonsson joined a crew of 11 treasure hunters, including President Ferdinand Marcos (1917–1989) of the Philippines, to locate the gold that had been plundered by Japanese officers during World War II and hidden on the islands. Jonsson was instrumental in locating several mineshafts containing more than $2 billion in gold. Jonsson and a number of the other treasure hunters recalled later how the mine shafts were filled with the sorrowful spirits of the men and women the Japanese military had enslaved to do the digging.

Throughout the 1970s and 1980s, Jonsson joined numerous treasure hunters who sought the watery graves of ships that had gone down with cargo on board. Although he continued to be successful in these quests, Jonsson received little income from these enterprises.

❋ DELVING DEEPER

Psi-Stjarna. [Online] http://paranormal.se/topic/olof_jonsson.html. 23 November 2002.

Margaret Harrell's website. [Online] http://www.marharrell.com/Pages/NDonO1.html.

Seagrave, Sterling. *The Marcos Dynasty*. New York: Harper & Row, 1988.

Steiger, Brad. *The Psychic Feats of Olof Jonsson*. Englewood Cliffs, N.J.: Prentice-Hall, 1971.

NOSTRADAMUS (1503—1566)

On December 14, 1503, Michel de Nostredame began a life that was destined to be filled with political intrigues, Renaissance rationalism, and mysticism. Born in Saint-Remy in Provence, France, Nostradamus came from a long line of Jewish ancestors who had first come to Europe during the Dispersion. Sometime before his birth, Nostradamus's parents had publicly converted to Roman Catholicism because of a papal edict decreeing disfavor to all those who were not of the Christian faith.

However, during their son's formative years, the religious practice of the family had become a curious blend of Catholic and Jewish customs. In addition, there was a strong current of mysticism in the family. Young Michel's grandfather was considered one of the most influential astrologists on the entire continent.

When he was old enough, Nostradamus was sent off to study liberal arts at Avignon. His great interest was in studying astrology, and this prompted his practical-minded father to reconsider the choice of vocation he had made for his son. The next time Nostradamus was sent to school it was to Paris, and there he studied to become a man of medicine. After almost four years of intensive study, Nostradamus passed his examinations and was allowed to establish a practice. His plans to continue study for the doctorate were disrupted when the plague struck Southern France.

Nostradamus is said to have been successful in his treatment of the Black Death, even though some of his fellow doctors complained that his methods were unorthodox. Later he returned to the University of Paris and there earned his doctorate. He accepted a position at the university and also married.

His unorthodox interests and unquenchable desire to travel made him unhappy in the university setting, but his deep affection for his family enabled him to achieve some satisfaction. After his wife had borne him two children, another outbreak of the plague swept his family away. Grief stricken, Nostradamus abandoned his practice and set about wandering across Europe. It was during this period that he first began to cultivate his prophetic powers.

As he wandered, he made predictions which would later make him famous. While traveling in Italy, Nostradamus saw a young Franciscan monk coming toward him. He was an ex-swineherd named Felice Peretti from Ancona. As the young monk passed, the prophet bent one knee to the ground devoutly, in an attitude of deep respect. Afterwards, Nostradamus's traveling companions questioned him about his strange behavior. His reply was that he must submit himself and bend a knee before His Holiness. In 1585, Cardinal Peretti became Pope Sixtus V (1520–1590).

Everywhere the seer went he was in great demand. Once, visiting a noble family in France, he spotted two pigs running together side by side. Nostradamus told his host that that evening they would eat the black one, and the wolf would eat the white one.

The host decided on a plot to foil the prophet. He ordered the cook to slaughter the white pig and serve it for supper. The cook did as he was ordered. But while he had his back to the spitted carcass, a wolf cub that the family had been attempting to domesticate stole up to it and began making a meal of the freshly killed animal. Eventually the cook chased the cub away, but he knew that he could not put an apple in a mutilated pig's mouth and drop it on the master's table. So the cook had the other pig, the black one, butchered and prepared for the master's table that evening.

NOSTRADAMUS *believed he was guided in his prophecies by the angel Anael.*

That evening at dinner, the noble Frenchman explained to his guest how he had arranged to fool him by ordering the cook to prepare the white pig and not the black one. As respectfully as possible, Nostradamus disagreed. The cook was summoned to settle the matter, and the entire story was brought to light, showing the exact fulfillment of Nostradamus's prediction.

Later in his life, the great prophet was summoned to give a reading for Catherine de Medici (1519–1589), the queen mother and controller of France. She was concerned for her children, and no prophet in his right mind would have told her what was to happen to them even if he could have envisioned it. Catherine's children were all destined to die young as the result of political intrigues.

Perhaps because of the nature of the inspiration Nostradamus received, but more likely because of public response, the prophet began to hide his predictions in obscure poetic language. It would have been sheer folly to tell

Michel Nostradamus.

(CORBIS CORPORATION)

will obey no laws. Skeptic James Randi's translation, however, points out that "Hister" refers to a geographical region, rather than a person.

Some believe that Nostradamus foresaw the downfall of Communism in a quatrain that says "the law of More" (a widely read treatise on communal living in Nostradamus's time) will be seen to decline because of "another much more attractive doctrine." But the seer missed his target on another interesting prophecy that had to do with a masculine woman, who, at the time of the double eclipse in July and August 1999, would rise to power in Russia.

According to some interpreters, Nostradamus foresaw the decline of the papacy in the year 2000. While some may argue that such a decline has begun, others will counter that in many ways the papacy has a greater world influence in the twenty-first century that it has enjoyed for quite some time. Another quatrain tells of the next-to-last pope declaring Monday as his day of rest and wandering far because of a frantic need to deliver his people from economic pressures.

A last great battle, in which the "barbarian empire" shall be defeated, is determined by some interpreters of Nostradamus as being predicted for the year 2332. In this last battle of **Armageddon,** a young German leader will force the warring nations to lay down their arms and observe a lasting world peace. Nostradamus and a host of other prophets have designated Palestine as the site for this last desperate warfare.

Perhaps the controversial prophet's most unusual prediction was fulfilled in June 1566. That month, although Nostradamus had not suffered an unhealthy day in his life, he died after a short illness. Nostradamus had previously informed his physician that he would die on June 25, and he upheld his reputation as a seer by doing so.

the ruthless Catherine de Medici that all her children were destined for miserable deaths. His only recourse was to disguise the ugly truth in poetry and preserve his own skin.

In his astrological studies, which he turned to late in his career, Nostradamus, who believed he was guided in his prophecies by the angel Anael, also resorted to poetic quatrains, four-line verses, arranged in groups of 100 (Centuries). According to many Nostradamus scholars and enthusiasts, a large number of prophecies contained in these quatrains were fulfilled. Those who believe in his prophetic powers insist that Nostradamus foresaw airplanes, rockets, submarines, and many great historic events. Other more skeptical researchers believe the prophecies to be nonsensical gibberish.

In a famous quatrain that many feel refers to Adolf Hitler (1889–1945), Nostradamus writes that a son of Germany named "Hister"

✵ DELVING DEEPER

Cheetham, Erika. *The Final Prophecies of Nostradamus.* New York: Berkley Publishing Group, 1990.

Crockett, Arthur. *Nostradamus: Unpublished Prophecies the Untold Story.* New Brunswick, N.J.: Inner Light, 1983.

Hogue, John. *Nostradamus: The Complete Prophecies*. Element Books, 1997.

Randi, James. *The Mask of Nostradamus: The Prophecies of the World's Most Famous Seer*. Buffalo, N.Y.: Prometheus Books, 1993.

Seligmann, Kurt. *The History of Magic*. New York: Pantheon Books, 1948.

MOTHER SHIPTON

Often called the world's most famous prophetess, Mother Shipton was born in a cave beside the River Nidd in North Yorkshire, England in 1488. Previously known as Ursula Sontheil, she would display supernatural powers by the age two that earned her the nickname of Child of the Devil.

Although little is known about the rest of her youth, stories circulated about an incident that occurred early in her childhood. Upon returning to her house after doing an errand, her foster mother found the door wide open and Ursula missing. Reporting dreadful wailing and strange noises coming from the house, the neighbors told a story of an invisible force that wouldn't let them enter the kitchen. Together, they all returned to the house to discover the girl sitting in the kitchen. Completely naked, Ursula was sitting on the iron bar in the chimney from which the cooking hooks were suspended, pleased that she had wreaked havoc. From that time on, gossip spread and rumors abounded about her growing uncanny abilities.

In addition to being mischievous, Ursula made rhymes or prose of events or circumstances that would often come true. She suffered from a physical deformity that made her a victim of merciless teasing, and she soon developed what seemed a power to reap revenge on those who did so. For the most part, Ursula was an oddity, and said to even be feared by many.

Accused of using witchcraft in order to make a man fall for her, she married Toby Shipton, a carpenter, in 1512. Ursula Shipton continued to tell fortunes and predict events. Her fame spread throughout Europe, for her predictions in riddle that forecast such events as the Fire of London in 1666, the defeat of the Spanish Armada in 1588, and future technology. Born fifteen years before Nostradamus, it is reputed that she predicted the end of the world and even predicted her own end, with her death in 1561.

Although the first known edition of Mother Shipton's prophesies appeared in print in 1641, (*The Propheceyes of Mother Shipton…Fortelling*

Drawing of the famous witch Mother Shipton. (CORBIS CORPORATION)

the Death of Cardinall Wolsey, the Lord of Percy, and others, As Also What Should Happen in Insuing Times), by an anonymous author, eighty years after her death, it was also published in London by Richard Lowndes. It was a 1684 edition by Richard Head and edited by Charles Hindley, which included her earliest biographical data. Both Hindley and Head, in later years, said the whole thing was a hoax and they made up and invented most of the details of her life.

There is controversy as to whether or not Shipton ever really existed outside of legend. Some say thirteen of her prophecies were accurate and fulfilled; while others say she may have been a real person, but her prophecies were all part of the legend and were written after the events had already come true.

⚜ DELVING DEEPER

Shipton, Mother. *Mother Shipton's Fortune Teller; Or, Future Fate Foretold by the Planets*. New York: Padell Book Co.: 1944.

Harrison, W. H. Holmes. *Mother Shipton Investigated. The Result of a Critical Examination of the Extant Literature Relating to the Yorkshire Sybil*. London: Holmes Publishing Group LLC: 2001.

Windsor, Diana. *Mother Shipton's Prophecy Book: The Story of Her Life and Most Famous Prophecies*. London: Wolverson Publishing: 1988.

Weed, Joseph J. *Complete Guide to Oracle and Prophecy Methods*. New York: Parker Publishing. 1975.

Glass, Justine. *They Foresaw the Future. The Story of Fulfilled Prophecy*. New York: G. P. Putnam's Sons. 1969.

SCRYING/CRYSTAL GAZING/CRYSTALOMANCY

For many centuries, those who would divine the future have assisted their clairvoyant abilities by crystal gazing, known technically as scrying. This method of divination is of such vast antiquity that it would be impossible to state exactly where it originated. It is known that both the ancient Egyptians and Babylonians scryed by means of gazing into low, open stone dishes filled with palm oil. But who can say for certain when the first diviner entered into an altered state of consciousness while gazing into a pool of water, a crystal globe, the surface of a polished gem, or any transparent object and received what he or she believed to be a vision of the future?

The practice of scrying consists of fixedly gazing into a crystal ball, often placed upon a black cloth in order to shut out all brilliant highlights and reflections.

In place of a crystal ball, scryers will occasionally use the surface of a pool or a glass or saucer full of water, ink, oil, or other liquids. Such surfaces, when used by scryers for the purpose of divination, are known under the name of "speculum." In other instances, scryers will utilize a large piece of natural quartz crystal to serve as their window into other dimensions.

In their instructions to those who would be scryers or crystal gazers, practitioners of the art advise the apprentice to make their mind a blank. They should gaze, rather than stare, steadily at the crystal, blinking as little as possible. It is also advised that they should not extend such steadfast gazes for more than five minutes at a time. If their eyes begin to water, this may be taken as an indication that their time limit has been reached. They should then end their experimentation without delay.

Sooner or later, the accomplished scryers promise, the crystal ball or the scrying device will cloud over and, when this passes, small figures may be seen moving about in the crystal itself. A varying panorama, not unlike

Predicting the future using a crystal ball and tarot cards. (PHILIP PANTON/FORTEAN PICTURE LIBRARY)

miniature motion pictures, will develop, and certain scenes portraying the future or the past will be played out before their eyes. Such pictures and scenes—whether they are of familiar or strange locations—do not actually appear in the ball, crystal, or liquid; they are merely projected into the object by the subconscious mind of the scryers.

If beginners are unable to see anything in the crystal or the liquid, the experienced practitioners remind them that they can attempt to train their latent ability. They suggest various exercises, such as strengthening their visual memory by first looking at a certain object in the room and then trying to project it, mentally, into the crystal. Neophytes might also close their eyes for a few minutes, thinking intensely of someone well known to them, and then trying with their eyes open to visualize a picture of that person in the crystal.

❋ DELVING DEEPER

Gibson, Walter B., and Litzka R. Gibson. *The Complete Illustrated Book of the Psychic Sciences.* Garden City, N.Y.: Doubleday and Co., 1966.

Petrie, Jodra. *Tell Fortunes and Predict the Future.* New York: Award Books, 1968.

Post, Eric G. *Communicating with the Beyond.* New York: Atlantic Publishing, 1946.

TEA LEAF READING (TASSEOGRAPHY)

A centuries-old method of divining the future involves the interpretation of the fragments of tea leaves at the bottom of a client's cup. The first rule to follow in tea leaf or tea cup reading, also known as tasseography, is to brew the tea in a pot without a strainer in order to allow sufficient bits of leaves to enter the cup. Obviously, tea bags will not work at all. For those who prefer reading coffee grounds, the same rule applies: fresh-brewed coffee—no instant coffee or coffee bags. The rest of the rules that follow regarding tea leaf reading are also those required for the interpretation of coffee grounds.

The best results in a reading will be obtained from a white or light-colored cup with a wide top. The person whose fortune is to be read must drink the tea, leaving a little in the bottom of the cup. Once the tea has been drunk, the subject of the reading should slowly move the cup from left to right three times, thereby distributing some of the leaves around the sides of the cup.

At this point, most tea leaf readers may sit for a few minutes in silence, allowing the psychic rapport to be better established with the client. When they feel a mental connection has been made, the readers will take the cup from the client and begin an interpretation of the symbols made by the bits of leaf within the cup. There are some readers who prefer to have their client shake the cup to be certain the leaves are scattered around its surface and then place it upside down on the saucer. When the cup has been emptied, it is handed to the reader for interpretation of the leaf particles. Whichever method the individual reader prefers, they all agree that the first impression upon looking into the cup is the most important.

Experienced readers take in the total pattern of the leaves and envision the various symbols in terms of the whole picture before picking up on individual details. Again, there is little dogma among tea leaf readers. For some, the rim of the cup represents the future; the bottom, the past. For others, the rim represents the present, the sides predict the future, and the bottom foretells the very distant future. There seems some consensus that the cup's handle stands for the client's home life and personal environment, so the nearer the symbol to the handle, the sooner it will occur.

If the reader sees some of the specks of tea leaves as forming numbers, these may be interpreted as representing time—hours, days, weeks, months, depending upon other impressions received by the reader. If the reader envisions some bits of leaves as letters of the alphabet, they usually represent people close to the client. Very small specks, appearing as dots, indicate a journey for the client. Larger dots indicate money coming soon. Leaf residue that appears to be arranged in a wavy line suggest uncertainty. Straight lines represent a definite course of action that must be followed carefully. If the reader interprets any specks as stars or tri-

Tea leaf reading.

(FORTEAN PICTURE LIBRARY)

angles, the indication is good fortune; circles, great success; squares, a need to be cautious.

The reputation of any tea leaf reader is dependent upon his or her innate psychic ability and an imaginative interpretation of the meaning of the symbols that have been formed by the scattered bits of leaf. Here are some suggested interpretations of tea leaf imagery that seem somewhat common among tea leaf and coffee grounds readers:

- *Angel:* Good news is on the way. Someone is watching out for your best interests.

- *Ant:* You are an industrious person, but there is more hard work ahead for you.

- *Axe:* Someone near to you may be planning to stab you in the back with lies or deceit.

- *Bear:* Trouble ahead.

- *Bell:* Good news. Perhaps a wedding day will soon be set.

- *Bird:* There is a journey to be planned soon. It will be pleasant and productive.

- *Cat:* Keep your eye on a treacherous friend or relative.

- *Clouds:* If the flecks are scattered, troubles will soon be over. If they are solidly grouped, financial woes will soon materialize.

- *Flies or other insects:* Minor annoyances will soon become major problems if not dealt with immediately.

- *Flowers:* Love or an important honor is about to come to you.

- *Frog:* Be ready to make a dramatic change in your life.

- *Heart:* There is someone close to you in whom you may always confide.

- *Horseshoe:* Go ahead with your plans. The outcome will be fortunate.
- *Hour glass:* Take more time to make your decision.
- *Knife:* Avoid misunderstandings with those closest to you. Be more mindful of your health. Beware of a potential lawsuit.

A TEA *leaf reader's reputation is dependent upon their innate psychic ability and an imaginative interpretation of the meaning of symbols.*

- *Moon:* If it appears full, there is romance ahead for you. A half moon represents a time to leave old projects for new. The quarter moon warns against making hasty decisions.
- *Ring:* There is an approaching marriage or engagement for you or someone close to you.
- *Snake:* A small misfortune will only slightly impede your plans for success, for you will easily overcome its ill effects.
- *Wheel:* You or someone close to you are about to receive great advances in work and will soon receive much needed financial increases.
- *Woman:* Your great desire is for love and a happy family life.

❖ DELVING DEEPER

Cirlot, J. E. *A Dictionary of Symbols*. New York: Barnes & Noble, 1993.

Gibson, Walter B., and Litzka R. Gibson. *The Complete Illustrated Book of the Psychic Sciences*. Garden City, N.Y.: Doubleday and Co., 1966.

Petrie, Jodra. *Tell Fortunes and Predict the Future*. New York: Award Books, 1968.

Woodruff, Maurice. *The Secrets of Foretelling Your Own Future*. New York: Signet, 1969.

MAKING THE CONNECTION

clairvoyant Someone who has an ability or insight to perceive or see objects, events or actions in a supernatural way, beyond the normal senses.

cosmos From the Greek *kosmos* meaning "order, universe, ornament." The entire universe as regarded in an orderly, harmonious and integrated whole.

deity From late Latin *deitas* "divine nature," and *deus* "god." A divine being or somebody or something with the essential nature of a divinity, such as a god, goddess.

The Dispersion From the Greek *diaspora* meaning to scatter or disperse. Refers to the period in history when the Jewish people were forced to scatter in countries outside of Palestine after the Babylonian captivity.

haruspicy A method of divining or telling the future by examining the entrails of animals.

horoscope From Greek *horoskopos*, literally meaning "time observer" and from *hora* meaning "time, or hour," referring to the time of birth. A diagram or astrological forecast based on the relative position in the heavens of the stars and planets in the signs of the zodiac, at any given moment, but especially at the moment of one's birth.

neophyte From the Greek *neophutos* meaning "newly planted." A person who is a new convert to a religion or religious community. Somebody who is a beginner at an endeavor or task.

soothsayer From Middle English, literally meaning "somebody who speaks the truth." Someone who claims to have the ability to foretell future events.

CHAPTER 8
OBJECTS OF MYSTERY AND POWER

An object of mystery and power can be an everyday object that an individual believes brings good luck or fortune, ranging from an item of clothing that was worn when some great personal success was achieved, to an antique necklace passed on from generation to generation by a revered member of the family tree. In addition to such items of personal significance, individuals prize objects that reportedly brought victory or good fortune to heroes of long ago. Still others search for mysterious relics imbued with supernatural attributes that have accomplished miracles so that such powers might be theirs.

INTRODUCTION

bjects of power and mystery range from ancient stone structures with puzzling origins and purposes, to legendary lost relics that reportedly reappeared centuries later, to everyday objects that are believed to have special powers that will bring good fortune to the bearer.

Salt, for example, represents life and health to many people: it has been used as a flavor enhancer and food preservative since ancient times. A superstition for new parents in Europe and the Americas involves placing salt in a baby's cradle to protect the infant until it is baptized; a similar custom in some Middle Eastern countries calls for babies to be rubbed with salt to protect them from demons. It's bad luck in many cultures to spill salt, but there is a quick way to recover: toss a pinch of salt with the right hand over the left shoulder in order to stave off any bad luck resulting from the salt spill. Throwing salt over one's left shoulder is also believed to be a way to ward off the devil, who is said to look over the left shoulder of people; the salt tossed over the shoulder goes into the devil's eyes.

Some people keep or carry a certain object they believe brings them good luck and helps ward off bad fortune. Those items are based on superstition, religious belief, cultural practices, or personal associations. A "good luck charm," an object that symbolizes some important event, or a sacred religious item all possess some significance that combines with personal conviction to bring a sense of power, protection, and influence. The word "charm," however, did not always refer to an object of good luck. In the past, a charm was an incantation or inscription meant to result in an act of magic.

Amulets and talismans are objects intended to attract good luck and ward off bad luck. An amulet is most often a stone or a piece of metal with either an inscription or figures engraved on it. When talismans are crafted, the maker usually follows a ritual in order to infuse the talisman with a certain power. For example, a talisman crafted for a particular individual might be made of a metal corresponding to the qualities associated with a person's astrological sign.

The metal would have to be melted and forged during a positive astrological cycle.

Just as powerful in stirring the imagination are items associated with Judaism and Christianity that were lost in ancient times and were claimed to be recovered later. No physical evidence is available to determine that such objects ever existed, but they continue to be pursued. Sometimes, distinctions between what is real or imagined become blurred. The Holy Grail is never mentioned in the Bible, for example, but by medieval times it was popularized as "the holiest relic in Christendom" through Le morte d'Arthur by Sir Thomas Malory (fl. 1470). Tales of knights questing for the Holy Grail actually preceded a full account of the history of the grail. Yet, so powerful is the legend that the term "Holy Grail" is commonly used nowadays to describe an elusive, ultimate achievement. It is questionable as to whether the Holy Grail ever existed as a physical object, but it continues to inspire the imagination.

When it comes to things of mystery and power, then, the human imagination usually plays a key role in broadening the mystery and making it more powerful. Even when science provides data or physical proof that something mysterious can be explained, the ability to understand the impact of the explanation requires imagination, and often a change in outlook. Such is the power of objects of mystery: imagination and skill was used to create them, and imagination is required to begin to comprehend them by the more advanced human race of many centuries later.

❋ DELVING DEEPER

Bracken, Thomas. Good Luck Symbols and Talismans: People, Places, and Customs. Philadelphia: Chelsea House Publishers, 1997.

Budge, E.A. Wallis. Amulets and Talismans. New York: Collier Books, 1970.

Mintz, Ruth Finer. Auguries, Charms, Amulets. Middle Village, N.Y.: Jonathan David Publishers, 1983.

Nelson, Felicitas H. Talismans & Amulets of the World. New York: Sterling Publishers, 2000.

Pavitt, William Thomas. The Book of Talismans, Amulets, and Zodiacal Gems. New York: Samuel Weiser, 1970.

Walker, Barbara G. The Woman's Dictionary of Symbols and Sacred Objects. Edison, N.J.: Castle Books, 1988.

Amulets

The word "amulet" comes from the Latin (*amuletum*), an indication of the power Romans invested in amulets as protection against evil spells. Prehistoric amulets representing fertility and animals have been found near some of the oldest known human remains. Archaeologists have also unearthed shells, claws, teeth, and crystalline solids dating to 25,000 B.C.E.; engraved with symbols and sporting small holes, the objects were probably worn as necklaces.

Animals have been used as symbols in amulets since the earliest times. Modern amulets include a rabbit's foot; when rubbed it is activated to bring luck. The wishbone from the breast of a bird is believed to make wishes come true to the person lucky enough to hold the larger half when the bone is broken with a partner, a common practice at Thanksgiving Day dinners in the United States. Metal representations of wishbones and rabbit's feet have become popular amulets in contemporary times.

By the time the Roman Empire was established in the first centuries B.C.E., however, amulets had a long history of being worn for luck and protection. Egyptians considered amulets necessary for protection of the living and the dead. An amulet with a heart on it was often placed with the dead to help represent them in judgment about their fate in the afterlife. Likenesses of scarabs (a kind of beetle) were also prominent. A scarab encloses an egg in mud or dung and rolls it along to a spot where it can be warm and safe. Egyptians considered this a metaphor for the journey of the sun each day. The scarab amulet became a common emblem for regeneration and was placed with the dead.

Sumerians, who inhabited Mesopotamia (present-day Iraq) and were contemporaries of the Egyptians, had amulets inscribed with images of animals and gods. They also inscribed such images on seals for everything from pottery to vaults to doors: the emblem on the seal represented a guardian spirit that would bring bad luck to those who opened the sealed compartment without permission of the owner.

Ancient Amulets of the Middle East

Ancient Assyrians, Egyptians, Babylonians, Arabs, and Hebrews placed great importance in amulets:

- *Frog*—protected fertility
- *Ankh*—everlasting life
- *Udjat*—health
- *Scarab*—resurrection after death

Some of the Egyptian amulets are massive—a stone beetle at Karnak measures five feet long by three feet wide and weighs more than two tons.

Source:

"Amulets History" [Online] http://www.paralumun.com/amulet. htm. November 11, 2002.

The treasures of King Tutankhamen of Egypt (c. 1370–1352 B.C.E.) abound with crystals in the form of gems and jewels. They were intended for personal adornment, but they also had symbolic meaning: they were believed to possess mystical and religious powers. Today, crystals are still worn for decorative purposes in the form of gems and jewels; those who believe in the mystical powers of crystals wear them as amulets.

Many amulets have religious significance. Ancient Jews wore amulets around their necks that contained slips of parchment on which the laws of God were written. The Torah, comprising five books of the Old Testament of the Bible, is among the copies of holy books including the Bible (Christians), Vedas (Hindu), the Koran (Muslims), and the Avestar (Zoroastrians) believed by the faithful to

Amulets at the Wat Market. (CORBIS CORPORATION)

words "Hear O Israel, the Lord Our God Is One God" on the doorposts of their homes. An amulet with those words continues to be attached to doors in many modern Jewish households, or worn as a gold chain around the neck for good luck.

Early Christians inscribed the word *ichthys* (Greek for "fish") on their amulets because the word contained in Greek the initials for Jesus Christ, Son of God, Savior. The fish symbol has been important to Christians ever since.

A simple cord is perhaps the plainest amulet of them all. Wrist, ankle, and neck cords are popular in contemporary times and have a long history. Unlike other amulets, which when lost or broken are believed to end luck or protection, cords release magic to come true when they break naturally from wear. An amulet lost or broken might be a reason for despair, but a broken cord should signal the beginning of good fortune.

✤ DELVING DEEPER

Bracken, Thomas. *Good Luck Symbols and Talismans: People, Places, and Customs*. Philadelphia: Chelsea House Publishers, 1997.

Budge, E. A. Wallis. *Amulets and Talismans*. New York: Collier Books, 1970.

Mintz, Ruth Finer. *Auguries, Charms, Amulets*. Middle Village, N.Y.: Jonathan David Publishers, 1983.

Nelson, Felicitas H. *Talismans & Amulets of the World*. New York: Sterling Publishers, 2000.

Pavitt, William Thomas. *The Book of Talismans, Amulets, and Zodiacal Gems*. New York: Samuel Weiser, 1970.

bring good luck and to ward off evil. A favorite contemporary Muslim amulet consists of a square-inch miniature of the Koran enclosed in metal and worn around the neck. Muslims also believe they gain power by wearing amulets inscribed with a form of the name of Allah.

EGYPTIANS *considered amulets necessary for protection of the living and the dead.*

Amulets are frequently mentioned in Talmudic literature where they are called *kemiya* and often consist of a written parchment or root of herbs worn on a small chain, a ring, or a tube. Many such amulets had healing purposes: they were considered legitimate only after having worked successfully in healing on three different occasions. Another kind of parchment amulet was the *mezuzah*, a Hebrew word for door post. Moses (14th–13th century B.C.E.) commanded Israelites to inscribe the

BELLS

Bells have been associated with mystical occurrences and the spirit world since ancient times. Goddess images were frequently cast in the shape of bells. Ancient Jews wore bells tied to their clothing to ward off evil.

The ringing of bells or death knells for the deceased is an old custom. Some authorities believe that the ringing of bells at times of death originated in the practice of seeking to frighten away the evil spirits that lurk beside a corpse, waiting the opportunity to seize the newly released soul. In ancient times bells were rung only when important people died, but with the advent of Christianity it became the custom to ring death during burial services for all church members.

In medieval times, church bells were rung during epidemics with the hopes of clearing the air of disease. It was generally believed that church bells had special magical or spiritual powers, especially because of their position, suspended between heaven and Earth, guarding the passageway between the material and nonmaterial worlds, frightening away demons. The sacred bell of the Buddhists, the *ghanta*, serves that spiritual expression in a similar manner, driving away the negative entities and encouraging the positive spirits to manifest. The very sound of a bell is a symbol of creative power.

People along the west coast of Africa used to tie a bell to the foot of an ill child to ward off evil, and food was placed nearby to lure those spirits away. In contemporary times, bells above the door of a shop alert the shopkeeper that customers have entered. That practical function is predated by the use of bells over doors to keep evil spirits from entering into a home or shop.

❀ Delving Deeper

Bracken, Thomas. *Good Luck Symbols and Talismans: People, Places, and Customs.* Philadelphia: Chelsea House Publishers, 1997.

Gaskell, G. A. *Dictionary of All Scriptures and Myths.* Avenel, N.J.: Gramercy Books, 1981.

Walker, Barbara G. *The Woman's Dictionary of Symbols and Sacred Objects.* Edison, N.J.: Castle Books, 1988.

BLOODSTONE

Carnelian is a red-colored variety of chalcedony that for many centuries has been known as "bloodstone" and credited with the power to stem loss of blood from wounds or excessive menstrual flow. Although some have declared that its name was derived from the Latin *carne,* "flesh," most authorities maintain that the origin of the bloodstone's common European version, carnelian, lies in the word *cor,* "heart."

The blood redness of carnelian made it highly desired among ancient Egyptians who used it to represent the blood or virtue of the goddess Isis and placed it within the body cavity of a mummy. The Egyptian jewelers also favored the bloodstone as an addition to their heart amulets and proclaimed it as a symbol of the heart-soul of the goddess.

Carnelian is called the Mecca stone by many Muslims and is carried by them as an object that may assist in fulfilling all wishes for perfect happiness. While many authorities state that the "sardis" mentioned as the first stone in the breastplate of Aaron, Moses's brother, was a ruby, others suggest that it was a carnelian, or bloodstone.

CARNELIAN *is called the Mecca stone by many Moslems.*

Some bloodstones are greenish in color, with bright red flecks of jasper within them that look like flecks of blood. In folk medicine it matters little which bloodstone one employs, for in the mind of the practitioner, the stone is certain to halt the flow of blood and promote healing. And for the practical magician, the use of a bloodstone in rituals and incantations is believed to greatly increase the realization of all desires.

❀ Delving Deeper

Kunz, George Frederick. *The Mystical Lore of Precious Stones.* San Bernardino, Calif.: Borgo Press, 1986.

Pavitt, William Thomas. *The Book of Talismans, Amulets, and Zodiacal Gems.* New York: Samuel Weiser, 1970.

Walker, Barbara G. *The Woman's Dictionary of Symbols and Sacred Objects.* Edison, N.J.: Castle Books, 1988.

CANDLES

Candle burning has been associated with religious and magical ceremonies since earliest antiquity. To light a candle in respectful remembrance of a person who has died is a common practice in many religions. The light of a single candle is held by many to be symbolical of the illumination of the soul in the midst of earthly despair or of death.

Ancient Romans honored Juno Lucina, Mother of the Light, whenever a candle was lit to spread its light and sweet scent into the darkness. Juno Lucina controlled the sun, moon, and stars, and granted to newborn children the "light" of their spirit. Each year during the winter solstice a festival of lights was celebrated in her honor. This winter celebration became the Christian feast of Santa Lucia (Saint Lucy), which is still observed in Sweden with a young woman wearing a crown of candles and portraying the *Lussibruden* or Lucy Bride.

The custom of the lighting of the Yule candle also has its roots in the pagan observance of the winter solstice. Whereas Christians light an oversized candle that they hope would burn through the night from Christmas Eve to the dawn of Christmas Day to bring good luck for the coming year, the Scandinavians of old ignited a bundle of kindling and conducted a religious ceremony that was designed to encourage the sun to return from the long night of darkness.

For many centuries, candles have been very popular in the practice of certain rites of magic. In the Middle Ages, it was believed that a candle formed in the image of a woman and burned with the proper incantation could bring love to a man seeking the favor of a particular lady. According to tradition, a red-colored candle brought about the best results. First, according to the charm, the candle was to be anointed with perfume to signify femininity. Then, after the candle had burned for a few minutes a brief invocation was offered to loving spirits to bring the man's love to him forevermore. The invocation was to be made at sunset—once over the flame of the candle, then repeated over the smoking wick. The spell was to be repeated on consecutive sunsets until the candle had been consumed.

A black candle formed in the shape of a skull was often used in ceremonial magic to dispel curses. The skull-candle was to be burned at midnight and a proclamation, which had been formally written on paper, was to be read above the flame, demanding the removal of any curse that had been set against the magician. The candle was to be anointed with oil and was to be burned precisely at midnight.

It was believed that power and success might be gained through the ritual burning of a candle with oil and setting before it an incense offering of sandalwood or myrrh. The candle was lighted, and the magician concentrated on a mental image of the goal that he or she most wished to attain.

If a Magi felt that he had become the unwelcome recipient of a candle spell, he believed that he might reverse its effect through an ancient Medieval candle burning ceremony. For five consecutive nights, the magician was careful to light two large, black candles just as the sun was phasing into dusk. As the candles burned, the supplicant recited an invocation that called upon benevolent spirits to remove the curse from his head and to redirect it toward whomever had summoned the powers of darkness to cast a malediction against him. The ritual required that two candles must be allowed to be completely consumed each night.

✴ DELVING DEEPER

Buckland, Raymond. *Advanced Candle Magic: More Spells and Rituals for Every Purpose*. St. Paul, Minn.: Llewellyn, 1999.

Cooper, Phillip. *Candle Magic: A Coveted Collection of Spells, Rituals & Magical Paradigms*. New York: Weiser, 2000.

Riva, Anna. *Candle Burning Magic*. Toluca Lake, Calif.: International Imports, 1995.

Telesco, Patricia. *Exploring Candle Magick: Candle Spells, Charms, Rituals & Divinations*. Franklin Lakes, N.J.: Career Press, 2001.

Walker, Barbara G. *The Woman's Dictionary of Symbols and Sacred Objects*. Edison, N.J.: Castle Books, 1988.

CAULDRON

Cauldrons were used in various Celtic rites. Some cauldrons were believed to possess magical qualities: they would not boil the meat of a coward or an unrighteous person; they granted divine inspiration; or they provided great quantities of food. Early Celts used cauldrons in rites of fertility, and "cauldrons of plenty" were associated with abundance. The mead in the cauldron of the Celtic goddess Cerridwen gave divine wisdom, and that of the goddess Branwen promised regeneration.

Cauldrons in Celtic cultures may have also been used in acts of human sacrifice. The Gundestrup Cauldron, recovered from a peat bog in present-day Denmark dating from around 100 B.C.E., has a carved image of a victim being plunged into a cauldron.

The following ritual goes back to the early Middle Ages and has become a legendary magical method of gaining a desired lover's affection. It requires a cauldron of the first rain water in April. As the water boils, the following ingredients are to be collected and stirred into the brew: seven hairs from a blood snake (an old colloquialism for sausage prepared in the gut and/or hide of a pig), seven feathers from an owl, seven scales from a snake, a hair from the object of love and a bit of his nail paring. When all the ingredients have been incorporated into the cauldron, the magical "stew" must be allowed to boil briskly for seven minutes. At the end of this time, the magician must permit the brew to cool before he or she sprinkles it upon the intended lover. The brew is meant to warm the lover up a bit, not to scald him or her.

✤ Delving Deeper

Cooper, Phillip. *Candle Magic: A Coveted Collection of Spells, Rituals & Magical Paradigms*. New York: Weiser, 2000.

Hope-Simpson, Jacynth, ed. *Covens & Cauldrons: A Book of Witches*. London: Beaver Books, 1977.

Walker, Barbara G. *The Woman's Dictionary of Symbols and Sacred Objects*. Edison, N.J.: Castle Books, 1988.

CRYSTALS

Crystals were prized in many ancient cultures, and they remain so today—both for their scientific and their mystical qualities. Crystals have practical uses in radios, lasers, and computers, among other devices; and traditional Native American healers and New Age practitioners of alternative medicine believe that they have marvelous curative powers.

Ancient Greeks valued quartz crystal for its beauty and believed it had supernatural powers. The Greeks thought that the mineral

A woodcut of witches at a cauldron. (CORBIS CORPORATION)

quartz with its crystalline structure was water frozen so thoroughly that it could never be thawed, and they called quartz, "krystallos," from the word "kryos," which means icy cold. *Krystallos* became "crystal" in English during the Middle Ages to refer to stones with structures like quartz. Atoms and molecules in crystals are always arranged in tidy rows. These repeated, orderly patterns give crystals their beautiful sparkle and special shapes.

Some crystals, when compressed, develop electrical charges (piezoelectricity) at their ends, and others develop similar charges when heated (pyroelectricity). Both of those properties are evident in quartz and make the mineral useful in sonar and radio, for amplifying electric current, and to help make possible the solar battery that converts sunlight into electrical energy.

Lithium crystals are an energy source in the popular *Star Trek* television and movie series to fuel the starship *Enterprise*. On Earth, lithium is the lightest known metal and is often used in storage batteries.

Marcel Joseph Vogel, born in San Francisco in 1917, was revived after being pronounced dead at the age of six from pneumonia. At this time, Vogel encountered a near-death experience (NDE). It caused him to question the meaning of life. Every day, from the age of six, he walked to early morning Mass to pray and questioned the purpose of his existence.

At age 12, an answer came as a "voice" that told Marcel he would be a "phosphor chemist" doing work in luminescence. Majoring in chemistry and physics at the University of San Francisco, Vogel found little written, or taught, in the field of luminescence. So he translated articles he found written in German on phosphors. Due to deteriorating health, he left college and completed his education privately, with Dr. Peter Pringsheim, a German professor.

Pringsheim and Vogel published a book, *The Luminescence of Liquids and Solids and Their Practical Application* (1943). Vogel published other papers and formed his own corporation, Vogel Luminescence. The company pioneered in the manufacturing of fluorescent paints, oils, crayons, chalk, Day-Glo colors, invisible ink, and tagging and tracing powders—used to detect bacteria and disease, including cancer. He worked part-time for IBM and he became a senior research scientist in 1957. He remained with IBM until 1984, when he founded his own lab, Psychic Research, Inc.

Vogel's work with human–plant communication experiments led to his discovery of an intelligent matrix existing in crystal/liquid crystal with an ability to store, amplify, and transfer information, and that crystal can be altered during its growth stage. Seventeen years of research in this area led to his faceted crystal inventions, useful in laser applications. Vogel was also working on the structuring of water for purification purposes, and the structuring of wines to rapidly age them.

MARCEL VOGEL, MAN OF CRYSTAL VISION

SOURCES

Vogel, Marcel, and Peter Prigsheim. *The Luminescence of Liquids and Solids and Their Practical Application.* New York: Wiley-Interscience, 1943.

Vogel-cut Crystals by Lifestream Associates. [Online] http://www.vogelcrystals.com.

Stephen Quong-Vedic Astrologer: Healing Crystals [Online] http://www.jyotisha.com/Healingcrystals.htm.

Crystal Distributing Company. [Online] http://www.heartsharmony.com/vogel.htm.

Crystal Wings. [Online] http://www.crystalwings.com/vogelc.html.

The verifiable qualities of crystals are showcased in numerous applications in modern technology, but the mystical qualities of crystals are more difficult to explain and depend more on belief. Since the days of ancient Egypt, crystals have been believed to have healing properties and the ability to rid the body of negative energies. Crystals are believed to be able to store images and thoughts, serving as keepers of knowledge of the past. Among other attributes reputed of crystals is the ability to store and discharge light; to receive impressions from humans, who are able to program crystals for certain functions; to emit frequencies; and to become reenergized by sunlight and moonlight. Clear quartz is said to attract positive energy, and small wands with crystals mounted at both ends can supposedly locate pain or illness in a body.

Some mystics claim that inhabitants of the legendary continent of **Atlantis** used crystals to produce psychic energy and establish interstellar communication. Some believe that a powerful crystal energy source ultimately destroyed Atlantis. The popular twentieth century mystic **Edgar Cayce** (1877–1945) told his followers about his visions of the great crystals that powered Atlantis, and he referred to the healing capacities of crystals. Cayce taught that crystals possessed an energy within themselves that could be transmitted to people and be of great assistance in meditation, healing, and the achievement of higher levels of consciousness.

In 1976, **medium/channel** Frank Alper founded the Arizona Metaphysical Center in Phoenix and began channeling spirit messages that outlined methods of crystal therapy. In *Exploring Atlantis* (1982), three volumes of spirit directives on the powers of crystals, Alper outlined techniques that were followed with careful attention by New Age enthusiasts around the world. Within a very short time, crystal therapists were applying the ancient healing exercises that Alper's channeled messages described as having originated in ancient Atlantis.

New Age believers in crystal power were told by a number of channelers that all people had within themselves a Higher Self that was the ultimate expression of their personality. This Higher Self could become a conduit

Crystal necklaces for healing and well-being. (CORBIS CORPORATION)

between themselves and a source of divinity that had the power to activate a crystal for the purpose of healing. Those who wished to focus the healing abilities inherent in crystal were told that they must activate their crystal by breathing their "intent" to help others into the crystal. The process of activation involved their taking their crystal in the left hand. According to New Age channeling, the act of holding one's crystal in the left hand will stimulate the creative, intuitive process in the right brain hemisphere. Once this has occurred, the supposed vortex of energy in the crystal begins interacting with the individual's electromagnetic field and will start to increase the field energy around him or her.

When the energy field has been activated, the individual is to begin to breathe into the crystal the intention to be able to heal the physical bodies of those who request a healing. The individual healer must remember always that the crystal will magnify his or her intention and thereby serve as a powerful healing instrument.

In addition to its use in healing, crystals have always been popular as devices utilized in scrying, the ancient fortune telling technique of foreseeing future events in a clear surface. Pure quartz crystals polished into spheres became popular for divining purposes during the Middle Ages, and such crystal balls are still used by various contemporary psychic readers to obtain glimpses of the future.

❀ DELVING DEEPER

Conway, D. J. Crystal Enchantments. Santa Cruz, Calif.: Crossing Press, 2000.

Cunningham, Scott. Cunningham's Encyclopedia of Crystal, Gem & Metal Magic. St. Paul, Minn.: Llewellyn Publications, 1987.

Gienger, Michael. Crystal Power, Crystal Healing: The Complete Handbook. New York: Sterling Publications, 1998.

Jones, Wendy. Magic of Crystals. West Sunbury, Pa.: Harper House Books, 1996.

Simpson, Liz. Book of Crystal Healing. New York: Sterling Publications, 1997.

Sullivan, Kevin. The Crystal Handbook. New York: New American Library, 1996.

FAIRY CIRCLES

In most traditions, especially in the British Isles and Scandinavia, the fairy folk were supernormal entities who inhabited a magical kingdom beneath the surface of the earth. Fairies have always been considered to be much akin to humans, yet something more than mortal person. As many of the ancient texts declare, the fairies are "of a middle nature between Man and Angel." One factor has been consistent in fairy lore—these so-called "middle folk" continually meddle in the affairs of humankind, sometimes to do them good, sometimes to do them ill.

NATIVE *American tribes have similar stories of interactions with entities they call the "pukwudjinis."*

Tales have been told with endless modifications and variations, but it remains essentially a story of a fairy outwitting a greedy human. Less widely known are the many stories in which the person who discovers the fairies at their work is whisked away by them to the fairy kingdom, from which he or she may return much later as an old person believing that only a day or so has gone by.

In *The Science of Fairy Tales* by Edwin Sidney Hartland, published in London in 1891, the account is given of a shepherd who went out one day to look for his cattle and sheep on the mountain and seemingly disappeared into thin air. After about three weeks, the search parties had abandoned hope of ever finding him again. His wife had given him up for dead, and it was at that time that he returned. When his astonished wife asked him where he had been for the past three weeks, the man angrily said that he had only been gone for three hours. When he was asked to describe exactly where he had been, he said little men who closed nearer and nearer to him until they formed a small circle surrounding him. They sang and danced and so affected him that he got lost.

Near Bridgend is a place where a woman is said to have lived for 10 years with the fairy folk and who upon her return insisted that she had not been out of the house for more than 10 minutes.

The Germans, the Irish, the Scots, the English, and the Scandinavians have no end of such accounts of fairies interacting with people and stealing time. There are variants of these tales in Wales, in the Slavic countries, and in Japan and China. Stories are told of men and women who returned years, sometimes even generations, after they had stepped into a fairy circle and been enchanted by the singing and dancing of the wee people. Additional anecdotes are told of those who coupled with fairy folk and produced a hybrid of human and fairy individuals.

In Scotland the story is repeated of a man who went with his friend to enter his first child's birth in the record books and to buy a keg of whiskey for the christening. As the two men sat down to rest, they heard the sound of piping and dancing. The father of the newborn child became curious, and spotting some wee folk beginning to dance, he decided to join them.

His friend fled the spot, and when the new father did not return for several months, the friend was accused of murdering him. Somehow he was able to persuade the court that he should be allowed a year and a day to vindicate himself. Each night at dusk, he went to the spot where his friend had disappeared to call out his friend's name and to pray. One day just before the term ran out, he saw his friend dancing merrily with the fairies. The accused man succeeded in grabbing him by the sleeve and pulling him out. The bewitched man snapped angrily because his friend would not let him finish the dance. The unfortunate friend, who would face the gallows if he could not bring the enchanted man home, told the celebrating father that he had been dancing for 12 months and that he should have had enough. When rescued from the fairies' circle, the man would not believe the lapse of time until he found his wife sitting by the door of his home with their year-old son in her arms.

Several Native American tribes have similar stories of interactions with entities they call the "pukwudjinis," the little vanishing people. The tribespeople also refer to the medicine or magic circle. If anyone stepped inside

one, he or she could disappear for months or years or a lifetime.

✤ DELVING DEEPER

Bord, Janet. *Fairies: Real Encounters with Little People*. New York: Dell Publishing, 1998.

DuBois, Pierre. *The Great Encyclopedia of Fairies*. New York: Simon & Schuster, 2000.

Keightley, Thomas. *The World Guide to Gnomes, Fairies, Elves, and Other Little People*. New York: Random House, 2000.

Rose, Carol. *Spirits, Fairies, Leprechauns, and Goblins: An Encyclopedia*. New York: W. W. Norton & Co., 1998.

Spence, Lewis. *The Fairy Tradition in Britain*. London: Rider and Co., 1948.

GARLIC

Some naturally formed amulets can be worn or kept to ward off evil. Garlic reportedly keeps one safe from vampires, and also repels evil spirits. For garlic to perform that function in Mexico, it must be received as a gift. Some Roman soldiers wore garlic for extra protection when they went into battle.

It is possible that the tradition of garlic as an agent capable of warding off creatures of

A T. H. Thomas drawing from the book *British Goblin* (1880) by Wirt Sikes of a man being pulled back before entering a fairy circle. (FORTEAN PICTURE LIBRARY)

Some people use garlic to ward off vampires. (CORBIS CORPORATION)

darkness grew out of the simple fact that heavy consumption of garlic greatly affects the breath odor of those who have liberally partaken of the herb. In the ancient mystery religions, which emphasized the goddess and fertility rites, those who had eaten heavily of garlic were ostracized from worship.

❋ DELVING DEEPER

Allison, Lynn. *The Magic of Garlic*. Boca Raton, Fla.: Cool Hand Communications, 1993.

Mintz, Ruth Finer. *Auguries, Charms, Amulets*. Middle Village, N.Y.: Jonathan David Publishers, 1983.

Nelson, Felicitas H. *Talismans & Amulets of the World*. New York: Sterling Publishers, 2000.

HAND OF GLORY

One of the most macabre of all occult preparations was the Hand of Glory, a magic light made from the hand of a dead man. Once the hand had been severed from a corpse—often taken from the body of a hanged highwayman swinging on a gallows—it was to be slowly dried in an oven. When it was judged as quite dry, it was to be soaked in the melted fat of a black tomcat. Each finger served as a separate candle, and twisted human hair wrapped around the fingers served as wicks.

Although used as a protection against evil by those common folk who somehow managed to acquire such a grisly deterrent of the forces of darkness, the Hand of Glory was a favorite acquisition of burglars and thieves who believed that as long as the fingers burned the persons whose house they invaded would remain fast asleep and allow them to conclude their thievery undetected. There was even a little rhyme to be said when the hand was lit:

> Let those who rest more deeply sleep;
>
> Let those awake their vigils keep.
>
> O, Hand o' Glory shed thy light,
>
> Direct us to our spoils tonight.
>
> Flash out thy light, O skeleton hand,
>
> And guide the feet of our trusty band.

The only way to stop the power of the hand once it had been ignited was to douse it with either milk or blood. According to belief, water alone was incapable of extinguishing the flames of a Hand of Glory.

❋ DELVING DEEPER

Cavendish, Richard. *The Black Arts*. New York: Capricorn Books, 1968.

Opie, Iona, and Moira Tatem. *A Dictionary of Superstitions*. New York: Barnes & Noble, 1999.

Steiger, Brad, ed. *The Occult World of John Pendragon*. New York: Ace Books, 1968.

HORSESHOES

Horseshoes have long been popular in folk magic as an instrument of bringing the owner good luck—provided the object is worn out and found, rather than new and purchased.

In some countries the horseshoe is hung with the open end downward as a fertility symbol, but in Ireland, Britain, and the United States it is commonly hung with the open end pointing upward, so luck won't run out. A great debate rages: should a horseshoe be hung with its ends pointing downward, so luck can pour out in a steady, unending stream, or is it better placed upward, to collect, store, and bestow luck?

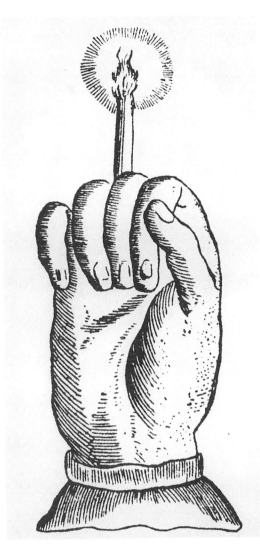

"The Hand of Glory" from Albertus Parvus Grimoire. (FORTEAN PICTURE LIBRARY)

In Italy, a horseshoe is hung by the door, not above the door, as it is elsewhere, so it can be touched by whomever passes over a threshold. In Mexico, horseshoes are wrapped up in bright colored threads. In Turkey, horseshoe charms are manufactured to help ward off the evil eye.

✤ DELVING DEEPER

Bracken, Thomas. *Good Luck Symbols and Talismans: People, Places, and Customs.* Philadelphia: Chelsea House Publishers, 1997.

Budge, E. A. Wallis. *Amulets and Talismans.* New York: Collier Books, 1970.

Mintz, Ruth Finer. *Auguries, Charms, Amulets.* Middle Village, N.Y.: Jonathan David Publishers, 1983.

Nelson, Felicitas H. *Talismans & Amulets of the World.* New York: Sterling Publishers, 2000.

Pavitt, William Thomas. *The Book of Talismans, Amulets, and Zodiacal Gems.* New York: Samuel Weiser, 1970.

KNIFE

The original cutting implements used by humans consisted of pieces of flint or other stone that had been chipped to form an edge. Such bits of stone evolved into the knife, among the first tools to be developed by humankind. Eventually, the stone blade became longer; the handle was wrapped with leather to avoid accidentally cutting the hand; and the knife was carried everywhere its owner went.

In the martial encounters between tribes, the spear, which is a knife with a long handle, and the club were favored in order to keep some distance between combatants. But when things got up close and personal, the knife came into play. Thus when the arts of warfare evolved and bronze weapons were used, the sword—a large and long knife—together with the spear and club were considered honorable implements of war. The knife was deemed the last resort of the gentleman or the sole weapon of the brigand and the assassin. In the days of chivalry, the knights bore swords and lances for self-defense while peasants and outlaws carried knives to protect themselves. The knife was a kind of secret weapon, and therefore considered base by those who faced one another with swords or lances. Men and women of any means whatsoever used knives primarily for cutting their food before they ate their meals with their fingers. Forks were unknown as table utensils until well into the eighteenth century, and table knives were a rarity until about the same time. People carried their own serviceable knives so they were always prepared to dine.

In witchcraft, the ceremonial knife is referred to as the athame.

In various systems of magic, from the times of human and animal sacrifice to ceremonial rituals, the knife has played an extremely important role. The magic circles of protec-

Chinese jade knife, c.
2500–2000 B.C.E.
(CORBIS CORPORATION)

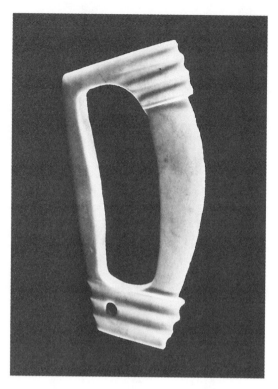

Chinese jade knife, c.
2500–2000 B.C.E.
(CORBIS CORPORATION)

tion that surround the magus and the sorcerer must be drawn with the magician's special knife, blessed by an invocation to a deity. In witchcraft, the ceremonial knife is referred to as the athame.

Knives are used in various divination practices simply by spinning them and seeing toward which object, number, person, and so forth, the blade points. Other traditions believe it is bad luck to spin a knife on the table, fearing that it symbolizes death for the one to whom it points.

While magicians use their magic knife to stir their potions, many individuals believe that those who use a knife to stir their tea, coffee, or food will summon strife. To drop a knife while eating, some people believe, is a sign that unexpected company will soon arrive. Others fear that to drop a knife will bring illness to the household. With the knife having played such an important and integral role in the societal and spiritual development of humankind, it is little wonder that there should be many superstitions regarding its use and misuse.

❋ DELVING DEEPER

Cavendish, Richard. *The Black Arts*. New York: Capricorn Books, 1968.

Gaskell, G. A. *Dictionary of All Scriptures and Myths*. New York: Gramercy Books, 1981.

Opie, Iona, and Moira Tatem. *A Dictionary of Superstitions*. New York: Barnes & Noble, 1999.

Walker, Barbara G. *The Woman's Dictionary of Symbols and Sacred Objects*. Edison, N.J.: Castle Books, 1988.

LOVE KNOTS

The expression "tying the knot" when one speaks of the marriage vows seems to have almost universal meaning. Africans tell of similar "knot-tying" love spells in their own tribes. Somehow it seems the most natural kind of symbolism to visualize the binding of one's self to the object of one's love while the fingers weave the knots and the lips chant a soulful litany. Here is how the ancient love spell of the seven knots was woven:

The magician would take a length of cord or ribbon that would sustain seven knots strung out at a distance of about an inch from one another. According to the ritual, the first knot was to be tied in the middle of the cord with the admonition that the two lovers remain bound to each other from that moment and that their love was in the circle that bound them.

At about the distance of one inch, the conjurer formed the second knot to the right of the first, telling the lovers that their love would endure with the strength of steel. The third knot was tied to the left of the first knot and the lovers were told that they would not be able to break away from one another, even though from time to time their passion might waver. The fourth knot was placed to the right with the message that all good spirits and the Holy Light would always keep the image of the other in the lovers' mind. The fifth knot was done to the left, assuring fidelity throughout their lifetimes. The sixth knot was bound on the right, binding the exclusivity of their affections, one to the other. The last knot, the seventh, was secured to the left and the officiator declared that the two should stand always within the circle of their love and happiness, unable to be separated by any power of Earth.

The incantation completed, the maker of the ritual would then bind the two ends of the cord together and wear it in the manner of a garter upon her or his left arm above the elbow. The "seven-knot-love-garter" was to be worn to bed for seven alternate nights. Upon the fourteenth day, the charm was either to be burned in offering to good spirits or to be hidden in a secret place.

❀ Delving Deeper

Bracken, Thomas. *Good Luck Symbols and Talismans: People, Places, and Customs.* Philadelphia: Chelsea House Publishers, 1997.

Budge, E. A. Wallis. *Amulets and Talismans.* New York: Collier Books, 1970.

Mintz, Ruth Finer. *Auguries, Charms, Amulets.* Middle Village, N.Y.: Jonathan David Publishers, 1983.

Nelson, Felicitas H. *Talismans & Amulets of the World.* New York: Sterling Publishers, 2000.

Pavitt, William Thomas. *The Book of Talismans, Amulets, and Zodiacal Gems.* New York: Samuel Weiser, 1970.

Mandrake Root

Mandrake, also known as *mandragora officinarum*, has a long tap-root that resembles a human form. This resemblance created the superstition that it literally shrieked when it was uprooted. Those who heard the scream were to die, or, if it didn't kill them, it caused them to go insane.

This relative of the potato family was a popular anaesthetic during the Middle Ages. In the Elizabethan Age it was used as a narcotic.

❀ Delving Deeper

"The Mandragora Plant—Myths and other Information." [Online] http://www.wordfocus.com/ anesthes-wrd-hist.html#mandragora. November 11, 2002.

Maypole

The ancients in Great Britain and Northern Europe believed that May 1 was the boundary day between summer and winter and that on this day a war took place between the two seasons to determine which would prevail. It became customary to stage a mock war between two people, one to represent winter; the other, summer. Summer always managed

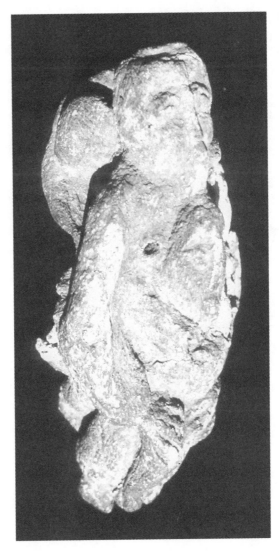

Mandrake root shaped like mother with child. (RAYMOND BUCKLAND/FORTEAN PICTURE LIBRARY)

to win and was promptly crowned King of the May. In triumph he held aloft green branches decorated with beautiful May flowers and sang an old folk song, the essence of which seems to have been, "I have won, I bring you summer!"

Later, as the custom evolved, a young tree was cut down and decorated with ribbons and flowers. This tree was set up triumphantly in the village and everyone danced around it. The Druids worshipped the tree, and it is possible that the Maypole originated with them. But long before the time of Charles I (1600–1649) in England the tree had given way to the pole. Huge poles were planted in the ground and decorated with green branches and flowers. Long streamers were attached to the top, and each dancer held on proudly to his or her end of the ribbon.

✤ DELVING DEEPER

Bracken, Thomas. *Good Luck Symbols and Talismans: People, Places, and Customs.* Philadelphia: Chelsea House Publishers, 1997.

Budge, E. A. Wallis. *Amulets and Talismans.* New York: Collier Books, 1970.

Eichler, Lillian. *The Customs of Mankind.* Garden City, N.Y.: Doubleday, 1937.

Mintz, Ruth Finer. *Auguries, Charms, Amulets.* Middle Village, N.Y.: Jonathan David Publishers, 1983.

Nelson, Felicitas H. *Talismans & Amulets of the World.* New York: Sterling Publishers, 2000.

MIRROR

The first mirror was quite likely a quiet pool in which one caught a fleeting reflection of an image of oneself. The early Greeks had mirrors that were made of circular pieces of polished bronze, sometimes with richly adorned handles. The early Egyptians also had bronze mirrors, highly polished dishes, usually with graceful and decorative handles.

Since early times the mirror has been used in divination, in attempts to read the future or the past. In ancient Greece divination performed by means of water and a mirror was so popular and so widely practiced that it was given a definite name—"catoptomancy." There are still seers and fortune-tellers called "scryers" who "see" the past and the future in crystals and mirrors.

An early belief was that one saw the will of the gods in the mirror. To break a mirror accidentally, therefore, was interpreted as an effort on the part of the gods to prevent the person from seeing into the future. This was construed as a warning that the future held unpleasant things.

It was not until 1688 that glass mirrors were invented. In that year, a Frenchman,

Louis Lucas, invented plate glass that, backed with the proper alloy, formed a mirror that for the first time gave both sexes a true reflection of their appearance.

One of the most common of modern superstitions is that to break a mirror invites death, or seven years of bad luck. This old folk belief originated with the Romans about the first century C.E. They believed that the health of a person changed every seven years, and as the mirror reflected the health or the appearance of the person, to break a mirror would be to shatter one's health for a period of seven years. Among highly superstitious people the breaking of the mirror came to be looked upon as a death omen. Somehow this superstitious belief has prevailed and still exists even among educated people.

Man and woman hanging mistletoe.
(CORBIS CORPORATION)

🕱 DELVING DEEPER

Bracken, Thomas. *Good Luck Symbols and Talismans: People, Places, and Customs*. Philadelphia: Chelsea House Publishers, 1997.

Budge, E. A. Wallis. *Amulets and Talismans*. New York: Collier Books, 1970.

Eichler, Lillian. *The Customs of Mankind*. Garden City, N.Y.: Doubleday, 1937.

Mintz, Ruth Finer. *Auguries, Charms, Amulets*. Middle Village, N.Y.: Jonathan David Publishers, 1983.

Nelson, Felicitas H. *Talismans & Amulets of the World*. New York: Sterling Publishers, 2000.

MISTLETOE

Mistletoe is another natural amulet. It is commonly hung in homes during Christmastime; the custom of kissing under the mistletoe goes back to ancient Europeans, who believed mistletoe brought fertility, healing, and luck. They hung it in homes and barns. Mistletoe was sacred as well to Celts. It is a parasitic plant that grows on trees without forming roots in the earth. This quality led Celts to venerate mistletoe as a divine substance.

For many centuries, people around the world have created many folklore beliefs about mistletoe:

• Central Australian aborigines believed that the *ratapa*, spirits of unborn children of their tribe, lived in trees, rocks, and sprigs of mistletoe.

• The Japanese chopped mistletoe, leaves, and millet, and offered prayers for a good harvest.

• Swedes hung a mistletoe besom (broom) in the house as a charm against lightning.

• Swedes used mistletoe rods to locate treasure in the earth. The rod was supposed to quiver, like a divining rod, when it was over the treasure.

• Austrians hung mistletoe over the doorstep to protect people in the house from nightmares.

• Since ancient times, a kiss under the mistletoe was a pledge of love and a promise of marriage.

• The kiss of friendship was given under a mistletoe to signify a truce. Enemies who met under the mistletoe in the forest were to lay down their arms, exchange friendly greetings, and keep a truce until the following day.

🕱 DELVING DEEPER

Budge, E. A. Wallis. *Amulets and Talismans*. New York: Collier Books, 1970.

Mintz, Ruth Finer. *Auguries, Charms, Amulets*. Middle Village, N.Y.: Jonathan David Publishers, 1983.

"Mistletoe." [Online] http://www.celticattic.com/ olde_world/myths/mistleoe.htm. November 11, 2002.

Nelson, Felicitas H. *Talismans & Amulets of the World.* New York: Sterling Publishers, 2000.

Pavitt, William Thomas. *The Book of Talismans, Amulets, and Zodiacal Gems.* New York: Samuel Weiser, 1970.

RINGS

The ring as a pledge can be traced back to great antiquity. "And Pharaoh said unto Joseph, 'See I have set thee over all the land of Egypt.' And Pharaoh took off his ring from his hand, and put it upon Joseph's hand" (Genesis 41:42).

Similar use of signet rings as symbols of respect and authority is mentioned in several parts of the Bible, and it would appear that rings were commonly worn by persons of rank at that period, and that rings were bestowed upon others either as gifts or for the purpose of transferring authority.

Rings worn only as ornaments were common in early Egypt, in Greece, and even among less civilized peoples. In antiquity, it was the custom among people of the lower classes to break a piece of gold or silver to seal the marriage pact. One half of the token was kept by the man, the other half by the woman. This custom came before the exchange of rings. In ancient Ireland, for instance, it was the custom for the man to give the woman he wanted to marry a bracelet woven of human hair. Her acceptance of it was symbolic of accepting the man, of linking herself to him for life.

In England, rings were exchanged to seal the verbal contract of betrothal.

It appears that the ring as a love pledge existed at an early period. It was customary in the early Middle Ages to make a solemn betrothal by means of a ring to precede matrimony. In England, rings were exchanged to seal the verbal contract of betrothal. In Italy the use of the ring was widespread, and the

diamond was the favorite gem. The diamond remains the favorite gem for the engagement ring in modern times. Indeed, many people think only of the diamond in connection with rings of betrothal. According to an old superstition, the sparkle of the diamond is supposed to have originated in the fires of love. Therefore the diamond engagement ring is considered by many persons as the only true engagement ring, portending love and happiness throughout life.

✢ **DELVING DEEPER**

Eichler, Lillian. *The Customs of Mankind.* Garden City, N.Y.: Doubleday, 1937.

Mintz, Ruth Finer. *Auguries, Charms, Amulets.* Middle Village, N.Y.: Jonathan David Publishers, 1983.

Nelson, Felicitas H. *Talismans & Amulets of the World.* New York: Sterling Publishers, 2000.

SALT

In Finnish mythology, the mighty god of the sky, Ukko, struck fire in the heavens. A spark from this celestial fire fell into the ocean and turned to salt. Another old legend is that the oceans are made up of the tears of all those who have suffered since the world began; and as tears are salt, the oceans' waters are salt.

Salt was used long before the contemporary era, and it was highly valued by those who included it in their diet. Salt was probably being traded even in Neolithic times. The Israelites believed that no meal was complete without a bit of salt to help digest it. Homer (9th–8th century B.C.E.) called salt divine, and Plato (c. 428–348 or 347 B.C.E.) described it as a substance valued by the gods.

At one time salt was regarded as being almost as valuable as gold, and soldiers, officials, and working people in Greece and Rome received all or part of their pay in salt. Money paid for labor or service was termed "salarium," the origin of the word "salary,"—money paid for services rendered. From this custom of paying with salt comes also the popular phrase "to earn one's salt."

It was a custom in early times to place salt before strangers as a token or pledge of friendship. "Take a pinch of salt with me" was the popular method of inviting a friend or acquaintance to one's home to partake of one's hospitality.

In many Asian countries salt was offered to guests as a token of hospitality, and if any particles fell to the ground while being presented it was considered an omen of ill luck. The belief was that a quarrel or a dispute would follow.

Among the Germans there is the old saying, "Whoever spills salt arouses enmity." The ancient Romans believed that to spill salt was to cause quarrels or disputes, and when salt was spilled it was the custom to exclaim, "May the gods avert the omen!" Another old tradition says that if salt is thrown over the left shoulder, it will appease the devil, who will otherwise make enemies of friends whenever salt is spilled.

According to some authorities, the widespread notion that the spilling of salt produces evil consequences is supposed to have originated in the tradition that Judas overturned a salt shaker at the Last Supper as portrayed in Leonardo da Vinci's (1452–1519) painting. But it appears more probable that the belief is due to the sacred character of salt in early times.

These old salt superstitions are found in many widely separated countries. Long ago they captured the public fancy, and they have survived. There are still many people who believe that to spill salt is an omen of a quarrel or bad luck, and that to toss a bit of the salt over the left shoulder is to cancel the negative consequences.

Salt crystals. (CORBIS CORPORATION)

❈ Delving Deeper

Cavendish, Richard. *The Black Arts*. New York: Capricorn Books, 1968.

Eichler, Lillian. *The Customs of Mankind*. Garden City, N.Y.: Doubleday, 1937.

Gaskell, G. A. *Dictionary of All Scriptures and Myths*. New York: Gramercy Books, 1981.

Mintz, Ruth Finer. *Auguries, Charms, Amulets*. Middle Village, N.Y.: Jonathan David Publishers, 1983.

Silver

Silver is said to offer protection and enhance one's psychic qualities. Silver was associated with the moon in Roman and Chinese cultures, and was considered divine (rather than a naturally formed metal) by Incas of South America. Egyptians coveted silver because it was not found in their region.

Silver bullets are reportedly good for killing vampires, werewolves, and ghosts. Another metal, brass, is especially good for amulets since it is believed to repel evil spirits.

❈ Delving Deeper

Cavendish, Richard. *The Black Arts*. New York: Capricorn Books, 1968.

Cunningham, Scott. *Cunningham's Encyclopedia of Crystal, Gem & Metal Magic*. St. Paul, Minn.: Llewellyn Publications, 1987.

Gaskell, G. A. *Dictionary of All Scriptures and Myths*. New York: Gramercy Books, 1981.

Kunz, George Frederick. *The Mystical Lore of Precious Stones*. San Bernardino, Calif.: Borgo Press, 1986.

Pavitt, William Thomas. *The Book of Talismans, Amulets, and Zodiacal Gems*. New York: Samuel Weiser, 1970.

Stones for Healing and Energy

Perhaps the most popular amulets in folk magic are the 12 birth stones. These semiprecious gems, mounted in rings and pendants, have enjoyed widespread appeal for centuries. Because most people are familiar with these stones, the magic powers of each is as follows:

Agate. This stone may appear as striped or clouded quartz, and is astrologically associated with the sign Gemini. An agate amulet is believed to promote good health. An agate ring bestows wealth and honor; also, it can be used to obtain favors from people in high positions. Legend has it that any person who gazes upon this gem will be compelled to speak the truth and cannot maintain secrecy.

Amethyst. This gem, a purple variety of quartz, is traditionally considered to be the Aquarian birthstone. An amethyst ring is usually worn for protection against sorcery and the evil eye. An amethyst pendant prevents depression and supposedly bestows spiritual visions.

Bloodstone. Also known as heliotrope, this variety of quartz is the Piscean birthstone. Worn as a pendant, it allegedly prevents miscarriage and other illness during pregnancy. Mounted in a ring, the amulet reportedly promotes creativity. Worn to bed, bloodstone may bestow pleasant dreams and clear visions of the future.

Diamond. This precious gem is astrologically associated with the sign of Aries. A diamond amulet traditionally symbolizes enduring love and happiness in a marriage. Given as a gift, the gem is believed to strengthen emotional bonds and promote loyalty. A diamond pendant may be worn to obtain honor and friendship. Mounted in a ring, the amulet insures lasting marriage and financial success.

Emerald. Traditionally associated with the astrological sign Taurus, this precious green gem has several unique properties. An emerald pendant is thought to afford women protection against assault. Mounted in a ring, the stone promotes domestic stability and fortune. According to legend, this amulet may be used to combat epilepsy, depression, and insanity.

Garnet. This semiprecious gem is the birthstone of Capricorn people. Early Egyptians and Phoenicians used the stone extensively. It reputedly healed snakebite and food poisoning by absorbing foreign chemicals in the blood through the skin. A garnet pendant is usually worn to arouse the passionate love of the opposite sex. A garnet ring reputedly combats fear and pessimism. Argument and eventual separation of two lovers is thought to result when garnet is given as a gift.

Opal. This semiprecious gem is associated with the astrological sign Libra. Worn as a ring, this amulet reputedly alleviates indigestion and other stomach disorders. Also, it instills tranquility and joy. An opal pendant is worn to attract happiness in love, fortune and favorable judgment in court. The opal amulet is believed to take on a dull gray appearance when minor illness is forthcoming. A sickly yellow hue presages injury by accident.

Ruby. This popular birthstone, which is associated with the astrological sign Cancer, reputedly promotes mental health and tranquility. A ruby pendant is thought to combat depression and enable the wearer to overcome sorrow. A ruby amulet worn as a ring bestows knowledge, health, and wealth. This stone should never be given as a gift, as it is thought that discord and broken relationships will result.

Sapphire. This deep blue corundum is astrologically associated with the sign Virgo. A sapphire pendant is a reputed cure for fever, seizures, and delusions. Mounted in a ring, the gem bestows wisdom and compassion. When danger is imminent, this amulet reportedly takes on a chalky appearance, which remains until the hazard has subsided.

Sardonyx. The birthstone of Leo people, this gem is a popular remedy for impotence. Ancient occultists believed that a sardonyx amulet could be worn to alleviate this affliction in less than a week. Mounted in a ring, sardonyx has no power; however, worn as a pendant, the stone combats sterility. Given as a gift, the sardonyx amulet is thought to guarantee the recipient's fidelity.

Topaz. This gem is the birthstone of Scorpio people. Some medieval occultists insisted that a topaz amulet promoted psychic sensitivity and facilitated control of destiny. A topaz pendant reputedly bestows honor, happiness, and inner peace in addition to the above benefits. Mounted in a ring, the gem insures promotion and financial success.

Turquoise. The birthstone of Sagittarians, turquoise has been worn in amulets since the earliest times. Native Americans considered the stone sacred, and medieval sorcerers used it in various magic rituals. Modern authorities claim that a turquoise amulet is an effective deterrent against illness and injury. Worn as a pendant, the stone also protects its bearer from a violent death. A turquoise ring is said to have the power to allow the wearer to rekindle old love affairs.

In addition to the 12 birthstones, other gems of magical and healing significance warrant consideration. These are:

Amber. This gem, which has been used for magical purposes from time immemorial, is primarily a health aid. An amber pendant reportedly cures diseases of the blood, poor circulation, and prevents heart attack. Mounted in a ring, this stone is believed to combat malfunction of the kidney and protect the wearer against heat stroke and suffocation.

Beryl. This opaque stone usually comes in yellow, pink, green, or white. Worn as a pendant, it is claimed to promote happy marriage and honesty. Given as a gift, it is a popular deterrent to unfaithfulness. A beryl ring is frequently worn to insure good health during pregnancy.

Carnelian. This reddish quartz gem was highly popular with Old World occultists. Early Chaldeans gave their stone to enemies and thereby rendered them harmless.

Chrysocolla. This stone is recommended for treatment of diabetes and asthma and is said to build inner peace and strength and to attract prosperity and good luck.

Coral. This stone occurs in a variety of colors and is allegedly invaluable to careless people. As an amulet, it is said to take on a chalky white appearance when in close proximity with sick people. A coral ring or pendant may also be worn to promote health and wisdom.

Jade. Throughout history, magicians have used this gem as a deterrent to sorcery and demonic possession. Jade is therefore considered to be one of the most potent protective device known to humankind. Modern occultists claim that a jade pendant may be worn to achieve these effects, and that a ring combats tragedy and depression.

Jet. Perhaps one of the most powerful amulets known, this lustrous black gem holds an important place in the legends of various cultures. In ancient Greece, occultists believed that it was a sacred substance, and in Assyria it was considered to be the gods' favorite jewel. Medieval legend credits the jet amulet with supernatural powers. The person wearing this stone supposedly attains complete control of the natural elements—fire, air, earth, and water.

Lapis Lazuli. This stone has long been valued as an aid to cleanse the mind and body of toxins and promote psychic abilities.

❋ DELVING DEEPER

Cavendish, Richard. *The Black Arts.* New York: Capricorn Books, 1968.

Cunningham, Scott. *Cunningham's Encyclopedia of Crystal, Gem & Metal Magic.* St. Paul, Minn.: Llewellyn Publications, 1987.

Kunz, George Frederick. *The Mystical Lore of Precious Stones.* San Bernardino, Calif.: Borgo Press, 1986.

Pavitt, William Thomas. *The Book of Talismans, Amulets, and Zodiacal Gems.* New York: Samuel Weiser, 1970.

Walker, Barbara G. *The Woman's Dictionary of Symbols and Sacred Objects.* Edison, N.J.: Castle Books, 1988.

TREES

Many trees and plants are used as objects of power. Hazel, the wood of choice for magic wands, was commonly used for divining rods as a means for locating sources of underground water so that wells could be dug. A hazel rod was used by St. Patrick (fifth century C.E.) to draw out the snakes of Ireland, which he then cast out to sea.

H AZEL *is the wood of choice for magic wands.*

To the Druid and other magicians, trees are a good source of radiant vitality and may be drawn upon for relief, and even cure, of backache conditions. Many who are attuned to nature seek to create a tree charm to bring them strength. The prospective charm maker

selects a suitable tree, strong, upright, free from distortions, and of good size. Ash, spruce, and birch are recommended. For best results, the tree should be situated as far away from human contamination as possible.

Once a proper tree has been selected, the magician makes friends with it by touching it, talking to it, and thinking into it. The tree should be circled nine times while the magus touches it gently with his or her fingertips. Upon the completion of the encirclement, the magician takes a final position to the north, leans back against the tree, and reaches his or her hands behind so that they might touch the bark of the tree. In this position, the magus chants:

> O Tree;
> Strong Tree; King Tree:
> Take thou this weakness of my back.
> Give me strength instead.
> That I may be as upright as thyself
> Between the Heavens (look up)
> And the Earth beneath (look down).
> Secure from storm

And blessed in every branch.
May this be so!

The magician repeats the incantation until a feeling of rapport is established with the tree. When it is felt that the treatment is over, the magician breaks contact gently and thanks the nature spirits for their help.

❋ DELVING DEEPER

Cavendish, Richard. *The Black Arts*. New York: Capricorn Books, 1968.

Cirlot, J. E. *A Dictionary of Symbols*. Translated by Jack Sage. New York: Barnes & Noble, 1993.

Gaskell, G. A. *Dictionary of All Scriptures and Myths*. New York: Gramercy Books, 1981.

Gifford, Jane. *The Wisdom of Trees: Mystery, Magic and Medicine*. New York: Sterling Publications, 2000.

Paterson, Jacqueline Memory. *Tree Wisdom*. Great Britain: Thorson Publishing, 1997.

VOODOO DOLLS

To accomplish the placing a curse or a spell upon an individual, many magic traditions utilize a wax or cloth image to represent a hated enemy or a desired loved one. To properly effect such a spell or curse, it is generally required to obtain some personal bit of the object of one's intentions, i.e., nail parings, hair, excrement, saliva; and mix this in with soft wax or sew it in the cloth. Once this has been accomplished, the wax or pieces of cloth may be shaped into the form of either a male or female figure.

In the popular mind the so-called voodoo doll is the most well-known of such effigies, and many tourists have brought such souvenirs home from their visits to New Orleans or Haiti where **Voudun** (Voodoo) is practiced as a religion. Over the years, the portrayal of a voudun priest or priestess sticking pins into a doll that represents someone who has incurred their wrath has become so common that such effigies or puppets are known collectively as voodoo dolls. Actually, such figures have no role in the religion of voodoo, and the practice of sticking pins in dolls or poppets (puppets) is a custom of Western European witches, rather than the Haitian or Caribbean practitioners of voudun. Perhaps the misunderstanding arose when outsiders who witnessed

Replica voodoo doll.
(KLAUS AARSLEFF/FORTEAN
PICTURE LIBRARY)

certain rituals saw the followers of voudun sticking pins in the figures of saints or guardian spirits. Such acts are done not to bring harm to anyone, but to keep the good force of magic within the object.

One method of effigy cursing calls for the magician to fashion a wax or cloth skeleton and to inscribe the name of the intended victim on its back. The image is then pierced with a thorn or a sharpened twig in the area corresponding to the victim's body part that the sorcerer desires to inflict with pain. Once pierced, the skeleton is wrapped in a shroud and prayed over as if it were a deceased person. When the death-rites have been accomplished, the effigy must be buried in a spot over which the intended victim is certain to walk.

Waxen and cloth images may also be used to bring about unions of love, as well as terrible deeds of hatred and revenge. In order to weave a love spell with wax effigies, the magician fashions two hearts of wax, baptizes them with the lovers' names, and then joins the hearts together with three pins. The images are then given to the one who desires such a union so that she or he might press the wax hearts to her or his own heart.

EVERY *magic tradition in every culture utilizes a wax or cloth image to represent a hated enemy or a desired loved one.*

When magicians are convinced that they themselves have been cursed, they might form an image, or puppet, to represent the one who has cast the malign spell. Once the magicians have fashioned such a puppet, they bury the box containing the puppet under a thin layer of soil. Over the soil, they light a bonfire and chant their wish that the curse set against them will be consumed along with the flames that burn the puppet representing the one who cursed them.

Witchcraft puppet.

(FORTEAN PICTURE LIBRARY)

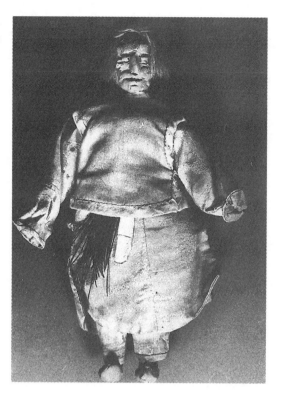

✤ DELVING DEEPER

Bracken, Thomas. *Good Luck Symbols and Talismans: People, Places, and Customs.* Philadelphia: Chelsea House Publishers, 1997.

Budge, E. A. Wallis. *Amulets and Talismans.* New York: Collier Books, 1970.

Mintz, Ruth Finer. *Auguries, Charms, Amulets.* Middle Village, N.Y.: Jonathan David Publishers, 1983.

Nelson, Felicitas H. *Talismans & Amulets of the World.* New York: Sterling Publishers, 2000.

TRIBAL EMPOWERMENT

In *Black Elk Speaks* (1932), John G. Neihardt told of accompanying Black Elk, the aged holy man of the Oglala Sioux, to Harney Peak, the same place where the spirits had taken Black Elk in a vision when he was young. Neihardt wrote that as those who stood by watched, thin clouds began to gather out of a clear sky. A scant chill rain began to fall, and there was low, rumbling thunder without lightning. With tears running down his cheeks, Black Elk chanted that the Great Spirit, the Six Powers of the World, heard his prayer to preserve his people. According to Neihardt, Black Elk stood for a few minutes in silence, his face uplifted, weeping in the rain, and then the sky was once again cloudless.

While those witnesses who observe such apparent control over the weather by a tribal shaman consider it magic, the practitioners themselves regard such abilities as empowerment. The tribal medicine men and women use forces that have been here for all time for the benefit or needs of their people. In their view, magic is not magic if one understands it. Their medicine power enables them to will something into existence because they have need of it.

When evolving humankind existed in a less technological state in tribes around the world, there was a conscious or unconscious awareness that humans were a part of nature, part of one whole. And conversely, the whole was part of humankind. Because of this oneness, humans understood that they were a part of the power of creation and of all the creatures that walked, swam, or took flight.

To be a recipient of tribal empowerment, the practitioner, the shaman, or the priest must live their commitment every moment of every day. They must believe in the unity and the cooperation of all forms of life. When they are forced to take the life of an animal in order to survive, they kill only after uttering a prayer, beseeching the group spirit of that animal to understand that such an act was necessary in the turning of the great wheel of life.

When those tribal initiates who seek empowerment have displayed the proper attitude of receptivity, they must go alone into the wilderness to fast, to receive their **spirit guide,** and to receive a secret name and a sacred song. Perhaps the guide will also grant special powers of healing or prophecy to the supplicants.

The recipient of tribal empowerment is able to obtain personal contact with the invisible world of spirits and to pierce the sensory world of illusion which veils the great mystery. Often this gift is heightened by the intoning of the personal mantra, the personal song, the holy syllables that attune him or her with the eternal sound, the cosmic vibration of all creation.

A crucial element in tribal empowerment is the ability to rise above linear time. Most people have accepted the conventional concept of time as existing in some sort of sequential stream flowing along in one dimension. In solitary, mystical experience, those recipients of tribal empowerment are able to enter a reality of time that is not clock-measured or clock-controlled and that places their psyches in a dimension beyond linear time and space.

The ethnologist Ivar Lissner believed that in the sophistication of the modern world, people must not forsake the heritage of spirituality that has been bequeathed to humankind over hundreds of thousands of years. Humans must never allow the materialist or the pure technologist to dictate the fate of humanity. In his view, surveying the contributions made over the centuries by those nontechnological societies and their tribal empowerments, humankind must be guided by "great, universal minds which are closer to the secrets of the transcendental and throw more into the scales than mere weight of technological progress."

❀ DELVING DEEPER

Gill, Sam D., and Irene F. Sullivan. *Dictionary of Native American Mythology*. New York: Oxford University Press, 1992.

Gregor, Arthur S. *Amulets, Talismans, and Fetishes*. New York: Scribner, 1975.

Harner, Michael. *The Way of the Shaman*. New York: Bantam Books, 1982.

Lissner, Ivar. *Man, God and Magic*. New York: G. P. Putnam's Sons, 1961.

Neihardt, John G. *Black Elk Speaks*. New York: William Morrow, 1932. Reprint, New York: Pocket Books, 1972.

CRYSTAL SKULLS

Crystal skulls are fashioned from large pieces of crystal, usually from the mineral quartz. They are often life-sized and bear the same distinguishing characteristics as a human skull with eye sockets, a nasal cavity, and a rounded cranium. The most exquisite crystal skulls have finely crafted jaws with removable mandibles.

In addition to claims of paranormal activity, controversy concerning crystal skulls centers on their origins. More than a dozen of them were claimed to have been discovered in Mexico and Central America and are dated by

their founders or those who currently possess them as being hundreds, perhaps thousands of years old. Common methods for dating artifacts can neither confirm nor refute claims about when these crystal skulls were crafted, but, generally speaking, skulls sculpted with metal tools cannot be more than a few centuries old if they originated in Mexico and Central America.

CRYSTAL *skulls are believed to awaken the human consciousness to a higher level of being.*

Some crystal skulls are attributed to the Mayan culture that thrived in southern Mexico and Central America during the first millennium C.E. However, as established through studies of recurring symbols, artifacts, or references in hieroglyphics, there is no known cultural tradition among the Mayans that relate to crystal skulls or any kind of skull worship or fascination. There is some evidence of skulls being symbolically important in Aztec culture, which flourished earlier and further north than Mayan civilization, yet there are far fewer claims among crystal skull enthusiasts that connect the objects to Aztec culture. Radio-carbon testing is not applicable to crystal, because the method works only on previously animate objects.

Crystal skulls are credited by believers for having the ability to awaken human consciousness to a higher level of being. Some people assert that they experience a psychic connection when viewing a crystal skull, and commonly declare that they were infused with positive energy. Skulls of quartz crystal, like other quartz objects, are believed by mystic crystal enthusiasts to have the ability to record events, thoughts, and emotions that occur in their presence.

Some believers in mystical qualities of crystals credit ancient peoples with having crafted crystal skulls. According to them, ancients used the skulls to predict the future, to control the weather, as healing devices, as oracles to receive cosmic wisdom, as receivers of universal knowledge, and as a tool meant for future use to gain divine knowledge.

There is a crystal skull on display at the London Museum of Mankind, and the Paris Crystal Skull is on display at the Trocadero Museum. Both skulls can be traced back to Mexico, where records show they were purchased in the 1890s. The London Museum acquired its skull through Tiffanys of New York in 1898. Tests conducted in 1995 revealed scratches from steel tools, perhaps a jeweler's wheel, confirming the skull must be of modern origin. The date of the skull was moved from ancient Aztec times to the more recent period after the Spanish conquest of Mexico in 1520. Night workers at the museum reportedly refused to work near the skull unless it was covered, citing vibrations, colors appearing in the skull, or a simple association of skulls and death.

The Amethyst Crystal Skull and the Mayan Crystal Skull were found in Guatemala in the early 1900s. The latter skull received its name because it was found at the site of Mayan ruins. "Maya" is kept by a psychic who uses the skull to assist her in readings.

Two skulls exhibit particularly exquisite craftsmanship. The Rose Quartz Crystal Skull, found along the Guatemala-Honduras border, includes removable mandibles, as does the Mitchell-Hedges skull, the most famous and notorious of crystal skulls. Named after its founders and keepers, F. A. Mitchell-Hedges (1882–1959) and his daughter Anna (1910–), it is considered the finest example of a crystal skull. Fashioned from clear quartz, the Mitchell-Hedges Crystal Skull is realistic in size (the cranium approximates that of an average female adult), and its jaws were formed from the same piece of crystal as the skull. The jaws fit neatly into sockets and maintain a perfect balance with the skull.

The two biggest mysteries of the Mitchell-Hedges skull concern the craftsmanship used to make it and the story surrounding its discovery. The skull is believed to have been formed from a large block of crystal that was carved into a rough shape of a skull and then smoothed into its final shape with water and a solution of silicon-crystal sand or, perhaps,

through some unknown technology. There are no scratches on the Mitchell-Hedges skull that would indicate the work of metal tools. Shafts within the skull are said to channel light from the base of the skull to the eye sockets in a manner similar to modern optic technology, and the sockets have concave forms that reflect light to the upper cranium. Internal prisms and light tunnels are believed to be the reason why objects are magnified and brightened when held beneath the skull.

Like other crystal skulls, the Mitchell-Hedges skull reportedly changes color, sometimes clouding up white, and other times growing from a small patch of black to intensely black. Many of those who have viewed it report strange visions when looking in, and some have detected a faint hum or a scent. Like other mystical crystal objects, the Mitchell-Hedges version has been reputed to have oracular and healing powers, to be able to accumulate natural magnetism, and to amplify and transmit energy. Its keeper and early publicist, F. A. Mitchell-Hedges, also claimed it had the power to kill, citing several of his enemies who died before he did.

Mitchell-Hedges was an explorer and gambler who wrote books about his searches for remnants of lost tribes and the lost continent of **Atlantis** (*Lands of Wonder and Fear*, 1931) as well as his encounters with sea monsters (*Battles with Giant Fish*, 1923, and *Battles with Monsters of the Sea*, 1937). In 1927, Mitchell-Hedges and his daughter Anna were clearing debris atop a temple in the ancient Mayan city of Lubaantum (modern-day Belize) when Anna discovered what became known as the Mitchell-Hedges Crystal Skull on her seventeenth birthday. Weeks later, near the same site, she found the jaw of the skull.

Mitchell-Hedges did not publicize the skull until 1943, when he began referring to it as the Skull of Doom and claimed it was 3,600 years old. Curiously, he barely mentioned the skull in his autobiography, *Danger, My Ally* (1954). After he died in 1959, daughter Anna became the keeper of the skull.

It is now generally accepted that Anna Mitchell-Hedges did not discover the fabled crystal skull in the ruins of a Mayan city in

1927, but Mitchell-Hedges bought the artifact at an auction at Sothebys in London in 1943. Such claims have been verified by records at the British Museum, which had bid against Mitchell-Hedges for ownership of the object.

In 1970, the Mitchell-Hedges skull was examined by art conservator and restorer Frank Dorland. He claimed to have seen a spirit after studying the skull late at night in his home. According to Dorland, tests conducted at Hewlitt-Packard laboratories in Santa Clara, California, vouched for its craftsmanship including an absence of scars that would indicate metal tool work, and evidence that it was cut against the crystal axis. The validity of the tests has been questioned, as has the whole story of how the Mitchell-Hedges Crystal Skull was found and how far back it dates.

Jo Ann and Carl Parks became owners of the famous Texas Crystal Skull, whom they affectionately call Max, in 1980 when a Tibetan healer bestowed the artifact on them in payment of a debt. Admittedly unaware at first of the significance of this object, Carl and Jo Ann, residents of Houston, placed the skull in a closet for the next seven years. Not until they came into contact with F. R. "Nick" Nocerino of Pinole, California, one of the world's foremost authorities of crystal skulls and director of the Society of Crystal Skulls, did they learn what an important artifact it was. Nocerino had been searching for that skull since the 1940s. He knew of its existence, but its actual location had sent him on a quest that had led him around the world.

Of the 13 crystal skulls known to researchers that are the actual true size of a human head, Max is the largest, weighing 18 pounds compared to the others, which weigh nine to 11 pounds. Max was found in a Mayan tomb at a site in Guatemala, and it has been estimated that Max came from a 50-to-60-pound piece of crystal that was more than a half a million years old. Other than Max and the crystal skull owned by Anna Mitchell-Hedges of Canada, all the others, each differing somewhat in size and detail, are held in museums or private collections.

People claim that being in Max's proximity provokes images and visions within them.

They believe to see scenes from the past history of Earth, and frequently they perceive UFO-related scenes and messages. "Whether you believe any of that or not, if you simply look at the artifact on a scientific and archaeological level, you cannot help being overwhelmed and awed at the skilled worksmanship that was involved in creating him," Jo Ann Parks has commented.

The British Crystal Skull on display at the London Museum of Mankind is considered to be a nineteenth-century artifact. Scientists, at least, are convinced that all evidence weighs toward recent origins of all crystal skulls. Until convincing evidence that a known civilization venerated such an object, or that crystal skulls are remnants of a vanished civilization, belief in special qualities of the skulls are in the minds of beholders of mysticism.

❋ DELVING DEEPER

Bryant, Alice. *The Message of the Crystal Skull: From Atlantis to the New Age*. St. Paul, Minn.: Llewellyn Publications, 1989.

Garvin, Richard M. *The Crystal Skull: The Story of the Mystery, Myth and Magic of the Mitchell-Hedges Crystal Skull*. New York: Doubleday, 1973.

Gienger, Michael. *Crystal Power, Crystal Healing: The Complete Handbook*. New York: Sterling Publications, 1998.

Sullivan, Kevin. *The Crystal Handbook*. New York: New American Library, 1996.

FETISHES

Fetishes (from the Portuguese word *feitio*, meaning artificial, or false) are distinguished from amulets and talismans by supposedly being endowed with human thoughts or feelings, or infused with a spirit. Drawings of animals on cave walls by prehistoric people were believed to infuse humans with the qualities of strength, speed, or other attributes associated with that animal. Today, fetishes carved of wood or stone by Native Americans of the Southwest have the same purpose. Fetishes carved in the likeness of an animal are given as gifts, with the recipient supposedly gaining some of the qualities of that animal. Fetishes from the Zuni tribe are particularly sought after in modern times, sustaining a tribal tradition stretching back in time for centuries.

Fetishes are important in the vodoun religion, originating in western Africa as small pouches or chests, or items worn as amulets, and evolving into doll fetishes that were believed to possess the spirit of the person on whom the doll was modeled. That mystical practice of vodoun practitioners was misrepresented and generally overdramatized as a horror element of voodoo in popular culture, in movies, television shows, and fiction.

DRAWINGS *of animals on cave walls were believed give humans the qualities of strength, speed, or attributes of that animal.*

Egyptians had dolls called *shawabtis* that were occasionally buried with the dead for their use in the afterlife. A central African tribe called the Bakongo had a fetish called *Nkosi*.

Unlike an amulet, which works automatically to bring luck or ward off misfortune, the Nkosi was believed to work only through an elaborate ceremony, where its power to identify the party guilty of a crime was coaxed and sometimes forced into action. That is the nature of fetishes, and what distinguishes them from amulets and talismans. Fetishes have personalities that must be appealed to in some way in order for them to work; amulets, invested with power based on the material and inscriptions, are supposed to work automatically; and talismans work automatically if they were crafted following a specific, ritualistic practice.

✳ DELVING DEEPER

Bracken, Thomas. *Good Luck Symbols and Talismans: People, Places, and Customs.* Philadelphia: Chelsea House Publishers, 1997.

Budge, E. A. Wallis. *Amulets and Talismans.* New York: Collier Books, 1970.

Mintz, Ruth Finer. *Auguries, Charms, Amulets.* Middle Village, N.Y.: Jonathan David Publishers, 1983.

Nelson, Felicitas H. *Talismans & Amulets of the World.*
    New York: Sterling Publishers, 2000.

Megaliths

Around Carnac, in the Brittany region of France, stand more than 4,000 stones dating back 6,000 years. Some of them stand individually, some are aligned in rows, and some mark the sites of chambered graves beneath nearby mounds. Intricate burial chambers in Ireland, like many of the 12,000 ancient chambered burial sites beneath mounds in northern Europe, have arrangements of stone or markings that correspond with lunar and solar cycles. All of those ancient structures and arrangements of large stones are examples of a megalith (from the Greek "megas" meaning large, and "litho" meaning stone), a term used most specifically in reference to stone structures erected for ceremonial, astronomical, and religious purposes, and as monuments. Megalith building (placing large stones in a specific site) dates back to at least 5000 B.C.E. Many of the most famous megaliths were erected between then and 1500 B.C.E. The communities that erected them eventually faded into the recesses of history, but the megaliths they left behind continue to tantalize the imagination.

Adding to the mystery of these ancient structures is the supposition that they were erected by people not credited with possessing the knowledge and technology needed to move massive stones. Even if large labor forces were available, most megalithic structures demanded keen architectural and mathematical skills for planning and erection. Additionally, many ancient megaliths seem to have had sophisticated uses as solar and lunar calendars and as astronomical observatories. In fact, the discipline of archaeoastronomy (the study of astronomy among ancient societies) has become a burgeoning field of study during the past few decades, with ancient megaliths often serving as the focus of the discipline.

As ancient megaliths are studied, a greater appreciation for the skills and knowledge of prehistoric civilizations comes forth. Missing pieces of the puzzle of human development remain, however, fueling more speculation and theories. Perhaps survivors from vanished civi-

White witch Kevin Carlyon working with crystals at Stonehenge. (KEVIN CARLYON/FORTEAN PICTURE LIBRARY)

lizations passed knowledge on to inhabitants of distant lands. As the old myths sometimes suggest, the megalith builders themselves may have known magic secrets of levitation and of transforming and reassembling solid materials. UFO enthusiasts argue that visitors from outer space may have directed the erecting of megaliths, particularly since so many megalithic sites were devised with the intention of viewing and charting the skies above.

Ancient megaliths are generally divided into five categories:

1. alignments, stones placed in rows and other non-circular shapes;

2. burial chambers, underground chambers usually covered by a mound of some kind;

3. monoliths (from the Greek; "mono" means single, "litho" is stone), single standing stones, also called menhirs;

4. monument memorials to gods or community leaders; and

5. stone circles.

The greatest concentration of aligned megaliths is in the Carnac area of Brittany, France, where megaliths are aligned in rows in three different fields. Le Menec has two stone circles at either end of 12 rows of megaliths. The tallest stones stand 13 feet in height, and the stones dwindle in size moving from west to east, totaling 1,099 megaliths. Kermario has 10 rows and 1,029 megaliths. One tall menhir, in which five serpents are engraved, serves to signal a nearby tumulus, an earthen mound that covers a chambered grave. The third field, Kerlescan, has 13 rows of aligned megaliths that form the shape of a barrel.

MANY *ancient megaliths appear to have had sophisticated uses as solar and lunar calendars and as astronomical observatories.*

The megaliths of Carnac first underwent radio-carbon dating techniques in 1959. At that time it was expected the results would show the megaliths were erected during the first or second century B.C.E., for it was generally believed that the megalith builders had come from the eastern Mediterranean region from Egypt, or Mycea (a civilization that preceded ancient Greece). The radiocarbon test, however, pushed the megalith builders back as far as 4650 B.C.E. All previous theories about the origins of the Brittany megaliths were undermined. The structures originated with pre-Roman and pre-Celtic civilizations, and they were older than similar structures in the eastern Mediterranean region from which the engineering expertise to erect the megaliths was previously believed to have originated.

The question of how the megaliths were positioned at sites where they stand is baffling. Modern-day tests conducted on moving the megaliths from quarries to nearby sites showed that it was possible for the primitive societies to move and erect the megaliths using rope or simply pushing the stones. Such effort, however, would have required coordinating the labor of hundreds of workers. One test during the 1970s showed that 200 people could move a 30-ton stone two to three miles in a few days by rolling the stone over logs.

Some monoliths (single blocks or large pieces of stone) are formed naturally and gain mythical importance based on their sublime appearance. In the Australian desert stands the world's largest monolith, Uluru (also called Ayers Rock), which reaches about a thousand feet high. Uluru is venerated by aborigines (native people of the area), who believe the ground beneath it is hollow and is a source of energy called Tjukurpa Dreamtime. According to their belief, all life as it is today is part of one vast unchanging network of relationships that can be traced to the spirit ancestors of the Dreamtime. The great spirits walked along the earth and literally sang material objects into existence.

The Uluru monolith extends downward more than three miles beneath the surface. Approximately 500 million years ago it was part of the ocean floor at the center of present-day Australia. Depending on the time of day and the atmospheric conditions, Uluru can dramatically change color, from a deep blue to glowing red. The area draws a variety of visitors, from those seeking to tap mystical energy, to tourists bussed in and out for a couple hours' worth of viewing time.

Among natural monoliths with mysterious qualities are "healing stones," usually a large stone with a hole through it. The Men-an-Tol in Cornwall, England, is one of several examples of a stone reputed to have healing properties. According to legend, people can be cured of back and leg pains by passing through the hole in the stone.

❖ DELVING DEEPER

Burl, Aubrey. *Megalithic Brittany: A Guide to over 350 Ancient Sites and Monuments.* London: Thames and Hudson, 1985.

Daniel, Glyn Edmund. *Megaliths in History.* London: Thames and Hudson, 1972.

Lancaster Brown, Peter. *Megaliths, Myths, and Men: An Introduction to Astroarchaeology.* New York: Dover, 2000.

Michell, John F. *Megalithomania: Artists, Antiquarians, and Archaeologists at the Old Stone Mountains.* Ithaca, N.Y.: Cornell University Press, 1982.

Mohen, Jean-Pierre. *The World of Megaliths.* New York: Facts on File, 1990.

RUNES

Although the various markings on objects of stone and wood known as runes are commonly referred to as an ancient alphabet of the Northern European Germanic and Scandinavian people, they do not really constitute a language as such. The runes are essentially symbols with particular meanings that were used to convey brief magical inscriptions and were often used in rites of divination. The word "rune" means "secret," especially as it might apply to a hidden wisdom, and the various symbols were inscribed on a wide variety of objects to give them power. The runes were used to send secret messages, to cast spells, to divine the future, and to communicate with the spirit world.

Some scholars say that some of the symbols used in the mystical runic markings may have originated as far back as Paleolithic times and been combined in historic times with certain characters from an old Etruscan alphabet. Certain traditions attribute the runes to the *Volsungr*, an ancestral tribe of heroic and semidivine beings that settled in Northern Europe just prior to the Ice Age. According to some of the legends of the Volsungr, the godlike beings gave the magical symbols as a gift that might assist lesser humans in their struggles to survive in the harsh environment of Ice Age Europe. In the Old Norse religion, it was Odin, the father of the gods, who, seeking higher wisdom, hung upside down from the World Tree for nine days before he received the rune symbols as the answer to his quest.

When the runic symbols were placed on small rocks or blocks of wood, the Old Norse cast them to predict the success of a hunting or fishing expedition, when to plant crops, or what course their children might follow throughout their lives. In the eleventh century when Christianity began to replace the old

Viking religion and Latin became the written language of the educated, the runes were not replaced, but gained an even stronger reputation for containing magical powers. While the priests of the new religion frowned upon any supernatural connotations attributed to the runes, the symbols remained as integral designs in folk art, jewelry, and wearing apparel. In recent years, the casting and reading of runes—the "Viking Oracle"—has again become a popular tool of divination.

✤ DELVING DEEPER

Blum, Ralph. *The Book of Runes: A Handbook for the Use of an Ancient Oracle.* New York: St. Martin's Press, 1993.

Davidson, H. R. Ellis. *Pagan Scandinavia.* New York: Frederick A. Praeger, 1967.

Gordon, Stuart. *The Encyclopedia of Myths and Legends.* London: Headline Publishing, 1994.

Karcher, Stephen. *The Illustrated Encyclopedia of Divination.* Rockport, Mass.: Element Books, 1997.

Sawyer, Brigit. *The Viking-Age Rune Stones: Custom and Commemoration in Early Medieval Scandinavia.* Oxford: Oxford University Press, 2001.

TALISMANS

The word "talisman" comes from the Arabic and means "to make magical marks." An amulet can be a found object, a common item, or one bought in a store. A talisman, on the other hand, is inscribed with pictures, words, letters, or mystical signs and is crafted for a specific function. When properly designed, talismans are believed to bring love, treasures, and health, and can allow one to communicate with the dead. Talismans must be crafted following a specific ritual based on the intended use, and the recipient's astrological sign, religion, or other qualities are often taken into consideration.

TALISMANS *are often used by members of secret societies.*

Talismans are intended to remain mysterious. While amulets often feature recognized symbols to bring protection or luck, talismans

Bone pendants. (CORBIS CORPORATION)

cloth to animal parts, created in a ritualistic practice and intended to bring money, love, or good health to the wearer.

❋ DELVING DEEPER

Bach, Marcus. *Inside Voodoo*. New York: Signet, 1968.

Bracken, Thomas. *Good Luck Symbols and Talismans: People, Places, and Customs*. Philadelphia: Chelsea House Publishers, 1997.

Gregor, Arthur S. *Amulets, Talismans, and Fetishes*. New York: Scribner, 1975.

Mintz, Ruth Finer. *Auguries, Charms, Amulets*. Middle Village, N.Y.: Jonathan David Publishers, 1983.

Nelson, Felicitas H. *Talismans & Amulets of the World*. New York: Sterling Publishing, 2000.

TOTEMS

Among the shamanic teachings of the traditional Native Americans, the totem represents the physical form of one's spirit helper, his or her guardian or guide. The totem entity may in some ways be comparable to the concept of a guardian angel or **spirit guide** that presents itself on the physical plane in the form of an animal.

Traditional Native Americans believed that the great mystery prepared the land as a place where all things that swam, walked, crawled, and flew were to mingle in harmony. Gifts were bestowed upon each creature, with abilities to learn lessons from one another. The native people accepted their kinship with all of nature and believed that each entity performed its specific talents according to its abilities. Therefore, it was advantageous for all humans to learn the identity of their totem and to receive its lessons in order to make their lives more complete.

In the shamanistic tradition, all creatures are called relatives and are considered brothers, sisters, parents, and so forth. All nonhuman entities are regarded as "people," and everyone has an important role to perform in the larger system of life.

It was the totem animal that guided shamans through the portal that led to the other world, to the mysterious transcendent reality beyond the material world, the dimension that lay beyond time and space. For all the members of the tribes, their own totem animal

have inscriptions meant to be secret or specific only to the individuals wearing them. Talismans must be crafted at a proper time and in a proper way to be effective; injury is believed to result from carelessness in the making or wearing of talismans.

Talismans are often used by members of secret societies. Kabbalists, for example, combined a complicated system of knowledge that utilized elements of numerology and astrology to create magic squares that protect against sorcery. Magic squares feature letters that spell out the name of God or numbers arranged in rows and columns that produce an equal sum when added in various sequences.

The magic triangle, another talisman, is based on the belief that systematic reductions of an inscription, line by line, create power that can ward off evil spirits and heal maladies. The mystical word "Abracadabra," for example, was used in medieval Europe as a chant to reduce fever. Each time the word was spoken in the chant, a letter was dropped. As the chant reduced, the fever was dispelled. Such talismans were especially popular during the Great Plague that swept through London during the mid-1660s.

A talisman of **vodun,** called gris-gris, is a small cloth bag filled with items from herbs to gave them their spiritual power and provided them with their own instrument of passage into the spirit world. Their totem animal would guide them in the purification of their spirit, helping them to achieve self-discipline through fasting, prayer, and the emptying of their hearts of all earthly desires. Although many in the Judeo-Christian tradition prefer to emphasize the charge that humans shall have dominion over all animals, it might be mindful to also take serious notice of Job 12:7–8: "Ask the animals, and they will teach you, or the birds of the air, and they will tell you; or to speak to the earth, and it will teach you, or let the fish of the sea inform you."

Although totems are most often associated with Native Americans, many cultures have at some time in their past used animal totems. Local sport teams use names such as the Tigers, Lions, Bears, Cardinals, and Falcons. Various religions and sects use expressions like the Lamb of God, the Dove of the Holy Spirit, and the Lion of Judah. People through history have even had such surnames as Bear, Beaver, Wolf, Crane, Crow, Drake, Finch, Fish, Fox, Hawk, Robin, Pike, Lamb, Partridge, and Salmon.

For many centuries, humans have allowed animals to be both surrogates and teachers. The ethnologist Ivar Lissner has pondered the provocative mystery of why those anonymous Franco-Cantabrian cave artists of more than 20,000 years ago never left mankind any clearly defined self-portraits that would show the exact physical appearance of human ancestors. Aside from a few Venus-type mother-goddess statuettes, people are left with a rather bizarre collection of ghostly creatures with the heads of animals and birds, strange half-human, and half-animal entities.

Lissner suggested that the Stone-Age artists really were portraying themselves, "…but in the guise of intermediary beings who were stronger than common men and able to penetrate more deeply into the mysteries of fate, that unfathomable interrelationship between animals, men, and gods." The ancient cave painters may have been saying that "…the road to supernatural powers is easier to follow in animal shape and that spirits can only be reached with an animal's assistance."

Totem pole. (CORBIS CORPORATION)

For countless centuries, those people who trust their totems have relied upon the assistance of their personal animal totem to lead them to higher spiritual awareness.

✤ DELVING DEEPER

Gill, Sam D., and Irene F. Sullivan. *Dictionary of Native American Mythology*. New York: Oxford University Press, 1992.

Gregor, Arthur S. *Amulets, Talismans, and Fetishes*. New York: Scribner, 1975.

Harner, Michael. *The Way of the Shaman*. New York: Bantam Books, 1982.

Lissner, Ivar. *Man, God and Magic*. New York: G. P. Putnam's Sons, 1961.

Steiger, Brad. *Totems: The Transformative Power of Your Personal Animal Totem*. San Francisco: HarperSanFranciso, 1997.

THINGS OF SACRED POWER

Things of sacred power associated with Judeo-Christian history as recorded in the Bible and in various apocryphal texts have enraptured believers for centuries. Whether pilgrims seek the physical remains of Noah's Ark or the cup from which Jesus (c. 6 B.C.E.–c. 30 C.E.) drank Passover wine at the Last Supper, great controversies over the physical existence of certain objects mentioned in the Bible have persisted for thousands of years and continue in the new millennium.

So prevalent is the belief that Noah's Ark can be located on the slope of the tallest mountain in Turkey, Agri Dagi (**Mt. Ararat**), that some travel agencies include participation in expeditions to search for the ark as part of tour packages to Turkey. Several ark sightings on Mt. Ararat occurred during the twentieth century. During a thaw in the summer of 1916, a Russian Imperial Air Force lieutenant flying over Mt. Ararat reported seeing half the hull of some sort of ship poking out above surface of a lake. A photograph taken in 1972 by the Earth Research Technical Satellite (ERTS) is said to reveal an unusual feature at 14,000 feet on Mt. Ararat. It was reported to be the same size as the Ark. In the 1980s, former NASA astronaut James Irwin participated in expeditions up the mountain, but he found only the remnants of abandoned skis. With the breakup of the former Soviet Union, expeditions up the mountain intensified during the 1990s, and the search for Noah's Ark continues.

As described in the Old Testament book of Exodus, the Ark of the Covenant, a wooden chest covered with gold, is said to contain such sacred relics as the tablets of law from God that Moses (14th–13th century B.C.E.) brought back from Mt. Sinai. The ark possessed supernatural powers and served as a means through which God could express his will to the Israelites. It was last known to have rested in the Temple of Solomon in Jerusalem, but ever since Babylonian forces conquered the city in 587 B.C.E. the whereabouts of the Ark of the Covenant has been a mystery. Interest in the Ark of the Covenant has inspired generations of those who would recover the sacred relic. In medieval times the **Knights Templar** supposedly came into possession of the ark.

A whole mythology has been built around the legendary Holy Grail, said to be the drinking vessel of Jesus at the Last Supper before his crucifixion and resurrection. The legend of the grail has been perpetuated through literature since the twelfth century, particularly in tales involving knights of Camelot who served the legendary King Arthur of Britain. Through the inspirational recounting of the various quests, Christian teachings and virtues are presented. In modern times, the Holy Grail persists as a symbol of an ultimate achievement, a higher order of being for which people search.

Another thing of sacred power that has inspired generations of Christians is the **Shroud of Turin,** which is discussed in an earlier chapter. The Bible mentions a "clean linen cloth" (Matthew 27:59) in which the dead body of Jesus was wrapped following his crucifixion. Several cloths purported to be the one mentioned in the Bible have been made public through the centuries. The Shroud of Turin is a linen cloth that bears the image of a bearded, crucified man. The claims that the image on the Shroud of Turin was that of Jesus were first made public in the fourteenth century. The Shroud has been controversial ever since—embraced as authentic by believers, and written off as a forgery by skeptics. Each time evidence seems to weigh heavily against the authenticity of the Shroud, a new finding renews the controversy and inspires believers.

Perhaps a greater stretch for the skeptical mind is the belief that the lance that pierced Jesus' side has been preserved down through the centuries as a symbol that will bring vast political power to the one who possesses it. Nevertheless, when Christian crusaders discovered the lance in the Church of St. Peter in Antioch during the First Crusade in 1098, they used it as a symbol to rally their forces and defeat the Saracens. From that time onward, European monarchs coveted the Holy Lance as a sign that their reigns would be far-reaching and long-lasting. Fortunately, the power of the **Spear of Destiny** ebbed when it fell into the possession of the Nazis and their leader, Adolf Hitler (1889–1945).

This section will examine these objects of sacred power and discuss why they have been deemed so precious and holy by believers down through the centuries.

✤ DELVING DEEPER

Bernstein, Henrietta. *The Ark of the Covenant, the Holy Grail*. Marina del Ray, Calif.: DeVorss Publications, 1998

Goodrich, Norma. *The Holy Grail*. New York: HarperCollins Publishers, 1992.

Hancock, Graham. *The Sign and the Seal*. London: Heinemann, 1992.

Weston, Jessie L. *From Ritual to Romance*. Mineola, N.Y.: Dover Publications, 1997.

THE ARK OF THE COVENANT

Ever since the Babylonian Captivity of Jerusalem in the sixth century B.C.E., the whereabouts of the Ark of the Covenant has been a mystery. As described in the Old Testament of the Bible, the ark served as the visible sign of God's presence to the Israelites. The Israelites would rally and vanquish their foes when the ark was brought to sites of battle, and death came to those in the presence of the ark who were enemies of God, betrayed their allegiance to God, or who simply forgot about the ark's immense power. According to the Bible, the ark was last known to have rested in the Temple of Solomon in Jerusalem. Whether it was destroyed, stolen, moved, or remained hidden after Babylonian forces conquered the city and leveled the temple in 587 B.C.E. is not known.

Another mystery concerning the ark is its contents. The ark is said to contain numerous sacred relics, including the tablets of law from God that Moses (14th–13th century B.C.E.) brought back from Mt. Sinai; Aaron's rod, a kind of rounded stick that miraculously grew leaves as a sign of God's trust in Aaron, brother of Moses; and/or a specimen of manna, the mysterious food that had provided an unending source of nourishment to the Israelites as they wandered in the desert. Additionally, the ark possessed a supernatural power that awed and overwhelmed those who viewed it, and it served also as a means through which God could express his will.

The idea of the ark was expressed by God to the Israelites and was then made into a material object by skilled craftsmen in about 1462 B.C.E. They built a chest (about 2 cubits in length and 1 cubits in height or about 3 feet, 9 inches in length, 2 feet, 3 inches in height) using setim (acacia) wood overlaid with the purest gold. The outside of the ark had a gold rim and four golden rings, one on each corner of the chest. Two poles made of setim and covered with gold ran through the gold rings on either side; the poles were used to lift the ark and were never removed from the rings. The ark had a cover of gold on which two cherubim faced each other, each with wings spread. The oracle (word, or commands) of God would issue from the ark from a cloud between the two cherubim (Exodus 25:19–22).

THE *Ark of the Covenant was last known to have rested in the Temple of Solomon in Jerusalem.*

The ark originally provided safety to the Israelites in their journey to the Promised Land. The power of the ark was manifested several times and enemies were scattered. When priests carrying the ark stepped into the River Jordan, the water stopped flowing and all the Israelites were able to cross. At the battle of Jericho the ark was carried by a procession around the walls of the city for seven days, after which the walls came down and the Israelites won the battle.

After losing a series of battles with the Philistines, the Israelites brought the ark to a battle site, hoping for inspiration and wanting to strike fear into the Philistines. However, the Philistines won the battle and secured possession of the ark. The Philistines viewed their capture of the ark as a victory over the Israelites and their God. The ark was treated as a trophy, but several disasters fell upon the Philistines, including the rapid spread of a plague and an invasion of mice wherever the ark was placed. The Philistines eventually built a cart on which they placed the ark and representations of their afflictions; they yoked two cows to the cart and set it forth. The cart made its way to the territory of Israel, where the ark came into the possession of the Bethsames. A large number of Bethsames fell dead when they failed to show respect for the ark. Fearful of the ark's power,

the Bethsames offered it to the inhabitants of nearby Cariathiarum, who took it in their possession with proper sacraments.

Later, when David (d. 962 B.C.E.) became king of Israel and established Jerusalem as the holy center of the nation, the ark was to be moved there. Along the way, however, a cart carrying the ark was jostled and the ark began sliding off. Forgetting about the ark's strange powers, a man who reached out to secure it was struck dead. The ark was then housed at a nearby site outside the city, where it was the object of veneration for several months before the journey to Jerusalem was completed. The ark was taken once from Jerusalem to inspire David's army in its battle against the forces of Absalom.

Eventually, the ark was placed in the new Temple of Solomon in Jerusalem. It was occasionally taken away from the temple for a battle or ceremony, but soon the ark was not allowed

to leave the temple. As decades passed, the sacredness and powers of the ark were largely forgotten. When Jerusalem was invaded and taken by Babylonians led by King Nebuchadnezzar II (c. 630–562 B.C.E.; the Babylonian Captivity of Jerusalem is dated from 587 B.C.E.), the whereabouts of the ark became a mystery. It was either destroyed along with the city or, as suggested in Kings 4:25, taken to Babylon as one of the spoils of victory.

Some biblical scholars theorize that those Israelites still faithful to God were forewarned about the fall of Jerusalem and moved the ark to safety. Jeremiah is said to have moved the ark to a cave on Mt. Sinai, the mountain in Egypt where Moses first spoke with God. The Talmud, the ancient, authoritative history of the Hebrews, indicates that the ark was kept in a secret area of the Temple of Solomon and survived the destruction and pillaging of Jerusalem. The Temple of Solomon was rebuilt on its original foundation after the

Babylon Captivity. Around 150 B.C.E., a successor of Alexander the Great invaded Jerusalem and took valuable items from the new temple, but the ark was not mentioned among them.

One account has the illegitimate son of Solomon and Sheba stealing the ark about 1000 B.C.E. and hiding it in Aksum, Ethiopia, where it was guarded by a monk in a church. Other stories have the ark being transported during a Hebrew migration to Abyssinia (Ethiopia) that preceded the Babylonian Captivity. There, according to that version, the ark remained on an island in Lake Tana. With the spread of Christianity throughout the Roman world by 300 C.E., Abyssinia was largely Christian. Later, during the sixteenth century, fierce battles were waged by invading Muslim armies on the Christian empire of Abyssinia, causing much destruction, including the razing of monasteries on the island Tana Kirkos, where the ark was believed to have been kept. A cathedral was built after the Muslim armies retreated, and there, according to this legend, the ark remains safe.

In December 2000, Erling Haagensen and Henry Lincoln published their thesis that the Ark of the Covenant and the **Holy Grail** were both hidden in sites on the Baltic Sea island of Bornholm about the year 1170.

Interest in the Ark of the Covenant has recurred through the centuries. In medieval times the **Knights Templar** supposedly came into possession of the ark. In contemporary times, interest in the ark was renewed with the 1981 film *Raiders of the Lost Ark,* where it is the object of a search just prior to World War II (1939–45) between Nazi forces and an American archaeologist named Indiana Jones. The ark is found and, as in the Bible, its power kills (literally melts) all of those who do not pay it proper respect. In the film, as in the Old Testament, the presence of the ark brings destruction to the wicked and to the vain. In *Raiders of the Lost Ark,* the relic eventually ends up in an undistinguished crate in an overstocked U.S. government warehouse waiting to be archived.

In December 2001, Rev. John McLuckie found a wooden tablet representing the Ark of the Covenant in a cupboard in St. John's Episcopal Church in Edinburgh, Scotland. Rev. McLuckie, who had lived in Ethiopia, recognized the artifact as sacred to Ethiopia's Orthodox Christians, and arranged to have the tablet returned in a special ceremony in 2002.

✦ DELVING DEEPER

Bernstein, Henrietta. *The Ark of the Covenant, the Holy Grail.* Marina del Rey, Calif.: DeVorss Publications, 1998.

Deevey, Edward S. "Ancient Wonders Abound in Ethiopia." *International Travel News* 23, no. 11 (January 1999): 23.

"Ethiopian Artifact Found in Cupboard." *BBC News,* December 6, 2001.[Online] http://news.bbc.co.uk/hi/english/world/africa/newsid_1695000/1695102.stm.

Hancock, Graham. *The Sign and the Seal: The Quest for the Lost Ark of the Covenant.* New York: Crown, 1992.

Heverly, Lorry. "Where Is the Ark of the Covenant?" *Christian Science Monitor.* (March 30, 2000): 18.

Starck, Peter. "Are the Holy Grail and Ark of the Covenant Hidden on Baltic Sea Island?" [Online] http://www.rense.com/general6/baltic.htm

CROSSES

Christians wear crosses to remember the crucifixion of Jesus Christ (c. 6 B.C.E.–c. 30 C.E.) and because they believe that nothing unholy can stand in the presence of the cross. The cross as a Christian amulet dates back to the fourth century, when the Roman emperor Constantine (d. 337) adopted it as his symbol instead of the traditional Roman Eagle. That act symbolized the conversion of Rome to a Christian empire.

THE *cross as a Christian amulet dates back to the fourth century.*

But amulets with crosses date back to Mesopotamia and Egypt, and served as a symbol long before associations of the cross with the crucifixion of Jesus Christ. Native Americans already had amulets with crosses by the time of first contact with Europeans. European adventurers, beginning with Christopher Columbus (1451–1506), assumed that Christians had arrived previously when they saw the crosses on Native Americans, but they were really viewing a people who invested belief in the power of a universal symbol. Crosses and circles are among the symbols and figures worn for protection and prosperity by humans since the earliest times. Such crosses often signified the four directions, the four forces (earth, water, air, and fire), and, when enclosed in a circle, the oneness of life.

✤ Delving Deeper

Bracken, Thomas. *Good Luck Symbols and Talismans: People, Places, and Customs.* Philadelphia: Chelsea House Publishers, 1997.

Gregor, Arthur S. *Amulets, Talismans, and Fetishes.* New York: Scribner, 1975.

Mintz, Ruth Finer. *Auguries, Charms, Amulets.* Middle Village, N.Y.: Jonathan David Publishers, 1983.

Nelson, Felicitas H. *Talismans & Amulets of the World.* New York: Sterling Publishing, 2000.

THE HOLY GRAIL

The Holy Grail is most often identified as a serving dish or a chalice that was used by Jesus (c. 6 B.C.E.–c. 30 C.E.) during the Last Supper. The word "grail" may have originated from "garalis," which derives from the medieval Latin word "cratalis" (a mixing bowl). Garalis became "greal" in medieval French, "grail" in English. Another possible origin for the word is based on the writings of a Christian monk named Helinandus, who served the Cistercian order as a chronicler and died around 1230. He wrote of a hermit who around the year 717 saw a vision of a dish used by Jesus Christ at the Last Supper. The hermit supposedly wrote a book in Latin and called the dish "gradale." In French, gradale meant a wide and deep dish on which various meats are placed; it is similar to the word "greal" ("pleasant"). Greal was the word used to describe the dish in French tales, and it became "grail" in English.

In the history that developed after grail stories emerged, Joseph of Arimathea came into possession of the vessel following the crucifixion of Jesus. As the story continues, Joseph of Arimathea was imprisoned for several years for expressing his faith that Jesus was the Messiah, the son of God. After being released, he traveled to Britain and took the grail with him. When he died, the grail passed on to his descendants. The grail had magical qualities for the righteous, providing food and assurances of the grace of God. A few generations later, because of some transgression and a general lack of humility and virtue by keepers of the grail, the powers of the vessel were lost and its existence was virtually forgotten.

The legend of the grail has been perpetuated through literature since the twelfth century, particularly in tales involving knights of Camelot who served the legendary King Arthur of Britain. Stories of their quests to find the Holy Grail blend supernatural adventures, love stories, Christian myth, and the lore of Celts, a people who occupied much of Europe until the spreading of the Roman Empire.

King Arthur, the legendary ruler of ancient Britain, was most likely based on a figure from around 500 or earlier. According to Celtic lore, Arthur helped stave off invasions by Angles and Saxons, Germanic tribes that subsequently conquered Britain in the fifth century. Arthur became more established as a historical figure during the 1100s, when a book written by Geoffrey of Monmouth (c. 1100–1154), *History of the Kings of Britain,* included details of his heroic reign. Much of Geoffrey's material was gathered from folktales and contains historical and chronological inaccuracies. However, Geoffrey's work was popular and was translated from its original Latin into French (by a poet named Wace) around 1155 and into Middle English (by a poet named Layamon) a few years later. Between 1160 and 1180, the French poet Chretien de Troyes (fl. 1170) wrote five major works about Arthur and his knights based on history and legend.

Chretien helped introduce and popularize the grail legend, but he died before completing a full account of the mysterious and powerful object kept in the Grail Castle. In his version, Arthur's knights Gauvain (Gwain in English) and Perceval (Percival in English, Parzeval and Parsifal in German) journey to the castle where the grail is kept. Chretien's unfinished manuscript was continued by others.

Around 1200, the German poet Wolfram von Eschenbach (c. 1170–c. 1220) wrote a grail legend, *Parzeval*, about a youth who sets out to become a knight in King Arthur's court. Along the way the title character stops at the castle of the Fisher King, where Parzeval witnesses a procession bearing a glowing object (the grail) and a spear (the one that wounded Christ). In the presence of the grail, the Fisher King is struck dumb. Parzeval fails to inquire about the mysterious procession and the objects. Since Parzeval had a pure soul, he could have spoken in the presence of the grail and used its magical powers to heal the infirm Fisher King. Only much later, after many wanderings, does Parzeval learn about the true nature of the grail and his missed opportunity. He returns to the castle of the Fisher King, who is revealed to be his uncle, heals him, and restores the king's land, which had become barren when he became infirm.

Later stories concerning the Holy Grail reflect the influence of Christianity, most notably *Morte d'Arthur* by the fifteenth-century English writer Sir Thomas Malory (fl. 1470). In this most famous collection of Arthurian tales, the grail becomes the object of a quest among the knights of the roundtable at King Arthur's castle, Camelot. Sir Galahad, who is completely without sin, eventually realizes the grail quest. He is in the company of Sir Bors and Sir Percival (Parzeval), two other virtuous knights, but Sir Galahad, as an emblem of Christian virtue, alone achieves the grail.

Arthurian legends and the grail may be based to some extent on Celtic lore. The Holy Grail might well have been developed from references to magic cauldrons that appear in many Celtic myths and practices. In her book *From Ritual to Romance* (1920), Jessie Weston traced some similarities between Celtic myths and grail legends. Some Celtic fertility rituals,

and the Last Crusade (1989). Whether magical or divine, the grail persists as a symbol of a higher order of being for which people are searching, a striving toward some ultimate achievement.

✤ DELVING DEEPER

Bernstein, Henrietta. The Ark of the Covenant, the Holy Grail. Marina del Rey, Calif.: DeVorss Publications, 1998.

Goodrich, Norma Lorre. The Holy Grail. New York: HarperCollins Publishers, 1992.

Starck, Peter. "Are the Holy Grail and Ark of the Covenant Hidden on Baltic Sea Island?" [Online] http://www.rense.com/general6/baltic.htm

Weston, Jessie L. From Ritual to Romance. Mineola, N.Y.: Dover Publications, 1997.

for example, were designed to ensure the health and vigor of a community leader: the physical welfare of the land was connected with that of the king. The silence and sterility of the Fisher King in a tale like Parzeval, then, would indicate some transgression and physical failure of the king that affected his land. Celtic legends have references to the Fisher King as the leader of a barren land, referred to as the Waste Land and "the land laid waste." Other noted studies that trace Celtic sources for grail stories include The Grail: From Celtic Myth to Christian Symbol (1963), by Roger S. Loomis, and The Evolution of the Grail Legend (1968), by D. D. R. Owen.

THE legend of the Holy Grail has been perpetuated through literature since the twelfth century.

The legendary Holy Grail remains nearly as popular in modern culture as it was during the period from 1150 to 1250. Back then, grail stories were a hit in the courts of France, England, and Germany. Nowadays, books about grail adventures are popular, as are films ranging from Monty Python and the Holy Grail (1975), to Excalibur (1981), to Indiana Jones

PHILOSOPHER'S STONE

At the center of the alchemist's quest was the legendary philosopher's stone, a magical piece of the perfect gold, which could immediately transform any substance it touched into gold as pure as its own nature. The Emerald Tablets of the great **Hermes Trismegistus** spoke of such a marvelous catalyst, and ever since that secret knowledge had been made known to certain individuals, the philosopher's stone had become the symbol of the alchemical pursuit. According to tradition, **Albertus Magnus** actually came to possess such a wonder of transmutation, and **Helvetius** was given a small piece of the philosopher's stone by a mysterious man in black.

Some alchemists believed that the stone was somehow hatched like a chick from an egg if one could only find the proper ingredients with which to create the substance of the shell and the "yolk." Others believed that the philosopher's stone, that most marvelous of all catalysts, oozed somehow out of the moon or from one of the stars and fell to Earth where it solidified into the magical stone of transformation.

As the works of more of the alchemists have come to light, it becomes clear that the philosopher's stone wasn't really a stone at all—even though it is always referred to as such. Sometimes the catalyst of transmutation is described as a divine child, an angel, a drag-

The use of the prayer wheel as a mystical practice dates back to at least 400 C.E. in China. The idea itself of the prayer wheel might have originated as a play on words of *"turn the wheel of the daharma"*—a classical metaphor used for Buddha's teaching activity.

There are many types and sizes of prayer wheels. The most common one is a simple hand-held metal or wooden object, from four to six inches long, with a cylindrical body and a metal or wooden axle that serves as a handle at one end, while the other end is wrapped with a roll of paper on which a mantra or prayer is written. The prayer or mantras are repeated in a row, with the length of paper sometimes reaching twenty yards or more. An ornate cover protects the spool of prayers; the prayers cycle and turn with each rotation of the wrist, due to a weighted cord or chain. It is customary to turn prayer wheels in homes first thing in the morning and last thing before bed in the evening, and many people carry and rotate one while walking throughout the day.

Most common in Tibet, they are sometimes even referred to as "Tibetan Prayer Wheels" or *"Mani,"* derived from the mantra or prayer *"Om Mani Padme Hum."* Tibetan Buddhists believe these words sacred and its recital, silently or out loud, evokes a powerful, spiritual and benevolent blessing. Traditionally, even though the wheel itself and its practical uses for carts were known from other cultures, the Tibetans considered the wheel very sacred and did not allow its use for *any* other purpose other than that of the prayer wheel.

Ironically, in recent years the reverse is true, as much of Tibetan culture has had to seek refuge outside its homeland. Now the wheel is used largely for trucks, cars, busses, and tanks, and the spiritual uses of the wheel and other practices are severely restricted.

The Prayer Wheels in Asia

Sources:

Ladner, Lorne. *The Wheel of Great Compassion.* Boston: Wisdom Publications: 2000.

Lama, His Holiness the Dalai. Translated by Jeffrey Hopkins. Foreword by Tenzin Gyatso. *The Meaning of Life.* Boston: Wisdom Publications: 2000.

Rinpoche, Dagyap. *Buddhist Symbols in Tibetan Culture: An Investigation of the Nine-Best Known Groups.* Boston: Wisdom Publications: 1995.

Philosopher's stone and
the serpent of alchemy
from the 1622 edition of
Philosophia Reformata
by J. D. Mylius. (FORTEAN
PICTURE LIBRARY)

on, an elixir, a tincture, or an as-yet unknown chemical compound.

Many alchemists began to consider that somehow the philosopher's stone was not a thing at all, but a system of knowledge. Once the alchemist truly perceived the reality that lay behind the symbols, he would achieve an intellectual and spiritual level wherein he would become one with the power that existed within the mysterious goal for which he searched so long. Once he understood what the philosopher' stone represented, he would have found it at last—and he would have become one with it.

Many scholars have since insisted that the true alchemists sought not to turn base metals into gold, but to transform the dense material of their physical bodies into a spiritually evolved immaterial entity. In this perspective, the philosopher's stone becomes the Holy Spirit that mystically transmutes humans into true manifestations of God on Earth.

✤ DELVING DEEPER

Cavendish, Richard. *The Black Arts*. New York: Capricorn Books, 1968.

De Saint-Didler, L. *Hermetical Triumph: The Victorius Philosopher's Stone*. Edmonds, Wash.: Holmes Publishing Group, 2001.

Kelly, Edward. *The Stone of the Philosophers*. Edmonds, Wash.: Holmes Publishing Group, 1990.

Smith, Patrick. *A Light from Out of the Darkness: On the Composition of the Stone of the Philosophers*. Edmonds, Wash.: Holmes Publishing Group, 2001.

THE SPEAR OF DESTINY

The Spear of Destiny, also known as the Holy Lance, is in Christian tradition the spear that the Roman soldier Longinus thrust into the side of Jesus (c. 6 B.C.E.–c. 30 C.E.) as he hung on the cross. ("Then came the soldiers and brake the legs of the first and of the other which was crucified with him. But when they came to Jesus and saw that he was dead already, they brake not his legs: But one of the soldiers with a spear pierced his side and forthwith came out blood and water" [John 19: 32–34 KJV]). Christian knights discovered the Holy Lance at Antioch during the First Crusade in 1098. The sight of the sacred artifact in the Church of St. Peter so inspired the beleaguered Christian soldiers that they rallied and routed the Saracens from the city. From that time forth, according to legend, whoever claims the spear and solves its secret holds the destiny of the world in his hands for good or evil.

Although there are a number of relics in various European churches that claim to be the genuine Holy Lance, the spear that is on display in the Weltliches Schatzkammer Museum (the Hapsburg Treasure House Museum) in Vienna has been considered the most authentic and it has found a home there for 250 years. It is also known as Constantine's Lance, and it was employed as a symbol of the imperial power of Holy Roman emperors at the time of their coronation in much a similar manner as the orb and scepter are used in the coronation of the monarchs of Great Britain. According to Trevor Ravenscroft in *The Spear of Destiny* (1997), a 19-year-old Adolf Hitler (1889–1945) was first led to the lance in 1908 and from the moment of his first encounter with it in the museum, it became "the central pivot" in his life and the "very source of his ambitions to conquer the world." In addition to Constantine (d. 337), Hitler found that as many as 45 emperors had owned the lance before the great Charlemagne (742–814) had possessed it. Frederick the Great of Germany (1194–1250), who founded the Teutonic Knights on which Hitler allegedly based his SS, had also been an owner of the Spear of Destiny at one time. Ravenscroft claimed in his book that Hitler would often visit the museum, stare at the Holy Lance, and enter

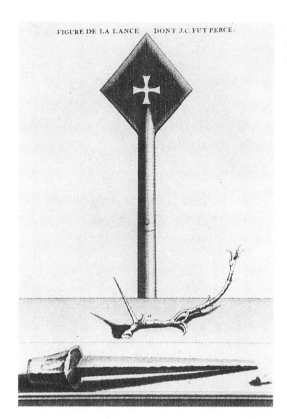

FIGURE DE LA LANCE   DONT J.C. FUT PERCE.

into a **trance state** in which he would view his future glory as the master of the Third Reich.

Thirty years later, on March 14, 1938, Hitler arrived in Vienna to oversee the annexation of Austria. He also observed the transfer of the Hapsburg Crown Jewel collection, which included the Holy Lance, from Vienna to Nuremberg, the Nazis' favorite city. With the Spear of Destiny now safely ensconced in Germany, Hitler declared that the war could begin in earnest. The lance would be well protected in the hall of St. Katherine's Church, where it had once rested for nearly 400 years.

However, later in the war when Allied bombers damaged a portion of St. Katherine's, the many treasures looted by the Nazis and stored there were taken to another hiding place. In the chaos and confusion, the Holy Lance was inadvertently left behind.

The Spear of Destiny fell into the hands of U.S. soldiers on April 30, 1945. A few hours after the Holy Lance passed from Nazi possession on to its next claimant to world power, Adolf Hitler committed suicide in his Berlin bunker. Later, the United States officially returned the Holy Lance to Austria, along with the other treasures that the Nazis had stolen. Today, the Spear of Destiny stands again in the Hapsburg Treasure House Museum in Vienna.

✤ DELVING DEEPER

Anderson, Ken. *Hitler and the Occult*. Amherst, N.Y.: Prometheus Books, 1995.

Angebert, Jean-Michel. *The Occult and the Third Reich*. New York: Macmillan Publishing, 1974.

Ravenscroft, Trevor. *Spear of Destiny*. New York: Red Wheel/Weiser, 1987.

Ravenscroft, Trevor, and Tim Wallace-Murphy. *The Mark of the Beast: The Continuing Story of the Spear of Destiny*. New York: Red Wheel/Weiser, 1997.

Sklar, Dusty. *The Nazis and the Occult*. New York: Dorset Press, 1989.

SWASTIKAS

The swastika has an evil association in the twentieth century, but it has a long, rich positive history, for the meaning of the word *svastika* in Sanskrit means "good fortune" or "well-being." Swastikas were the symbol of the supreme God in ancient, southeast Asia and were used by Native Americans as a sign for good luck. Swastikas appear among artifacts of ancient Rome and Greece. Buddha's (c. 563–c. 483 B.C.E.) footprints were said to leave impressions in the shape of swastikas. To Central Americans long before contact with Europeans, the swastika represented good luck, long life, and prosperity. The symbol appears on Navajo blankets and on ancient Chinese coins.

THE *earliest known swastikas date from 2500 or 3000 B.C.E. in India and Central Asia.*

Helene Petrovna Blavatsky, founder of the **Theosophical Society,** included the swastika in the seal of the society. Rudyard Kipling (1865–1936) combined the symbol in a circle with his signature to form his personal logo. Coca-Cola once issued a swastika pendant for patrons of its soft drink. The Girls' Club published a magazine entitled *The Swastika*; and until 1940, just before the United States entered World War II, the Boy Scouts awarded a swastika badge.

The earliest known swastikas date from 2500 or 3000 B.C.E. in India and Central Asia. It was the German archaeologist Heinrich Schliemann, who, during his excavation of Homer's Troy on the shores of the Dardanelles (1871–75), presumed that the swastikas he found on certain artifacts were somehow linked to religious symbols of his ancestors.

By 1914, the Wandervogel, a militarist anti-Semitic German youth group, began using a curved swastika on a cross as its insignia. In 1920, a dentist named Friedrich Krohn, a member of the Nazi Party, designed the official symbol of the party, the flag with a black swastika in its center. Adolf Hitler's (1889–1945) contribution to the insignia was to reverse the direction of the swastika so it appeared to spin clockwise. From that time onward, a once great symbol of good fortune became the most potent icon of racial hatred and violence the world has ever known.

✤ DELVING DEEPER

Boxer, Sarah. "One of the World's Great Symbols Strives for a Comeback." *The New York Times on the Web*, July 29, 2000.

Bracken, Thomas. *Good Luck Symbols and Talismans: People, Places, and Customs*. Philadelphia: Chelsea House Publishers, 1997.

Gregor, Arthur S. *Amulets, Talismans, and Fetishes*. New York: Scribner, 1975.

MAKING THE CONNECTION

Invocation The act of calling upon or appealing to a higher power such as a deity, spirit, or God for assistance. A form of prayer, inviting God's presence, at the beginning of a ceremony or meeting. In black magic, can be the casting of a spell or formula to invite an evil spirit to appear.

manna The food miraculously supplied to the Israelites by God, according to the Old Testament, as they wandered in the wilderness during their flight from Egypt. Spiritual nourishment or something of value received of divine origin or unexpectedly.

sarcophagus From the Greek *sarx* meaning "flesh," and Greek *sarkophogos*, literally meaning "flesh-eater." Originally a kind of limestone that had properties to aid in the rapid decomposition of the deceased bodies and was used in the making of coffins. Eventually came to mean any stone coffin, especially one with inscriptions or decorated with sculpture and used as a monument.

CHAPTER 9
PLACES OF MYSTERY AND POWER

This chapter visits many sites sacred to world religions, examines the theories of lost civilizations, and evaluates places that harbor ancient mysteries—both legendary and real.

INTRODUCTION

Throughout their history of cultural and religious development, humans have always discovered or created places that are special to them—sites where they might gather to participate in social rituals or where they might retreat for solitude and reflection. In such places, many people claim to experience a sense of the sublime, something larger than life. Others, while in a solemn place of worship or in a beautiful natural setting, attest to feeling a special energy that raises their consciousness and perhaps even heals their physical body.

Mysterious megaliths (from the Greek: "mega" means large, "lithos" means stones) are those placed at a site by ancient people who left no records explaining how they managed to lift and transport stones weighing several tons. Such sites include the standing stones of Brittany, the Bighorn Medicine Wheel in Wyoming, the monoliths of Zimbabwe, and the monuments of Easter Island. All of these places were ostensibly significant to an ancient society or religion, but many were long abandoned by the time they became known to the larger world, and the meaning of the megaliths remains unexplained.

The most popularly known megalithic structures are probably Stonehenge in Great Britain and the complex of pyramids and the Great Sphinx in Egypt. Like many ancient megalithic structures, those sites have been examined, written about, mythologized, and speculated upon for centuries, yet they still continue to conceal old secrets and occasionally yield surprising information that forces new historical interpretations of past societies.

Rising up on a plateau called Giza, 10 miles west of present-day Cairo, Egypt, the Great Pyramid, its two companion pyramids, and the Sphinx are probably the world's oldest and best-known enigmas. Among the mysteries of the pyramids are the questions of where the immense amount of rock forming them (11 million cubic yards of stone for the Great Pyramid alone) was quarried, and how it was moved and then erected into an astonishingly precise structure. Academic debates are ongoing concerning what surveying methods and equipment were used to ensure that the landscape was level and that measurements were accurate. Many researchers argue about the number of workers needed for such an undertaking and wonder how such an army of laborers could be mobilized, housed, and fed.

Other mysteries surrounding the pyramids are the contentions that the structures are situated at cardinal points on the compass, and their numerous astronomical uses show knowledge of mathematics in advance of other civilizations. In addition, the body of the pharaoh Khufu (Cheops) for whom the tomb was built, and precious objects that usually surround the bodies of royalty in Egyptian tombs, have never been found. In fact, all three of the pyramids at Giza were allegedly erected as tombs, yet not a single body has been found in any of them.

Other places have become mysterious sites because things have happened there that are impossible to document fully, yet physical evidence remains that promotes further speculation. The claimed miraculous healings at Lourdes, the accounts of spiritual illumination at Jerusalem and Mecca, and the sacred visions at Taos provide testimonies of faith and wonder that must be assessed by each individual.

This chapter also deals with accounts of vanished civilizations—places where ruins are found that offer mute evidence to the majesty and glory of prior cultures. No one can dispute the evidence of the Mayan temples, the splendor of Tiahuanaco, the mystique of Angkor Wat, but scholars fiercely debate the intricacies of the purpose of certain of these structures and the lifestyles of their inhabitants. Uncertainty also persists about why so many of these ancient peoples suddenly chose to abandon settlements that they labored so hard—sometimes for centuries—to build. The Mayans of Mexico and Central America left behind immense structures that were eventually overrun by the surrounding rainforest. In present-day Bolivia, the amazing structures of Tiahuanaco were constructed and abandoned before the great Inca dynasty conquered the area in the fifteenth century. The Great Houses of the Anasazi in the southwestern area of the present-day United States were left behind more than five centuries before they were seen by the first white settlers.

Some sites acquire a reputation for being eerie because of their appearance or because of events that are alleged or rumored to have happened there. The Nazca Lines of Peru and various so-called "spirit pathways" are cloaked in mystery as to their actual purpose as places of worship, initiation, or contact with alien beings. Lines where spirits or natural energies pass have been traced in Great Britain (where they are called Ley lines) and Germany (where they are called holy lines). Based on the idea that earlier civilizations were more attuned to mysterious Earth energies and built their sites along those lines, proponents of leys attempt to recreate those lines by tracing alignments of ancient sites. Many ancient structures were erected with consideration for the surrounding landscape and adjacent structures. In that sense, the community erecting the structure viewed the area as a sacred landscape. The landscapes were integral to rites performed there.

More than 2,500 years ago, a legend first began to spread about an ideal society of the past that enjoyed an abundance of natural resources, great military power, splendid building and engineering feats, and intellectual achievements far advanced over those of other lands. Called Atlantis, this ancient society was described as existing on a continent-sized area with rich soil, plentiful pure water, abundant vegetation, and such mineral wealth that gold was inlaid in buildings. In the ensuing centuries, no evidence of Atlantis has been found, but its attributes have expanded to include engineering and technological feats that enhance its legendary status in the popular imagination. Atlanteans are commonly thought by enthusiasts to have had cosmic connections with extraterrestrial life.

The truth behind such alleged places of mystery and power as the Bermuda Triangle, an area off the coast of Florida where ships and aircraft are said to vanish without a trace; El Dorado, the city of gold which drove the Spanish conquistadors on endless fruitless searches; and Avalon, the mystical place where the legendary King Arthur was taken after receiving mortal wounds in battle are also examined. Although the stories of Camelot, Arthur, and the Knights of the Round Table are only myths, there are actual sites on which Avalon may well have been based. Some sources suggest that Avalon lies off the coast of Great Britain or is possibly the island of Greenland. Others have considered Arran, an island off the coast of Scotland, as a possible model for Avalon.

Sometimes legends really do come to life. The Lost City of Willkapanpa the Old, a principal city rumored to consist primarily of Incan rulers and soldiers, was not discovered until 1912 when a historian from Yale University found the site now known as Machu Picchu hidden at 8,000 feet in altitude between two mountains, Huayana Picchu ("young mountain") and Machu Picchu ("ancient mountain") in Peru. The ridge overlooks a sacred river and valley called Urubamba. The most accepted view of Machu Picchu is that it was a religious sanctuary that served high priests and "virgins of the sun" (Incas worshipped the sun). Even though many mysteries abound about Machu Picchu, many researchers have been inspired to call it "the eighth wonder of the ancient world."

Everyone has his or her own special and private place of mystery, power, and wonder. This chapter shall explore those sites—both sacred and secular—that have fascinated and inspired men and women for thousands of years.

☙ DELVING DEEPER

Gaddis, Vincent H. *Invisible Horizons: True Mysteries of the Sea.* Philadelphia: Chilton Books, 1965.

Gordon, Stuart. *The Encyclopedia of Myths and Legends.* London: Headline Books, 1993.

Harpur, James, and Jennifer Westwood. *The Atlas of Legendary Places.* New York: Konecky & Konecky, 1997.

Ingpen, Robert, and Philip Wilkinson. *Encyclopedia of Mysterious Places.* New York: Barnes & Noble, 1999.

Kusche, Lawrence D. *The Bermuda Triangle Mystery—Solved.* New York: Harper and Row, 1975.

Larousse Dictionary of World Folklore. New York: Larousse, 1995.

Spence, Lewis. *The History of Atlantis.* New York: University Books, 1968.

ANGKOR WAT

Angkor Wat, in present-day Cambodia, formed part of the capital of the Khmer Empire from 802 until 1295, and is probably the largest religious monument ever constructed. Built over a 30-year period with sandstone and laterite (a dense, porous, iron-bearing soil that can be quarried like stone), the rectangular structure (2,800 by 3,800 feet) faces west, in Hindu belief the direction taken by the dead when going to their next life.

At the center of the complex stands a temple with five lotus-shaped towers, a larger central tower, and four smaller surrounding towers. They represent the five peaks of Mount Meru, the mountain where a pantheon of Hindu gods reside and from which, according to Hindu belief, all creation comes. Three square terraces surrounds the central tower. The entire complex is surrounded by a moat more than three miles long and rimmed by a causeway that leads to four gateways into the temple complex. Decorating the causeway are carvings that depict divine serpents, known as nagas.

Angkor Wat was taken by the Cham army from northern Cambodia in 1177, after which the complex began to fall into ruin. It was reclaimed, but not inhabited, in 1181. Pillaged by Thai invaders in the fifteenth century, the ruins were somewhat refurbished and expanded by later rulers of Cambodia. Angkor Wat was intermittently inhabited by Buddhist monks, and the former Hindu temple subsequently became a destination for Buddhist pilgrims from all over the world.

❄ DELVING DEEPER

Ingpen, Robert, and Philip Wilkinson. *Encyclopedia of Mysterious Places*. New York: Barnes & Noble, 1999.

MT. ARARAT

According to Genesis 8:4, after seven months and 17 days afloat in the ark upon the waters of the great deluge that destroyed all life on Earth, Noah, his family, and his massive living cargo of livestock came to rest upon the mountains of

E ach year since the eighth century, Hindu pilgrims have traveled to one of the four sacred cities—Hardvar, Prayag, Ujjain, and Nasik—each located on a different sacred river—to seek forgiveness of sins as they bathe in the holy waters. According to Hindu mythology, the four cities became consecrated by the four drops of the nectar of immortality that fell upon them from the vessel that the gods used to carry the elixir of life away to heaven.

The ancient city of Prayag, now known as Allahabad, is a city of about 900,000 located on the Ganges River in southeast Uttar Pradesh in North India. Allahabad is called the Titharaja, "King of Tithras" (King of the Holy Cities), for it is located where three sacred rivers meet—the Ganges, the Yamuna, and the mythical Sarasvati, known as Sangam. (The Sarasvati, according to tradition, flowed from the Himalayas before it transferred its magical powers to the Ganges and disappeared into the north Indian desert.) The very act of bathing at the confluence (the Triveni) is believed to bestow a triple blessing upon the Hindu pilgrim.

THE SACRED CITY OF ALLAHABAD

SOURCES:

"Allahabad." *India Food and Fun.*
[Online] http://www.indiafoodandfun.com/travel/allahabad.htm.
Crim, Keith, ed. *The Perennial Dictionary of World Religions.* San Francisco: HarperSanFrancisco, 1989.

Ararat, near the headwaters of the Euphrates River in what is today eastern Turkey. So prevalent is the belief that Noah's Ark can be located on the slope of the tallest mountain in Turkey, Agri Dagi (Mt. Ararat), that some travel agencies include participation in expeditions to search for the ark as part of tour packages to Turkey. Two thousand years earlier, in the first century B.C.E., native Armenians of the region routinely declared that remnants of the ark could still be seen. The same declaration was made in the thirteenth century, as recorded in the notes of adventurer Marco Polo (1254–1324). Armenians told him of the ark as he crossed through the region during travels that took him as far east as China from his native Venice, Italy. Several claims of sightings of the ark in the twentieth century make it a modern-day mystery as well.

The rugged environment of the area that includes Mt. Ararat makes it difficult to sustain an expedition. Six to eight weeks of favorable weather are the most searchers can hope for as they try to maneuver along the treacherous paths of the 16,000-foot high mountain, where glaciers and deep pockets of snow have little time to begin thawing before the return of cold weather.

Even if the ark can be located on Mt. Ararat, the elements work against being able to reach it and excavate around it. Several years of drought might be needed to melt snow and lower water levels in areas where the ark is most often thought to rest. Meanwhile, some ark researchers believe the vessel landed further east, and others claim the ark came to rest in present-day Ethiopia. Others doubt whether the ark ever existed.

Mt. Ararat, Turkey.
(KLAUS AARSLEFF/FORTEAN
PICTURE LIBRARY)

According to the Bible (Genesis, 6–10), God had become angered at the wickedness of humans and was determined "to end all flesh." He called on Noah, whom God deemed a just man, and told him to build a large barge with three interior decks. The barge was to be constructed of wood and sealed with bitumen. Its length was to be 300 cubits (about 450 feet), its width 50 cubits (about 75 feet), and its height 30 cubits (about 45 feet). The ark would be able to survive the deluge through which God would wipe out life.

In the first century B.C.E., native Armenians declared that remnants of Noah's Ark could still be seen.

The ark held Noah's family—his wife, their three sons, and the sons' wives—and at least two animals from every species to populate the earth again. All the food needed for their survival was provided for them. The ark and its inhabitants survived the deluge by sailing on the floodwaters, and all aboard returned to the land to repopulate the earth after the rain stopped and the water receded. What happened to the ark after it came to rest and all those aboard disembarked safely is not mentioned in the Bible.

Questions persist about where the ark finally landed. The Bible cites the mountains of Ararat, which could designate a region (then known as Armenia) or a specific mountain peak. Some biblical scholars locate it in Kurdistan, an area that encompasses Mt. Ararat

and parts of present-day Turkey and Iran. The Babylonian account of the Deluge in the Epic of Gilgamesh names Mt. Nisir in that region. After the ark came to rest, according to the Gilgamesh epic, pilgrims would scrape off bitumen (a sealant against water) and make charms of it to guard against witchcraft.

Most evidence and sightings are based on locations on Mt. Ararat. As the Christian religion spread in the first century, the Christians of Apamea, in Phrygia, built the monastery of the ark, where a feast was celebrated annually to commemorate Noah's disembarking. Marco Polo, in journals of his journey to China in 1271, wrote, "In the heart of Greater Armenia is a high mountain, shaped like a cube (or cup), on which Noah's ark is said to have rested, whence it is called the Mountain of Noah's Ark." Identifying the place as Mt. Ararat, Marco Polo wrote, "On the summit the snow lies so deep all the year round that no one can ever climb it; this snow never entirely melts, but new snow is for ever falling on the old, so that the level rises."

Several ark sightings on Mt. Ararat occurred during the twentieth century, though none of them have been documented well enough to satisfy skeptics. During a thaw in the summer of 1916, according to one account, a Russian Imperial Air Force lieutenant noticed a half-frozen lake in a gully on the side of Mt. Ararat. World War I was raging and the Russian pilot was flying high-altitude tests to observe Turkish troop movements. Flying nearer to the lake, he saw half the hull of some sort of ship poking out above the lake surface. He reported it to his captain. The captain was flown over the site. Believing it was Noah's Ark, preserved because it was encased in ice most of the year, the captain sent a report to the Russian tsar at St. Petersburg. The tsar sent two corps of engineers up the mountain. It was nearly a month before the ark was reached.

Measurements by the engineers were allegedly taken and drawings and photographs were made, but none of those were ever officially documented. According to accounts, the photographs and reports were sent by courier to the attention of the tsar, but Nicholas II (1868–1918) apparently never received them. The Russian Revolution was underway in 1917, and the results of the investigation were never reported publicly.

According to another story, the Turkish Air Force in 1959 conducted an aerial survey of the Ararat region. A photograph revealed the outline of a ship on one of the lower slopes of Mt. Ararat (just over 6,000 feet). The ship's dimensions were similar, though somewhat larger, than those of the ark. Another alleged aerial sighting was made in 1960. A Turkish army pilot and a liaison officer reported seeing evidence of an enormous, rectangular barge on the southeast slope at about 13,000 feet altitude.

A photograph taken in 1972 by the Earth Research Technical Satellite (ERTS) revealed an unusual feature at 14,000 feet on Mt. Ararat. It was reported to be the same size as the ark. The existence of the photograph is disputed, however. Even if it does exist in the files of a U.S. government agency, it has apparently been given no special designation to accommodate search requests: a request for "satellite image of ark," for example, brings the reply, "no responsive records."

In the 1980s, former NASA astronaut James Irwin participated in expeditions up the mountain, bringing much publicity to the search for the ark. He found only the remnants of abandoned skis. With the breakup of the former Soviet Union, expeditions up the mountain intensified during the 1990s. Previously, expeditions were considered a security threat by the Soviet government because the region bordered the former Soviet Union.

The search for Noah's Ark continues, as do questions concerning how best to understand the story of Noah and the ark: should the Bible's description of the ark, the extent of the deluge, and the capability of lodging every species of animal and bird be taken literally, or is the message most important? The deluge occurred, according to the Bible, because God had become disgusted with the wickedness of humankind. Those searching for the ark with the hope of making great profits probably missed that most enduring legacy of the story, a moral that persists regardless of whether or not physical remnants of the ark have been, or can be, found.

✤ DELVING DEEPER

Fasold, David. *The Ark of Noah*. New York: Wynwood Press, 1988.

Harpur, James and Jennifer Westwood. *The Atlas of Legendary Places*. New York: Konecky & Konecky, 1997.

Kite, L. Patricia, ed. *Noah's Ark: Opposing Viewpoints*. San Diego: Greenhaven Press, 1989.

Toumey, Christopher P. "Who's Seen Noah's Ark?" *Natural History*, 106, no. 9 (October 1997): 14–17.

ATLANTIS

More than 2,500 years ago, a legend first began to spread about a society of the past that enjoyed an abundance of natural resources, great military power, splendid building and engineering feats, and intellectual achievements far advanced over those of other lands. Called Atlantis, it was described as a continent-sized area with rich soil, plentiful pure water, abundant vegetation and animals, natural hot springs for health and vigor, and such mineral wealth that gold was inlaid in buildings and was among the precious metals and stones worn as jewelry. Slaves performed manual labor, allowing a large elite to pursue knowledge, enjoy sporting events, and continually improve upon an already thriving society.

THE idea of Atlantis was first expressed in the works of Plato.

In the ensuing centuries, no conclusive evidence of Atlantis has been found, but its attributes have expanded to include additional engineering and technological feats that enhance its legendary status in the popular imagination. In 1882, Ignatius Donnelly (1832–1901) published *Atlantis: The Antediluvian World,* arguing that all civilization is an inheritance from Atlantis. Listing numerous parallels between ancient cultures spaced far away from each other, Donnelly argued that their commonness resulted from contact with Atlanteans.

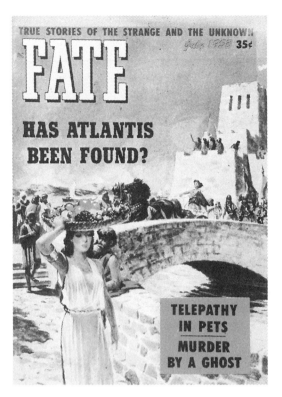

firmly believe that the inhabitants of the lost continent had cosmic connections with extraterrestrials and may actually have been a colony established on Earth by alien explorers.

Since Atlantis was first described, claims have been made that certain members of the civilization escaped destruction during its catastrophic final days and managed to impart their knowledge to other peoples of the world, helping civilize primitive societies, passing on the secret of written language, and supervising construction of some of the world's most mysterious structures of the ancient world. The pyramids of Egypt and the Americas, the Sphinx in Egypt, and the megaliths of western Europe are among the structures attributed to the genius of Atlanteans.

According to most accounts, Atlantis was suddenly destroyed by a cataclysm of earthquakes and floods and swallowed up by the sea. No definitive remnants have ever been found, and the exact location of the "lost continent" remains debatable. The idea of Atlantis was first expressed in the works of Plato (c. 428–348 or 347 B.C.E.), the Greek philosopher, who stressed that a perfect world exists in Ideas. For example, a shoe, according to Plato, exists as an idea before a craftsperson makes the material object identified as a shoe. The material world, then, is a reflection of ideas, never quite reaching the perfection of ideas, but which serve as models for which the adepts might strive.

While Plato used the model of Atlantis to represent a world of perfect order in contrast to all that was imperfect in the world around him, he labeled the story of Atlantis "literally true"—a significant declaration. For Plato was suspicious of fiction and art. If ideas are the primary reality, and the material world is a reflection of ideas, then art, as a reflection of the material world, is twice removed from reality, according to Plato. His claim that the Atlantis story is literally true helps sustain the continuing legend of Atlantis. It remains a legend, or an Idea, however, until some material proof shows that Atlantis existed in the material world. Aristotle (384–322 B.C.E.), another of the great Greek philosophers, viewed the Atlantis legend as fiction.

Similarities do indeed exist among various ancient cultures, as do significant differences. Flood myths and sun worship, for example, might be based on a shared teaching, or they might be separate reactions to beneficent and destructive elements of nature. Pyramids were built in Egypt and the Americas, but they are also significantly different in their structures. The walls of pyramids in the Americas did not converge to form a true point, as they did in Egypt; rather, the walls reached a certain level upon which a platform was built and often a temple erected. If Atlantis did indeed fall somewhere between 8500 and 9500 B.C.E., what accounts for the long time lag until the pyramids were erected in Egypt (generally dated around 2500 B.C.E.) and North America (generally dated after 200 C.E.)?

Since the 1800s, Atlanteans have been credited for having had the technology to generate electricity, build flying machines, and harness nuclear power for energy and warfare—all developed more than 9,000 years before such things came into being in modern society. Other claims have Atlanteans knowledgeable about a formidable death ray, secrets for levitation, and pure forms of energy through crystals. Many Atlantis enthusiasts

Plato's writings comprise several letters and 25 dialogues. His views and those of his mentor, Socrates (c. 470–399 B.C.E.), were presented as dramatic conversations exploring such topics as truth, the origin of the world and its composition, the purpose of humankind, and what an individual should choose as an aim of life. Atlantis is discussed in two of Plato's dialogues, *Timaeus* and *Critias*. *Timaeus* provides a description of the island continent and how Atlanteans conquered all the known world except for the Athenians (Plato was an Athenian). *Critias*, named after the primary speaker in the dialogue, Plato's great-grandfather, presents a history of Atlantean civilization and describes the ideal society that flourished there. Critias notes that the stories were originally passed on by an ancestor, Solon (638–558 B.C.E.), a politician and poet who traveled widely. Critias and Solon were both ancestors of Plato.

Solon, as the story goes, was informed by Egyptian priests in the city of Sais, located in the Nile delta, that there was once a land even older in history than Egypt, which the Greeks acknowledged as being centuries older than their own society. The priests described a large island continent called Atlantis that prospered some 8,000 years earlier, which dates Atlantis before 8500 B.C.E. The continent was located beyond "the Pillars of Hercules," the Greek term for the rocks that form the Straits of Gibraltar, the westernmost point of the Mediterranean Ocean. Beyond the straits is the Atlantic Ocean.

There were several cities on the continent. The primary city, also called Atlantis, was located in the center of a series of concentric rings that alternated between rings of water and land. The water rings served as canals for trade and helped form a series of natural defenses that made an invasion of Atlantis extremely difficult.

The city of Atlantis, in the innermost circle, had palaces and temples where wise and powerful rulers lived. The ruling coalition descended from Poseidon, the Greek god of the sea. Poseidon and Clieto had five sets of twin sons, according to Greek mythology, each of which was given a region of Atlantis.

Nineteenth-century map of Atlantis. (FORTEAN PICTURE LIBRARY)

Atlas, the firstborn son, was given the largest province, which became the city of Atlantis, a name that derives from Atlas. The finest structure on the island, the Temple of Poseidon, honored the god and served as the home of the primary ruler.

Atlantis had a powerful army of professional soldiers, as did each of the other nine regions of the continent. The culture of Atlantis promoted learning, through which advances in engineering and science made the land bountiful, beautiful, and powerful. In addition to magnificent architectural structures, a network of bridges and tunnels linked the rings of land, and clever uses of natural

Floorbed of Atlantis.

cules" as the location of Atlantis. As late as the twentieth century, a belief persisted that a landbridge once existed in the ocean and ran between Europe and Africa and North and South America. Such a land-link concept helps explain similarities in flora and fauna existing on continents spread thousands of miles apart. The mid-Atlantic ridge, a series of undersea mountains, has been presented as a remnant of the land bridge, or as the remains of Atlantis.

resources provided security and abundance. Many groves provided solitude and beauty, racetracks were used for athletic competitions, and irrigation systems ensured great harvests.

In Plato's account, the people of Atlantis eventually became corrupt and greedy, putting selfish pursuits above the greater good. They began invading other lands with the idea of world domination. Angered by these developments, Poseidon set about destroying the civilization, battering the continent with earthquakes and floods until Atlantis was swallowed up by the ocean.

That description of the destruction of Atlantis has been linked by some to other cataclysmic events—stories of a great deluge in the Bible, the Epic of Gilgamesh, and flood myths in other societies. Some contend that the end of the Ice Age between 12,000 and 10,000 B.C.E. likely resulted in rises of water levels in various parts of the world and that earthquakes, volcanic eruptions, and climate changes, either incidental or associated with the Ice Age, occurred during the time identified with the destruction of Atlantis.

The location of Atlantis has been claimed on each of the seven continents, and in several spots in the world's oceans and seas. Additionally, many of the ancient world's wonders have been attributed to Atlanteans who, presumably, escaped the destruction of their homeland and spread their advanced engineering skills elsewhere.

The text of Plato's dialogue suggests the Atlantic Ocean "beyond the pillars of Her-

Jacques Collina-Girard of the University of the Mediterranean in Aix-en-Provence had been studying patterns of human migration from Europe into North Africa at the height of the last Ice Age, 19,000 years ago, when his reconstruction of the area revealed an ancient archipelago with an island at the spot where Plato wrote Atlantis existed. The island was named Spartel, and it lay in front of the Pillars of Hercules to the west of the Strait of Gibraltar at a time when the sea level was 130 meters lower than it is today. According to Collina-Girard (*New Scientist*, September 2001), the slow rise of post-glacial sea levels would gradually have engulfed the island and the archipelago 9,000 years before Plato.

While the concept of an island being swallowed by the sea in the area before the Pillars of Hercules seems a viable theory, there is as yet no evidence discovered to prove that a continent existed in the mid-Atlantic Ocean. The shallow waters around the northwest coast of Africa and extending to the Canary Islands is an area that may have been above the ocean at one time and has been suggested as a location for Atlantis, but no physical remains of human habitation have been located there.

Alan F. Alford, a leading authority on ancient mythology, spent five years investigating Plato's account of Atlantis, and, in December 2001, announced his conclusion that the myth of the lost continent took place only in Plato's mind. In Alford's theory, the Greek philosopher invented Atlantis as a metaphor for the ancient version of the contemporary "Big Bang Theory." Atlantis, as a symbol for a lost paradise, represented a kind of cataclysm of all cataclysms that brought about the beginning of all time.

The discouraging theories of the skeptical do little to diminish the enthusiasm of those who earnestly believe in the physical reality of Atlantis. The Atlantic Ocean location for the lost continent received renewed attention in the late 1960s, specifically the region near Bimini Island in the Bahamas, an island chain off the coast of the United States. Fueling the excitement over what appeared to be discoveries of actual roadways, walls, and buildings under the water was the fact that they were found in the exact location and at the same point in time as prophesied by **Edgar Cayce** (1877–1945), a psychic, whose "life readings" for clients revealed that many of their present-life psychological traumas were being caused by a terrible incident that the sufferer had experienced in a past life. Many of the presentlife traumas of his clients, according to Cayce, were due to the sufferings they had experienced as people who lived in Atlantis in a previous life.

Cayce helped popularize a modernized view of Atlantis as a superior civilization that had developed planes, submarines, x-ray, anti-gravity devices, crystals that harness energy from the sun, and powerful explosives. He theorized that an explosion in 50,000 B.C.E. blew Atlantis up into five islands; another occurred in 28,000 B.C.E.; and the third, the one described by Plato, occurred around 10,000 B.C.E. Cayce claimed that he had been an Atlantean priest from around 10,500 B.C.E. who had foreseen the coming destruction and sent some of his followers to Egypt. Those followers directed the building of the Sphinx and the pyramids.

In 1940 Cayce predicted that remnants of Atlantis would rise again near the Bahamas in the late 1960s. In 1967, two pilots photographed a rectangular structure in the ocean off the coast of Andros, the largest island of the Bahamas. Another configuration of stone, in the shape of a "J," was found by divers off the island of Bimini. The J-shaped formation was believed to be a road of stone. Extensive diving expeditions became common in the area, and some divers claimed to have seen remnants of temples, pillars, and pyramids. However, none were documented by extensive excavations.

The J-shaped structure became popularly known as the Bimini Road and was a cause of celebration among enthusiasts of Atlantis and Cayce. Geological tests, however, show that the J shape is actually a limestone beachrock. Fractures in the formation give it the appearance of a construction of blocks, but the entire formation shows the same grains and microstructure—a quality difficult to replicate in a series of blocks. Radiocarbon testing of shells in the stone show that the formation is relatively young—about two or three thousand years old, some 9,000 years younger than the alleged final destruction of Atlantis. Finally, the curve of the J parallels the beachline of the nearby island, showing it has been shaped by the same currents affecting the island.

The rectangular structure off the coast of Andros, on the other hand, was indeed manmade—it was a storage facility built in the 1930s where sponges could be deposited after they were collected in the surrounding ocean. Despite these explanations, enthusiasm over the Bahama site continues among believers.

Another theory suggests that Antarctica was once located in the mid-Atlantic and had a more temperate climate where a civilization once thrived. Antarctica, thus, has been claimed as the site of Atlantis and of a similar type of advanced civilization.

The question of where Atlantis was located still persists. Among the many possible sites for Atlantis on the seven continents or under the seas, two popular locations are based on areas that, like Atlantic Ocean regions "beyond the pillars of Hercules," can be related to Plato's time. One site is the island of Crete, where the thriving Minoan civilization fell into disarray around 1400 B.C.E. The other site is in present-day Turkey, known in ancient times as Anatolia, where associations with Atlas and his descendants were strong.

Little was known about Minoan culture before the discovery in 1900 of a great palace at Knossos on the island of Crete by the British archaeologist Sir Arthur Evans (1851–1941). He named the culture that created Knossos and thrived on Crete "Minoan civilization" after Minos, the legendary king of Crete. The palace at Knossos was probably damaged by an earthquake about 1700 B.C.E., a date that marked the end of one phase of the early history of Crete. Minoan civilization had regular contact and trade with ancient Egypt, which lies southeast, across the Mediterranean, from Crete. Crete, then, qualifies as a land far to the west (in those days) of Egypt where Atlantis was said to be by the Egyptian priests who spoke of the continent to Solon.

Archaeological excavations early in the twentieth century unearthed remarkable artifacts of Minoan civilization. Then, in 1939, Greek archaeologist Sypridon Marinatos (1901–1974) discovered pumice, volcanic ash, on Crete. Marinatos connected the ash to the tremendous eruption of a volcano on Thera, a nearby island. The eruption was reported in ancient histories. The explosion would have created havoc on Crete and perhaps a tidal wave that swept over the island. To illustrate that possibility, Marinatos likened the Thera explosion to the 1886 eruption of Mt. Krakatoa that could be heard a thousand miles away and created tidal waves that killed 36,000 people. The volcanic ash on Crete helped preserve excellent artifacts of Minoan civilization, including whole streets and houses as well as frescoes and pottery.

However, while Plato's text cites earthquakes and floods as having destroyed Atlantis, there is no mention of a volcano. The date of the Thera volcano, around 1500 B.C.E., does not match the period of the downfall of Atlantis, which Egyptian priests told Solon had occurred 8,000 to 9,000 years earlier. The 1500 B.C.E. date does coincide if the claim of 8,000 years is reduced to 800 years. That tactic was suggested by Greek geologist Angelo Gelanpoulous in 1969: he theorized that all dates and measurements related by Solon were exaggerated and were actually one-tenth as large as claimed. Gelanpoulous' theory provided some neat correlations, but they work only in a few circumstances.

Another problem with identifying the fall of Atlantis with the destruction of Minoan civilization is an inexact correlation between the eruption of Thera and the demise of ancient Crete, where Minoan civilization continued on for another century after the volcanic eruption.

In fact, during twentieth-century excavations, some volcanic ash was found beneath an elaborate palace, showing that construction soon continued after the eruption. Furthermore, there was no apparent disruption in trade between the Minoans and Egyptians. The volcanic eruption caused havoc on Crete, but it did not destroy Minoan civilization.

The kings of Knossos attained their greatest power about 1600 B.C.E., when they controlled the entire Agean area and traded extensively with Egypt. The subsequent destruction of Knossos and the collapse of Minoan culture coincided with the beginning of the most flourishing period of Mycenae civilization in Greece; this coincidence suggests that it may have been the warlike Mycenae who attacked and destroyed Minoan civilization.

Lydia, an ancient country of Asia Minor (now Turkey), was located in the valleys of the Hermus and Cayster rivers (now the Gediz and Büyükmenderes rivers). Known earlier by the name Maeonia, it had fertile soil, rich deposits of gold and silver, and a magnificent capital, Sardis. Lydia prospered as a powerful dynasty beginning about 685 B.C.E. During the sixth century B.C.E., Lydia attained its greatest splendor under the rule of King Croessus. The empire ended when the Persian ruler Cyrus the Great (c. 585–c. 529 B.C.E.) captured Sardis about 546 B.C.E. After the defeat of Persia by Alexander III (c. 356–323 B.C.E.), king of Macedonia, Lydia was brought under Greco-Macedonian control, and then in 133 B.C.E. it became part of the Roman province of Asia.

Lydia was across the Agean Sea from Greece. A legendary king of Lydia was named Tantalis: his name sounds similar to Atlantis, and he shared many mythic attributes among Lydians that the god Atlas had among Greeks. Like Atlas, Tantalis was a leader of the Titans, the group of gods who were overthrown by Zeus. In Greek mythology, Zeus punished Atlas by banishing him to the west and made to hold up the sky. A similar fate was shared by Tantalis in myths of Anatolia (an old name for the region in Asia Minor that includes Turkey).

According to that myth, Tantalis ruled over a fabulously wealthy city he founded on Mt.

Sipylus in Lydia. His city was shattered by earthquake and flood and was reputed to have sunk when he lost the favor of the Olympian gods.

During the 1990s ruins were found on the northern slope of Mt. Sipylus. The area had undergone several phases of change through the centuries. Among the ruins was a statue of the goddess Cybele that was dated around 1400 B.C.E., a time when the Hittite rule over the area was overthrown by locals affiliated with the Mycenae civilization of Greece. The area of Tantalis had been conquered, and perhaps razed. Or, it subsequently was buried during an earthquake, and eventually submerged by a lake. The area is in a major fault zone, and heavy earthquake damage to the cities of Lydia was documented in 17 C.E. Among the hardest hit of twelve ancient Lydian cities was Magnesia at Sipylus, in the region where Tantalis was located.

Lake Saloe in Turkey has long been identified with the lost city of Tantalis. The lake was pumped out in modern times to provide more land for farming. It is now a fertile plain with nearby rivers. An old caravan route was found, certainly not a remnant of a mighty empire, but the tantalizing prospect that Tantalis was Atlantis remains.

Enthusiasts of the lost continent were tantalized once again in December 2001 when explorers using a miniature submarine to probe the sea floor off the coast of Cuba announced their discovery of stone structures deep beneath the ocean surface that were suggestive of ruins left by an unknown human civilization thousands of years ago. Representatives of the Canadian-based Advanced Digital Communications, together with experts from the Cuban Academy of Sciences, said that the structures were discovered at a depth of around 2,100 feet and were distributed as if remnants of an urban area. Estimates of the ancient city under the sea were somewhere in the vicinity of 6,000 years, thereby making them about 1,500 years earlier than the great Giza pyramids of Egypt. Whether this new intriguing site proves to be Atlantis or evidence of a land bridge that once linked Cuba to mainland Latin America, it is certain to be controversial.

✸ DELVING DEEPER

Cawthorne, Andrew. "Explorers View 'Lost City' Ruins under Caribbean." *abcNews.com*, December 6, 2001. [Online] http://abcnews.go.com/wire/SciTech/reuters20011206_346.html.

Copley, Jan. "Sea Level Study Reveals Atlantis Candidate." *New Scientist*, September 19, 2001. [Online] http://www.newscientist.com/news/news.jsp? id'ns99991320.

Donnelly, Ignatius. *Atlantis: The Antediluvian World*. 1882. evised Edition. Ed. by Egerton Sykes. New York: Harper & Row, 1949.

Harpur, James, and Jennifer Westwood. *The Atlas of Legendary Places*. New York: Konecky & Konecky, 1997.

Hill, Amelia. "Myth of Atlantis All Took Place in Plato's Mind." *The Observer*, December 16, 2001. [Online] http://www.observer.co.uk/international/story /0,6903,619567,00.html.

Muck, Otto. *The Secrets of Atlantis*. New York: Times Books, 1978.

Plato. *The Timaeus and Kritias*. Trans. by Desmond Lee. London: Penguin Books, 1977.

Spence, Lewis. *The History of Atlantis*. New York: University Books, 1968.

AVALON

Avalon is the place where the legendary King Arthur was taken after receiving mortal wounds in battle. Although it is a mythical place, there are sites on which Avalon may well have been based.

Avalon is mentioned in a widely read text in *History of the Kings of Britain* (1138), written by Geoffrey of Monmouth (c. 1100–1154). Part fiction, part history, and partly based on Celtic folktales, Geoffrey's work was the first popular source to depict the exploits of King Arthur, a leader believed to have ruled in Britain during the fifth or sixth century. That era falls within the Dark Ages, a period after the Roman Empire retreated from northwestern Europe and the area was assailed by invaders from eastern Europe and Scandinavia. Not much is known about the history of that period.

Geoffrey's work helped bring attention to myths of the Celtic people, who were overwhelmed by Romans and then other invaders

< MERLIN AND VIVIEN &>

Merlin and Vivien, the fairy queen of Avalon. (FORTEAN PICTURE LIBRARY)

interpreted as the Atlantic Ocean, with Avalon possibly being the island of Greenland or a location in North America.

Geoffrey likely took the name from "Avallon," a Celtic term equivalent to "apple place." Celtic myths had identified a paradise in terms that translate to an "island of apples." The old Welsh language, where the word "Avallach" referred to a mythical island, is another possible source.

Arran, an island off the coast of Scotland, has been considered a possible model for Avalon. The name Arran derived from "Emhain of the Apple Trees." Another popular claim for the site of Avalon is Glastonbury, a longtime apple-growing area in England.

✠ DELVING DEEPER

Gordon, Stuart. *The Encyclopedia of Myths and Legends*. London: Headline Books, 1993.

Harpur, James, and Jennifer Westwood. *The Atlas of Legendary Places*. New York: Konecky & Konecky, 1997.

Ingpen, Robert, and Philip Wilkinson. *Encyclopedia of Mysterious Places*. New York: Barnes & Noble, 1999.

Larousse Dictionary of World Folklore. New York: Larousse, 1995.

THE BERMUDA TRIANGLE

The Bermuda Triangle, also called the Devil's Triangle, is an imaginary area that can be roughly outlined on a map by connecting Miami, Florida; San Juan, Puerto Rico; and the Bahamas, an island chain off the coast of the United States. Within that triangular area of the Atlantic Ocean have occurred a number of unexplained disappearances of boats and planes. Additionally, readings on directional devices do not operate normally inside the triangle.

Unusual events in that area date back in recorded history to 1493 and the first voyage of Christopher Columbus (1451–1506) to the New World. In his log, Columbus noted that his compass readings were askew within the area now called the Bermuda Triangle, and he and his crew were confused by shallow areas of sea with no land nearby.

during the first six centuries. His recounting of the exploits of King Arthur inspired a trend of tales written and told about Arthur and his knights. The tales were especially popular in the courts of Europe from about 1150 to 1250, and have enjoyed several revivals since.

After Arthur received mortal wounds in battle, he was tended to by a maiden and placed aboard a boat bound for Avalon. The location of Avalon, usually called an island, varies according to which of the many Arthurian tales is being read. Some sources suggest Avalon lies off the coast of Great Britain, or "across the sea," a term some have

The "Devil's Sea" and the Dragon's Triangle located in the Philippine Sea off China's eastern coast is known for vanishing ships and seamen similar to the legendary **Bermuda Triangle.** While sensational theories for the mysterious disappearances speak of extraterrestrials and lost kingdoms under the sea wreaking havoc, others believe that the region displays the same magnetic anomalies as the Bermuda Triangle. The area, which can be marked off on a map by connecting Japan, Taiwan, and Yap Island, has become known as the Dragon's Triangle after a centuries-old Chinese myth. According to the myth, dragons live deep beneath the surface and their movement can suddenly churn up waves, whirlpools, thick fog, and sudden storms.

In 1950, Japanese officials declared the triangle a danger zone for shipping. In 1952, a research vessel, the *Kaio Maru No. 5,* sent by the Japanese government to investigate the troubled waters, vanished without a trace, and 22 crewmen and nine scientists were lost.

Like the Bermuda Triangle, the Devil's Triangle area may be volatile, subject to sudden weather

JAPAN'S DRAGON'S TRIANGLE

changes and ocean swells not yet understood. Undersea volcanoes are believed to influence the area's sudden environmental changes. Others cite *mikakunin hiko-buttai,* Japanese for UFOs.

SOURCES:

Berlitz, Charles. *The Dragon's Triangle.* New York: Wynwood Press, 1989.

"The Dragon's Triangle." [Online] http://dragonsunlimited. tripod.com/index-8.html.

The term "Bermuda Triangle" was first used in an article written by Vincent H. Gaddis for *Argosy* magazine in 1964. Gaddis claimed that several ships and planes had disappeared without explanation in that area. The article was expanded and included in his book, *Invisible Horizons: True Mysteries of the Sea* (1965), where he described nine mysterious incidents and provided extensive detail. Many newspapers carried a story in December of 1967 about strange incidents in the Bermuda Triangle after a National Geographic Society news release brought attention to Gaddis's book. The triangle was featured in a cover story in *Argosy* in 1968, in a book called *Limbo of the Lost* (1969) by John Wallace Spencer, and in a documentary film, *The Devil's Triangle,* in 1971. Charles Berlitz's 1974 bestseller *The Bermuda Triangle* marked the height of the disaster area legend, but some of its sensationalized claims were quickly proved inaccurate.

THE *Bermuda Triangle is also known as the Devil's Triangle.*

As early as 1952, George X. Sands had noted in a report in *Fate* magazine that an unusually large number of strange accidents had occurred in the region associated with the Bermuda Triangle. That many of the accidents in the area are intriguing, and that the area does have some natural conditions that sailors and pilots need to be aware of, has not been challenged. However, neither statistics nor documented evidence indicates that the number of accidents is unusually high or without explanation.

In March 1918, during World War I, the *USS Cyclops* vanished in the Bermuda Triangle. That ship may have been a casualty of war, but the December 1945 disappearance of Flight 19, a training squadron of five U.S. Navy torpedo bombers, became the most notorious of disappearances associated with the Bermuda Triangle. The squadron left Fort Lauderdale, Florida, with 14 crewmen and disappeared after radioing in several distress messages. A seaplane sent in search of the squadron also vanished. Those two airplane disappearances were frequently cited as the Bermuda Triangle legend grew during the 1960s and 1970s.

THE *Bermuda Triangle has claimed over 1,000 lives during the twentieth century.*

Few of those stories included telling details. All of the crewmen of Flight 19 were in training, for example, except for their patrol leader, who had tried to withdraw from his flight duty that day because he was feeling ill. After his compass malfunctioned soon into the flight, the flight leader decided to navigate by landmarks below on the islands of the Florida Keys, with which he was familiar. Visibility became a problem because of a sudden storm, and the leader became disoriented. Flight 19 was still in radio contact with the Fort Lauderdale air base, but after some mechanical difficulties they failed to switch to an emergency frequency. Radio recordings indicate that some of the crew believed they were heading out over the Atlantic Ocean, instead of the Gulf of Mexico as their leader reported.

A search plane took off and was claimed to have disappeared into the Bermuda Triangle with Flight 19. The plane actually blew up 23 seconds after takeoff. Wreckage from Flight 19 has never been recovered.

Other aircraft that have disappeared in the area include a DC-3 carrying 27 passengers in 1948 and a C-124 Globemaster with 53 pas-

sengers in 1951. Among the ships often listed among the mysteriously disappeared are the *Mary Celeste* (1872), the Marine tankership *Sulphur Queen* with 39 men aboard (1963), and the nuclear-powered submarine *Scorpion* with a crew of 99 (1968). The *Mary Celeste* entered the list of supposed Bermuda Triangle mysteries many decades after its odd tragedy. The ship set sail from New York to Genoa, Italy, but was found sailing unmanned some 400 miles off course, off the coast of Africa. Personal articles of the crew were found and food storage areas showed no sign of upheaval. A tattered sail and a missing lifeboat suggested the boat had encountered a storm, but the ship's log, in which information was recorded as late as nine days before the ship was found, made no mention of any kind of catastrophe.

There is no evidence, however, that the *Mary Celeste* ever entered the area of the Bermuda Triangle. Still, the eerie, unanswered questions concerning its fate are often cited by those who attribute a malevolent force as being responsible for odd and tragic events of the triangle.

Nevertheless, there are many documented disappearances that occurred within the triangle. They include a four-engine Tudor IV airplane lost in 1948, with 31 aboard; an American freighter, the *SS Sandra* (1952), which sunk without a trace; a British York transport plane, disappeared in 1952, with 33 aboard; a U.S. Navy Lockheed Constellation airplane, vanished in 1954 with 42 aboard; a U.S. Navy seaplane, 1956, with a crew of 10; a French freighter in 1970; and a German freighter, *Anita*, lost in 1972 with a crew of 32.

Theories about why so many air and water ships disappeared in the Bermuda Triangle involve strange magnetic fields, time warps, the lost continent of Atlantis, and alien abduction. Other proposed explanations include physical forces unknown to science, a "hole in the sky," and an unusual chemical component in the region's seawater. Several books have suggested that an intelligent, technologically advanced race living in space or under the sea has been responsible for jamming equipment and leading ships and planes to disaster.

Bermuda Triangle.

(DEZSO STERNOCZKY/SUFOI)

Many books and articles play up mystery angles concerning vanished ships by depicting the disappearances as having occurred in calm weather and daylight. Such particulars of Flight 19 as an inexperienced crew, a faulty compass, a squadron leader who failed to follow instructions, and conditions of deteriorating weather and visibility are often not mentioned. Larry Kusche, a librarian at Arizona State University, examined claims of mysterious disappearances and recorded evidence from each example. The results, published in *The Bermuda Triangle—Mystery Solved*, showed that many of the accidents happened during raging storms, or were later explained.

The area known as the Bermuda Triangle is one of the two places on Earth where a magnetic compass does point towards true north, a phenomenon called compass variation. Navigators must compensate the amount of variation or the craft they are on will go off course. A region commonly called the "Devil's Sea" in the Pacific Ocean is the other area of compass variation.

The Gulf Stream that runs through the Bermuda Triangle area is swift and turbulent, and can quickly erase evidence of a disaster. The unpredictable Caribbean-Atlantic weather can suddenly change into thunderstorms or create waterspouts. Many short and intense storms build up quickly and dissipate quickly, undetected by satellite surveillance. The ocean floor has shoals around islands as well as some of the deepest marine trenches in the world. The interaction of the strong currents over reefs promotes a constant flux and the development of new, uncharted navigational hazards.

These factors can confuse even experienced sailors. A large number of pleasure boats travel the waters between Florida's coast and the Bahamas. The U.S. Coast Guard receives more than 8,000 distress calls per year, averaging more than 20 per day from that area, often from sailors who have run out of gas.

The Bermuda Triangle claimed more than 1,000 lives during the twentieth century. That averages to about 10 per year, a figure similar to other areas of high water traffic or volatile

natural conditions. Scientific evaluations of the Bermuda Triangle have concluded that the number of disappearances in the region is not abnormal and that most of the disappearances have logical explanations. Paranormal associations with the Bermuda Triangle persist, however, in the popular imagination.

❖ DELVING DEEPER

Berlitz, Charles. *The Bermuda Triangle*. New York: Doubleday and Co., 1974.

Gaddis, Vincent H. *Invisible Horizons: True Mysteries of the Sea*. Philadelphia: Chilton Books, 1965.

Gordon, Stuart. *The Encyclopedia of Myths and Legends*. London: Headline Books, 1993.

Kusche, Lawrence D. *The Bermuda Triangle Mystery—Solved*. New York: Harper and Row, 1975.

Spencer, John Wallace. *Limbo of the Lost*. New York: Bantam Books, 1973.

CHARTRES

The gothic cathedral that stands in the French town of Chartres is the sixth church or cathedral constructed on that site over 1,500 years. Although the present cathedral is recognized as a place for Christian pilgrimages, it is considered mysterious.

Before the Gauls inhabited this region on the River Eure about 60 miles southwest of Paris, some ancient priests of an unknown religion constructed a dolmen (two or more large upright stones with a space in between and covered by a large horizontal rock) and a well within a mound. The Druids, Celtic priests of Gaul and Britain, made the mound and dolmen a center for the study of their religion. Here a Druid priest had a vision of a virgin who would bear a child. To honor the

Cahokia Mounds State Historical Site in Illinois is the site of the largest prehistoric Native American city north of Mexico. The city covered six square miles of settlement and may have been inhabited by as many as 20,000 people sometime between 800 and 1400. The site includes Monks Mound, the largest earthwork in North America, rising 100 feet and consisting of four terraces that covered 14 acres and contained an estimated 22 million cubic feet of earth. Atop the great mound stood a ceremonial building 100 feet long and 50 feet high. Named for the Trappist monks who grew vegetables on the site circa 1809, it was later discovered that the mound served a forgotten people as both a temple and a palace.

It has been determined that the city was the principal ceremonial center of a vanished culture known as the Mississippian who occupied the area from around 1050 to 1250. At its peak around 1150, the city supported a population of as many as 20,000 people.

Many scholars believe that the customs of the Natchez people who inhabited the lower Mississippi Valley when French explorers encountered the tribe in the latter part of the seventeenth century may offer some insight into their ancestors. Unlike the other Native American tribes, the Natchez had distinct social classes who were governed by a ruler-priest known as the Great Sun, who was regarded as the representative of the Sun on Earth and was treated with godlike reverence by the members of his tribe. The Great Sun wore a headdress-crown of white swan feathers and was born aloft on a litter by devotees so his feet would not be defiled by contact with the earth. The Natchez, and it is supposed their vanished Mississippian predecessors, had elaborate funeral ceremonies which involved certain sacrifices. When Mound 72 was excavated, the burial pits of nearly 300 people were discovered, including what may have been as many as 53 young women who were sacrificed to honor the death of a great ruler-priest.

In 1961, Dr. Warren Wittry unearthed the remains of a circle of red cedar posts that may have been used as a solar calendar to note coming seasons and to

CAHOKIA AND ITS WOODHENGE

help determine when to plant and when to harvest crops. The discovery was dubbed "Woodhenge," in recognition to its similarity to the circular arrangement known as **Stonehenge** in Great Britain.

SOURCES:

Harpur, James. *The Atlas of Sacred Places*. Old Saybrook, Conn.: Konecky & Konecky, 1994.

Thomas, David Hurst. *Exploring Ancient Native America*. New York: Macmillan, 1994.

vision, an image of the virgin with the babe resting on her knee was carved from a peach tree and placed next to the well and the power point within the dolmen.

When the first Christians appropriated the area in the third century, they built the first church dedicated to Our Lady on the site of the dolmen, mound, and well and placed the image of the Black Virgin in the church's crypt. The Duke of Aquitania burned the first church in 743; Vikings destroyed the second in 858. The third and fourth churches were burned in 962 and 1020, and the first of the cathedrals was destroyed by fire in 1194. Each time the place of worship was burned or crumbled, faithful Christian townspeople, builders, and architects appeared to rebuild the structure. But the identity of the master builders who constructed the majestic Chartres Cathedral that stands there today remains unknown.

✤ DELVING DEEPER

Images of Chartres Cathedral. [Online]
  http://www.bluffton.edu/~sullivanm/chartreswest/
  centralportal.html.

Westwood, Jennifer, ed. *Mysterious Places.* New York: Galahad Books, 1987.

CURSUSES AND LEYS

There exists substantial evidence that some ancient societies wanted their landscapes to reflect the interconnectedness of life—imitating patterns they noticed in constellations, in changing seasons, or in rituals they performed. Ritual paths are found near some of Great Britain's ancient megalithic sites and are called cursuses. Unlike geoglyphs, which are marked clearly on the land, patterns formed by structures are detected by plotting them on the map of an area and looking for connections—literally, connecting the dots to determine whether or not a pattern emerges.

Ley lines is a term coined by Alfred Watkins (1855–1935), an Englishman who noticed in 1921 that several hilltops with ancient ruins on them in Herefordshire formed a straight alignment. He found several other instances where standing stones, burial mounds, and other ancient sites were aligned, criss-crossing the countryside. He called the straight alignments "leys" and published his findings in a book, *The Old Straight Track,* in 1925. The theory of ley lines promotes the belief that ancient structures in Great Britain were built on specific sites to form patterns and were so well aligned that if one continued in a straight line after walking from one structure to another one would soon find a third site.

Watkins believed that such alignments were intended as trade routes: the quickest way to get from one point to another is by a straight line. By the mid-twentieth century, however, leys became associated with cosmic lines of force—the belief that unknown forms of energy run in channels through the terrain. The practice of "ley hunting," plotting ancient sites and looking for patterns—straight lines, in particular—became popular in Great Britain during the twentieth century.

Reports of a curious feature found near megalithic sites in Great Britain date back to the 1720s, when William Stukeley (1687–1765), a British antiquarian, noticed parallel lines of banks and ditches at Stonehenge. He called the phenomenon a cursus, a Latin word for racetrack, since the lines were thought to run parallel and were joined at the ends to form an oval. The straight tracks he found were later dated as having been built in the same neolithic period as Stonehenge. Cursuses became a subject of study in the twentieth century when many more of them were discovered through aerial photography, and curiosity was piqued as to what their purpose might be.

The cursus at Stonehenge had chamber graves at both ends. So, too, did a cursus found at Dorset, England. The Dorset Cursuses follow a crescent pattern, each passing by chamber graves dated earlier than the ones at either end of the cursus. Other cursuses waver even further off the straight track, but all of them have burial graves at either end or point to graves or standing stones.

The Dorset Cursuses were called an "Avenue of the Dead" by archaeologist Richard Bradley, who suggested that ancients believed spirits of the dead passed along those lines, which he called avenues. Those wishing to communicate with the dead could meet them on the avenue. It is likely that the cursuses were used in ancient processional rituals in ceremonies honoring the dead.

In Britain, many of the ancient sites on ley lines were erected by Celts, a people who had rituals involving nature. Since the Celts were more attuned to the natural world than modern humans, according to those who believe in cosmic lines of force, their structures were purposefully erected on sites of pulsating energy. Some UFO proponents believe that ley lines were energy forces on which ships from outer space were able to harness energy and move quickly around Earth.

Ley hunting, the act of researching ancient sites to discover straight alignments, has also inspired detractors. Many supposed leys had sites built at various times and by various societies: a Celtic hill-fort from 200 B.C.E. might be followed on a ley by a Christian church erected in medieval times. Watkins countered by noting that Christian sites were often built on places of pagan worship. He also took a practical approach, believing the ley lines indicated trade routes, rather than cosmic lines of force. Interested in establishing sound criteria for leys, Watkins argued that leys involving three sites might just as likely be a chance occurrence as a planned pattern. Five aligned sites, he determined, were necessary to consider a purposeful pattern.

Many claims of ley lines were proven inaccurate: they were not quite straight, or they lumped together many different kinds of things from many different time periods. Even

though quite a few intriguing leys were discovered, the theory began losing support because of extravagant claims.

Ley hunting enjoyed a revival beginning in the 1970s. By then, much more information was known about prehistoric civilizations and their capacity for great engineering feats and mastering of sophisticated astronomical and mathematical techniques. The enthusiasm for the pastime was channeled through a magazine, *The Ley Hunter*, which Paul Devereux took over as editor in 1976. Devereux set up a system where all prospective leys could be catalogued and researched. Hundreds of claims were submitted and checked, and the results were published in *The Ley Hunter's Companion* (1979). Forty-one leys, each including at least four sites, were presented in that book as being worthy of further research. Virtually all of them failed the test of being straight alignments.

LEY *lines were previously believed to be trade routes.*

Meanwhile, statisticians showed that the possibility of chance alignments was greater than expected. Random patterns were just as likely to be straight as planned sites because of the large number of items available to be considered. The question concerning leys is whether the sites arise from random connection or whether they were planned to form a pattern. Even if they were not planned, a simple combination involving many sites will form patterns and several straight alignments.

Statistical methods based on rigorous standards for alignment and ensuring that sites on leys were from a certain time period all worked to compromise the theory of leys. Taking the practical and scientific approaches to the ley theory proved to be its undoing. Although the belief that many megaliths erected by neolithic peoples were placed along energy lines persists among a number of ley hunting enthusiasts, except for a few isolated cases, most claims do not match the criteria of straight alignment, and they often incorporate structures from vastly different eras.

✦ DELVING DEEPER

Michel, Aime. *Flying Saucers and the Straight Line Mystery.* New York: Criterion Books, 1958.

Watkins, Alfred. *The Old Straight Track.* New York: Ballantine Books, 1973.

EL DORADO

Europeans of the sixteenth century presumed that somewhere deep in South America was a vast city called El Dorado that contained unimaginable mineral riches. Several Spanish conquistadors made perilous, often deadly journeys to find it. Sir Walter Raleigh (1554–1618), the English raconteur, explorer, and visionary, claimed in a book he published in 1596 that he knew the whereabouts of El Dorado. But in spite of such valiant efforts, El Dorado seems to persist only as a symbol of the rapacious greed with which the English and Spanish beheld the New World.

THE *Chibcha people blew gold dust all over the new priest chief's body until he resembled a statue of pure gold.*

Europeans first learned of El Dorado through word-of-mouth tales that circulated among South America's indigenous peoples. There was a small grain of truth to the story: high in the eastern range of the Andes, in what is now Colombia, lived the Chibcha people. Geographically isolated, they mined gold and emeralds freely, and built a highly stratified and developed society. When they anointed a new priest-chief, they covered the man in balsam gum, and then blew gold dust all over his body through cane straws until he resembled a statue of pure gold. The new priest-chief then ceremonially bathed in Lake Guatavita, a sacred place to the Chibcha. This practice ended around 1480 when they

were subdued by another tribe. But the story of the "gilded one" became part of the oral folklore traditions in South America, and in its retellings, the tale took on added dimensions: the gilded one supposedly ruled over a vast kingdom where nearly everything was made from gold, silver, or precious stone.

Spanish colonization of Latin America began not long after the end of this practice. Francisco Pizarro (c. 1475–1541), who conquered the powerful Inca civilization in the 1530s in what is today Peru, saw the technically advanced and lavishly prosperous city of Cuzco that the tightly organized indigenous culture created. He believed that the continent held enormous mineral wealth, and he took bags of gold and stacks of silver bars back to Spain from his plunder of the Inca. Not long after the conquest, a messenger from an unknown Indian tribe appeared in Peru with a message for the Inca emperor, unaware the empire had been defeated. Interrogated by the Spanish, he told them he came from the Zipa people in the Bogota region, but knew of another kingdom, high in the mountains to the east, a tribe so rich that they covered their chief in gold.

The Spanish, who had already heard about the Chibcha, became increasingly certain that El Dorado, their translation of "the gilded one," really existed. Adding to the mystery was a rumor that a renegade Inca faction had managed to escape the violent Spanish conquest and had fled to the mountains. Supposedly they had migrated into the Amazon River jungle. There, according to folklore, was an empire richer than that of the Inca. The Spanish assumed that the rebels took large amounts of mineral wealth with them, and that this fugitive empire was flourishing somewhere in what is today Venezuela.

Between 1536 and 1541, the Spanish sent out five major expeditions in search of El Dorado. After the journeys proved fruitless, the Spanish became certain that El Dorado must lie in the northern part of the continent into which they had not yet ventured—the jungle basin between the Orinoco and Amazon rivers.

Meanwhile, another mysterious appearance of a man who spoke of a city of gold he called "Manoa" only fueled their desire. His name was Juan Martinez, and he had been a munitions master on board a Spanish ship exploring the Caroni River that branched off from the Orinoco at San Thome. His group headed deeper into the jungle, but the journey was aborted when its gunpowder stores exploded. Martinez was left behind in an open canoe as punishment for the accident.

He claimed to have met friendly Indians, who blindfolded him for days and led him to their kingdom, called Manoa, where everything in the royal palace was made of gold. Martinez said that riches had been given to him as a departing gift, but they had been stolen by Indians on his way back.

This story was told to Sir Walter Raleigh in England around 1586. Raleigh had established an ill-fated colony in North America on Roanoke Island and had fallen out of favor with Queen Elizabeth I (1533–1603). Wishing to restore his reputation and status at court, he set sail for South America. After arriving in March of 1595, Raleigh and his party spent weeks sailing along the Orinoco River, but found nothing but a massive Spanish anchor, which had been lost when Martinez's ship had exploded.

Raleigh brought back to England exotic flora and fauna and some blue-tinged rocks that hinted at great ore deposits. But when Raleigh told his extraordinary tales of the jungle, his enemies ridiculed him, claiming that he had been hiding in Cornwall the entire time. In response, he wrote a book, *The Discovery of the Large, Rich and Beautiful Empire of Guyana with a Relation to the Great and Golden City of Manoa*.

The book was absorbing, but the English expedition had not ventured into any parts of the Orinoco that the Spanish had not already explored. Raleigh claimed that the city of Manoa was on Lake Parìma, behind a mountain range. He provided a map so remarkably accurate that most atlases of South America showed the mythical lake for the next 150 years. Raleigh also wrote of a tribe of headless, club-wielding warriors with eyes and mouths on their torsos. That brought further discredit to his book, but it sold well, even in translation.

Raleigh's claims failed to interest Queen Elizabeth I or potential investors who might finance a further search for El Dorado. After the monarch died in 1603, Raleigh was imprisoned in the Tower of London by her successor, King James I (1566–1625), on charges of treason. Convinced in the very least that vast gold mines existed close to the Orinoco River, Raleigh continually petitioned for release; only when dire financial straits fell on Great Britain did the king allow Raleigh a second chance. Raleigh's 1618 expedition battled the Spanish, and Raleigh's son died in battle. When Raleigh returned to England empty-handed, he was jailed again, tried in secret, and executed on the 1603 treason charge.

The term "El Dorado" became part of Renaissance-era English culture; John Milton (1608–1674) wrote of it in *Paradise Lost*, and William Shakespeare (1564–1616) mentioned the headless warriors in *Othello*. El Dorado has become synonymous with a place of fabulous wealth or inordinately great opportunity. Accepted theory holds that El Dorado existed only in the minds of the Europeans who were eager to discover the quickest path to riches.

✤ DELVING DEEPER

Gordon, Stuart. *The Encyclopedia of Myths and Legends*. London: Headline Books, 1993.

Larousse Dictionary of World Folklore. New York: Larousse, 1995.

EASTER ISLAND

In one of the most remote spots on Earth, separated by more than two thousand miles of ocean from the nearest centers of civilization, is a lone, triangular-shaped island that occupies about 64 square miles of the Pacific Ocean, which spans 70 million square miles. On the island's southeast coast stand nearly a hundred huge, megalithic monuments carved in a stylized manner to resemble male human heads with elongated facial features. Some 800 additional statues remain in a quarry or scattered about the island.

The statues average about 13 feet in height, 5 feet in width, and weigh an average of 14 tons; they stand on stone platforms aver-

aging 4 feet in height. Islanders call the statues "moai," and the platforms are called "ahus," but the megaliths abound in mystery: who carved them and what is their significance?

EASTER *Island was reached by Dutch explorer Jacob Roggeveen in 1722.*

Inhabitants call the island Rapa Nui. Europeans have known it as Easter Island since the first recorded contact in 1722 by the Dutch explorer Jacob Roggeveen (1659–1729). The island is also known as Isla de Pascua in Spanish, the language of Chile, the South American country that annexed the island in 1888. But Chile, on the closest continent to Easter Island, lies 2,300 miles to the east. Tahiti, the nearest large island to the west, is 2,500 miles away from Easter Island. It is 1,500 miles to the nearest area of human habitation, Pitcairn Island. Another mystery,

then, is how the island came to be populated, and how the isolated island people managed to make and move the immense moai.

The island inhabitants could tell little about the moai to European visitors. Evidence of a once-thriving culture existed on the island, but when Roggeveen named the island on Easter Sunday, 1722 the several thousand Polynesian inhabitants were struggling for survival. At the time of this first contact with Europeans, islanders called their home Te Pito O Te Henua, which has been variously translated as "naval of the world," "end of the world," and "lands' end." The population and land were even more impoverished 50 years later when British explorer James Cook (1728–1779) arrived there. Islanders were readily willing to trade old, elaborate wood carvings for food and cloth. Noting that the statues were not part of the inhabitants' sacred rituals, Cook called them "monuments of antiquity" in his notes.

The engineering feat of moving moai from the quarry to their sites remains unexplained, particularly since there is no evidence of wheels or a pully system through which such massive blocks could be transported. No evidence of advanced engineering skills exists on the island. Islanders told Captain Cook and more modern visitors that the moai walked from the quarry to their sites on the ahus.

Some theorists have speculated that the monuments are remnants of the lost continent of **Mu.** According to that account, Lemurians, an intellectually advanced race of people, were responsible for crafting, moving, and erecting the monuments. The stones were moved from quarry to ahu using ancient secrets known to the Lemurians, perhaps involving levitation or the secret for liquifying stone.

The two most prominent theories with some scientific evidence have the island becoming inhabited by seafarers, moving east to west from South America or west to east from Polynesia, who settled on the island, established a thriving community, and erected the monuments. The east to west theory was popularized in the late 1940s by anthropologist Thor Heyerdahl (1911–2002) who made a daring journey across the Pacific in a primitive balsa wood craft called the *Kon Tiki*. By doing so, Heyerdahl successfully overturned the notion that prehistoric South Americans could not have made the ocean journey to Polynesian islands in the eastern-central Pacific Ocean. Heyerdahl's voyage with a crew of five took 101 days and covered 4,300 miles and proved that such a journey could be made. Favorable winds blow east to west across the south Pacific Ocean. Those winds cross Easter Island and keep it warm year round.

Beginning in the mid-1980s, anthropologist Jo Ann Von Tilburg made important contributions to the study of the Easter Island megaliths. Her research has been featured in documentaries on Easter Island broadcast on the Public Broadcasting System's *Nova* series, as well as The Learning Channel, Discovery Channel, The History Channel (appearing with Thor Heyerdahl), and the syndicated *Arthur C. Clarke's Mysterious World*. In 1998 she completed an experimental archaeology project using a computer to simulate the crafting and transporting of an average-sized moai. Her project showed that an average moia could be moved about six miles in under five days by a team of 70 people. In the simulation, the statues were laid on two long poles that form a track and were rolled forward over smaller logs within the track. Polynesians had long been adept with hinges and levers to help lift and prop large objects through their construction of large canoes. Such devices could be used to place the moai on the ahus.

The megaliths on Easter Island stand with their backs to the sea. Many archaeologists believe that signifies the edge of the Polynesian's world. The statues are believed to be the spirits of ancestors and high-ranking chiefs. That the faces are standardized perhaps indicates an archetype of a powerful individual. Van Tilburg suggests that the moai are positioned on platforms to indicate they are links between heavenly gods and the material earth. Polynesians erect such statues as "sky props" that help hold up the heavens, and their leaders are considered the props that hold up the community.

The monuments on Easter Island were believed to have been erected between 1400 and 1550, until radiocarbon dating in the 1990s pushed that date back some 700 years. A history can be sketched beginning around 400, with the arrival of Polynesians. The community on Easter Island fell into decline after 1550, and resources were nearly exhausted at the time of first contact with Europeans in the eighteenth century.

Geology professor Charlie Love, of Western Wyoming Community College, with a crew of 17 students, archaeologists, and islanders, spent much of the summer of 2000 attempting to solve the mystery of how the great stone heads, some weighing as much as 90 tons, had been moved from the quarry to the ceremonial centers on the coast of Easter Island. Although the roadways have not been firmly dated, Love agreed with previous estimates that the statue-moving activity ended about 1500. After several months of on-site investigation, Love readily conceded that the mysteries of Easter Island had not been solved.

✤ DELVING DEEPER

Deuel, Leo. *Conquistadors without Swords: Archaeologists in the Americas*. New York: St. Martin's Press, 1967.

"The Easter Island Mystery." [Online] http://www.discoveringarchaeology.com/ articles/122900-easter.shtml.

Heyerdhal, Thor. *Kon-Tiki: Across the Pacific by Raft*. 35th anniversary ed. Chicago: Rand McNally, 1984.

Ingpen, Robert, and Philip Wilkinson. *Encyclopedia of Mysterious Places*. New York: Barnes & Noble, 1999.

Van Tilburg, Jo Anne. *Easter Island Archaeology, Ecology, Culture*. Washington, D.C.: Smithsonian Institution Press, 1994.

GLASTONBURY

Glastonbury, in the Somerset region of England, seems always to have been a spiritual center, from Celtic May Day festivities, to Christian worship, to present-day New Age festivals. Human habitation dates back many centuries before the contemporary era, based on findings of flints, the remains of two lake villages that rose above the marshes on artificial islands, and hundreds of planks that formed walkways held by pegs driven into the soil. Those remnants date back to at least 2500 B.C.E., the same period in which many other sites, such as Stonehenge and Silbury Hill, the tallest prehistoric man-made mound in Europe, were being erected.

GLASTONBURY *Abbey was long established when it became a focal point for Arthurian legends in 1190.*

Romans conquered Great Britain during the first century B.C.E. and established wharves on nearby Bristol Bay, thus enabling Glastonbury to become a shipping area. A legend has it that Joseph of Arimathea, who is mentioned in the Bible as the person who pre-pared Jesus Christ (c. 6 B.C.E.–c. 30 C.E.) for burial after his crucifixion, landed in Bristol Bay and established the first Christian church at Glastonbury. Later, according to some accounts, he traveled by sea and landed in Great Britain, bringing with him the Holy Grail. Several centuries later, according to legends, King Arthur's knights undertook quests to find the lost Holy Grail.

When Joseph arrived in Glastonbury, according to tradition, he pushed his staff into the soil on a ridge called Wirral. That staff miraculously became a tree, the famous Glastonbury Thorn. It flowers around the beginning of winter, usually around Christmas time. It is not known when the original Glastonbury Thorn first appeared, but it was already centuries old and revered in the sixteenth century, when a Puritan cut it down because it represented a prideful icon of veneration. The Glastonbury Thorn is unlike any native species of tree in Great Britain and is reputed to be related to a thorn tree of the eastern Mediterranean area.

The most distinctive and highest of the hills in the area is the Glastonbury Tor ("tor" is an old word for "hill"). An imposing hill, the tor can be seen from as far as 25 miles away. A ruined tower of a Christian chapel is perched on the top of the tor. Nearby are the ruins of Glastonbury Abbey and, reportedly, the oldest Christian church in England.

Glastonbury Abbey, a Christian monastery, was long established at the site when it became a focal point for Arthurian legends in 1190. King Henry II (1133–1189) had claimed that a bard told him that King Arthur's bones were buried deep at Glastonbury. In 1190, two monks at the monastery had a vision about a site where Arthur was buried in Glastonbury. After digging a hole sixteen feet deep, they claimed that they uncovered two stone markers and a giant coffin. Inside the coffin were the bones of a man and a woman together with a tablet identifying the remains as those of King Arthur and his wife, Guinevere.

The find was widely heralded, but was also quickly regarded as a hoax and the authenticity of the grave strongly debated. Nevertheless,

the Norman kings, whose invading armies had conquered Britain a century earlier and were still attempting to solidify their power, embraced the find. By the sixteenth century, when King Henry VIII (1491–1547) dissolved all Christian monasteries in Great Britain, the bones and artifacts alleged to be Arthur's were looted and the authenticity of the burial find was generally disproved. In the popular mind, however, the claim continued to be taken seriously because of the area's associations with Arthurian legends. Even to this day, the Pomparles Bridge that spans the River Brue that runs through Glastonbury is reputed to be the site where Arthur's sword, Excalibur, was returned to the Lady of the Lake.

During the twentieth and into the twenty-first century, Glastonbury remains the site of official festivals and unofficial gatherings that celebrate its Celtic roots. Beltane Day, as the Celts called May Day, is celebrated with a festival for the rebirth of the sun.

✤ DELVING DEEPER

Gordon, Stuart. *The Encyclopedia of Myths and Legends*. London: Headline Books, 1993.

Harpur, James, and Jennifer Westwood. *The Atlas of Legendary Places*. New York: Konecky & Konecky, 1997.

Maltwood, Katherine E. *A Guide to Glastonbury's Temple of the Stars*. London: Clarke, 1929.

HOLLOW EARTH

Edmund Halley (1656–1742) is best known for having calculated the orbit of a comet that passes by Earth every 76 years. The comet known as Halley's made its first appearance under that name in 1682. During the next decade, Halley turned his attention away from the celestial in favor of the subterranean. He claimed that the Earth was hollow and populated by humans and beasts.

Halley's Hollow Earth idea was developed further during the eighteenth and nineteenth centuries, and sometimes backed by sound scientific reasoning. None of the claims of Hollow Earth proponents have been substantiated, however. Those still holding to the belief in the twenty-first century are part of a long history of people who believe human life exists beneath the surface of the Earth.

Halley's theory was based on the fact that the earth's magnetic field varies over time. Halley suggested that there were several magnetic fields, one of which emanated from a sphere within the earth. Halley eventually developed the idea that there were four concentric hollow spheres within the earth. He believed the inner earth was populated with life and had a luminous atmosphere. The aurora borealis, he concluded, was actually an emanation of radiant gases from within the earth that escaped through thin layers of crust at the poles.

EDMUND *Halley claimed the Earth was hollow and populated by humans and beasts.*

During the eighteenth century, Halley's Hollow Earth theory was adapted by two other famed mathematicians, Leonhard Euler (1707–1783), a Swiss, and John Leslie (1766–1832), a Scotsman. Euler abandoned Halley's concentric spheres idea. He postulated that a glowing core some six hundred miles wide warmed and illuminated the inner earth, where an advanced population thrived. Leslie, on the other hand, believed there were two concentric spheres within the earth each with their own sun, which he named Pluto and Proserpine after the Greek god of the underworld and his mate.

Perhaps the most enthusiastic proponent of the Hollow Earth idea was John Cleves Symmes, who was born in 1780 in New Jersey. He was named after an uncle who fought in the American Revolutionary War. Symmes fought in the War of 1812, after which he moved to St. Louis, Missouri, and established a trading post. He immersed himself in reading books in the natural sciences. By 1818 he was publicizing his version of the Hollow Earth, which had concentric spheres and received light and warmth from the sun through large holes in the planet open at each of the poles.

Symmes proved relentless in publicizing his views: he was a prolific lecturer and writer of letters and articles; wrote fictional accounts of the Hollow Earth, including *Symzonia: Voyage of Discovery* (1820), which he published under the pseudonym Adam Seaborn; and advocated expeditions to the poles. His Hollow Earth illuminated by openings at the poles became the most popularly known version, and one that would be tested as humans began struggling to reach the poles.

Symmes was able to impress two influential men who would take his cause further. James McBride, a wealthy Ohio man, wrote articles supporting the concentric spheres version of the Hollow Earth. He lobbied a U.S. senator from Kentucky to support a bill funding a proposed expedition to explore trade routes in the southern hemisphere (where McBride hoped the expedition would continue on to the open pole). The senator he had lobbied, Richard M. Johnson (1790–1850), later became vice president of the United States under Martin Van Buren (1782–1862). In 1828, President John Quincy Adams (1767–1848) indicated that he would approve funding for the expedition. However, when Adams left office in 1829, his successor, Andrew Jackson (1767–1845), stifled a bill funding the proposed expedition.

Symmes died in 1829, but his cause was continued by Jeremiah Reynolds, an Ohio newspaper editor. After the failure to get government funding for the expedition in 1829, Reynolds joined a crew sailing to the south seas to hunts seals, but seven years later in 1836, he helped renew efforts for funding of a Southern Hemisphere expedition. Reynolds spoke before Congress, emphasizing the national glory that would accompany scientific discoveries and expanded foreign relations, but he became so impatient with the methodical planning and a series of delays that he was fired from the crew.

What became known as the Wilkes expedition, named after its commander, Charles Wilkes (1798–1877), launched in 1838. When the expedition was completed in 1842, they had effectively mapped a landmass where Symmes had envisioned a large hole in the

earth. The world's seventh continent, Antarctica, was officially recognized for the first time.

The open poles theory promoted by Symmes had been effectively undermined, but the belief in the Hollow Earth would only grow more popular. In 1846, the remains of a woolly mammoth, a creature long extinct, were discovered perfectly preserved in ice in Siberia. So suddenly had it been frozen, that the mammoth had not yet digested pine cones it had recently eaten. It was theorized that the animal had been caught by a climate change, but many questioned that such a change could have happened so quickly and thoroughly. Some people believed the animal had wandered out from the Hollow Earth through a hole at the North Pole.

As late as 1913, even after the North Pole had been reached, Marshall Gardner published *A Journey to the Earth's Interior, or Have the Poles Really Been Discovered?* which claimed that many creatures thought to be extinct were still thriving within the earth. Gardner theorized that the interior earth was warmed by materials still spinning since earth's creation. Based on the law of centrifugal force, Gardner argued that earth was originally a spinning mass of matter. An outer layer of matter had hardened and continued to revolve around a central axis, while an inner layer also hardened and was warmed by heat continually generated by the earth's spinning.

That same year, William Reed published *The Phantom of the Poles* (1906), in which he promoted the idea that a ship can pass from outer Earth to inner Earth. The effect of gravity pulls a ship against the interior in the same manner as it works on the exterior. He claimed that some sailors had already passed into inner Earth without knowing it. Gravity had pulled them to the interior side, where a 600 mile-long sun continued to keep them warm, as the outer sun had done.

In between the woolly mammoth find and those publications of 1913, fascination in the Hollow Earth was exhibited by scientists and science fiction writers. Jules Verne (1828–1905) published *Journey to the Center of the Earth* (1864), in which characters enter the Earth's interior through the chimney of an inactive volcano in Iceland. In 1873, *The Coming Race*, a novel by the occultist Edward Bulwer-Lytton (1831–1891), was set in the Earth's interior, where an advanced civilization of giants thrived. In this story, the giants had built a paradise and discovered a form of energy so powerful that they outlawed its use as a potential weapon. The paradise is threatened, nevertheless; not by weapons, but by a lack of conflict that has resulted in general boredom.

One of the more interesting variations on the Hollow Earth theory during the late nineteenth century was expounded by Cyrus Read Teed (1830–1908). In *The Cellular Cosmogony, or The Earth, A Concave Sphere*, Teed claimed a civilization inhabited the concave inner surface of Earth. Dense atmosphere prevents viewing across the surface. The Moon, according to Teed, reflects the larger, uninhabitable surface of Earth.

Teed made a religion of his discoveries and changed his name to Koresh, the Hebrew equivalent of his given name, Cyrus. As the messiah of Koreshanity, he formed a church, started a magazine, *The Flaming Cross*, which continued to be published regularly into the 1940s, and founded a community on a 300-acre tract in Florida in 1894. He lived there with about 250 followers until 1908. Upon his death, his followers waited for him to rise again, as he had prophesied. After four days, health officials appeared on the scene and ordered his burial.

Hollow Earth theories continued to be promoted by enthusiasts even as explorers reached the North and South Poles during the first decade of the twentieth century. The open poles theory was further undermined when aviator Richard E. Byrd (1888–1957) became the first to fly over the North Pole (1926) and the South Pole (1929) and reported nothing but unending whiteness. In 1959, a U.S. submarine journeyed beneath the polar ice cap and actually surfaced at the North Pole, based on precise calculations. Since then, year-round research stations have been built on several sites at both poles. No large holes have been found.

Hollow Earth enthusiasts continue to believe. Teed's Concave Earth theory, for example, was tested during World War II (1939–1945) by a Nazi scientist. He aimed a camera at a 45-degree angle into the sky from an island in the Baltic Sea, hoping to catch an image of a British fleet on the other side of the concave Earth. The experiment was unsuccessful.

✠ DELVING DEEPER

Beckley, Timothy Green, ed. *The Smoky God and Other Inner Earth Mysteries.* New Brunswick, N.J.: Inner Light Publications, 1993.

Bernard, Raymond. *The Hollow Earth.* Mokelumne Hill, Calif.: Health Research, 1963.

Gordon, Stuart. *The Encyclopedia of Myths and Legends.* London: Headline Books, 1993.

Michell, John. *Eccentric Lives and Peculiar Notions.* San Diego, Calif.: Harcourt Brace Jovanovich, 1984.

JERUSALEM

Jerusalem stands in the middle of the nation of Israel, a holy city to three of the world's great religions—Judaism, Christianity, and Islam. Before Muslims underwent pilgrimages to **Mecca,** the most venerated holy place in all of Islam was the Dome of the Rock, a magnificent mosque built over the sacred rock where Abraham prepared to sacrifice his son Isaac to the Lord and where the Prophet Muhammad (c. 570–632) is believed to have ascended to Paradise. For the Jews, Jerusalem is the site of King David's (d. 932 B.C.E.) ancient capital of Judea and a massive wall, called the "Wailing Wall," which is all that remains of the great Temple that was destroyed by the Romans in 70 C.E.. Christian pilgrims revere the city as the place where Jesus (c. 6 B.C.E.–c. 30 C.E.) was crucified and is believed to have risen from the dead, and for more than 1,600 years they have visited the most revered of all Christian holy places, the Church of the Holy Sepulchre, which was built over what was believed to be Christ's tomb.

listings of the greatest architectural achievements of the world date at least as far back as the time of Herodotus (484–425 B.C.E.), who mentions such an inventory. Later Greek historians wrote about the great monuments of their time, and the list of seven ancient wonders of the world was finalized from among those opinions during the Middle Ages. The Seven Wonders include:

- *The Great Pyramid of Khufu (Cheops).* The oldest of the Seven Wonders and the only surviving one, constructed about 2630 B.C.E.

- *The Hanging Gardens of Babylon.* Part of the palace of King Nebuchadnezzar II and built about 600 B.C.E., it featured a series of terraces with stone arches. The terraces were filled with plants, and an elaborate tunnel and pulley system brought water from the nearby Euphrates River.

- *The Statue of Zeus.* Dated to the mid-fifth century B.C.E. and credited to the Greek sculptor Phidias, it was located at the Temple of Zeus at Olympia, Greece.

- *The Temple of Artemis at Ephesus in Greece.* Erected in 356 B.C.E. in a marshy area where several earlier temples had stood, it was destroyed by the Goths in 262.

- *The Mausoleum of Halicarnassus.* Built around 353 B.C.E., it was a marble tomb for King Mausolus of Caria in Asia Minor. It was damaged by an earthquake, and during medieval times its marble was used to fortify a castle.

- *The Colossus of Rhodes.* A 100-foot-high bronze statue of the Greek Sun god Helios, it was erected about 280 B.C.E. to guard the entrance to the harbor at Rhodes, a Mediterranean island, but it was destroyed about 55 years later.

- *The Pharos of Alexandria.* A lighthouse erected around 280 B.C.E., it fell into ruins by the mid-1300s because of a series of earthquakes. Located on an island in the harbor of Alexandria, Egypt, and rising 440 feet, it was the tallest building of the ancient world.

THE SEVEN WONDERS OF THE ANCIENT WORLD

SOURCES:

"Seven Wonders of the Ancient World." [Online] http://ce.eng.usf.edu/pharos/wonders.

"Seven Wonders of the World." [Online] http://library.advanced.org/23378.

According to Hebrew tradition, Jerusalem was chosen to be the earthly headquarters for the Lord's work among humankind in very ancient times, for Melchizedek, a priest, a survivor of the pre-flood world, the oldest living human at that time, was living there as King of Salem even before Father Abraham set out on his quest for the Promised Land. Obeying a commandment of the Lord, Melchizedek had come out of Babylonia to south central Canaan to build a city on the summit of the watershed between the Jordan River and the Mediterranean. Salem was constructed on the southeast hill of a mountain ridge with deep valleys on its east, south, and west sides. With the spring of Gihon at its feet to provide fresh water easily available for its inhabitants even during times of siege, the location of Salem made it a naturally impregnable fortress.

JERUSALEM *is the holy city to three of the world's great religions—Judaism, Christianity, and Islam.*

As the city of Jerusalem grew, it sprawled out over the two larger and three smaller hills of the ridge. With Egypt about 300 miles southwest; Assyria, 700 miles northeast; Babylon, 700 miles east; Persia, 1,000 miles east; Greece, 800 miles northwest; and Rome, 1,500 miles northwest, Jerusalem became a very cosmopolitan city with a steady flow of merchants and traders arriving from nations throughout the known world. David established Jerusalem as Israel's national capital in about 1000 B.C.E., and in about 950 B.C.E., his son Solomon built the magnificent temple that housed the **Ark of the Covenant.** The city and the temple were destroyed by the Babylonians in 586 B.C.E., but by the time that Jesus walked its streets in about 29 C.E., Jerusalem had been restored to its former glory. In 70, a series of Jewish revolts against Rome brought the imperial army to the walls of Jerusalem on the day of Passover. After a five-month siege, the city walls were brought down, the Temple of Herod destroyed, and Jerusalem was left in ruins and desolate.

In 135, Barocheba, a self-proclaimed messiah of the Jews, led another revolt against the Romans. He managed to gain control of the city and set about rebuilding the Temple, but his ambitious project was short-lived when the Roman army arrived in force and squelched the rebellion with great loss of life for the Jews. The conquerors decreed that no Jews could enter Jerusalem on pain of death, and a temple to Jupiter, father of the Roman gods, was built where the Temple had stood.

In 326, after the Roman emperor Constantine (d. 337) converted to Christianity, he traveled to the Holy Land to view the sacred sites for himself. Helena, his mother, received a vision that showed her the exact spot where Joseph of Arimathea, a wealthy follower of Jesus, had buried him after his crucifixion. The site lay beneath a temple to Venus that had been erected by a Roman army of occupation, but Constantine perceived the edifice as only a minor impediment. He ordered the temple of the goddess torn down and replaced by the Basilica of Constantine, the original Church of the Holy Sepulchre, near the Tomb Rotunda, which covered the tomb of Christ. In time, the Basilica, the tomb, and Calvary, the site of the crucifixion, were all brought under the roof of a vast Romanesque cathedral. For the next three centuries, Jerusalem remained a Christian city, and in the fifth century, it dominated Christendom as one of the seats of the Five Patriarchs, along with Rome, Constantinople, Antioch, and Alexandria.

In 638, a Muslim army under Caliph Omar Ibn al-Khattab (ruled 634–644) conquered Jerusalem. A devout follower of the Prophet Muhammad, the caliph was also tolerant of other religions. He ordered that the Church of the Holy Sepulchre be respected as a Christian place of worship and forbade it to be converted into a mosque. When he was taken to the Temple Mount, he was shocked to discover that the holy rock where Abraham had taken Isaac to be sacrificed, the place that had held the Ark of the Covenant in Solomon's Temple, and the spot where Muhammad had ascended to Paradise, lay exposed to the elements. After the area had been purified by prayers and a rainfall, the caliph ordered the Dome of the Rock to be built to shelter the sacred rock. The shrine with its massive dome gilded with gold mosaics was completed in 691.

The golden dome collapsed in 1016, but it was soon rebuilt. In 1099, Christian crusaders massacred the Muslim inhabitants of Jerusalem and converted the Dome of the Rock to a Christian shrine, replacing the crescent on the top of the dome with a cross and constructing an altar on the rock. The shrine returned to Muslim possession in 1187 when the great Muslim military genius Salah al-Din, known to the crusaders as Saladin, captured Jerusalem. In 1537, the Ottoman Turks replaced the gold mosaics on the outside of the dome with 45,000 Persian tiles. Today's visitor to the shrine will see the sunlight reflecting from sheets of gold-plated aluminum, imprinted with selected verses from the Koran, which were placed there during a complete restoration of the Dome of the Rock in 1956-1962. In 1967, the Old City of Jerusalem, including the Temple Mount, was seized by Israeli soldiers, but the Dome of the Rock remains available for worship by Muslims and visitation by others at scheduled times.

Interestingly, the Dome of the Rock plays a significant role in the end-time beliefs of Christian, Jewish, and Muslim Fundamentalists. Jews and Christians envision the site as one of the places in which **Armageddon,** the last great struggle between the forces of good and evil, will begin before the Messiah appears—or for the Christians, returns in a Second Coming. For the Muslims, it is here that Jesus will conquer the **Antichrist** and the chief eschatological figure, the Mahdi (Guided One) will appear to help destroy the forces of evil and to bring about the conversions of all Jews and Christians to Islam.

When the Muslims assumed control of the sacred rock of Abraham and the site of Solomon's Temple in the seventh century, the Jews began to focus their devotion on the huge blocks of stone along the western edge of the Old City, all that remained of the retaining wall of the temple built by King Herod

(73–4 B.C.E.). Herod had begun the construction of the Temple in 19 B.C.E. and the main building was completed about 18 months later. However, Herod's intentions to build the most magnificent of all temples in the history of the Jewish people did not cease at that time. Construction continued until about 64 C.E. For centuries, the wall has been a place where Jews might gather to mourn the destruction of the Temple and the onset of the great Jewish Exile. Because it is a place of tears and sorrow, the name "Wailing Wall" was attached to the ruins, and it has become a site for Jewish pilgrimages, especially during Passover, Sukkot, and Shavuot.

Since 1968, Jerusalem has been a city divided by uneasy truces and sporadic fighting. Perhaps as the twenty-first century progresses, a lasting peace can be achieved and Jerusalem may truly become the City of God.

✤ DELVING DEEPER

Halley, H. H. *Halley's Bible Handbook: An Abbreviated Bible Commentary.* 24th ed. Grand Rapids, Mich. Zondervan Publishing House, 1965.

Harpur, James. *The Atlas of Sacred Places.* Old Saybrook, Conn.: Konecky & Konecky, 1994.

Kunstel, Marcia, and Joseph Albright. *Their Promised Land: Arab and Jew in History's Cauldron—One Valley in the Jerusalem Hills.* New York: Crown Publishers, 1990.

Shanks, Hershel. *The City of David: A Guide to Biblical Jerusalem.* Washington, D.C.: Biblical Archaeological Society, 1975.

Starr, Chester G. *A History of the Ancient World.* New York: Oxford University Press, 1991.

Westwood, Jennifer. *Mysterious Places.* New York: Galahad Books, 1996.

KARNAK

On the banks of the Nile, between the ancient cities of Luxor and Thebes, lie the remains of Karnak, one of the most magnificent temple complexes ever constructed. In ancient Egyptian, Karnak means "the most select of places," and it became a religious center during the period known as the New Kingdom (founded c. 1550 B.C.E.). Dedicated to the sun deity Amon-Ra (also

Amun-Re) and built around 1500 B.C.E., Karnak consists of massive pillars, towering
columns, avenues of sphinxes, and a remarkable obelisk that stands 97 feet tall and weighs
323 tons. The Great Hypostyle Hall, one of
the largest single chambers ever built, covers
an area of nearly 54,000 square feet. The
entire Cathedral of Notre Dame could fit
comfortably within its walls.

Nearby ruins suggest that Karnak was considered a sacred site much earlier than the
time during the New Kingdom when it
became the center of worship for Amon-Ra.
The remains of temples dated c. 1971 B.C.E.
prove that predecessors of the devotees of the
ram-headed Amon-Ra also found the area to
be a special place to honor their gods.

The worship of Amon-Ra and the influence of Karnak remained strong until Akhenaton's reign in 1379–1362 B.C.E., when the
pharoah decreed all Egyptian gods banished
but one supreme being—Aten, the god of the
fully risen sun. Throughout all of Egypt the
images of all the gods were defaced and the
temples of Amon-Ra were desecrated or
destroyed. In addition to denigrating the

ancient gods of Egypt, Akhenaton moved his
capital city to Tel el Amarna, thus denying
the region of Thebes and Karnak their prestige as sacred ground. Akhenaton's crusade
against the plurality of Egyptian religion was
short-lived, however, and when he died, the
boy-king Tutankhamen (c. 1370–1352 B.C.E.)
spent his brief reign restoring the hierarchy of
the old gods, including Amon-Ra.

Construction on the Great Hypostyle Hall
was begun during the reign of Ramses I
(reigned 1320–1318 B.C.E.), continued by his
son Seti I (reigned 1318–1304 B.C.E.), and
completed by Ramses II, one of the longest-
reigning of Egyptian pharaohs (1304–1237
B.C.E.) and a devotee of Amon-Ra. Ramses II
also extended the temple of Amon by adding
a series of courtyards and ceremonial halls.

At the time of Ramses III (reigned 1198–
1166 B.C.E.), the size of the temple estates covered almost 700,000 acres of land, from the
Nile Delta in the north to Nubia in the south.
Eighty thousand servants and slaves were designated to serve Amon-Ra in Karnak, and
more than 5,000 statues reflected his glory
throughout the vast temple complex. Large
numbers of animals considered sacred to
Amon were kept on the site at Karnak,
including thousands of geese and rams and
over 421,000 head of cattle.

From about 1080 B.C.E. onward, Egypt suffered a number of invasions from the Nubians,
Libyans, Kushites, and Assyrians. Many of the
conquerors respected the sacred site at Karnak
and some, such as the Kushites, even added
some buildings of their own. However, even
those invaders who sought to carry away some
of the stone to implement building projects of
their own or even to deface some of the statu-
ary had not removed or destroyed enough of
Karnak to spoil the magic of the place for the
generations yet unborn. The whole of the
ancient site remains in good condition today,
and each year convinces thousands of tourists
from all over the world that Karnak is indeed
"the most select of places."

❋ DELVING DEEPER

Harpur, James, *The Atlas of Sacred Places*. Old Saybrook, Conn.: Konecky & Konecky, 1994.

Harpur, James, and Jennifer Westwood. *The Atlas of Legendary Places.* New York: Konecky & Konecky, 1997.

Ingpen, Robert, and Philip Wilkinson. *Encyclopedia of Mysterious Places.* New York: Barnes & Noble, 1990.

Michalowski, Kazimierz. *Karnak.* New York: Praeger Publishers, 1970.

Westwood, Jennifer. *Mysterious Places.* New York: Galahad Books, 1996.

LEMURIA AND MU

Lemuria and Mu are sometimes distinct and sometimes interchangeable names for a legendary lost continent, which, according to its proponents, existed in the Caribbean Ocean and had many of the attributes associated with **Atlantis.** The mysterious lost lands of Lemuria and Mu were conceived of during the nineteenth century, when the theory of evolution was introduced and was among the advances in the sciences that challenged conventional ways of understanding life. Archaeological discoveries among the ruins of the Egyptians, Mayans, and other societies were forcing new interpretations of history, and radical forms of mysticism, such as **Theosophy,** were becoming popular.

References to the lost continent of Mu can be traced back to 1864 and a French archaeologist named Charles-Etienne Brasseur de Bourbourg. He had become fascinated by hieroglyphics found on Mayan ruins that dated back several centuries. By the time Spanish explorers had reached the New World areas of Mexico and Central America in the 1500s, the great centers of Mayan civilization had long been abandoned and were being reclaimed by the rainforest.

Brasseur traveled to Spain to look at artifacts of Mayan civilization. In a library in Madrid he discovered a purported guide to Mayan hieroglyphics. Using the guide to decipher a rare Mayan manuscript, he learned about an ancient land that had sunk into the ocean after a volcanic eruption. Figures corresponding to letters "M" and "U" were connected with the lost land, and Brasseur determined that the lost continent was named Mu. Using

that same guide, however, later scholars were unable to decipher such a story, or to even make sustained and meaningful text from the hieroglyphics. It was not until the mid-twentieth century that a thorough guide to interpreting Mayan hieroglyphics was established.

BY the 1500s, the great centers of Mayan civilization were abandoned and were reclaimed by the rainforest.

Nevertheless, Brasseur's version of a lost continent won some favorable attention. An archaeologist named Augustus Plongeon (1825–1908) used a similar key to decipher hieroglyphics at one of the first excavations of Mayan sites. He allegedly uncovered a story about two brothers who vied for a queen named Moo (which he connected with Mu). One of the brothers was killed, and the other took power just before a catastrophe struck Mu. Queen Moo fled before the catastrophe. Speculations quickly added that she had reached Egypt, became revered as the goddess Isis, founded Egyptian civilization, and directed the building of the Sphinx.

In the mid-nineteenth century, Charles Darwin's (1809–1882) theory of evolution, *Origin of the Species,* was published. Although the theory became widely accepted among scientists, it was also extremely controversial. One point of contention concerned an animal and layers of sediment found in South Africa, the island of Madagascar, and India—all of which are in the same region but separated by expanses of water. The lemur, a predecessor of monkeys, had the same traits in each locale. According to Darwin's theory, the animal should have developed some unique traits respective to the different environments. Similarities in sediments in each of the areas also raised questions. Scientists began to speculate that a land bridge once existed in the Indian Ocean that connected the three areas.

English zoologist Phillip L. Schlater proposed the name Lemuria after the lemur for this former land now sunk in the Indian Ocean. The land bridge idea was supported by noted scientists, including German naturalist Heinrich Haeckel (1834–1919) and Alfred Russell Wallace (1823–1913), who developed a theory of evolution similar to Darwin's. Seas and continents were thought to be immobile in those days before the theory of continental drift, and no fossils of early humans had yet been found. Haeckel used Lemuria, which had sunk into the sea, to explain the absence of early human fossils. Lemuria became a respected term among educated people in Europe and America.

Thus, the lost continent of Lemuria began with science, but its renown spread and has been sustained through mysticism. Science has since discounted the land bridge and lost continent theories, and evidence of early humans was found during the twentieth century in Africa.

James Churchward (1832–1936) was among the first mystics to promote Lemuria as the lost continent of an advanced human race. Beginning in the 1870s, Churchward said Lemuria was a paradise of 64 million people, and that it was destroyed around 10,000 B.C.E. According to Churchward, Lemurians developed homes with transparent roofs, lived to be hundreds of years old, and were capable of telepathy, astral travel, and teleportation. Lemuria, according to Churchward, was about 5,000 miles long and 3,000 miles wide and stretched to the Pacific Ocean, where islands of the present day are former mountain peaks of the lost continent.

In the 1880s, **Helena Petrovna Blavatsky** (1831–1891) formed the **Theosophical Society** with psychic investigator Henry Steel Olcott. In her book *The Secret Doctrine* (1888), she claimed to have learned of Lemuria in *The Book of Dzyan*, which she said was composed in Atlantis and shown to her by survivors of that lost continent. Her source may have been Sanskrit legends that tell of the former continent of Rutas that sank beneath the sea.

Lemurians, according to Blavatsky, were the third of seven root races of humankind. They were hermaphrodites with psychic abilities and a third eye. Atlanteans, she stated,

were the fourth root race. They evolved from Lemurians after much of Lemuria sank, and they lived on the edge of the continent in the northern Atlantic. Atlantis sank around 8,000 B.C.E., according to Blavatsky, and its inhabitants fled to central Asia.

Rudolf Steiner (1861–1925), who founded **Anthroposophy,** was another proponent of Lemuria. Other mystics have envisioned the Elders of Lemuria, known as the Thirteenth School, who moved to an uninhabited plateau of Central Asia now called Tibet before the catastrophe that wiped out their land. They established a library and a school of spiritual adepts known as the Great White Brotherhood.

Certain land masses on the planet are supposedly the last remains of Lemuria, from Pacific islands (Fiji, Hawaii, and Easter Island) to the west coast of the United States. According to some Lemurian enthusiasts, in 1972 the ruins of a submerged Lemurian city was found between Maui and Oahu in the Hawaiian island chain and was covered up in a top-secret project by U.S. Naval Intelligence.

❁ DELVING DEEPER

Churchward, James. *The Cosmic Forces of Mu.* New York: Paperback Library, 1968.

———. *The Lost Continent of Mu.* New York: Paperback Library, 1969.

———. *The Sacred Symbols of Mu.* New York: Paperback Library, 1968.

LOURDES

The healing Grotto of Bernadette at Lourdes, France, was constructed on the site where 14-year-old Bernadette Soubrious (1844–1879) claimed to have conversed with Mother Mary in 1858. Since the time that the miracle occurred to the young miller's daughter, pilgrims have journeyed to Lourdes to seek healing from the waters of the natural spring that appeared in the grotto next to the Gave de Pau River. Consistently, for decades, an average of 200,000 people visited the shrine each year. The celebration of the 100th anniversary of Lourdes in 1958 brought more than two million persons into the small community in southern France. In the 1990s, annual attendance rose to more than five million per year.

On February 11, 1858, Bernadette Soubrious and her two sisters were gathering firewood outside Lourdes when she fell behind the younger girls. That was the first time that Bernadette saw the apparition of a lady dressed in white with a blue sash and a yellow rose on each foot standing in a grotto next to the river. The lady did not speak, but made the sign of the cross before she disappeared.

Bernadette returned to the grotto a second time, but it was not until the lady's third appearance that she spoke and asked Bernadette if she would like to meet her every day for two weeks. Bernadette enthusiastically agreed, and word of her visitations soon spread throughout the entire village. Crowds gathered to observe the girl and hear what messages she would relay from the lady. The apparition insisted again and again that priests must build a chapel in the grotto and that Bernadette was to drink from the spring there. Since there was no spring in sight, Bernadette began to scrape at the muddy ground until a spring bubbled forth with waters that were immediately believed to contain curative powers. Water from that same spring is still piped to a bathing house where pilgrims gather to receive its healing blessings.

Upset by the disturbances that she was causing in the town, the local police and civil authorities interrogated Bernadette, but they could not dissuade her from continuing her meetings by the grotto. The local parish priest, Father Peyramale, also did his best to convince Bernadette that she was only imagining the visions. Then, on March 25, after her sixteenth visit, the lady revealed her name to Bernadette, who, when questioned by the skeptical priest, relayed the lady's identity as "The Immaculate Conception." Because that title had been applied to Mother Mary by Catholic theologians only four years before and was only known to the clergy, Father Peyramale thought it highly unlikely that a teenaged girl who could not read or write and spoke only a crude, provincial form of French would know the phrase used to define the doctrine that declared Mary free from the taint of original sin.

Exterior view of a chapel in Lourdes, France. (CORBIS CORPORATION)

With the official endorsement of the clergy, the grotto at the edge of the river would soon support a healing chapel and begin to attract pilgrims from great distances. After 1866, when a railway line was completed to Lourdes, many thousands of those afflicted with various illnesses began to arrive in the little French town. In that same year, 22-year-old Bernadette Soubrious left for a convent in Nevers, hundreds of miles to the north. She died there in 1879.

AFTER *Bernadette's sixteenth visit, the lady revealed her name as "The Immaculate Conception."*

Since the 1860s, thousands of pilgrims have left their crutches and canes at the shrine. Thousands more claim to have been cured of advanced cancers. On May 3, 1948, the Bishop of Nice acted at the request of the Lourdes Medical Commission and declared Rose Martin's healing to be a miraculous cure. When Rose Martin arrived at Lourdes in 1947, her total weight was a scant 70 pounds. She had undergone surgery for cancer of the uterus in February 1947, and the cancer had continued to spread despite several subsequent operations. Doctors could prescribe only morphine to enable the suffering woman to endure the pain of her affliction.

On July 3, 1947, after three baths in the waters of the shrine, Rose Martin returned to her hotel. Her appetite had suddenly returned. The awful pain had disappeared. Several of her medical complications had vanished. In 1948, Madame Martin was examined by the medical bureau at Lourdes and declared to be totally free of cancer. In the interim she had gained 34 pounds. She had become the picture of health and vitality. More than 20 leading French doctors and surgeons confirmed the unusual healing. Annual checkups and subsequent physical examinations revealed that she remained free of the disease.

Dr. Alexis Carrel (1873–1944), an American surgeon who won the Nobel Prize in 1912 in physiology and medicine for his extensive work in suturing blood vessels, transplanting organs, and inventing the mechanical heart, witnessed a miracle healing firsthand when he visited Lourdes in the 1940s. Only an hour before a young woman named Marie Bailly

had been carried to the waters of Lourdes, Carrel had examined her and saw that she was dying of tuberculosis, a disease that had afflicted her for years. As he observed her, Carrel saw her pain-wracked body suddenly surge forward as if filled with a powerful force. Her paleness was replaced with a rosy hue, and as the surgeon and his colleagues watched in astonishment, they saw her swollen abdomen transformed from a misshapen lump and flattened to a smooth stomach. Her pulse calmed, her respiration returned to normal, and she asked for the first food she had been able to consume in almost a week. Marie Bailly was found to be cured of her terminal illness.

Although there are thousands of cures and healings claimed by men and women who have immersed themselves in the cold spring waters of the shrine, the Lourdes Medical Bureau has established certain criteria that must be met before they will certify a cure as miraculous:

- The affliction must be a serious disease. If it is not classified as incurable, it must be diagnosed as extremely difficult to cure.

- There must be no improvement in the patient's condition prior to the visit to the Lourdes shrine.

- Medication that may have been used must have been judged ineffective.

- The cure must be totally complete.

- The cure must be unquestionably definitive and free of all doubt.

Such stringent requirements set by members of the medical profession in order to qualify as a miraculous healing do little to deter the five million visitors each year who travel to the small town in the foothills of the Pyrenees in search of their own miracle.

✤ DELVING DEEPER

Carrel, Alexis. *Voyage to Lourdes*. New York: Harper & Brothers, 1950.

Cranston, Ruth. *The Miracle of Lourdes*. New York: McGraw-Hill, 1955.

Harpur, James. *The Atlas of Sacred Places*. Old Saybrook, Conn.: Konecky & Konecky, 1994.

Lourdes, France. [Online] http://www.lourdes-france.com/bonjour.htm. 2 May 2002.

Our Lady of Lourdes. [Online] http://www.catholic.org/mary/lourdes1.html. 2 May 2002.

MACHU PICCHU

At its height during the 1400s, the Incan empire was the largest in the world, stretching 2,500 miles north to south and supporting a population of more than ten million people. The temples, extensive roads, elaborate masonry, and treasures of gold and silver associated with the Incas date from around 1200 through the 1400s. The city of Cuzco became the powerful center of an empire that spread to encompass more than 100 small nations.

Roads were built to criss-cross the entire empire, running through valleys and along the sides of mountains. The Incas never developed the wheel, but the roads provided the means to move large amounts of stone and goods used to build and sustain great cities. Trained runners were used to communicate messages throughout the empire. The Inca cultivated maize and potatoes, domesticated the llama as a beast of burden, crafted boats of balsa wood to travel on rivers and streams, and built suspension bridges of rope, among their many accomplishments.

The empire was primarily expanded by three emperors, Pachacuti Inca Yupanqui and his descendants Topa Inca Yapanqui (ruled 1438–1471) and Huayna Capac (ruled 1493–1525). The latter's sudden death in 1525 came before he named a successor, and the nation became bitterly divided, a situation that still raged when the Spanish conquistador Francisco Pizarro (c. 1475–1541) and his army of about 400 men arrived in 1532. Lured by vast amounts of gold they found in Inca cities, the conquistadors kidnapped an Inca leader and held him for ransom. The ransom, estimated at about $50 million in gold and silver, was paid, but the leader was executed anyway.

DURING *the 1400s, the Inca empire was largest in the world, stretching 2,500 miles and supporting a population of over ten million people.*

Diseases such as smallpox, previously unknown in the New World, had begun spreading as early as the 1520s. The combination of disease, estimated to have killed two-thirds of the Incan population, and military reinforcements from Spain after Pizarro showed off the great treasures he had found, allowed the Spaniards to subdue the Incan empire, systematically sweeping through and plundering all the great Incan centers. They missed one, however, and it would remain lost to the world until 1912. The majestic site is called Machu Picchu, a city in the clouds that rests at 8,000 feet in altitude between two mountains, Huayana Picchu ("young mountain") and Machu Picchu ("ancient mountain"), and overlooks a sacred river and valley called Urubamba.

In 1911, Hiram Bingham (1875–1956), a historian from Yale University who was per-

forming research in Peru, was alerted by a local farmer, Melchior Artega, about ancient ruins high up in the mountains. Bingham followed the lead and rediscovered the site of Machu Picchu. He publicized his findings in 1912, and in April of 1913 *National Geographic* magazine devoted an entire issue to the site.

THE *Temple of the Sun is believed to have an astronomical significance.*

Even though many mysteries abound about Machu Picchu, what has been discovered about the site since 1911 has led some to call it "the eighth wonder of the ancient world." Machu Picchu features religious shrines and temples, baths and water systems, plazas, fountains, and elaborate masonry work. Stones are fitted so tightly in structures that they have withstood almost five hundred years of weathering and

the lush growth of vegetation. Machu Picchu, situated on a long, narrow strip between mountains and above a valley, has a series of open plazas, and was divided into three sections— agricultural, urban, and religious.

The agricultural section comprises a series of terraces bordered with irrigation channels. Crops were cultivated on levels above the channels to avoid erosion. The farm area is dotted with small buildings believed to be lookout huts. The urban area is on the part of the ridge that descends abruptly into the valley. A 67-step staircase rises up from the valley to the largest urban sector. Most of the structures have one room with solid walls of intricately fitted stones. The finest structures are believed to have housed high-ranking teachers. Many of the walls have niches the size of adult humans sculpted into them; the purpose of the niches is unknown.

A plaza with a large rock in the center separates the urban and religious areas. Among the structures in the religious center is the

Intihuantana Shrine, a temple carved from granite. The temple is considered a shrine to sun and stone, both of which were worshipped by Incas, and is also believed to have served as an astronomical observatory. Some of the buildings in the religious center are three-walled structures, including what is called the Great Central Temple and the Temple of the Three Windows. The latter building is believed to be associated with an Incan legend that their original ancestors emerged from a cave that had three windows. Also located in the religious center is the Temple of the Sun, a circular tower believed to have an astronomical orientation.

The most accepted view of Machu Picchu portrays it as a religious sanctuary serving high priests and "virgins of the sun." More than 80 percent of the graves found on the site contain the bones of females, considered to have been "chosen women." Machu Picchu was thought to have been visited by selected members of Incan royalty who were transported along special roads that could only be used with their permission. Since the roads were seldom used, few Inca knew about them. The conquistadors never found the way, nor did they find Incas who could lead them to the site. The reason why Machu Picchu was abandoned remains a secret lost to time.

✳ **Delving Deeper**

Deuel, Leo. *Conquistadors without Swords: Archaeologists in the Americas.* New York: St. Martin's Press, 1967.

———. *Flights into Yesterday: The Story of Aerial Photography.* New York: St. Martin's Press, 1969.

Harpur, James, and Jennifer Westwood. *The Atlas of Legendary Places.* New York: Konecky & Konecky, 1997.

Hodges, Henry. *Technology in the Ancient World.* New York: Alfred A. Knopf, 1970.

Irwin, Constance. *Fair Gods and Stone Faces.* New York: St. Martin's Press, 1963.

Mayan Temples

When the Spanish conquistadors claimed areas of Central America and Mexico in the sixteenth century, they discovered the ruins of a great civiliza-tion, that of the Mayans, who had vanished and left evidence of their lost grandeur in massive structures that had been over-whelmed by the surrounding rain forest. The native people could not explain the signifi-cance of the sprawling, vacant cities to the conquistadors. Unlike the great Incan cities, the Mayan centers had long been abandoned.

The ruins of the Mayans did not begin to reveal their secrets for 300 years. Since the nineteenth century, enough information has been gathered about the Mayan structures to sketch a history of their development, but the reasons why the great structures were suddenly abandoned, and the exact purposes of the massive and elaborate buildings, continue to remain trapped in the past.

The Mayan empire stretched south from the present-day Mexican states of Veracruz, Yucatán, Campeche, Tabasco, and Chiapas to almost all of Guatemala and parts of Belize and Honduras. Ruins in the Guatemalan highlands include Copán, a typical Mayan center with plazas, pyramids, a court for ball games, and blocks of stone inscribed with hieroglyphics. Tikal, another Mayan center in Guatemala, had more than 3,000 structures in a six-square-mile area. Vast palaces with hundreds of rooms, rows and rows of wooden huts, and increasingly larger buildings approaching the center of Tikal accommodated a surrounding community that may have numbered as many as 90,000 people.

Palenque is among the centers in the middle area of the Mayan region, where the rain forest is thickest. Among the finds there is the Temple of Inscriptions, a 65-foot-high pyramid. A secret passageway was found by archaeologists in 1952 that led to an elaborate tomb. Riches of jade, finely carved, life sized statues, and an elaborately sculpted sarcophagus were discovered. When modern archaeologists finally mastered Mayan hieroglyphics in the 1970s, inscriptions on the wall of the temple were deciphered. They identified the corpse as Sun Lord Pacal and described his life. Tracing references of dates with the Mayan calendar, another example of Mayan achievement, archaeologists were able to determine that Sun Lord Pacal was born in 603, ascended to the throne in 614, and died in 683. The 69 steps that run up the front of the temple each represent a year of his reign.

The Yucatan peninsula along the Gulf of Mexico forms the northernmost region of Mayan settlement. Among the ruins there are Chichen Itza, which feature a collection of pyramids, temples, and other common Mayan structures as well as an observatory where the movements of the Sun and Moon and the planets Mars, Venus, and Jupiter were charted. Further inland lies Uxmal, site of two temple pyramids, a complex of four buildings around a courtyard, and the Palace of Governors with magnificent terraces and a stone mosaic frieze more than 300 feet long (a mosaic consists of small, inlaid materials of various colors that form a pattern or a picture, and a frieze is a richly ornamented band or line on a building).

The various ruins were not excavated and examined until the latter half of the nineteenth century. They show that Mayans developed systems of mathematics, writing, and astronomy and erected monumental forms of architecture. Subsequent discoveries showed their calendar recorded dates as far back as 600 B.C.E. By the first century B.C.E., they specifically used a calendar that had 18 20-day months—matching the Mayan base-20 mathematical system (the contemporary mathematical system used in the West is base-10).

FROM 800 to 500 B.C.E., the Mayans began erecting modest burial monuments.

Because of the state of decline in which the conquistadors found Native Americans of the region, and fueled by cultural bias that made Europeans skeptical that less-advanced people could create such monumental structures, many early explorers believed that the engineering feats of the Mayans had been directed by peoples from the eastern Mediterranean region. Phoenicians and Egyptians had been seafaring people in ancient times. Perhaps they

had sailed across the Atlantic Ocean. Those who believed such theories speculated that the Mediterranean seafarers had directed the Mayans to build pyramids, taught them hieroglyphics, and brought them social order.

Variations on the theme of an external influence on the ancient Mayans continued to develop. Instead of Egyptians or Phoenicians, however, it was advanced Asians who first reached the Mayans and taught them secrets of architecture and mathematics, written language and astronomy. Or perhaps inhabitants of the legendary continent of Atlantis spread their knowledge to various peoples of the world, including the Mayans.

Excavations helped clarify some of the mysteries involving the Mayans. They had distinctive cultural traits evident in similarities of architecture—including pyramids, terraces, and ball courts—and artistic styles of paintings and pottery spread throughout their empire. When modern archaeologists learned how to read Mayan hieroglyphics by establishing meanings and patterns in the images, a history emerged that showed the Mayan centers were not occupied by peaceful astronomers and the large structures did not serve specifically as ceremonial sites. Instead, the hieroglyphics boasted of the accomplishments of a war-like elite. Many of the great Mayan buildings were monuments to great military leaders. Settlements with large structures served as centers for trade, but primarily for the accumulation of riches for the elite of Mayan society. Those who contributed to culture, artisans and astronomers among them, were highly esteemed, but a ruling elite held the riches and the power.

The Mayans learned to grow maize, beans, squash, and cacao. They raised cotton and developed a textile industry for spinning, dyeing, and weaving cloth, but they did not develop metal tools, domesticate large beasts of burden, and, in spite of building an elaborate system of roads, did not develop the wheel. Over the centuries, the Mayans domesticated the dog and the turkey, and they discovered how to mine copper, gold, silver, and jade, creating valuable and prized items.

From 800 to 500 B.C.E., the Mayans began erecting modest burial monuments, which by

Mayan temple in Tikel, Guatemala. (THE LIBRARY OF CONGRESS)

circa 400 B.C.E. to 250 C.E. had evolved into terraced, pyramidal shapes. The Mayan pyramids differ from those in Egypt, where the sides of the structures converge to form a pointed top. The pyramidal structures of the Mayans reach a certain height, then level off to form a flat platform on which temples were built.

Mayan civilization thrived until around 800 when a decline began. Tikal was abandoned, and the process of recording events stopped there by 900. Building began in another center, Seibal, in the southern lowlands in 830 but ended abruptly around 900. Uxmal showed more development around 850, but it was abandoned around 925. Chichen Itza was abandoned around 987. It was subsequently occupied, like some of the other centers, but new massive structures were not built and the old temples did not serve the same functions as they had in the past.

In 2000, near the present-day village of Cancuen, Guatemala, a Mayan palace was discovered in a long-abandoned city named the Place of Serpents that is estimated to cover an area as large as two football fields. With 170 high-ceiling rooms and 11 courtyards, the palace was revealed to have been a prosperous center of commerce and crafts. Inscriptions on the palace walls showed that it was completed by a leader named Tah ak Chaan, who ruled over Cancuen from 740 to around 790. Unlike other Mayan centers, there are as yet no indications that the rulers of the area engaged in warfare. There are no pyramids in the area, or outdoor plazas, and there appears to be a complete absence of religious symbols or any indications of the ceremonies evident in other Mayan centers. Rulers of the city appeared to specialize in commerce, not warfare, and a larger working-class group of people seemed to live in the Place of Serpents than at other Mayan centers. Hundreds of workshops where artisans plied their crafts were found.

What factors caused the demise of the Mayan empire remains a mystery. Destruction from earthquakes is evident in some Mayan centers, but not all, and earthquakes are not believed to have leveled any of the major centers. There is no evidence of mass burials that would indicate an epidemic, such as plague, small pox, or other infectious diseases that swept through Europe during the same time as the Mayan's golden era and downfall. An isolated disruption caused by conquerors from the north, a natural catastrophe, or war among leaders of Mayan centers would have affected trade routes that ran through the interior. Tikal, a major inland center dependent on trade, would certainly have been affected by such a disruption. Twice, in the sixth and ninth centuries, Tikal seems to have undergone some form of chaos.

The great success of the Mayan culture may be a plausible reason for their downfall. As the population grew, the stress on agriculture became greater, for an expanding population requires consistently more food production. Soil erosion or drought would have greatly affected the large settlements. A decrease in production would have led to malnutrition, increasing the likeliness of disease. Some human skeletal remains from the period show signs of malnutrition, but no conclusive evidence has been found to determine a sudden, widespread catastrophe.

Strange as it may seem, the Mayan calendar may have played an influential role in the culture's decline. The calendar was used for prophecy, as well as marking the date. The Mayan calendar begins with a date relative to 3114 B.C.E., when, according to the Mayans, the world began and the first Great Cycle got underway. Thirteen future cycles were recognized, and bad things often happened at the end of such cycles. For example, one cycle ended during the 500s, at about the same time that the city of Tikal went into decline. Another decline occurred in Tikal 256 years later, also at the end of a Great Cycle, and the city was all but abandoned.

Whatever happened to the Mayans was an event of such magnitude that it caused a fracture in the long-standing practices and social order of the entire culture. The great cities continued to be occupied for decades after the hieroglyphics stopped reporting triumphs, and then the majestic temples, stately pyramids, and massive edifices were abandoned completely to the surrounding jungle.

Whether or not the unknown dire events were prophesied or became self-fulfilling prophecies by the belief of a superstitious people accepting their fate is not known. According to Mayan prophecy, the end of the most current Great Cycle —2012— will end with a cataclysmic flood.

✤ DELVING DEEPER

Deuel, Leo. *Conquistadors without Swords: Archaeologists in the Americas*. New York: St. Martin's Press, 1967.

———. *Flights into Yesterday: The Story of Aerial Photography*. New York: St. Martin's Press, 1969.

Hodges, Henry. *Technology in the Ancient World*. New York: Alfred A. Knopf, 1970.

Irwin, Constance. *Fair Gods and Stone Faces*. New York: St. Martin's Press, 1963.

MECCA

Mecca, known to the Muslim faithful as *Umm al-Qura*, the Mother of Cities, is the holiest place in the Islamic world. It was here that Muhammad the Prophet (c. 570–632), the Messenger of God, the founder of the Muslim faith, was born in 570, and it is here within the Great Mosque that the Ka'aba, the most sacred shrine of Islam, awaits the Muslim pilgrim. Throughout the world, wherever they may be, all devout Muslims pray five times per day, each time bowing down to face Mecca. All able-bodied Muslims who have sufficient financial means and whose absence from their families would not create a hardship must undertake a pilgrimage, a *hajj*, to Mecca once in their lifetime during the Muslim month of Dhu-al-Hijah (the twelfth lunar month).

Physically, Mecca is located about 45 miles east of the Red Sea port of Jedda, a city surrounded by the Sirat Mountains. Born into a well-to-do family, Muhammad married Khadija, a woman of means, and became the manager of her caravans. It was when he was about 40 years old and was meditating in a cave on Mount Hira that he had the first of a series of visions of the angel Gabriel who instructed him concerning the oneness of God. Later, Muhammad's many revelations and visions

About the same time ley lines were first introduced by Alfred Watkins (1855–1935) in the 1920s, a German evangelical parson named Wilhelm Teudt proposed a similar theory he called *heilige linien* (holy lines) that linked a number of standing stones, churches, crosses, and other objects of spiritual significance in Germany. Teudt's holy line theory met the same fate as Watkins's ley lines. There were so many possibilities for connecting a variety of objects on a landscape that the odds were better of finding alignments than not finding them.

Teudt made another observation that had more lasting significance. He noted that an ancient chamber constructed in the naturally formed megaliths called the Externsteine had a circular window that formed a point where rays of light at the midsummer solstice shone through, and where the moon was visible when it reached its northernmost position. He believed the Neolithic peoples (before 2000 B.C.E.) had used the site as an astronomical observatory and a calendar.

The Externsteine, which lies at the approximate latitude as Stonehenge in Great Britain, is a natural site of five sandstone pillars rising 120 feet above an area filled with caves and grottoes. It served as a ritu-

THE ENERGIES OF HOLY LINES

al center for nomadic reindeer hunters, and later was the site of pagan rituals until the eighth century, when such rituals were forbidden by law. Christian monks took over the site and set up crosses and reliefs depicting biblical scenes. They abandoned it after about 1600. Many people continued to visit the Externsteine, claiming they were aware of its energy and that their physical ailments had been cured by walking among or rubbing against the stones.

SOURCES:

"Earth Mysteries." [Online] http://www.religionandnature.com/ encyclopedia/samples/Earth_mysteries.htm.

Magin, Ulrich. "Wilhelm Teudt and His Holy Lines." *The Ley Hunter.* No. 133. [Online] http://www.leyhunter.com/new/ win.htm.

would be collected into the sacred book of Muslims, the Qur'an (or Koran), but when he first began sharing the essence of his revelations with his fellow Meccans, they rejected the teachings and reacted with great hostility when he began to lecture them concerning their vices and pagan practices.

In 622, Muhammad left Mecca for Yathrib, which was later renamed Medina, City of the Prophet, where he began to amass many followers. After eight years of strife between the people of Mecca and Muhammad, he returned to the city of his birth with an army and met with little resistance when he proceeded to cleanse the Ka'aba of pagan idols and dedicate the shrine to Allah, the One God.

On the plains of Arafat in 632, Muhammad preached to an assembled crowd that tradition numbers as some 30,000 of his follow-

ers. After he had completed his message, he declared that he had now fulfilled his mission on Earth. Two months later, he died at Medina. Within 100 years, the Muslim faith had spread from Spain to India. In the twenty-first century, Islam is one of the world's largest religions with an estimated membership of 1.2 billion.

ALL *Muslims who are able to do so are required to make at least one pilgrimage (hajj) to Mecca during their lifetime.*

The pilgrimage (hajj) to the sacred city of Mecca and experience of worshipping at the mosque containing the Ka'aba is strictly limit-

Large crowd of Muslims making their pilgrimage to Mecca. (THE LIBRARY OF CONGRESS)

ed to those who follow the Islamic faith. There is an area of several miles around Mecca that is considered to be *haram* (restricted), and non-Muslims are forbidden to enter this sacred zone. Those Muslims who travel into this area as they progress toward the Mother of Cities must profess their having undergone a state of ritual purity and consecration. It is at this point that they set aside the clothes in which they have traveled and don a special article of clothing consisting of two seamless white sheets.

The hajj begins with a procession called the *tawaf*, which takes the pilgrim around the Ka'aba seven times. The Ka'aba is a cube-shaped structure that stands about 43 feet high, with regular sides from 36 to 43 feet. The building is draped in a black cloth (*kiswah*) that bears a band of sacred verses embroidered in gold and silver thread. In the southeastern corner of the Ka'aba is the sacred Black Stone, an ancient holy relic about 11 inches wide and 15 inches high that has been

mounted in silver. Muslims believe that Allah sent the Black Stone from heaven. It is the fortunate pilgrim who manages to break free from the press of the crowd and kiss the Black Stone. Because of the great mass of humanity crowding into the Ka'aba at any given moment, it had been decreed centuries ago that the gesture of a kiss toward the stone will suffice and merit a great blessing.

The second element of the hajj is the run seven times between two small hills, al-Safwa and al-Marwa, which are enclosed and connected with a walkway immediately adjoining the mosque courtyard. The third aspect of the pilgrimage involves walking about five miles to the town of Mina, then onward to the plain of Arafat, 10 miles farther to the east. The time of the journey is spent in prayer and meditation. As the pilgrims walk back toward Mina, they stop to throw small stones at three pillars, an act which symbolically recalls the three occasions when Abraham threw stones at Satan, who was tempting him to disobey

MEDICINE WHEEL OF THE BIG HORN MOUNTAINS

Above the timberline in the Big Horn Mountains of northern Wyoming exists a massive Medicine Wheel whose pattern of stones etches an imperfect circle with a diameter of about 25 meters. A group of stones about four meters in diameter establishes the hub of the wheel. Twenty-eight "spokes" angle out from the hub and connect with the outer rim. The Big Horn Mountains was significant to the Crow, the Sioux, the Arapaho, the Shoshone, and the Cheyenne Indians—but none of these tribes were known for building stone monuments. Bits of wood found in one of the six smaller groups situated unevenly about the rim indicates that the Medicine Wheel has been there since at least 1760 and was likely constructed around 1700. The monument has been known to non-natives for over a hundred years, but speculation about its true purposes has only inspired mysteries and tales.

John A. Eddy, a solar physicist and astronomer on the staff of the High Altitude Observatory, National Center for Atmospheric Research, in Boulder, Colorado, became interested in the site, especially after he discovered a large, crude pile of stones oriented to the summer solstice sunrise at over 11,000 feet on the Continental Divide. Interested by this discovery, he wanted to investigate just how much the pre-contact native people might have known of astronomy, and it occurred to him that the wheel might have been an observatory. Research over two summers on the site convinced him that the Big Horn monument may have been a primitive astronomical observatory that served its creators at least as well as **Stonehenge** served its primitive astronomers. The high altitude (9,640 feet) and the clear horizons of the monument make visible the marking of sunrise and sunset at the summer solstice. The accurate knowledge of the first day of summer would have been an important for a nomadic people whose lives depended on awareness of seasonal changes.

SOURCES:

Giese, Paula. "Stone Wheels and Dawn Stars Rising." [Online] http://www.kstrom.net/isk/starskno7.html.

Thomas, David Hurst. *Exploring Ancient Native America.* New York: Macmillan, 1994.

God's command to sacrifice his son. After they walk the five miles back to Mecca, the final stage of the hajj is achieved with a festival in which a sheep, goat, cow, or camel is sacrificed to commemorate the moment when God rescinded the command to Abraham to sacrifice his son and permitted him to slay a ram and offer its blood in Isaac's stead. The hajj concludes with a final procession around the Ka'aba. The hajj generally lasts about 13 days, but when as many as two million pilgrims crowd into Mecca to observe the annual event, it may last a day or two longer to accommodate the vast numbers of the faithful.

✤ DELVING DEEPER

Crim, Keith, general ed. *The Perennial Dictionary of World Religions*. San Francisco: HarperSanFrancisco, 1989.

Eerdmans' Handbook to the World's Religions. Grand Rapids, Mich.: William B. Eerdmans' Publishing Company, 1994.

Harpur, James. *The Atlas of Sacred Places*. Old Saybrook, Conn.: Konecky & Konecky, 1994.

Hixon, Lex. *Heart of the Koran*. Wheaton, Ill.: Theosophical Publishing Co., 1988.

Westwood, Jennifer. *Mysterious Places*. New York: Galahad Books, 1996.

THE NAZCA LINES

On the western side of the Andes mountain range are a modern town and a river named Nazca, as well as the mysterious remains of an ancient civilization also identified as the Nazca (sometimes spelled Nasca). Remnants of the Nazca civilization include a strip of impressive buildings, but they are more famous for leaving their mark on the earth in a different way—with geoglyphs, which literally means markings on the earth ("geo" for earth; "glyph" for a symbolic figure or character). Throughout a 150-square-mile area in the foothills of the Andes, the Nazca made long, straight, single lines that eventually cross other straight lines to form geometrical figures, such as trapezoids, triangles, and rectangles. Other lines lead to images of a bird, a whale, assorted human figures, and even such everyday objects as an ancient loom.

The Nazca Lines are located in an extremely arid area in Peru between the Andes mountain range and the Pacific Ocean. The territory lies between two rivers, the Nazca and the Grande, that border two valleys and an alluvial plain (a dry area composed of silt, sand, and gravel). Underground channels of water that surfaced to forms wells (puquios) were tapped by an ancient people long vanished by the time the lines were rediscovered in the 1920s.

The extent of the Nazca Lines was not appreciated until the 1930s, when pilots of the first airplane flights in Peru reported a more extensive and varied collection of geogylphs than had previously been known. The geoglyphs were originally thought to mark channels for water, but the reports from pilots indicated the lines were much more complex. Torriba Mejìa, a Peruvian archaeologist, introduced results of the first modern scientific examination of the area to an international conference of archaeologists in Lima, Peru, in 1939.

The layout of lines shows a sophistication with such geometrical figures as trapezoids—a rectangle where one end is larger than the other—triangles, and rectangles. Additionally, they lead to the more than 40 animal figures (including a monkey, a spider, a dog, a llama, and a bird with a tail 160 feet long) and some spiral patterns. The three most prominent explanations of the lines connect them either with the acquisition of water, with astronomical purposes, or with sacred rituals of the Nazca people.

The connections between the Nazca Lines and the acquisition of water dates to the rediscovery of the lines in the 1920s, when scientists were studying ancient irrigation techniques. A local myth about a huge sand dune called Cerro Blanco, which supposedly conceals a vast lake that feeds underground water channels, or that once erupted and watered the region, reflects the local preoccupation with water.

The "radiating centers" where many lines meet are located at bases of hills and at the elevated rim of a valley, where seasonal rivers run. Many lines parallel watercourses and often end abruptly, close to a river. A trapezoid appears at the edge of a river valley; the larger end of the trapezoid is located right near the edge where a seasonal river flows, perhaps serving as a marker.

This connection between the lines and sources of water has been interpreted in terms of religion, when ancient ritual processions were made to places where water can be expected to accumulate. The Nazca people, according to the theory, walked along the lines leading to areas from which water came, where they may have paid tribute to their gods or chanted prayers to them to bring them water.

The ancient Nazca people formed the lines by raking away the topsoil to uncover a lighter-colored clay, and they piled the topsoil along the sides of the yellow-white grooves. The results were grooves etched into the ground that remained lighter in color than the surrounding area. The densest concentration of Nazca Lines occurs in a place called Ingenio Valley, where seasonal rivers run from accumulated moisture in the Andes. The Ingenio Valley site became the focus for study by archaeologists, primarily to help trace irrigation routes to seasonal rivers.

Remains were found of two primary settlements, Cahauchi and La Estaqueria. Cahauchi had a complex of buildings two miles long and about two-thirds of a mile wide that included pyramids reaching 70 feet high, village squares, and cemeteries. Based on carbon dating of pottery found at the site, the community thrived from about 100 to 600. Similar pottery found along lines leading to Cahauchi date as late as 800, suggesting the center may have been abandoned by 600 but still remained an important ceremonial site for a couple of centuries afterward. Radiocarbon dating shows that La Estaqueria was begun after Cahauchi was deserted.

Historian Paul Kosok of Long Island University, New York, came to Nazca in 1941 to research the topic of irrigation among ancient civilizations. As he paused to rest on a hilltop, he noticed a line running directly to the setting Sun. The date was June 21, the day of the winter solstice in the southern hemisphere.

LEY LINES AND ENERGY ALIGNMENTS

In 1921, Alfred Watkins (1855–1935) coined the term "ley lines" when explaining his theory that such ancient sites around Britain as various stone circles, stone groupings, burial mounds, and places of worship had been deliberately constructed to form certain alignments between and across the landscape. Except for a few isolated cases, most ley claims did not match the criteria of straight alignment, and often incorporated structures from different eras.

Nevertheless, the belief that many megaliths erected by neolithic peoples were placed along energy lines persists. Others take a more practical view: such alignments could have served as signaling devices where watchers could provide advance alert miles away about approaching armies.

SOURCES:
"Ley Lines." [Online] http://www.mystical-www.co.uk/leylines.htm.
Hitching, Francis. *Earth Energy.* New York: William Morrow, 1984.

The line marked the point on the horizon where the Sun set and the line leading in the opposite direction corresponded with the sunrise on that day.

THE *Nazca Lines are located in Peru between the Andes mountain range and the Pacific ocean.*

Archaeologists began to link the geoglyphs with constellations: the figure of a large monkey was believed to correspond to the Big Dipper (or the Great Bear in northern climes), and other figures were believed to correspond to Pleiades and Orion. Maria Reiche, a translator and mathematician living in Lima, was

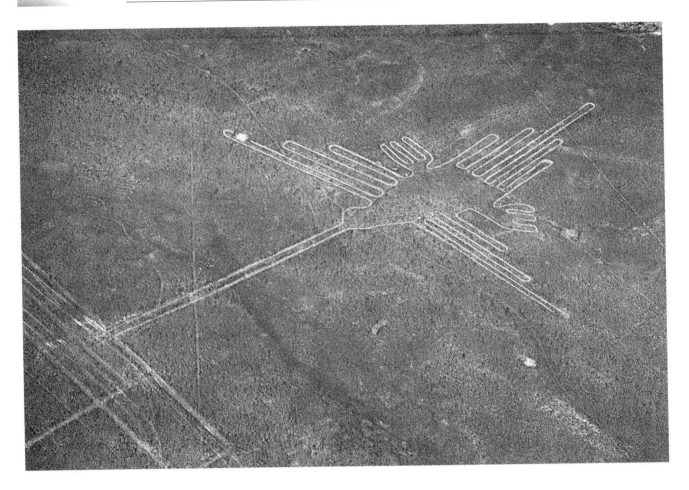

Aerial view of a Nazca line depicting a hummingbird.
(CORBIS CORPORATION)

brought to the site by Kosok. She remained there for the next 50 years and made the study of the Nazca Lines her life work, represented in *Contributions of Ancient Peru to the History of Geometry and Astronomy* (1993).

THERE *are over 800 Nazca lines made by an unknown culture.*

The theory that the Nazca Lines have astronomical purposes has been effectively challenged. In 1967, for example, Gerald Hawkins, an astronomer based at Boston University, used a computer to create a map of the sky over Nazca covering a 7,000-year period. The figures and lines on the ground were matched against actual settings of the solar system and constellations. Only 20 percent of the lines aligned with the rising and setting of the Sun and Moon for practical purposes, and

there was no consistency between figures and constellations.

Nevertheless, the lines that do match the rising and setting of the Sun suggest the lines could have served as a calendar. Being alerted about an upcoming season when the rivers were going to run, and when they would be dry, helped the community organize—knowing when to clear irrigation ditches, and when to plant seeds, for example.

During the 1970s, archaeologist Helaine Silverman of the University of Texas theorized that the lines were marked out only after a period of drought. The gods had failed, or perhaps, as she contended, priests living at the ceremonial center in Cahauchi lost the veneration of the people when prolonged drought set in. If indeed the lines were formed after Cahauchi fell into decline, she argued, the lines represent the practical purpose of a community struggling to tap a basic necessity.

The idea that the Nazca Lines served a spiritual function can encompass the water

and astronomy-related theories. Similar ancient lines found in present-day Bolivia, which borders Peru, were to be used in ritual processions. That rituals related to water took on spiritual dimensions in Nazca would hardly be surprising, for the area averages one-half inch of rainfall every two years.

In addition to geoglyphs that seem to correspond to constellations, a number of the figures resemble water animals (a frog, a duck, a whale, for example), all of which are replicated on Nazca pottery. In addition to rain dances and rituals, the Nazca, like many other ancient societies, had a priestly caste that included shamans. Entering trances or performing rituals to get in touch with animal spirits is a common practice among shamans, and the bestiary images of the Nazca could reflect the animals they respected and the animal spirits a shaman would want to tap.

In October 2001, Colgate University professor Anthony Aveni said that his 30-year aerial and ground survey of the more than 800 Nazca Lines had led him to conclude that the unknown culture that made the strange markings had been practicing water magic. According to the results of his research, the approximately 62 points where the lines converge occur at bends and kinks in rivers or high places in the Andes from which water would flow. The lines were intended to be walked on, by the people while they prayed to the gods to make the land fertile.

Monkey figure among the Nazca desert figures in Peru. (FORTEAN PICTURE LIBRARY)

❋ DELVING DEEPER

Deuel, Leo. *Conquistadors without Swords: Archaeologists in the Americas.* New York: St. Martin's Press, 1967.

———. *Flights into Yesterday: The Story of Aerial Photography.* New York: St. Martin's Press, 1969.

Faber, Lindsay. "The Nazca Lines—Professor Offers Theory on the Origins of Mysterious Mosaic." *Greenwich Time*, October 23, 2001. [Online] http://www. greenwichtime.com/news/greenwich/2001-10-23/article 1.shtml.

Hodges, Henry. *Technology in the Ancient World*. New York: Alfred A. Knopf, 1970.

Irwin, Constance. *Fair Gods and Stone Faces*. New York: St. Martin's Press, 1963.

THE GREAT PYRAMID (OF KHUFU), AT GIZA

When the Greek historian Herodotus (c. 484–between 430 and 420 B.C.E.) reported on the Great Pyramid of Khufu (Cheops, in Greek) during the fifth century B.C.E., his inquiry was impeded because the door leading into the pyramid was concealed. That door has since been found, but the results of passing through it and exploring the pyramid have opened up as many mysteries as those that have been explained.

Rising up on a plateau called Giza, 10 miles west of present-day Cairo, Egypt, the Great Pyramid, its two companion pyramids, and the **Sphinx** are probably the world's oldest and best-known enigmas. Among the questions swirling about the pyramids include the location of the sites from which the immense amount of rock forming them (11 million cubic yards of stone for the Great Pyramid alone) was quarried, and how it was moved and then erected into an astonishingly precise structure. What kind of surveying methods and equipment did the ancient Egyptians use to ensure that the landscape was level and their measurements were accurate? And how could the vast number of workers required for such an undertaking be mobilized, housed, and fed?

Other mysteries abound: the pyramids are situated at cardinal points on the compass, and numerous astronomical uses show knowledge of mathematics in advance of other civilizations. In addition, the body of the Pharaoh Khufu (Cheops) (twenty-sixth century B.C.E.) for whom the tomb was built, and precious objects that usually surround the bodies of royalty in Egyptian tombs, have never been found.

In fact, all three of the pyramids at Giza were erected as tombs, yet not a single body has been found in any of them. A baffling series of chambers, tunnels, and shafts, blocked passageways, corridors leading to empty spaces, and false leads confront pyramid explorers. The bodies of the pharaohs and their queens might still be buried somewhere in the pyramids—or, perhaps their remains fell victim to tomb robbing, a crime so old it is mentioned in Egyptian texts and on papyrus dating back centuries before Herodotus reported on the pyramids.

The Pyramid of Khufu, largest of ancient Egypt's 70 pyramids, stands 481 feet high, measures roughly 756 feet on each side, and covers 13 acres of land. If the blocks that form the pyramid were reduced to foot-sized square cubes and lined up, the cubes would stretch for 16,600 miles. It is generally agreed that all three pyramids at Giza, including those of the Pharaohs Khafre (Chephren, in Greek) and Menaure (Mycernius, in Greek) were built during the Fourth Dynasty of Egypt, which spanned from 2613 to 2494 B.C.E. It was a custom then that as soon as a new pharaoh ascended to the throne he began building a pyramid as a final resting place. The pyramid of Khufu is the grandest of them all and is the sole survivor among the Seven Wonders of the Ancient World.

Having been built within seven hundred years after Egyptian civilization became stabilized, the vast structure has inspired many theories. Egyptian records, in the form of hieroglyphics, provided some information about the pyramids (for whom they were built, for example), but much information was lost during subsequent periods of decline. So much was forgotten that Egyptians themselves were speculating about some of the purposes of the pyramids by the time Greek civilization began thriving, some fifteen hundred years after the period in which the Great Pyramid is believed to have been erected.

Speculation then and now casts the pyramid as a gigantic sundial and astronomical observatory, as a symbolic stairway to heaven, its shape simulating the way rays of sun spread from a cloud. Other scholars see the pyramid as a secret temple where rituals were performed that transformed new leaders into god-kings.

An astonishing employment of mathematics agreements bolster the mystery of the Great Pyramid. The distance of Earth to the Sun, for example, was believed to match the height in "pyramid inches" (slightly less than the common inch) of the pyramid multiplied by 10 to the 9th power (10 to 9 is also the proportion of height to width of the pyramid). The latitude and longitude lines that intersect at the pyramid run across more land than any others, leading some to believe that Giza and the monuments there represent the center of the inhabitable world. Ancient Egyptians would have had to determine the world was round in order to reach such a conclusion, a possibility accepted by some scholars. Lines extending northwest and northeast from the Great Pyramid neatly encompass the Nile Delta, the naturally formed area of deposits where the Nile River branches to flow into the Mediterranean. Deltas are formed by streams and become triangular-shaped, the same shape as the pyramids themselves.

The perfect pyramidal shape has been cited as the purpose of the Great Pyramid in that it embodies and represents a universal system of measurement in material form. One such set of calculations suggests the Egyptians were aware of the constant pi, the figure used to determine the circumference of a circle, some two thousand years before it was formulated by the Greek mathematician **Pythagoras** (c. 580–c. 500 B.C.E.).

Englishman John Taylor (1808–1887), a well educated editor who had read voraciously about Egyptian culture and the measurements of the pyramids, discovered a formula whereby dividing the length of the perimeter of a pyramid by twice its height produces 3.14159+, the numerical equivalent of pi (a constant figure used to determine the circumference of a circle: pi times a circle's diameter produces its circumference). Taylor believed that the Egyptians not only knew the formula for pi thousands of years before the Greeks, but he contended further that they knew the circumference of Earth and derived standard units of measure from Earth's circumference.

THE *Great Pyramid alone contains 11 million cubic yards of stone.*

The ratio of the pyramid's height to its perimeter, argued Taylor, is the same as the polar radius to Earth's circumference, 2π. He viewed that equation, embodied in the pyramid, as an expression of the wisdom of ancients. It was the biblical God, concluded Taylor, who had instructed the pyramid builders, just as God had instructed Noah to build the ark.

Astronomer Charles Piazzi Smyth conducted studies at the pyramid and came up with another startling conclusion, expressed in his book *Our Inheritance in the Great Pyramid* (1980). He claimed the pyramid was also an expression of time. Through his studies, Smyth devised a measurement called the pyramid inch—an ancient measurement within one-thousandth of a British inch. The perimeter of the structure in pyramid inches equals 365,200, or 1000 x 365.2. The latter figure is the number of days in a year. Smyth concluded that the pyramids were an expression of time spanning one thousand years.

In 1894, J. Norman Lockyer (1836–1920), director of the Solar Physics Observatory in London and founder of the journal *Nature*, published *The Dawn of Astronomy*. The book argued, based on his investigations, that ancient temples and monuments in Egypt were oriented for stellar observations and served as calendars—to determine the summer solstice, for instance.

Many centuries ago, ancient Roman and Arabian historians noted the interest of Egyptians in studying the heavens and the possible uses of the pyramids as astronomical tools. Egyptian hieroglyphics make numerous references to the stars. A constellation called Sahu (corresponding to Orion) was called the home for the dead, and two pharaohs who built pyramids outside of Giza have stellar associations in hieroglyphics (Nebka is "a star," and Djedefra is "a Sehetu star," or a star of Sahu).

THE largest pyramid of ancient Egypt is the Pyramid of Khufu.

During the ninth century, a caliph named Abdullah Al Mamun became convinced the Great Pyramid held astronomical charts, maps, and mathematical tables, as well as treasures. In 820, he gained entrance into the pyramid by breaking through the outer stone. After heating limestone bricks, workers doused them with cold vinegar, creating cracks in the pyramid that allowed the caliph's men to break through a wall and discover a passageway that led upward to the original entrance of the pyramid. Turning around, they descended until they located rooms identified as the King's chamber and another as the Queen's chamber. In the King's chamber they found an elaborate sarcophagus, but nothing was inside, as if it had never been used. The tombs had been looted, or they served as a purposeful deception, with the bodies and treasures located somewhere else in the pyramid. The mystery of the missing bodies and treasures continues to perplex to this day.

Subsequent findings and theories during the twentieth century tend to confirm astronomical and calendrical orientations of the Great Pyramid. The passageway discovered in the ninth century by Abdullah Al Mamun may have had an astronomical orientation as a kind of stationary telescope. The passage runs at an angle downward from the opening. From that corridor an ancient astronomer could watch and chart the passing night sky.

Two narrow shafts that were originally believed to provide ventilation in the pyramid may have had a similar astronomical purpose as the passage. It has been determined through calculations by astronomer Virginia Trimble, based on the angle of the shaft and the positions of stars from 3000 to 2400 B.C.E., that one of the shafts pointed to the Pole Star, which could have been used by Egyptians to determine the true north. Another shaft would have provided a view of the Orion/Sehu constellation every 24 hours during that same period in time.

Such findings and references contributed to a theory proposed by Robert Bauval and Adrian Gilbert in *The Orion Mystery* (1994). Noting that the third and smallest pyramid at Giza is somewhat out of line with the other two, they compared the alignment with that of three stars in the Orion constellation, and found a match. Bauval and Gilbert argued that two other pyramids also from the Fourth Dynasty—the Pyramid of Nebka (north of Giza) and the Pyramid of Djedefra (south of Giza)—together with the pyramids at Giza, form a pattern of five pyramids that align with five of the seven stars of Orion. However, the alignment does not fit quite precisely, and two corresponding pyramids are missing.

According to Herodotus, 100,000 men were needed to build the Great Pyramid. They were organized in groups that worked on the project for three-month stints. For many centuries it has been commonly believed that the workers were slaves forced to perform hard labor.

Modern scientific studies tend to support an ancient Egyptian civilization capable of acquiring the knowledge and the extended social system required for the building of such massive and sophisticated structures as the pyramids. Recent discoveries support a view that skilled engineers and masses of peasants were fed, housed, and clothed while performing work for a leader they revered as a god-king. Evidence that some of the laborers took great pride in their work is reflected in ancient graffiti. An inscription on one block of the pyramid has been translated as a signature for "The Craftsman Gang."

Egyptian civilization of the period had no beasts of burden and no wheel to assist in moving and erecting the 11 million cubic yards of stone used in the Great Pyramid. The transporting of the stone may not have been overwhelming, however. Limestone used for the pyramids distinctly matches a large bedrock on which the nearby Sphinx was sculpted. The limestone may have been quarried, moved, and then chiseled into blocks for the pyramid. A 50-foot drop-off, now filled in by sand, occurs just beyond the temples in front of the Sphinx, perhaps a result of quarried stone. Additional stone may have arrived through shallow boats. Dry canals have been discovered that lead from Giza to the nearby Nile River, where a harbor may have been located that was subsequently obscured by the steadily encroaching desert sands.

Contemporary experiments have demonstrated that the copper chisels and stone hammers used by workers were sufficient to chip away at limestone. Tests have determined that 2.5-ton limestone blocks can be transported a fair distance in a fair amount of time to match the estimated construction time of the Great Pyramid. In the experiments, quarried rock was fashioned into blocks and transported by rope pulled by 20 to 50 men.

Taking the view that the pyramids were built from the ground up, engineers have theorized that ramps were built as the level of building rose. Using water as a lubricant, workers pushed blocks up ramps and moved the stones into place. The ramp theory is popular, considering that 96 percent of the total mass of the Great Pyramid occurs in the bottom two-thirds of the structure. With the use of ramps, work actually became easier as the pyramid rose higher.

During the 1990s, archaeologists Mark Lehner and Zahi Hawass (1947–) developed theories for the pyramid building that reduced the workforce from the 100,000 laborers cited by Herodotus to a much smaller skilled crew of laborers that worked on the Great Pyramid year-round, but were joined by thousands of other workers only during the late summer and autumn months when the Nile River overflowed and drenched agricultural fields. When the annual flooding occurred, farmers and villagers left the fields to work on the Great Pyramid for their god-king.

Teams led by Lehner and Hawass found further remains of bakeries and buildings where fish may have been processed to help feed the workforce. They also discovered bones of young male cattle and evidence that grains were delivered to the site, rather than processed there. Beef from young male cattle was thought to be food only for the wealthy. The permanent crew of workers may have enjoyed the finest food and grains as reward for the skills they were employing to erect the pyramids.

In 1997, a grid of rooms was excavated. In addition to discovering more bakeries, and many molds used for bread, the crew found shops where artisans worked. One mudbrick wall led to another complex where a seal on a wall is believed to represent the Pharaoh Khafre (2558–2532 B.C.E.). Lehner believes an entire additional complex might be unearthed, which will provide more answers, and probably more questions, about the pyramids of Giza.

In July of 2000, two mini-replicas of the pyramids were unearthed at Giza in a spot between the Sphinx and the pyramids. They contained bodies of supervisors and laborers. "Ordinary people were also allowed to use the pyramid design to construct their own tombs," concluded Hawass, director of the Giza plateau. Inscriptions in the mini-pyramids identified one corpse as a building inspector. The upper level of the tombs were reserved for technicians and craftsmen, and the lower tombs housed bodies of workmen. Some of the bodies of workmen bore splints to repair broken bones. Among inscriptions were curses, and some frescoes showed laborers at work. "This care would not have been given to slaves," noted Hawass.

ACCORDING to Greek mythology, the sphinx was a half-woman, half-lion creature that guarded the gates of Thebes.

Lehner, an archaeologist associated with the Oriental Institute of the University of Chicago and the Harvard Semitic Museum, first traveled to Egypt during the 1970s. He

was inspired then by the theories of **Edgar Cayce** (1877–1945), who believed that the pyramids were actually thousands of years older than they were credited. Cayce was among those mystics who believed that people from the legendary, advanced civilization of Atlantis built the pyramids not long after 10,500 B.C.E., just prior to the time when their own homeland was destroyed by a natural or human catastrophe. Lerner, while searching for evidence of Cayce's prophecies, discovered, as have so many researchers before him, that there exist many intriguing possibilities to further broaden the mystery, and the achievement, of the pyramid builders.

✸ DELVING DEEPER

De Camp, L. Sprague. *The Ancient Engineers*. New York: Barnes & Noble, 1993.

Harpur, James, and Jennifer Westwood. *The Atlas of Legendary Places*. New York: Konecky & Konecky, 1997.

Hays, H. R. *In the Beginnings*. New York: G. P. Putnam's Sons, 1963.

Hodges, Henry. *Technology in the Ancient World*. New York: Alfred A. Knopf, 1970.

THE SPHINX

The Sphinx at Giza faces due east and is referred to in some Egyptian hieroglyphics as Hamachis, the god of the rising Sun. Later, Hamachis evolved into the name Hor-em-Akhet. The akhet is an Egyptian hieroglyph in the image of two triangles, both open at the base, connected by a line, which represents where the sun rises and sets—an image that comes to life when looking out from the Sphinx to the pyramids of Cheops and Cephren at sunset on the summer solstice. As the Sun sets between the pyramids, it highlights the image of two triangles (the pyramids) connected by a line (the earth).

The Sphinx has the head of a man in Egyptian headdress sporting a spiraling beard, a feature found on many likenesses of pharaohs. It has the body of a lion, with two paws resting beneath the head and chest, and it rises 66 feet high; the leonine body at rest behind stretches for 240 feet. The Sphinx, the largest surviving statue from the ancient world, was sculpted out of a large limestone bedrock, a stone soft enough to yield to copper chisels and stone hammers, common Egyptian tools. The distinctive limestone bedrock has bands of yellowish clay—the same kind of distinctive stone that appears in many of the blocks used to form the nearby pyramids. It is generally believed that after the limestone bedrock was quarried for stone used for the pyramids, the remaining block was sculpted into the Sphinx. A sudden, 50-foot drop not far from the Sphinx might indicate an area that was quarried for the pyramids.

It is commonly believed that the Sphinx was sculpted during the same era as the pyramids were built (about 2650 to 2550 B.C.E.). According to a traditional historical view, the Sphinx has been most often associated with the Pharaoh Khafre (2558–2532 B.C.E.), who is represented by—and is presumably buried in—the second largest of the three pyramids at Giza. At least two statues of Khafre have been found that bear a striking resemblance to the face of the Sphinx. Egyptian religion had taken on Sun worship shortly before Khafre's

I n 1587, a colony of 113 men, women, and children vanished from Roanoke Island. The English colonists who disappeared had remained on the island, situated off the coast of what is today North Carolina, while their governor, John White, sailed back to England to procure more supplies. When White returned in 1590, he found the settlement abandoned and overgrown.

Coming upon the deserted settlement, they found the letters "CRO" carved on a tree. In a wooden post that was new since White's departure, they found the word "CROATOAN" carved. The governor had allegedly told the settlers to leave that word if they relocated during his absence, and instructed them to carve a Maltese cross should the move have been made under threat.

One theory speculates they decided to settle inland along the Chowan River after navigating Albemarle Sound, located north and west of Roanoke. Still others assert that the colony headed to Croatoan, then intermarried with the tribespeople and eventually moved inland to become the Lumbee tribe. The

THE DESERTION OF ROANOKE

Lumbee, centered far inland near the border between the Carolinas, is one of the largest Native American groups east of the Mississippi.

SOURCES:

Lane, Ralph. "The Colony at Roanoke." [Online] http://www. nationalcenter.org/ColonyofRoanoke.html.

Miller, Lee. *Roanoke: Solving the Mystery of the Lost Colony.* New York: Arcade Publishing, 2001.

reign, and since pharaohs were viewed as god-kings, the association of Khafre and Hamachis is plausible. Tools and pottery discovered around the Sphinx are associated with the Fourth Dynasty, when each of the pyramid builders of Giza ruled. Nevertheless, the dating of the Sphinx remains a source of controversy, and even in ancient times, some sources dated it as preceding the pyramids.

In Greek mythology developed over two thousand years after the Egyptian use of hieroglyphics, a sphinx was a half-woman, half-lion creature that guarded the gates of Thebes, an ancient Egyptian city. A scourge fell upon the land that could only be lifted by solving a riddle posed by the sphinx: What begins life on four legs, lives most of its life on two legs, and ends life on three legs? In *Oedipus the King*, a play by the Greek dramatist Sophocles (c.

496–406 B.C.E.), the title character solves the riddle with the answer "a human," for an infant crawls on four legs before it begins to walk on two legs, then as an aged person, he or she walks with the use of a cane, or a third leg.

LIMESTONE *cannot be dated by modern techniques such as radiocarbon dating.*

In 1967, Herbert Ricke of the Swiss Archaeological Institute uncovered a temple at the foot of the Sphinx. Niches in the temple form sanctuaries dedicated to the rising and setting of the Sun, and a colonnade court in the temple features 24 pillars, which Ricke suggested represents the 24 hours in a day.

The Sphinx, in Ricke's opinion, represents the Sun god that peers into the sanctuaries of the temple.

The temple is situated on an east-west axis that points to the spring and autumn equinoxes. A second temple, constructed more than a thousand years later, is oriented toward the winter solstice. At the time the later temple was built, the Sphinx was buried up to its neck in sand and was called Hor-em-Akhet. The Sphinx itself forms an image of the akhet hieroglyphic when approached directly from Memphis, capital city during the Fourth Dynasty, when the pyramids and the Sphinx are believed to have been built. On the path from Memphis, the Sphinx appeared silhouetted between two pyramids.

The question of the age of the Sphinx was renewed during the end of the twentieth century. An article in *Omni* magazine (August 1992) detailed the work of Robert M. Schoch, a geologist whose research demonstrated that the limestone core of the Sphinx dates from 5000 B.C.E. and indicated that granite facing was added at the conventional time when the Sphinx is dated, around 2500 B.C.E. Schoch attributes the extremely weathered look of the Sphinx to erosion that began with heavy rains from the period between 5000 B.C.E. to 3000 B.C.E. Schoch's dating is based solely on geological evidence, rather than information from hieroglyphics or other histories. E. A. Wallis Budge, R. A. Schwaller de Lubicz, and John Anthony West all wrote extensively on the monuments at Giza, and all date the Sphinx before the pyramids.

West promotes a theory that an advanced, pre-Egyptian civilization was responsible for the Sphinx. He believes that much of the weathering took place because of rains and flood. West points to the period around 9000 B.C.E., when the end of the Ice Age may well have affected weather patterns. A great flood, perhaps the one recounted in the biblical story of Noah, affected the Sphinx, and afterward all the structures at Giza show erosion by wind and the slow but steady encroachment of desert.

Schoch, a science professor specializing in geology at Boston University, was hired by West to explore the erosion of the Sphinx from a geological standpoint. During his first trip to Giza, Schoch noticed extreme erosion in two temples located in front of the Sphinx. Where the granite covering of the temples had slipped off, the exposed limestone beneath was extremely weathered. The granite facing suggested to Schoch that the Sphinx was restored, not constructed, during the reign of Khafre.

Subsequent studies led Schoch to conclude that the Sphinx was constructed in stages and that the structure has undergone several restorations. The head and part of the body were originally carved as far back as 5000 B.C.E. The body was completed and the face restored by chiseling away weathered limestone during Khafre's reign. However, pushing the original date of the Sphinx to 5000 B.C.E. and attributing its erosion primarily to water creates problems, for that time period predates the development of mastabas, tombs that were built before the pyramids during the period between 5000 B.C.E. and 3000 B.C.E. and that show no signs of weathering because of water.

Schoch's findings have been widely disputed by other geologists. Since the limestone cannot be dated by modern techniques (radiocarbon dating can only be used to determine

S edona, Arizona, located about 120 miles north of Phoenix, is hailed as being one of the most mystical places; in recent years it has become a New Age center. Many metaphysicians have maintained that there is a spiritual city that exists in another dimension directly above Sedona. According to these seers, the ethereal city focuses energy down on the area.

Sedona has become a region of spiritual pilgrimage since 1983 when metaphysical leader Richard Sutphen began holding seminars near the vortexes, those mysterious areas of electromagnetic anomalous energy. Many New Age teachers believe that the Sedona area retains powerful energies from the ancient Native Americans or even from pre-Amerindian civilizations and that these forces exert an influence on contemporary psychic-sensitives.

The various vortexes that many sensitive individuals believe to exist in Sedona appear to be areas of some kind of unidentified electromagnetic phenomenon that certain people insist aids them in meditation,

SEDONA'S SECOND CITY

inspiration, and revelation. UFOs, ancient Atlantean super science, Indian spirits, and ethereal inhabitants of other dimensions have also been suggested as the origin of the vortexes.

SOURCES:

Sedona Online. [Online] http://www.sedona.net.

Sutphen, Richard. *Sedona: Psychic Energy Vortexes.* Updated ed. Malibu, Calif.: Valley of the Sun Publishing, 1996.

the age of things that were once animated), the age of the Sphinx continues to be considered in the context of other monuments, and the date of 2500 B.C.E. still holds weight among Egyptologists. Reconstruction is apparent, but evidence shows that a renovation occurred around 1500 B.C.E. as ordered by Thutmose IV, who had the Sphinx rescued from being buried by desert sand.

John Anthony West argues that the Sphinx was created by refugees from Atlantis, the legendary continent that was supposedly destroyed around 9500 B.C.E. Graham Hancock and Robert Bauval, coauthors of *The Orion Mystery* (1994), credit wanderers from an advanced civilization that once thrived on the continent of Antarctica before it was frozen over during a global catastrophe at the end of the last Ice Age. Cataclysmic floods,

they say, wiped out the connection of the Sphinx with an ancient, advanced civilization.

Psychic **Edgar Cayce** (1877–1945) prophesied that answers to the mysteries of the Sphinx and ancient civilizations would someday be yielded by the Sphinx. According to Cayce, a secret passageway leads from one of the Sphinx's paws to its right shoulder where there exists a Hall of Records that contains the wisdom of a lost civilization and the history of the world.

✾ DELVING DEEPER

Hodges, Henry. *Technology in the Ancient World.* New York: Alfred A. Knopf, 1970.

Darwish, Adel. "Sphinx May Disintegrate within 25 Years by Bungled Restoration." *Independent News,* March 18, 2001. [Online] http://www.independent.co.uk/news/World/Africa/2001-03/sphinx 18031.shtml.

De Camp, L. Sprague. *The Ancient Engineers*. New York: Barnes & Noble, 1993.

Hodges, Henry. *Technology in the Ancient World*. New York: Alfred A. Knopf, 1970.

Ludvigsen, Freja. "Osiris' Grave Said Detected Near the Sphinx by Hawass Team." Translated by Stig Agermose. *EkstraBladet*, January 24, 1999.

STONEHENGE

"The more we dig, the more the mystery seems to deepen," said William Hawley (1851–1941), the official archaeologist of Stonehenge following World War I (1914–18). He was reporting to the press about his underfunded historical project that seemed to be languishing. Hawley wasn't able to make much progress in understanding Stonehenge by the time he wearily gave up the task around 1925. Since then, many others have tried, and much information has been gained. Still, old legends and theories about Stonehenge seem to carry as much validity as information based on careful tests performed with the best in modern equipment. As Hawley observed, each new discovery seems to broaden the sublime aura of Stonehenge.

Located on Salisbury Plain in England, Stonehenge is a site of concentric rings of stone, an avenue, and paths leading to nearby burial sites. The stone circles are situated on a henge, an area enclosed by a bank and ditch; the surrounding circular ditch is 340 feet in diameter and five feet deep. There are four stone alignments—two are circles and two others are horseshoe-shaped patterns. The outer circle is about 100 feet in diameter and originally consisted of 30 upright stones (17 still stand), weighing an average of 25 tons and linked on top by a ring of stones. The stones, composed of Sarsen, a kind of sandstone, average about 26 feet in height. Pairs of standing stones are topped by a series of lintels—a term that describes an object that rests across two pillars, similar to the top part of a doorway. Such pairs of standing stones with a third horizontal lintel joining them at the top are called trilithons. All the stones were smoothed and shaped. The lintels are locked in place by sculpted, dovetail joints, and the edges were smoothed to maintain a gentle curving appearance.

A second ring consists of bluestones, a smaller-sized stone. Within that circle are five linteled pairs of Sarsen stones in a horseshoe shape. Another horseshoe, consisting of bluestones, is at the center. An avenue outlined with parallel banks and ditches 40 feet apart leads into the henge. A single standing stone, called the Heel Stone, is positioned in the center of the avenue just outside the outer circular ditch.

Several of the upright stones were toppled during the Roman occupation of Britain between 55 B.C.E. and 410 C.E. Two upright stones and a lintel fell in 1797, and two more in 1900. The five stones that fell since 1797 were put back in place in 1958 to restore the look Stonehenge had between 400 and 1797.

Several theories have emerged about when Stonehenge was erected and the purposes it served. Stonehenge begins being mentioned in recorded history during the twelfth century, most notably by Geoffrey of Monmouth (c. 1100–1154) in his *History of the Kings of Britain*. Geoffrey's history freely mixes documented events with folklore and contains many chronological inaccuracies. Still, his fanciful story of how Stonehenge was erected on Salisbury Plain remained popular for centuries. Geoffrey credited Stonehenge to Merlin, a wizard most often associated with the legendary King Arthur. In Geoffrey's account, Merlin was asked by Ambrosius Aurelianus, brother of Uther Pendragon and uncle of King Arthur, to erect a monument to commemorate the site where several hundred British nobles were murdered by Saxons. Merlin used magic to transport the stones from Ireland, where they had been erected in the form of Stonehenge after having been brought from Africa by giants. The formation of stones was called the Giants Dance.

Later theories emerged to overshadow Geoffrey's tale. Stonehenge was credited as the work of the Mycenae, a civilization that thrived in the Aegean Sea area of the eastern Mediterranean region before the rise of Greece in the first millennium B.C.E. The

Mycenae connection fit together with a theory that prevailed into the twentieth century that ancient megaliths throughout western Europe were designed and erected by members of eastern Mediterranean cultures, from which modern languages, histories, and other forms of culture emerged. In the second half of the twentieth century, however, advanced techniques for dating ancient objects showed that Stonehenge actually preceded the rise of Mycenean cuture.

The most popular modern theory connects Stonehenge with Celtic culture that thrived in Britain before the Romans came. A priestly caste among the Celts called the Druids were believed to have supervised construction of Stonehenge and other stone circles in the region. Druids were keepers of lore and leaders of ceremonial rites among Celts. They have been associated with magic powers, human sacrifice, and various mystical rites, but many of those attributes were bestowed on them by non-Celtic historians and are, therefore, suspect. As Christianity spread through Great Britain by the fourth century, Celtic culture and the Druids were eventually overwhelmed.

Under the supervision of Druids, the theory goes, Stonehenge was a sacred ceremonial site. The famous Slaughter Stone at Stonehenge, which shows traces of red after a rain, was believed to have been an altar where Druids performed human sacrifices. It was subsequently discovered that the redness derives from iron minerals in the Slaughter Stone.

William Stukeley (1687–1765) perpetuated the Druid link to Stonehenge in the 1740s with his book, *Stonehenge: A Temple Restor'd to the British Druids* (1740). Stukeley identified the avenue leading into Stonehenge as a procession route. Back during the 1720s, he had discovered parallel lines of banks and ditches near Stonehenge. He called the phenomenon a cursus, a Latin word for racetrack, since he thought the lines were joined at the ends to form an oval.

Stukeley contributed to a growing trend in Great Britain to recognize ancient Britons, especially Druids, as "bards" (poets) living in communion with nature. Stukeley himself "went Druid" and joined an order that prac-

ticed secret Druidic rites, and he assumed the name of Chyndonax after a fabled French Druid priest.

STONEHENGE *is located on Salisbury Plain in England.*

Sir J. Norman Lockyer (1836–1920), who was once director of the Solar Physics Observatory in London and the founder of the journal *Nature*, published *The Dawn of Astronomy* in 1894. The book argued that ancient temples in Egypt were aligned for stellar observations and as calendars—to determine the summer solstice, for instance. His findings were controversial, but they helped spur further studies of the astronomical interests of ancient societies. Lockyer came to the same conclusion about ancient Britons as he had of Egyptians after studying Stonehenge and nearby pre-historic, megalithic structures. Lockyer believed that Stonehenge served as a calendar. It was known that Celts had divided their year into eight parts. According to Lockyer, Stonehenge and other megalithic sites were used to determine key points of the year, such as the coming of warm weather for planting. Lockyer viewed Druids, the keepers of Celtic lore and knowledge, as astronomer priests responsible for devising the megalithic calendars.

The astronomical orientation of Stonehenge, meanwhile, was largely ignored by archaeologists. However, it received a tremendous boost during the 1960s and 1970s when Boston University astronomer Gerald Hawkins studied the site and used a computer to compare historical solar and lunar alignments with vantage points in Stonehenge. He published his findings in 1963 in *Nature*, then in an expanded version in a book, *Stonehenge Decoded* (1965), which offered the most convincing scientific evidence yet that Stonehenge served as an astronomical observatory, specifically as a calendar.

When one stands in the middle of Stonehenge and looks through the entrance of the avenue on the morning of the summer sol-

Cuzco, the ancient capital of the Incan empire in what is now Peru, was fortified by the massive structure of Sacsahuaman on a hill above the city. This walled citadel resides on top of a cone-shaped hill 12,000 feet above sea level. Its vast residential palaces, storehouses, inner forts, paved courtyards, and 50,000-gallon reservoir present a persistent puzzle to architects and engineers. Although the Incas are given credit for having built Sacsahuaman from 1438 to 1500, guidebooks state that the "basic structure" may have been lying in ruins, awaiting new inhabitants, when the Incas claimed the fortress.

Some of the boulders that are part of the fortress have been estimated at more than 20 tons, and the largest is 12 feet thick and 25 feet tall. The quarries that yielded the stone for Sacsahuaman are located about 20 miles from the city. It still puzzles researchers as to how the Incas moved the massive boulders across rivers, down deep ravines, then up to the mountaintop site of Sacsahuaman.

SACSAHUAMAN AND THE SKILLED STONECUTTERS

Some archaeologists have stated that the Incas were skilled stonecutters. In Sacsahuaman, the massive stones fit together so precisely that a mechanic's thickness gauge cannot be inserted between the rocks in the walls. Some archaeologists have argued that stones can be worked to fit closely together; that is, stones roughly cut can be shaped to fit by being rubbed together.

SOURCES:
Deuel, Leo. *Conquistadors Without Swords*. New York: St. Martin's Press, 1967.

"Sacsahuaman." [Online] http://www.snowcrest.net/goehring/inca/sacs. html.

stice, for example, the Sun will rise above the Heel Stone, which is set on the avenue. If one stands in the entrance and looks into the circle at dusk of that day, the Sun will set between a trilithon. According to Hawkins, the use of Stonehenge as a calendar probably evolved from painstaking trial and error experiments with wooden poles to a permanent form with the standing stones. Hawkins's work was greeted with great interest and much skepticism. Nevertheless, along with other studies around the same time, it helped spur a trend for greater scientific research into Stonehenge and confirmed a new discipline, archaeoastronomy, the study of the use of astronomy among ancient societies.

Credit for Stonehenge to the Celts continued until the 1950s, when radiocarbon testing determined that Stonehenge dated from about 3000 B.C.E. and that work was begun on the

site even before the Celts migrated into Britain from the European continent. Subsequent studies have revealed that Stonehenge was built in waves of construction spanning several centuries. Smaller stones were brought to the site around 2600 B.C.E. and the largest stones arrived around 2100 B.C.E. The last work on the site dates from around 1800 B.C.E.

Though information has come forth about when Stonehenge was erected, the identity of its builders remains unknown—and where the stones came from and how they were moved into place, are yet other matters to be investigated. The Sarcens likely came from Marlborough Downs, a quarry site about 18 miles northeast of Stonehenge. How the stones could be moved from by a prehistoric people without the aid of the wheel or a pulley system is not known. The most common theory of how prehistoric people moved megaliths has them creating a track of logs on which the large stones were rolled along.

Another megalith transport theory involves the use of a type of sleigh running on a track greased with animal fat. Such an experiment with a sleigh carrying a 40-ton slab of stone was successful near Stonehenge in 1995. A dedicated team of more than 100 workers managed to push and pull the slab along the 18-mile journey from Marlborough Downs.

To erect the slab, the group dug a hole. The slab was pushed over the hole until it fell in. Then, a team pushed while another pulled by rope to make the slab stand upright. The hole was filled after the process was repeated with a second slab. The lintel stone that forms the top of the trilithon was pushed up a ramp and then maneuvered into place on top of the two pillars. Engineers at the test site believed that levers may have been used to raise the lintel stone, and timber put underneath; the process was repeated until the lintel stone rested on timber at the necessary height to push it in place to complete the trilithon.

Whether such methods were actually used during the construction is not known. Still, human sweat and ingenuity were shown as a legitimate alternative to Merlin's magic and other theories about how Stonehenge was erected.

✦ **DELVING DEEPER**

Bahn, Paul G., ed. *100 Great Archaeological Discoveries.* New York: Barnes & Noble, 1995.

De Camp, L. Sprague. *The Ancient Engineers.* New York: Barnes & Noble, 1993.

Harpur, James, and Jennifer Westwood. *The Atlas of Legendary Places.* New York: Konecky & Konecky, 1997.

Hodges, Henry. *Technology in the Ancient World.* New York: Alfred A. Knopf, 1970.

TAOS PUEBLO

In 1992, Taos Pueblo in New Mexico was admitted to the World Heritage Society as one of the most significant historical cultural landmarks in the world, thereby joining such sites as the Taj Mahal, the **Great Pyra-**

Fortress of Sacsayhuman near Cuzco, Peru. (KLAUS AARSLEFF/FORTEAN PICTURE LIBRARY)

mids, and the Grand Canyon. For many Native Americans and proponents of New Age mysticism, Taos Pueblo is also one of the primary spiritual structures on the North American continent, and it is a sacred place that does not yield its secrets to anyone other than members of the Pueblo.

The main part of the Pueblo looks much as it did when it was built with sun-dried adobe bricks around 900 years ago. The two five-story houses, the *Hlauuma* (North) and the *Hlaukwima* (South), are believed to be the oldest continuously inhabited communities in the United States. Although there are more than 1,900 Taos Indians living on the 99,000 acres belonging to the Pueblo, only about 150 people live within the Pueblo itself on a full-time basis. Because the Pueblo traditions forbid the utilities of running water and electricity, many choose to live in more modern homes outside the old walls. Still others prefer to live near the fields that they work on Pueblo land.

The religion of the Taos Pueblo people is extremely complex, yet as many as 90 percent of them also practice Roman Catholicism, finding no conflict between the two forms of spiritual expression. St. Jerome (Geronimo) has been the patron saint of the Pueblo since the church dedicated to him was first built there in 1619. The original church was destroyed in 1680, rebuilt on the same site, demolished again during the War with Mexico in 1847, and restored again in 1850.

Evidence of the seamless fit between Catholic and traditional Pueblo ceremonies

can be seen in the calendar of festivals for the year. For example, dances celebrating the turtle, deer, or buffalo are interspersed with dances honoring St. Anthony, St. Jerome, and the Virgin Mary. All of these events are considered serious religious ceremonies. Cameras are forbidden, and the Tribal Council asks that visitors render the same respect toward the dances and rituals as they would during a solemn service in their home churches.

Each year the Tribal Council, a group of 50 male elders, appoints a tribal governor and a war chief. The tribal governor and his staff are responsible for the civil and business interests of the tribe, and the war chief and his men see to the security of the mountains, the Pueblo, and the land holdings outside of the old city walls.

While some tribal members work in the nearby town of Taos, many of them staff the traditional craft and art concessions at the Pueblo. Pottery, silver jewelry, and paintings by local artists have been world famous, and ever

since the beginning of the twentieth century, scores of non-Indian painters, writers, and photographers have visited Taos and made it their home. In the 1960s and 1970s, Taos became a revered scene for the counterculture, the so-called "hippies," and many stayed on to become contributive members of the community.

In 1970, the U.S. Government returned 48,000 acres of mountain land, including the sacred Blue Lake, to the people of Taos Pueblo. The federal government had confiscated the land in 1906, declaring the area to be part of the National Forest lands. Such desecration of holy land had caused great spiritual turmoil among the tribe, for Blue Lake was perhaps the most important of the ritual sites their people visited for ceremonial purposes. When the land was returned to the tribe after years of constant lobbying by the Pueblo leaders, the tribe felt that a good part of their spiritual and cultural well-being had been restored to them. Today, Blue Lake and the nearby mountains are off-limits to all but members of the Taos Pueblo.

Taos Pueblo welcomes visitors except during those times when tribal rituals require privacy; however, there are a number of ceremonies and powwows that are open to the general public.

When visiting the Pueblo, one must keep in mind that the tribal members regard themselves as a sovereign nation within the United States and that their primary objective as a tribe is to preserve their ancient traditions. The Tribal Council has posted a number of rules that must be observed at all times and indicated certain areas that are strictly off-limits to all visitors.

❀ DELVING DEEPER

Deloria, Vine. *God Is Red*. New York: Grosset & Dunlap, 1973.

Fergusson, Erna. *Dancing Gods: Indian Ceremonies of New Mexico & Arizona*. Albuquerque: University of New Mexico, 1931, 1957, 1966.

Horka-Follick, Lorayne Ann. *Los Hermanos Penitentes*. Los Angeles: Westernlore Press, 1969.

Steiner, Stan. *The New Indians*. New York: Dell Publishing, 1968.

"Taos Pueblo: A Thousand Years of Tradition." *Taos Vacation Guide*. [Online] http://www.taosvacationguide.com/history/pueblo.html. 2 May 2002.

TIAHUANACO

The Inca civilization of South America, unlike the Mayan, was still at its height when conquistadors arrived. One of the conquistadors, Cieza de Leon (1518–1560), followed trails from the coast of Peru into the foothills of the Andes and learned from natives about the ruins of a once great city high in the mountains. He presumed that it was an old Inca settlement like those the Spanish found elsewhere in what is now Peru. In 1549, heading inland from Lake Titicaca, which separates Peru from the land-locked nation of Bolivia, de Leon found the remains of the fabled city of Tiahuanaco, which were far greater than he had expected.

The site of the ancient city features large artificial mounds and massive, carved stones, including an enormous entrance called the Gateway of the Sun. Carved from a single block of stone weighing 10 tons, the Gateway features intricate decorations, including a god-figure often identified as Viracocha, who figured prominently in the mythology of the region.

THE *entrance called the Gateway of the Sun weighs 10 tons.*

A terraced monument called Akapana, measuring 650 by 600 feet and rising 50 feet high, has a pyramidal shape that levels off to form a high platform. Within that platform are sunken courtyards. Seen throughout Tiahuanaco are skillful examples of masonry and the brilliant use of metals, including copper clamps that hold massive blocks of stones together.

The Gateway of the Sun stands on the northwest corner of a platform temple called Kalasasaya, which is adjacent to a semi-underground temple; the temples form part of an astronomical observatory. Some standing stones placed on the site weigh up to 100 tons. Among other remarkable feats, the residents of Tiahuanaco devised a drainage and sewer system. At 12,500 feet of elevation, Tiahuanaco was the highest city of the ancient world.

As soon as Cieza de Leon reported the remarkable discovery, Tiahuanaco became one of the world's great mysteries, for the local Aymara Indians insisted that the ruins were there long before the great Inca civilization came to the area and conquered it around 1450. Christian missionaries followed Cieza de Leon to the ruins, and these men of learning soon doubted whether the Aymara people could ever have been capable of the craftsmanship and engineering such massive structures required. Legends began to be spread by the missionaries that the structures had been erected in the distant past by giants.

Scientists date the civilization that occupied Tiahuanaco to 300—when a community first began to settle in the area—to 900, when some kind of disruption occurred and Tiahuanaco was abandoned. Those dates match the claim of the Aymara Indians that Tiahuanaco

The Puma Punka temple at Tiahuanaco, Bolivia. (KLAUS AARSLEFF/FORTEAN PICTURE LIBRARY)

and that Tiahuanaco was once a major port city. The ancient citizens of Tiahuanaco were members of a superior culture who had introduced a golden age to the area. The founders of Tiahuanaco were taller and had distinctive facial characteristics quite apart from the high-cheekboned visages of today's dwellers of the high plateau.

In Posnanksy's view, the most startling tale told by the few artifacts left in the city was of a New World civilization that was amazingly similar to that of ancient Egypt. The Calassassayax (house of worship), he believed, was so similar to the Egyptian temple of Karnak in design and layout that its relative dimensions made it almost a scale model of the Old World structure. The stones used in the temple at Tiahuanaco are fitted and joined with their joints and facing parts polished to make a nearly perfect match. The Incas did not build in such a manner, but the ancient Egyptians did.

And then there were the buildings constructed of massive, polished stones, many tons in weight, that had been placed in such a manner that only a people with advanced engineering methods could have designed and transported them. If this were not enough of an impossible situation, the particular andesite used in much of the Tiahuanacan construction can only be found in a quarry that lies 50 miles away in the mountains.

The surgeons of Tiahuanaco were skilled in trepanning the brain, as were the Egyptian physicians. Posnansky uncovered skulls with well-healed bone grafts, which offered silent testimony to the skill of the ancient doctors and their knowledge of anatomy. Some archaeologists receptive to Posnansky's theories argue that the credibility of cultural coincidence is stretched considerably when related to brain operations. It is possible to accept the fact that two widely separated cultures, such as the Egyptians and the unknown people of Tiahuanaco, may have developed a form of brain operation, but that both cultures used identical instruments and methods, seems unusual to say the least. The instruments are of high-grade copper and include drills and chisels. In themselves they indicate an advanced degree of metallurgy, knowledge of simple machinery, and development of surgi-

was built and lay in ruins before the Incas came. Other theorists blend scientific finds and local myths, perpetuating the notion that a white race, perhaps Egyptians or Phoenicians, brought civilization to the high plain.

The argument that Tiahuanaco thrived more than 10 thousand years before the dates established by scientific testing was fostered by Arthur Posnansky in his book, *Tiahuanaco: The Cradle of American Man* (1945). Noting that the platform temple Kalasasaya was used as an astronomical observatory, Posnansky determined that it pointed precisely to solstice alignments in 15,000 B.C.E. Taking into account the very gradual shifting of Earth's axis, Posnansky postulated that arid plain was once below water, part of Lake Titicaca, cal practices far more detailed than can be expected in primitive societies.

Posnansky's theories won a popular readership, but were not widely accepted among scientists. At sunrise on dates of the equinox, for example, the Sun appears on the staircase of Kakassasaya. There is no need to believe that it was built at a precise time to point to a precise astronomical alignment. The port city idea was also quickly disputed. Areas that would have been submerged included neighborhoods of dwellings that share similar dates with the larger structures, and the surrounding countryside where farms were located also would have been underwater.

Radiocarbon dating suggests instead that Tiahuanaco was founded around 400, and after three centuries of gradual settlement, the city was abandoned around 1000. In the interim, the settlement had grown from a ceremonial center to a major city inhabited by 40,000 to 80,000 people.

Regular archaeological excavations have been underway in Tiahuanaco since 1877. The semi-subterranean temple next to the Akapana yielded a 24-foot tall monolith in 1932. That find and the generally arid climate helped sustain the idea that Tiahuanaco served primarily as a ceremonial center. Later finds, however, showed that it had been a thriving city, and dates for the time settlement and abandonment were established. Why the place was abandoned, however, remains a mystery to conventional archaeologists.

However, according to Posnansky, it was the climactic changes at the end of the Ice Age that contributed to flooding and the destruction of Tiahuanaco, wiping out its inhabitants and leaving the great structures in ruins. Posnansky died in 1946, convinced that he had traced the influence of Tiahuanaco on the native culture as far north as the coastal deserts of Peru and as far south as Argentina.

Most other archaeologists take much more conservative views. As with the Mayans, they argue, the ancient Indians of Tiahuanaco might have had too much of a good thing. There is evidence that they were victims of a natural catastrophe, but it was a prolonged drought, rather than Posnansky's great flood, that probably overwhelmed them. Drought conditions set in for an extended period, and the Aymara could no longer support a massive population and large-scale construction projects. People began abandoning the city around 1000. The Incas conquered communities remaining in the area around 1450. Then the Spanish came to Tiahuanaco about one hundred years after the Incas had moved in.

Still the questions remain: just who were the natives that thrived at Tiahuanaco and how did they construct such elaborate structures?

The Aymara, meanwhile, still live in the region. They outlasted the early Spanish settlers around Tiahuanaco, who never quite mastered the area's harsh conditions. The plain became a desert again after the Spanish farmed it, for they never learned to use a technique of the ancient dwellers of Tiahuanaco. The mysterious unknown people farmed on raised fields, which were filled and built up with soil from surrounding areas. Canals between the fields kept them watered, and by farming on raised fields the crops were kept safe from the danger of frost and erosion by water.

❋ DELVING DEEPER

Bahn, Paul G., ed. *100 Great Archaeological Discoveries*. New York: Barnes & Noble, 1995.

Deuel, Leo. *Conquistadors without Swords: Archaeologists in the Americas*. New York: St. Martin's Press, 1967.

———. *Flights into Yesterday*. New York: St. Martin's Press, 1969.

Irwin, Constance. *Fair Gods and Stone Faces*. New York: St. Martin's Press, 1963.

MAKING THE CONNECTION

archipelago From the Greek *arkhi*, meaning "chief or main" and *pelagos* meaning "sea." Any large body of water that contains a large number of scattered islands.

bitumen Any of a variety of natural substances, such as tar or asphalt, containing hydrocarbons derived from petroleum and used as a cement or mortar for surfacing roads.

cubit From the Latin *cubitum*, meaning forearm or elbow. An ancient unit of length, based on the distance from the tip of the middle finger to the elbow which approximated 17 to 22 inches.

druid Someone who worships the forces of nature as in the ancient Celtic religion. Can also refer to a priest in the Celtic religion.

frieze From the Latin *phrygium (opus)*, meaning work or craftmanship. A decorative architectural band, usually running along a wall, just below the ceiling, often sculpted with figurines or ornaments.

fulcrum From the Latin *fulcire*, meaning "to prop up or support." The part of something that acts as its support.

geoglyphics Lines, designs, or symbols left in the earth, such as those in Egypt, Malta, Chile, Bolivia, and Peru with a mysterious, ancient, and puzzling origin.

hieroglyphics A system of writing that uses pictures or symbols such as that in ancient Egypt.

Ice Age Any of the periods of extreme cold or glacial epochs in the history of Earth when temperatures fell, resulting in large areas of Earth's surface covered with glaciers; the most recent one occurring during the Pleistocene epoch.

megalith A very large stone that is usually a part of a monument or prehistoric architecture.

GLOSSARY

abductee Someone who believes that he or she has been taken away by deception or force against his/her will.

aboriginal Refers to a people that has lived or existed in a particular area or region from the earliest known times or from the beginning.

abyss From late Latin *abyssus* and Greek *abussos*, which literally means "bottomless," stemming from *bussos*, meaning "bottom." A gorge or chasm that is inconceivably deep, vast or infinite, such as the bottomless pit of hell or a dwelling place of evil spirits.

alchemy From Greek, *khemeia* to Arabic, *alkimiya* via medieval Latin *alchimia* and Old French, fourteenth century *alquemie*, meaning "the chemistry." A predecessor of chemistry practiced in the Middle Ages and Renaissance principally concerned with seeking methods of transforming base metals into gold and the "elixir of life."

alien A being or living creature from another planet or world.

amnesia The loss of memory which can be temporary or long term and usually brought on by shock, an injury, or psychological disturbance. Originally from the Greek word *amnestos*, literally meaning not remembered and from a later alteration of the word *amnesia* forgetfulness.

anomalous Something strange and unusual that deviates from what is considered normal. From the Greek *anomalos*, meaning uneven.

anthropology The scientific study of the origins, behavior, physical, social, and cultural aspects of humankind.

Antichrist The antagonist or opponent of Jesus Christ (c. 6 B.C.E.–c. 30 C.E.), who is anticipated by many early as well as contemporary Christians to lead the world into evil before Christ returns to Earth to redeem and rescue the faithful. Can also refer to any person who is in opposition to or an enemy of Jesus Christ or his teachings, as well as to those who claim to be Christ, but in fact are false and misleading.

anthroposophy A spiritual or religious philosophy that Rudolph Steiner (1861–1925), an Austrian philosopher and scientist, developed, with the core belief centering around the human accessibility of the spiritual world to properly developed human intellect. Steiner founded the Anthroposophical Society in 1912 to promote his ideas that spiritual development should be humanity's foremost concern.

apocalypse From the Greek *apokalupsis,* meaning "revelation." In the Bible, the Book of Revelation is often referred to as the Apocalypse. Comes from many anonymous, second-century B.C.E. and later Jewish and Christian texts that contain prophetic messages pertaining to a great total devastation or destruction of the world and the salvation of the righteous.

apothacary From the Greek *apotheke* meaning "storehouse." A pharmacist or druggist who is licensed to prescribe, prepare and sell drugs and other medicines, or a pharmacy—where drugs and medicines are sold.

apparition The unexpected or sudden appearance of something strange, such as a ghost. From the Latin *apparitus,* past participle of *apparere,* meaning to appear.

archaeologist A person who scientifically examines old ruins or artifacts such as the remains of buildings, pottery, graves, tools, and all other relevant material in order to study ancient cultures.

archipelago From the Greek *arkhi,* meaning "chief or main" and *pelagos* meaning "sea." Any large body of water that contains a large number of scattered islands.

Armageddon From late Latin *Armagedon,* Greek and Hebrew, *har megiddo, megiddon,* which is the mountain region of Megiddo. Megiddo is the site where the great final battle between good and evil will be fought as prophesied and will be a decisive catastrophic event that many believe will be the end of the world.

astral self Theosophical belief that humans possess a second body that cannot be perceived with normal senses, yet it coexists with the human body and survives death.

astronomy The scientific study of the of the workings of the universe—of stars, planets, their positions, sizes, composition, movement behavior. Via the Old French and Latin from Greek *astronomia,* meaning literally star-arranging.

automatic writing Writing that occurs through either an involuntary, or unconscious, trance-like state with the source being the writer's own unconscious self, from a telepathic link with another, or from a deceased spirit wishing to communicate a message.

banal Boring, very ordinary and commonplace. From the French word *ban,* originally used in the context of a mandatory military service for all or common to all.

barter The exchange or the process of negotiating certain goods or services for other goods or services.

Bedouin A nomadic Arabic person from the desert areas of North Africa and Arabia. Via Old French *beduin,* ultimately from Arabic *badw,* or desert, nomadic desert people.

betrothal The act of becoming or being engaged to marry another person.

Bhagavad Gita From Sanskrit *Bhagavadgi ta,* meaning "song of the blessed one." A Hindu religious text, consisting of 700 verses, in which the Hindu god, Krishna, teaches the importance of unattachment from personal aims to the fulfillment of religious duties and devotion to God.

bipedal Any animal that has two legs or feet. From the Latin stem *biped,* meaning two-footed.

birthstone Each month of the year has a particular precious gemstone or a semiprecious stone associated with it. It is believed that if a person wears the stone assigned their birth month, good fortune or luck will follow.

bitumen Any of a variety of natural substances, such as tar or asphalt, containing hydrocarbons derived from petroleum and used as a cement or mortar for surfacing roads.

black magick The use of magic for evil purposes, calling upon the devil or evil spirits.

blasphemy Something said or done which shows a disrespect for God or things that are sacred. An irreverent utterance or action showing a disrespect for sacred things or for God.

cadaver A dead body that is usually intended for dissection. From the Latin *cadere*, meaning to fall or to die.

charlatan From the Italian *ciarlatano*, via seventeenth-century French *ciarlare*, meaning "to babble or patter" or "empty talk." Someone who makes elaborate claims or who pretends to have more skill or knowledge than is factual, such as a fraud or quack.

chieftain The leader of a clan, tribe, or group.

clairvoyance The ability to visualize or sense things beyond the normal range of the five human senses. From the French word *clairvoyant*, meaning clear-sighted and *voyant*, the present participle of *voir* to see.

conjurations The act of reciting a name, words or particular phrases with the intent of summoning or invoking a supernatural force or occurrence.

conquistadores From the Latin *conquirere* meaning "to conquer." Spanish soldiers or adventurers, especially of the sixteenth century who conquered Peru, Mexico, or Central America.

consciousness Someone's mind, thoughts or feelings, or can be referring to the part of the mind which is aware of same. The state of being aware of what is going on around you, either individually or the shared feelings of group awareness, feelings or thoughts.

conspiracy A plan formulated in secret between two or more people to commit a subversive act.

contactee Someone who believes to have been or is in contact with an alien from another planet.

cosmic consciousness The sense or special insight of one's personal or collective awareness in relation to the universe or a universal scheme.

cosmic sense The awareness of one's identity and actions in relationship to the universe or universal scheme of things.

cosmology The philosophical study and explanation of the nature of the universe or the scientific study of the origin and structure of the universe.

cosmos From the Greek *kosmos* meaning "order, universe, ornament." The entire universe as regarded in an orderly, harmonious and integrated whole.

coven From the Anglo-Norman, mid-seventeenth century "assembly" and from *convenire* meaning convene. An assembly of or a meeting of a group of witches, often 13 in number.

cryptomensia A state of consciousness in which the true source or origin of a particular memory is forgotten or is attributed to a wrongful source or origin.

cryptozoology The study of so-called mythical creatures such as the Yeti or Bigfoot, whose existence has not yet been scientifically substantiated.

cubit From the Latin *cubitum*, meaning forearm or elbow. An ancient unit of length, based on the distance from the tip of the middle finger to the elbow which approximated 17 to 22 inches.

deity From late Latin *deitas* "divine nature," and *deus* "god." A divine being or somebody or something with the essential nature of a divinity, such as a god, goddess. When the term is capitalized, it refers to God in monotheistic belief or religions.

demarcation The process of setting borders, limits or marking boundaries. From the Spanish *demarcacion*, literally meaning, marking off.

demon possession When low-level disincarnate spirits invade and take over a human body.

desecration When something sacred is treated in a profane or damaging manner.

discarnate The lack of a physical body. Coined from *dis-* and the Latin stem *carn*, meaning *flesh*.

The Dispersion From the Greek *diaspora* meaning to scatter or disperse. Refers to the period in history when the Jewish people were forced to scatter in countries outside of Palestine after the Babylonian captivity.

dogma From Greek stem word *dogmat*, meaning "opinion" or "tenet," and from *dokein*, "to seem good." A belief or set of beliefs, either political, religious, philosophical, or moral and considered to be absolutely true.

druid Someone who worships the forces of nature as in the ancient Celtic religion. Can also refer to a priest in the Celtic religion.

ecclesiasticism Principles, practices, activities, or body of thought that is all-encompassing and adhered to in an organized church or institution.

ecstatic Intense emotion of pleasure, happiness, joy or elation.

electrodes Two conductors through which electricity flows in batteries or other electrical equipment.

electroencephalograph A device or machine that through the use of electrodes placed on a person's scalp, monitors the electrical activity in various parts of the brain. These are recorded and used as a diagnostic tool in tracing a variety of anything from brain disorders, tumors or other irregularities to dream research.

electroencephalographic dream research Researching dreams using a electroencephalograph to aid the researcher in the brain activity of the one being studied.

electromagnetic Of or pertaining to the characteristics of an electromagnet, which is a device having a steel or iron core and is magnetized by an electric current that flows through a surrounding coil.

elemental spirits A lower order of spirit beings, said to be usually benevolent and dwell in the nature kingdom as the life force of all things in nature, such as minerals, plants, animals, and the four elements of earth, air, fire and water; the planets, stars, and signs of the zodiac; and hours of the day and night. Elves, brownies, goblins, gnomes, and fairies are said to be among these spirits.

elixir Something that is a mysterious, magical substance with curative powers believed to heal all ills or to prolong life and preserve youthfulness. From the Arabic *al-iksir* and the Greek *xerion*, meaning dry powder for treating wounds.

enchantments Things or conditions which possess a charming or bewitching quality such as a magical spell.

encode To convert a message from plain text into a code. In computer language, to convert from analog to digital form, and in genetics to convert appropriate genetic data.

enigma From Greek *ainigma* "to speak in riddles" and *ainos*, meaning "fables." Somebody or something that is ambiguous, puzzling or not easily understood and might have a hidden meaning or riddle.

ephemerality Refers to the state of something living or lasting for a markedly short or brief time. The nature of existing or lasting for only a day, such as certain plants or insects.

eschatology Comes from the Greek word *eskhatos* meaning "last" and *-logy* literally meaning "discourse about the last things." Refers to the body of religious doctrines concerning the human soul in relation to death, judgment, heaven or hell, or in general, life after death and of the final stage or end of the world.

evocation The act of calling forth, drawing out or summoning an event or memory from the past, as in recreating.

exorcism The act, religious ceremony, or ritual of casting out evil spirits from a person or a place.

extraterrestrial Something or someone originating or coming from beyond Earth, outside of Earth's atmosphere.

false memory Refers to situations where some therapies and hypnosis may actually be planting memories through certain suggestions or leading questions and comments; thereby creating memories that the patient or client believes to be true, but in reality they are not.

fanatical Extreme enthusiasm, frenzy, or zeal about a particular belief, as in politics or religion.

Five Pillars of Islam In Arabic, also called the *arkan*, and consists of the five sacred ritual duties believed to be central to mainstream Muslims' faith. The five duties are the confession of faith, performing the five daily prayers, fasting during the month of Ramadan, paying alms tax, and performing at least one sacred pilgrimage to Mecca, the holy land.

foo fighter A term coined by pilots who reported sightings of unconventional aircraft that appeared as nocturnal lights during World War II. A popular cartoon character of the time, Smokey Stover, often said "Where there's foo there's fire" and it became the saying to describe the strange phenomena.

frieze From the Latin *phrygium (opus)*, meaning work or craftmanship. A decorative architectural band, usually running along a wall, just below the ceiling, often sculpted with figurines or ornaments.

fulcrum From the Latin *fulcire*, meaning "to prop up or support." The part of something that acts as its support.

Geiger counter An instrument named after its inventor, German physicist Hans Geiger (1882–1945), that is used to measure and detect such things as particles from radioactive materials.

geoglyphics Lines, designs, or symbols left in the earth, such as those in Egypt, Malta, Chile, Bolivia, and Peru with a mysterious, ancient, and puzzling origin.

Gestalt therapy A type of psychotherapy that puts a emphasis on a person's feelings as revealing desired or undesired personality traits and how they came to be, by examining unresolved issues from the past.

Gnostic From the Greek, *gnostikos*, meaning "concerning knowledge." A believer in Gnosticism, or relating to or possessing spiritual or intellectual knowledge or wisdom.

guardian angel A holy, divine being that watches over, guides, and protects humans.

hallucinations A false or distorted perception of events during which one vividly imagines seeing, hearing or sensing objects or other people to be present, when in fact they are not witnessed by others.

haruspicy A method of divining or telling the future by examining the entrails of animals.

heresy The willful, persistent act of adhering to an opinion or belief that rejects or contradicts established teachings or theories that are traditional in philosophy, religion, science, or politics.

heretic From the Greek *hairetikos*, meaning "able to choose." Someone who does not conform or whose opinions, theories, or beliefs contradict the conventional established teaching, doctrines, or principles, especially that of religion.

hieroglyphics A writing system of ancient Egypt that uses symbols or pictures to signify sounds, objects, or concepts. Can also refer to any writing or symbols that are difficult to decipher. The word comes from an ancient Greek term meaning "sacred carving."

hierophant From the Latin *hierophanta* and Greek *hierophantes*, meaning literally a "sacred person who reveals something." An ancient Greek priest who revealed or interpreted the sacred mysteries, or holy doctrines, at the annual festival of Eleusis.

hoax An act of deception that is intended to make people think or believe something is real when it is not.

Homo sapiens Mankind or humankind, the species of modern human beings.

horoscope From Greek *horoskopos*, literally meaning "time observer" and from *hora* meaning "time, or hour," referring to the time of birth. A diagram or astrological forecast based on the relative position in the heavens of the stars and planets in the signs of the zodiac, at any given moment, but especially at the moment of one's birth.

hypnagogic Relating to or being in the state between wakefulness and sleep where one is drowsy. From the French *hypnagogique* meaning literally leading to sleep.

hypnopompic Typical of or involving the state between sleeping and waking. Coined from *hypno* and Greek *pompe*, meaning a sending away.

hypnosis The process of putting or being in a sleeplike state, although the person is not sleeping. It can be induced by suggestions or methods of a hypnotist.

hypothesis A theory or assumption that needs further exploration, but which is used as a tentative explanation until further data confirms or denies it. From the Greek *hupothesis* meaning foundation or base.

Ice Age Any of the periods of extreme cold or glacial epochs in the history of Earth when temperatures fell, resulting in large areas of Earth's surface covered with glaciers; the most recent one occurring during the Pleistocene epoch.

incantation From fourteenth-century French, *cantare*, meaning "to sing" via Latin— *incantare*—"to chant." The chanting, recitation or uttering of words supposed to produce a magical effect or power.

incarnation A period of time in which a spirit or soul dwells in a bodily form or condition. One of a series of lives spent in a physical form.

indigenous From a mid-seventeenth century word *indigena*, literally meaning "born-in," and from *gignere*, meaning "to beget." Inborn, intrinsic, or belonging to a place, such as originating, growing, or living in an area, environment, region, or country.

Inquisition Fourteenth century, from Latin *inquirere* via Old French *inquisicion*, meaning "to inquire." In the thirteenth century, Roman Catholicism appointed a special tribunal or committee whose chief function was to combat, suppress and punish heresy against the church. Remaining active until the modern era, the official investigations were often harsh and unfair.

insurrectionist Someone who is in rebellion or revolt against an established authority, ruler, or government.

intergalactic Something that is located, or is moving, between two or more galaxies.

Invocation The act of calling upon or appealing to a higher power such as a deity, spirit, or God for assistance. A form of prayer, that invites God's presence, at the beginning of a ceremony or meeting. In black magick, can be the casting of a spell or formula to invite an evil spirit to appear.

ions An atom or group of atoms that are electrically charged through the process of gaining or losing one or more electrons. From the Greek *ion* meaning moving thing; and from the present participle of *ienai* meaning to go —from the movement of any ion toward the electrode of the opposite charge.

jinni In Islamic or Muslim legend, a spirit that is capable of taking on the shape of humans or animals in order to perform mischievous acts or to exercise supernatural power and influence over humans. From the Arabic *jinn*, which is the plural of *jinni*.

Kabbalah body of mystical Jewish teachings based on an interpretation of hidden meanings contained in the Hebrew scriptures. Kabbalah is Hebrew for "that which is received," and also refers to a secret oral tradition handed down from teacher to pupil. The term Kabbalah is generally used now to apply to all Jewish mystical practice.

karmic law Karma is the Sanskrit word for "deed." In the Eastern religions of Buddhism and Hinduism all deeds of a person in this life dictate an equal punishment or reward to be met in the next life or series of lives. In this philosophy, it is a natural moral law rather than a divine judgment which provides the process of development, enabling the soul into higher or lower states, according to the laws of cause and effect to be met.

knockings/rappings Tapping sounds said to be coming from deceased spirits in an attempt to communicate with or frighten the living.

left-hand path In occult tradition, a practitioner who practices black magic.

leprous From the Greek, *lepros*, meaning "scale." Something resembling the symptoms of or relating to the disease of leprosy, which covers a person's skin with scales or ulcerations.

loa A spirit that is thought to enter the devotee of the Haitian voodoo, during a trance state, and believed to be a protector and guide that could be a local deity, a deified ancestor or even a saint of the Roman Catholic Church.

lupinomanis Having the excessive characteristics of a wolf, such as being greedy or ravenously hungry.

lycanthropy The magical ability in legends and horror stories of a person who is able to transform into a wolf, and take on all of its characteristics.

magus A priest, wizard, or someone who is skilled or learned, especially in astrology, magic, sorcery, or the like.

manitou A supernatural force, or spirit that suffuses various living things, as well as inanimate objects, according to the Algonquian peoples. In the mythology of the Ojibwa of the eastern United States, Manitou is the name of the supreme deity, or God, and means "Great Spirit."

manna The food miraculously supplied to the Israelites by God, according to the Old Testament, as they wandered in the wilderness during their flight from Egypt. Spiritual nourishment or something of value received of divine origin or unexpectedly.

materialization Something that appears suddenly, as if out of nowhere. In the paranormal it might be a ghost or spirit that suddenly appears to take on a physical form.

medium In the paranormal, someone who is able to convey messages between the spirits of the deceased and the spirits of the living.

megalith A very large stone that is usually a part of a monument or prehistoric architecture.

Mesopotamia Greek word, meaning "between two rivers." An ancient region that was located between the Tigris and Euphrates rivers in what is today, modern Iraq and Syria. Some of the world's earliest and greatest ancient civilizations such as Ur, Sumer, Assyria, and Babylonia were developed in that region.

messiah A leader who is regarded as a liberator or savior. In Christianity, the Messiah is Jesus Christ (c. 6 B.C.E.–c. 30 C.E.), in Judaism, it is the king who will lead the Jews back to the Holy Land of Israel and establish world peace.

metaphysical Relating to abstract thought or the philosophical study of the nature of existence and truth.

metrology The scientific system or study of measurements. From the Greek *metrologie*, meaning theory of ratios and *metron*, or measure.

mortician An undertaker or one who prepares dead bodies for burial and funerals.

narcolepsy A condition where a person uncontrollably falls asleep at odd times during daily activities and/or for long extended periods of time. Hallucinations and even paralysis might also accompany this condition.

near-death experience A mystical-like occurrence or sensation that individuals on the brink of death or who were dead, but brought back to life, have described which includes leaving their physical body and hovering over it as though they were a bystander.

neo-paganism Someone who believes in a contemporary or modernized version of the religions which existed before Christianity, especially those with a reverence for nature over the worship of a divine or supreme being.

neophyte From the Latin *neophytus* and Greek *neophutos* or *phuein*, "to plant" or "cause to grow"—literally meaning "newly planted." A beginner or novice at a particular task or endeavor. Somebody who is a recent convert to a belief. A newly ordained priest, or someone who is new to a religious order, but who has not yet taken their vows, so is not yet a part of the order.

neuron The basic functional unit of the nervous system a cell body that consists of an axon and dendrites and transmit nerve impulses. A neuron is also called a *nerve cell*. Via German from Greek *neuron*, meaning sinew, cord, or nerve.

Novena of Masses In the Roman Catholic Church, the recitation of prayers or devotions for a particular purpose, for nine consecutive days. From the Latin *nus*, meaning nine each and from *novem*, meaning nine.

Old Testament The first of the two main divisions of the Christian Bible that corresponds to the Hebrew scriptures.

omen A prophetic sign, phenomenon, or happening supposed to foreshadow good or evil or indicate how someone or something will fare in the future—an indication of the course of future events.

oracle Either someone or something that is the source of wisdom, knowledge or prophecy. Can also refer to the place where the prophetic word would be given. Via French from the Latin *oraculum*, from *orare* to speak.

paleoanthropology The study of humanlike creatures or early human beings more primitive that Homo Sapiens, usually done through fossil evidence.

paleontology The study of ancient forms of life in geologic or prehistoric times, using such evidence as fossils, plants, animals, and other organisms.

Pan In Greek mythology the god of nature or of the woods, fields, pastures, forests, and flocks. Is described as having the torso and head of a human, but the legs, ears, and horns of a goat.

paranormal Events or phenomena that are beyond the range of normal experience and not understood or explained in terms of current scientific knowledge.

parapsychologist One who studies mental phenomena, such as telepathy or extrasensory perception, the mind/body connection, and other psi or paranormal factors that cannot be explained by known scientific principles.

parapsychology The study or exploration of mental phenomena that does not have a scientific explanation in the known psychological principles.

Passover The seven or eight days of a Jewish festival that begins on the fourteenth day of Nissan and commemorates the exodus of the Hebrews from their captivity in Egypt. From the Hebrew word *pesa*, meaning to pass without affecting.

pharaoh From the Hebrew *par'oh*, Egyptian *pr-'o*, and Latin and Greek *Pharao*, meaning literally "great house." An ancient Egyptian title for the ruler or king of Egypt, often considered a tyrant and one who expected unquestioning obedience.

pharmacologist The study of or science of drugs in all their aspects, including sources, chemistry, production, their use in treating ailments and disease, as well as any known side effects.

phenomena Strange, extraordinary, unusual, even miraculous events, or happenings to persons or things. From the Greek *phainomenon*, that which appears, from the past participle of *phainein*, to bring to light.

philanthropist Someone who is benevolent or generous in his or her desire or activities to improve the social, spiritual or material welfare of humankind. From the late Latin, ultimately, Greek *philanthropos*, humane; *philos*; loving and *anthropos*, human being.

philanthropy From the Greek *philanthropos*, meaning "humane," and from *philos*, meaning "loving." An affection or desire to help improve the spiritual, social, or material welfare of humanity through acts of charity or benevolence.

physiognomy From *phusis* meaning "nature, character" and *gnomon*, "to judge." The art of judging a person's character or temperament by their physical features, especially facial features.

physiology The study of the functioning and internal workings of living things, such as metabolism, respiration, reproduction and the like. From the Latin word *physiologia* and the Greek *phusiologia*, and *phusis* meaning nature.

precognition The ability to foresee what is going to happen in the future, especially if this perception is gained through other than the normal human senses or extrasensory.

predator Any organism or animal that hunts, kills, and eats other animals. Can refer to a ruthless person who is extremely aggressive in harming another. From the Latin *praedator* and *praedari*, meaning to seize as plunder.

psi The factor or factors responsible for parapsychological phenomena. Derived from the Greek letter *psi* which is used to denote the unknown factor in an equation.

psyche The soul or human spirit or can refer to the mental characteristics of a person or group or nation. Via Latin from Greek *psukhe* meaning breath, soul, mind and from *psukhein* to breathe.

psychiatrist A doctor who is trained to treat people with psychiatric disorders.

psychoanalysis The system of analysis regarding the relationship of conscious and unconscious psychological aspects and their treatment in mental or psycho neurosis.

psychoanalyst One who uses the therapeutic methods of psychiatric analysis, such as dream analysis and free association, as developed by Sigmund Freud (1856–1939) to treat patients in order to gain awareness of suppressed subconscious experiences or memories that might be causing psychological blocks.

psychokinesis The ability to make objects move or to in some way affect them without using anything but mental powers.

pulsar A star generally believed to be a neutron star and that appears to pulse as it briefly emits bursts of visible radiation such as radio waves and x-rays.

putrefy Causing something to decay, usually indicating a foul odor. From the Latin stem, *putr*, meaning rotten, plus *facere*, to make.

Qur'an The sacred text, or holy book, of Islam. For Muslims, it is the very word of Allah, the absolute God of the Islamic faith, as revealed to the prophet Muhammad (c. 570 C.E.–632 C.E.) by the archangel Gabriel.

rectory The house or dwelling that a rector (clergyman) lives in.

reincarnation The reappearance or rebirth of something in a new form. Some religions or belief systems state that the soul returns to live another life in a new physical form and does so in a cyclical manner.

resurrection The act of rising from the dead or returning to life. In Christian belief, the Resurrection was the rising of Jesus Christ from the dead after he was crucified and entombed. Resurrection also refers to the rising of the dead on Judgment Day, as anticipated by Christians, Jews, and Muslims.

retrocognition The mental process or faculty of knowing, seeing, or perceiving things, events, or occurrences of things in the past, especially through other than the normal human senses as in extrasensory.

right-hand path In occult tradition, a practitioner who practices white magic.

rite Originally from an Indo-European base meaning "to fit together" and was the ancestor of the English words *arithmetic* and *rhyme* via, the Latin *ritus*. A formal act or observance as a community custom, such as the rite of courtship. Often has a solemn, religious or ceremonial meaning, such as the rite of baptism.

Sabbath From the Greek *sabbaton*, and the Hebrew *sabba*, both meaning "to rest." A day of rest from work and for religious worship. In Christianity, Sunday is the observed day of worship while Saturday is observed in Judaism and some Christian denominations.

Sanskrit Sanskrit is an ancient Indo-European language and the language of traditional Hinduism in India. Spoken between the fourteenth and fifth centuries B.C.E., it has been considered and maintained as a priestly and literary language of the sacred Veda scriptures and other classical texts.

Santeria From Spanish *santeria* meaning "holiness." A religion which originated in Cuba by enslaved West African laborers that combines the West African Yoruba religion with Roman Catholicism and recognizes a supreme God as well as other spirits.

sarcophagus From the Greek *sarx* meaning "flesh," and Greek *sarkophogos,* literally meaning "flesh-eater." Originally a kind of limestone that had properties to aid in the rapid decomposition of the deceased bodies and was used in the making of coffins. Eventually came to mean any stone coffin, especially one with inscriptions or decorated with sculpture and used as a monument.

sauropod Any of various large semi-aquatic plant-eating dinosaurs that had a long neck and tail and a small head. From the suborder *Sauropoda,* a Latin word meaning lizard foot.

schizophrenia A severe psychiatric disorder which can include symptoms of withdrawal or detachment from reality, delusions, hallucinations, emotional instability, and intellectual disturbances or illogical patterns of thinking to various degrees. The term comes from Greek words meaning "split mind."

seance A meeting or gathering of people in which a spiritualist makes attempts to communicate with the spirits of deceased persons, or a gathering to receive spiritualistic messages.

semidivine Possessing similar or some of the characteristics, abilities, or powers normally attributed to a deity and/or existing on a higher spiritual level or plane than common mortals yet not completely divine.

shaman A religious or spiritual leader, usually possessing special powers, such as that of prophecy, and healing, and acts as an intermediary between the physical and spiritual realms.

shamanic exorcism When a shaman, or tribal medicine-holy person, performs a ceremonial ritual to expel the disincarnate spirits from a person.

shapeshifter A supposed fictional being, spirit or something that is able to change its appearance or shape.

shofar A trumpet made of a ram's horn, blown by the ancient and modern Hebrews during religious ceremonies and as a signal in battle.

soothsayer From Middle English, literally meaning "somebody who speaks the truth." Someone who claims to have the ability to foretell future events.

soul The animating and vital principal in human beings, credited with the faculties of will, emotion, thought and action and often conceived as an immaterial entity, separate from the physical body. The spiritual nature of human beings, regarded as immortal, separable from the body at death, and susceptible to happiness or misery in a future state. The disembodied spirit of a dead human being.

spell A formula or word believed to have magical power. A trance or a bewitched state.

spirit control The guide that mediums contact to receive messages from deceased spirits, or another name for spirit guide as used in mediumship.

spirit guide A nonphysical being or entity which possibly can be an angel, the higher self, the spirit of a deceased person, a higher group mind, or a highly evolved being whose purpose is to help, guide, direct, and protect the individual.

spittle Something that looks like or is saliva, which is secreted from the mouth.

stigmata Marks on a person's body resembling the wounds inflicted on Jesus Christ (c. 6 B.C.E.–c. 30 C.E.) during his Crucifixion on the cross.

subversive To cause the ruin or downfall of something or to undermine or overthrow principles, an institution, or a government.

supernatural Relating to or pertaining to God or the characteristics of God; a deity or magic of something that is above and beyond what is normally explained by natural laws.

superstition The belief that certain actions and rituals have a magical effect resulting in either good or bad. From the Latin stem *superstition*, and *superstes*, meaning standing over or in awe.

taboo Something that is forbidden. In some cases can refer to something being sacred, therefore forbidden, such as in Polynesian societies. From the Tongan *tabu*, said to have been introduced into the English language by Captain James Cook in the late eighteenth century.

talisman An object such as a gemstone or stone, believed to have magical powers or properties. From the Greek *telesma*, meaning something consecrated, *telein*, to complete, and *telos*, result.

Tanakh From the Hebrew *tenak*, an acronym formed from *torah*. It is the sacred book of Judaism, consisting of the Torah—the five books of Moses, *The Nevi'im*—the words of the prophets, and the *Kethuvim*—the writings.

telepathy Communication of thoughts, mental images, ideas, feelings, or sensations from one person's mind to another's without the use of speech, writing, signs, or symbols.

theory of evolution The biological theory of the complex process of living organisms, how they change and evolve from one generation to another or over many generations.

therianthropic Used to describe a mythological creature that is half human and half animal. Coined from the Greek *therion*,

meaning small wild animal, and *anthropo*, meaning human being.

totem An animal, bird, plant, or any other natural object that is revered as a personal or tribal symbol.

transference The process of change that happens when one person or place is transferred to another.

transience A state of impermanence, or lasting for only a brief time. Remaining in a place only for a short time, or the brief appearance of someone or something.

transmutation The act of transforming or changing from one nature, form, or state into another.

tribulation Great affliction, trial, or distress. In Christianity, the tribulation refers to the prophesied period of time which precedes the return of Jesus Christ to Earth, in which there will be tremendous suffering that will test humanity's endurance, patience, or faith.

UFO Literally an unidentified flying object, although the term is often used by some to refer to an alien spacecraft.

UFOlogist Someone who investigates the reports and sightings of unidentified flying objects.

Valhalla In Norse mythology, when the souls of heroes are killed in battle, they spend eternity in a great hall, which is called Valhalla. From the Old Norse *valhall*, literally meaning hall of the slain.

Valkyrie One of the 12 handmaids of Odin in Norse mythology who ride their horses over the battlefield as they escort the souls of slain heroes to Valhalla. From the Old Norse *Valkyrja*, meaning literally chooser of the slain.

vision From the Latin *vis*, to see. Faculty of sight or a mental image produced by imagination. Can refer to a mystical experience of seeing as if with the eyes, only through a supernatural means such as in a dream, trance, or through a supernatural being, and one which often has religious, revelatory, or prophetic significance.

voodoo From Louisiana French, *voudou* or *vodu*, meaning "fetish." A religion mainly practiced in the Caribbean countries, especially Haiti, that is comprised of a combination of Roman Catholic rituals and animistic beliefs involving fetishes, magic, charms, spells, curses, and communication with ancestral spirits.

white magick The use of magic for supposed good purposes such as to counteract evil.

Wiccan Someone who is a witch, a believer or follower of the religion of Wicca.

wizard A variant of the fifteenth century word *wisard*, meaning "wise." Someone professing to have magical powers as a magician, sorcerer, or a male witch. In general, someone who is extremely knowledgeable and clever.

zoology The scientific branch of biology that studies animals in all their characteristics and aspects. From the Greek *zoologia*, literally the study of life and from *zolion*, or life form.

Zoroaster A Persian prophet (c. 628 B.C.E.– c. 551 B.C.E.) and the founder of an ancient religion called Zoroastrianism whose principal belief is in a supreme deity and of the existence of a dualism between good and evil. Derived from the Greek word *Zarat* or *Zarathustra*, meaning camel handler.

The Cumulative Index, found in each volume, is an alphabetic arrangement of all people, places, images, and concepts found in the text. Names of publications, movies, ships, television programs, radio broadcasts, foreign words, and cross-references are indicated by italics.

The page references to the subjects include the Arabic volume number as well as the page number. Main entries are designated by bold page numbers while images are denoted by italics.

Cumulative Index

A

Johnson, Richard M., 2:240

Johnston, Roy, 3:91

Jones, Ernest, 3:179

Jones, Jim, 1:313, 315, *319*

Jones, Tommy Lee, 3:277

Jonsson, Olof, **2:158,** 3:178–179

Joseph of Arimathea, 2:204, 238

Josephson, Brian, 3:162

Josselyn, John, 3:93

Jourdemaine, Margaret, 2:100

Jouret, Luc, 1:318

Journey to the Center of the Earth (Verne), 2:242

Juan Diego (16th c. Aztec), 1:188, 244

Judaism
  afterlife, 1:14–15
  amulets, 2:169–170
  Apocalypse, 1:182
  blessing meals, 3:220
  burials and funerals, 3:224
  Dead Sea Scrolls and link with Christianity,
    1:46
  demons, 1:196–197
  divination of Hebrews, 2:150
  dreams, 3:117
  exorcism, 1:206
  hospitality and charity, 3:215
  Jerusalem, importance of, 2:242, 244, 245
  mourning, 3:228
  prayer, 1:228–229
  reincarnation, 1:48–49
  soul, 1:4, 5, 14
  wedding ceremonies, 3:211–212
  See also Hebrew beliefs and customs;
    Kabbalah

Judas Iscariot, 3:197–198

Judges, dream symbolism, 3:129

Judgment Day. *See* Final Judgment

Judgment (tarot), 2:132

Juggler (tarot), 2:130

Julius II, Pope, 2:125

Jung, Carl G., 3:*128*
  astrology and, 2:125
  on dreams, 3:119, 128–129
  ghostly encounter of, 3:3
  on Gnosticism, 1:280
  Kabbalah and, 2:142
  near-death experience of, 1:27
  on reincarnation, 1:59

Juno Lucina (Roman deity), 2:172

Justice (tarot), 2:131

"JW" (alien being), 1:305–306

K

Ka. See Ba and *ka*

Ka'aba (Mecca, Saudi Arabia), 2:256, 257–258,
  260

*Kabbala Dnudata Seu Dotrina Hebraeorum
  Transcendentalis et Metaphysica Atove
  Theologica* (Rosenroth), 2:142

Kabbalah, **2:141–142, 144**
  Golem and, 3:74
  magic squares and, 2:198
  on meditation, 3:150
  Pico della Mirandola, Giovanni, and, 2:70
  on reincarnation, 1:48
  tarot and, 2:129

Kaio Maru No. 5 disappearance (1952), 2:227

Kali (Hindu deity), 2:32, 33

Kamau, Johnstone. *See* Kenyatta, Jomo

Kampman, Reima, 1:67–68

Kane, Margaretta. *See* Fox sisters

Kaplan, Aryeh, 3:74

Kaplan, Stephen, 3:81

"Kaptar." *See* Yeti

Kardec, Allen, **1:143–144**

Karloff, Boris, 3:*74*, 109, 112

Karma, 1:6, 11, 55

Karnak (Egypt), **2:245–247**

"Katie King" (spirit control). *See* Cook, Florence

Katter, Reuben Luther, 2:124

Keel, John A., 3:264, 277

Kelly-Hopkinsville (KY) UFO sightings (1955),
  3:243–244

Kelsey, Denys, 1:58

Kelsey, Morton, 1:197–198, 223

Kennedy, John F., assassination of, 2:35, 156

Kenya, food kinship, 3:216

Kenya, Mau-Mau activity, 2:27–30

Kenyatta, Jomo, 2:30

Kepler, Johannes, 2:125

Key, dream symbolism, 3:129

Key of Solomon (ceremonial text), 2:107

Keyhoe, Donald E., 3:*254*, 254–255

Khafre (Pharaoh of Egypt), 2:268–269

al-Khattab, Omar Ibn, 2:244–245

Khomeini, Ayatollah, 1:182

Khul, Djwhal, 1:281

Kibwetere, Joseph, 1:314

Kikuyu Central Association, 2:30

Kikuyu people, 2:27, 29

Kilnapp, John W., 3:148

Kim, Young Sik, 3:52

Kimathi, Dedan, 2:29–30

Yogananda, Paramahansa, 1:47

"Yossele" (Golem of Prague), 3:76

You Were Born Again to Be Together (Sutphen), 1:59

Young, Sherry and Terry, 3:180

Yule candle, 2:172

Z

Zachariah (Hebrew prophet), 3:250

Zadikel (angel), 2:58

Zamora, Lonnie, 3:265–266

Zaphkiel (angel), 2:58

Zeitoun (Egypt) holy apparitions, 1:187, 190

Zell, Oberon, 2:73, 74

Zell, Tim. *See* Zell, Oberon

Zener cards, 3:163, 169

Zeta I and II Reticuli, 3:275–276

Zeuglodon, 3:87, 96

Zeus, statue of, 2:243

Zeus (Greek deity), 1:267

Zhengxin, Yuan, 3:68

Zinsstag, Lou, 3:272

Zodiac, 2:*120*, 121–123, 124

Zohar, 2:142

    See also Kabbalah

Zolar (astrologer), 2:123–124

Zombi, 2:55–56

Zombies of the Stratosphere (film). *See Satan's Satellites* (film)

Zoroaster (Persian religious leader), 1:288, 2:70–71

Zosimus of Panapolis, 2:42

Zulley, Jurgen, 3:121

Zulu people, burial customs, 3:226

Zuni people, fetishes, 2:193

Zuoguian, Feng, 3:68